Sleep and Dreaming

Also by Jacob Empson

HUMAN BRAINWAVES

Sleep and Dreaming

Third Edition

JACOB EMPSON

With a chapter by
Michael Wang

palgrave

First edition 1989 published by Faber & Faber
Second edition 1993 published by Harvester Wheatsheaf

This edition published 2002 by
PALGRAVE
Houndmills, Basingstoke, Hampshire RG21 6XS and
175 Fifth Avenue, New York, N.Y. 10010
Companies and representatives throughout the world

PALGRAVE is the new global academic imprint of
St. Martin's Press LLC Scholarly and Reference Division and
Palgrave Publishers Ltd (formerly Macmillan Press Ltd).

ISBN 0–333–94764–9 hardback
ISBN 0–333–94765–7 paperback

This book is printed on paper suitable for recycling and
made from fully managed and sustained forest sources.

Cataloguing-in-publication data

A catalogue record for this book is available
from the British Library.

A catalogue record for this book is available
from the Library of Congress.

10   9   8   7   6   5   4   3   2   1
11   10   09   08   07   06   05   04   03   02

Typeset in Great Britain by
Aarontype Ltd, Easton, Bristol

Printed and bound in Great Britain by
Creative Print & Design (Wales), Ebbw Vale

'The division of one day from the next must be one of the most profound peculiarities of life on this planet. It is, on the whole, a merciful arrangement. We are not condemned to sustained flights of being, but are constantly refreshed by little holidays from ourselves. We are intermittent creatures, always falling to little ends and rising to little beginnings. Our soon-tired consciousness is meted out in chapters, and that the world will look quite different tomorrow is, both for our comfort and our discomfort, usually true. How marvellously too night matches sleep, sweet image of it, so neatly apportioned to our need. Angels must wonder at these beings who fall so regularly out of awareness into a fantasm-infested dark. How our frail identities survive these chasms no philosopher has ever been able to explain.'

(Iris Murdoch, *The Black Prince*)

Contents

Preface to the Third Edition

The first edition of this book was published in 1989, and the second edition was published in 1993 by a different publisher. This third edition, with a different publisher again, has been brought up to date and has considerably more new material than the previous edition, as well as a chapter on the psychological treatment of insomnia, written by my colleague Professor Michael Wang, who also contributed more informally to the chapter on children's sleep problems. Being published by Palgrave – formerly Macmillan Press – brings me full circle as my first book, *Human Brainwaves*, was published by Macmillan in 1983.

This book is intended to provide answers to many of the questions that people ask about dreaming and sleep, or at least answers to questions that can be addressed from a scientific perspective. When people discover that I have been involved in sleep research they often insist on telling me one of their dreams. I tend to reply by telling them one of mine. This sidesteps the issue of attempting to provide an instant dream analysis for them. Like other people's children, other people's dreams are so much less interesting than one's own! This book does not provide simple formulae for interpreting dreams, although there is careful consideration of how dreams arise.

I hope it succeeds in being both an authoritative and a readable introduction to what is known about the psychology of sleep, including the experience of sleep and its psychophysiology. The techniques for recording and scoring sleep stages in the laboratory were established in the late 1960s, using EEG (brain-wave) and other psychophysiological measures. This development was crucial in providing a universal frame of reference that has survived for over 40 years. It has allowed the accumulation of a body of knowledge about sleep and dreaming that is largely internally consistent and uncontroversial – an achievement of scientific success scarcely matched in other branches of psychology during the same period. Books have of course been written, but some of the best are now somewhat dated or out of print, and some of the more recent ones have confined themselves to contemporary work. *Sleep and Dreaming* provides an account of what we have come to know about the subject, regardless of when the research was done.

As with the first two editions, the book is organized into four sections, but following the suggestion of one of the publisher's referees there have been some changes in the detail of their organization. Part I describes the context of sleep research, starting with an examination of beliefs about sleep in contemporary Britain, in other cultures and in antiquity. The historical account (in Chapter 2) of the development of electrophysiological measures is intended to provide an understandable introduction to them. This inevitably involves the use of some technical terms, but, as elsewhere in the book, jargon is avoided wherever possible and technical usages of words are explained as they appear.

Part II is concerned with the experience of sleep, including dreaming. The discovery of REM (rapid eye movement) sleep has allowed us to predict mental activity from EEG and other psychophysiological recordings in a way that is virtually impossible in the awake subject. Answers have been provided to questions such as how long dreams last during this state of sleep and whether everybody dreams. Some progress has also been made towards establishing the provenance of the content of dreams – such as the events of the previous day, or the dreamer's daytime preoccupations. We are a long way from fully understanding the nature and function of consciousness while we are awake, so not surprisingly there are many aspects of sleeping consciousness that remain a mystery. Advances in neurophysiology have however provided clues about the brain mechanisms that govern the generation of dreaming, and recent theories linking the psychological reality of dreaming to these processes are described in Part II.

Part III is devoted to the physiology and psychophysiology of sleep. Chapter 6, on the physiology of sleep, is rather technical, but by defining new terms as they arise, and providing a glossary I have tried to maintain a balance between readability and authoritativeness. The consequences of experimental sleep disturbance, either by reducing sleep, denying it altogether or selectively depriving subjects of particular sleep stages, are considered in Chapter 7. Experimental evidence of perceptual and attentional processing during sleep is assessed in Chapter 8, together with overt behaviours during sleep, such as sleepwalking and sleeptalking. Part III also includes an account of the sleep of animals, and ends with a chapter on theories about the functions of sleep.

Part IV, on problems with sleep, consists of three chapters: adult sleep disorders; the psychological treatment of insomnia (by Professor Michael Wang); and childhood sleep problems and their management.

This book is intended to be accessible to anybody with an interest in the subject, as well as being useful to students who wish to take their interests further. While virtually every assertion is supported by referenced evidence that can be followed up by the student, the general reader should have no difficulty reading straight through the chapters.

One reviewer was kind enough to say of the first edition, 'Empson has the scope of a textbook without actually writing a textbook, the final aim of the science communicator, while for professionals there are enough references to follow up evidence but not enough to choke the text.' It is hoped that this edition is as accessible as the first two for the general reader, while remaining useful as a source book for the student and professional reader in respect of the treatment of evidence and references to sources. In the second edition I tried to achieve this by following Nathaniel Kleitman's example (in his monumental *Sleep and Wakefulness*, the second edition of which was published over 35 years ago) in using numbered references and a comprehensive alphabetical list of all the references at the end of the book. This system proved very difficult to implement, and sometimes made the details of citation tricky for the reader to follow. This edition does include a full reference section, which serves as a useful list of sources in itself, particularly for students and professional readers, but it has reverted to the more usual Harvard convention of citing the authors' names and dates of publication in the text (for example, Jenkins and Dallenbach, 1924), which, while sometimes unwieldy, does have the virtue of unambiguous clarity.

Thanks and acknowledgements for the first edition

I would like to thank John Henry Jones for reading an early draft of Chapter 1. His literate and well-informed suggestions were invaluable. Chris Singleton provided me with much material on childhood sleep disorders, as well as some helpful comments on a draft of the chapter on childhood sleep problems. I would also like to thank my colleagues Ray Meddis and Jim Horne for the many opportunities over the years to discuss (and frequently dispute) the functions of sleep. My own initiation into sleep research 30 years ago was at Ian Oswald's laboratory in Edinburgh, and while our paths now rarely cross, his untiring work during a long career remains an example and an inspiration.

I would like to thank the staff of Regents Park Zoo for allowing me to photograph their giraffes sleeping, as well as for the practical help provided by the keepers of the Cotton Terrace. These photographs would not have been possible without Kelvin Murray's photographic expertise and help from James Blofeld.

Thanks and acknowledgements for the second edition

I am very grateful indeed to my assistants at the sleep laboratory, who have helped with the preparation of this edition. Caroline Crichton, Linda MacDonald and David Alford did a great deal of work for me in the library, finding the latest papers, and also helped with the redrawing of many of the illustrations as well as the creation of new ones.

Thanks and acknowledgements for the third edition

I am very grateful to Simone de Lacy of the Guy's and St Thomas' Hospital Sleep Disorders Centre for providing photographs of the Centre's facilities, used in this book to illustrate modern techniques of recording and scoring sleep stages. Thanks also go to my editor at Palgrave, Frances Arnold, who has been most encouraging, and to the two anonymous referees for their constructive and helpful criticisms.

Jacob Empson

Acknowledgements

The extract from *The Black Prince* by Iris Murdoch, published by Chatto & Windus is used by permission of the Random House Group Limited. The extract from *The Strings are False* by Louis MacNeice is included with the permission of Corinna MacNeice, representing the MacNeice literary estate. The *Clerihew* by W. H. Auden appears by permission of Faber & Faber. Figures 2.2 and 2.4 are photographs kindly supplied by the Sleep and Respiratory Services Manager at Guy's and St Thomas' Hospital, Simone de Lacy, and used with permission. Figure 5.1, illustrating J. A. Hobson's model of conscious states, appears with the permission of the American Psychological Association. Figure 6.1 is reprinted from J. Aschoff, 'Circadian rhythms in man', *Science*, 148, 1427–32 (1965) with permission from the American Association for the Advancement of Science. Figure 6.5 from the *Journal of Clinical Investigation*, appears with the permission of the Rockefeller University Press. Figure 6.3 appears with the permission of the American Physiological Society. Figure 12.4, illustrating the effects of two benzo-diazepines on sleep, appears with permission Springer-Verlag & Co. John Wiley & Sons Limited have permitted the inclusion of Figures 2.9, 11.1, and 12.2. These comprise the charts showing sleep times at different ages from R. L. Williams, I. Karakan, and C. J. Hursch, *Electroencephalography (EEG) of Human Sleep: Clinical Applications*, New York: Wiley, 1974; the evolutionary tree postulated by R. Meddis, 'The evolution of sleep', in A. Mayes (ed.), *Sleep Mechanisms and Functions*, Wokingham: Van Nostrand, 1983; and a table from K. Spiegel and A. Azcona (1985) 'Sleep and its disorders', in M. S. J. Pathy (ed.), *Principles and Practice of Geriatric Medicine*, London: Wiley, respectively.

Every effort has been made to contact the copyright-holders, but if any have been inadvertently omitted the publishers will be pleased to make the necessary arrangements at the earliest opportunity.

A Note on Michael Wang

Michael Wang is Professor of Clinical Psychology at the School of Medicine and Director of the Doctoral Clinical Psychology Training Course at the University of Hull. He also holds honorary consultant appointments at local hospitals and community National Health Service trusts. He is a recognized expert in the neuropsychological examination of traumatic brain injury, is a registered cognitive-behavioural psychotherapist, and has worked as a clinical psychologist for more than 20 years.

He has a longstanding clinical and research interest in consciousness and loss of consciousness, having been involved in the assessment and treatment of sleep disorders with Jacob Empson for more than a decade, and has published widely on the topic of cognitive function during general anaesthesia.

Part I
The Context of Sleep Research

1

The Obvious: Beliefs About Sleep and Dreaming

Sleep folklore

For all the time we spend doing it – about a third of our lives – we have very little natural insight into the sleeping process. Even the simple act of observing a sleeper normally requires forgoing sleep oneself. Typically the object of scrutiny is either a child in bed or our spouse asleep in front of the television. And what is there to see? They may twitch, shift to an apparently more comfortable position, but their eyes remain closed and they remain unresponsive. They offer no clues about whatever mental activity is going on, apart from occasional mumblings. On rare occasions they might talk more coherently, but what is said is seldom sensible.

Our memory of our own sleep is usually confined to one or two confusing and ill-recalled dreams, and some individuals even claim never to dream. The quality of sleep is normally judged by the degree of oblivion achieved, in the same way that digestion is counted as most satisfactory when we are least aware of it. Sleep has no obvious rationale, except that we do it when we feel sleepy or tired, and after doing it we are 'rested' – and do not feel sleepy any more.

If you ask a roomful of people whether anybody has had no sleep in the previous 24 hours, it is very rare indeed to find a serious candidate. During the 30 years in which I gave lectures on sleep and dreaming to numerous groups of sixth formers as well as undergraduate students I had only one positive response to this question. We all sleep, and as a rule we do it at night in one long session of up to nine or 10 hours, and during the day we stay awake.

About one third to a half of the usable space in any private house is taken up by special rooms devoted to sleeping. It is most unusual for anybody to do it in the kitchen, the hall, the bathroom or the dining room, although naps may be taken in the living room. But doing the whole thing – removing daytime clothes, putting on special sleeping garments, emptying the bladder, cleaning the teeth and finally laying on the purpose-built sleeping furniture – is something that is only done in rooms specially built for the purpose. In many households it is conventional for everybody to retire at the same time, and to reemerge simultaneously in the morning, with scant toleration being shown

to individuals who do not conform. A sleepless alien might legitimately conclude that earthlings' central preoccupation is this peculiar sort of inactivity.

What are the obvious truths about sleep? What do most people believe it is
for, what do their dreams and other experiences during sleep signify, and what
will happen to them if sleep is disturbed or prevented? A survey I conducted
among Hull University students and staff about their beliefs about sleep and
dreaming is reported fully in the appendix at the end of the book. They were
asked to indicate whether various assertions (such as 'An hour's sleep before
midnight is worth two afterwards') were true, possibly true or untrue. Some
of the questions concerned frequency, so answers ranging from 'Never' to
'Always' were available to assertions such as 'Dreams can foretell the future'.
Relevant findings are referred to in this chapter as being from the 'Hull survey'.

The analogy between resting after physical exertion and the relief from
sleepiness offered by sleep is very compelling, and many people would agree
with it. In the survey of students and graduates at Hull, over two thirds agreed
with the statement 'Exercise improves the quality of sleep'. This belief demonstrates the widely held assumption that sleepiness is equivalent to physical
fatigue. To generalize this into an implicit theory – development of the need
for sleep is contingent on accumulating physical fatigue during the course of
the day.

There are plenty of folk remedies for improving sleep, and maxims, adages
and proverbs concerning sleep give some insight into received views. My Afri-
kaaner grandfather was fond of repeating that 'a man needs six hours, a
woman seven, and a bloody fool eight' hours of sleep – a sentiment that nicely
incorporated both his simple male chauvinism and the Calvinist abomination
of indulgence. The common English proverb 'Early to bed and early to rise,
makes a man healthy, wealthy and wise' is less concerned with self-denial than
with a prescription for regular habits. Similarly the Welsh 'Go to bed with the
lamb and rise with the lark' allows a generous amount of time asleep, and is
more concerned with its timing.

The idea that sleep is especially important for growing children, that it may
somehow be essential to growth and development, has always been prevalent.
The notion that 'one hour's sleep before midnight is worth two afterwards' has
been perennially invoked to get children to bed early (although only 10 per
cent of the survey sample believed it to be true). Young ladies proverbially
make sure they have their 'beauty sleep' – the statement 'a good night's sleep
improves one's appearance' was endorsed by over two thirds of the sample.
Similarly, improvement from infectious illnesses accompanied by fever has
been commonly held to be intimately connected with sleeping, so that a fever
typically 'breaks' during the night, when the temperature reaches a maximal
high, and then reverts to near-normal as the patient falls into a deep restorative sleep. The common sense view of sleep is that it is good for you because
it enables recovery from fatigue, is essential for growth and is crucial for
recovery from illness.

Coexisting with this view of sleep as a benign restorative is a certain
apprehensiveness about it. We are obviously vulnerable during sleep. This is
primarily a physical vulnerability to enemies, both animal and human, because

of our obliviousness to our surroundings and the confused, inert state we can be in when we first wake up. The vampire legend, for example, gains much of its power from the helplessness of the sleeping victim. At one time the collective solution to this sort of worry was to employ somebody to patrol the streets all night, calling out 'Three o'clock and all's well!' or whatever, at regular intervals, providing reassurance to citizens sleeping in their beds and even more so to insomniacs.

Apprehension is also aroused by the fact that during sleep we seem to lose control of our minds. Consciousness during wakefulness in a sane person is pretty well ordered and familiar. The happy impression (perhaps totally illusory) that we have when awake that we are somehow in control of our mental processes deserts us when we are dreaming. On the contrary, while asleep our consciousness seems to happen to us, rather than being under our control. This is particularly disturbing for people who subscribe to the Christian view that sinful thoughts are as wicked as the corresponding deeds, since we sometimes dream of performing venial if not mortal sins.

In order to understand what is 'obvious' about sleep and dreaming it is necessary to examine some of the conventional ideological baggage that most Westerners carry about with them, and its historical origins. It will also be useful to examine the idea that preliterate societies, either in antiquity or those existing in the contemporary world, have more (or more far-fetched) mystical ideas about dreaming than our own.

Dreaming in antiquity

Prescientific thinking about sleep and dreaming is often said to have revolved around two notions: of the soul leaving the body during sleep, and of the body being visited by spirits – gods and demons offering revelations and glimpses into the future, or wandering nightmares.

In classical Europe and the Middle East dreams were often taken as portents of the future or guides for action. The Assyrian poem 'The Epic of Gilgamesh' is regularly punctuated by dreams, both the hero's and his great friend Enkidu's. They foretell events, providing a sort of rationale for the extraordinary exploits, failures and tragedy of Gilgamesh. The poem dates from the third millenium BC and is a eulogistic account of the life of King Gilgamesh of Uruk in Mesopotamia. It clearly ranks as the first written literature of any consequence. It is also remarkable for its universality and its enduring appeal after five millenia. (The tablets on which it was recorded were discovered in the mid-nineteenth century, and their decipherment was not largely completed until the end of that century.) It starts:

O Gilgamesh, Lord of Kullab, great is thy praise. This was the man to whom all things were known; this was the king who knew the countries of the world. He was wise, he saw mysteries and knew secret things, he brought us a tale of the days before the flood. He went on a long journey, was weary, worn-out with labour, and returning engraved on a stone the whole story.

N. K. Sanders' (1960) summary of the plot of the epic sets the scene:

> When the story begins he is in mature manhood, and superior to all other men in beauty and strength and the unsatisfied cravings of his half-divine nature, for which he can find no worthy match in love or in war; while his daemonic energy is wearing his subjects out. They are forced to call in the help of the gods, and the first episode describes how they provide a companion and foil. This was Enkidu, the 'natural man', reared with wild animals, and as swift as the gazelle. In time Enkidu was seduced by a harlot from the city, and with loss of innocence an irrevocable step was taken towards taming the wild man. The animals now rejected him, and he was led on by stages; learning to wear clothes, eat human food, herd sheep, and make war on the wolf and lion, until at length he reached the great civilized city of Uruk.

Enkidu's arrival at Gilgamesh's court was announced to Gilgamesh in two dreams. In the first Enkidu was symbolized by a meteor falling from heaven, whose attraction to Gilgamesh was mysteriously 'like the love of a woman', and when it was shown to his mother she pronounced it his brother. In his second dream he found an axe on a street in his city. Again, he was deeply drawn to it, loved it like a woman and wore it on his side. His mother Ninsun, a minor goddess, interpreted both these dreams for him, identifying the meteor and the axe as a new friend he was about to make.

Gilgamesh and Enkidu became inseparable companions. When Gilgamesh later dreamt that Enlil, the father of the gods, had decreed his destiny, it was Enkidu who interpreted it for him, explaining that it indicated his certain mortality as well as the gifts of unexampled supremacy over the people and victory in battle. When the two embarked on a mission against the giant Humbaba they both had dreams that were highly significant to their project. These were apparently induced, or incubated, by Gilgamesh, who dug a well, went up to the mountain and poured fine meal on the ground before saying 'O mountain, dwelling of the gods, bring me a favourable dream'. Encouraged by their interpretations of each other's dreams they set off to cut down Humbaba's cedar forests.

As well as killing Humbaba they also slaughtered a semidivine bull, the Bull of Heaven, which belonged to Ishtar, the Queen of Heaven and patroness of Uruk. Enkidu now dreamt that they had offended the gods so deeply that one of them must die, and he promptly succumbed to a fatal illness. During his illness he dreamt of the afterlife, where kings, rulers and princes were reduced from their high station to fetching and carrying as servants, and only the high priests, gods and one or two favoured dead kings were allowed to preserve their earthly privileges.

After Enkidu's death Gilgamesh wandered far and wide in his grief, encountering amongst others the proverbial survivor of the great flood, Utnapishtim, who told him how, in a dream, he had been warned by a god of the imminent deluge and instructed to build a great boat, aboard which he was to take the seed of all living creatures. Because of his obedience he had been granted the gift of eternal life. Gilgamesh went on to search for the secret of immortality, and according to the legend he almost succeeded.

Gilgamesh did not have any significant dreams after Enkidu's death, and despite his continuing effort to penetrate the mysteries it became increasingly apparent that his powers had waned and the gods had turned against him. As a test of his strength Utnapishtim challenged him to stay awake for six days and seven nights:

> But while Gilgamesh sat there resting on his haunches, a mist of sleep like soft wool teased from the fleece drifted over him, and Utnapishtim said to his wife, 'Look at him now, the strong man who would have everlasting life, even now the mists of sleep are drifting over him.'

Despite his human limitations he managed to retrieve the underwater thorn that would give immortality, although it was stolen from him by a serpent on his journey back to Uruk. The epic ends with his death in his own city, which he was largely responsible for building:

> This too was the work of Gilgamesh, the king, who knew the countries of the world. He was wise, he saw mysteries and knew secret things, he brought us a tale of the days before the flood. He went on a long journey, was weary, worn out with labour, and returning engraved on a stone the whole story.

It is impossible to do justice to the beauty of the poem in such a brief account. As Sanders (ibid.) says, it is a mixture of pure adventure, morality and tragedy, and Gilgamesh is the first tragic hero of whom anything is known. It is clear that even five thousand years ago in Mesopotamia people had achieved a degree of subtlety of belief that defies analysis into one or two dogmas. The recognition and acceptance of the mysteries of mortality, earthly hubris, privilege and their futility were carried through two thousand years, as this epic was copied and repeated in various versions. The role of dreaming in all this was to provide a channel of communication for the gods to inform and warn those few mortals who were sufficiently significant to attract their attention, at critical moments in their lives. Presumably most people's dreams were not interpreted as messages from deities, as even Gilgamesh was only favoured with two or three of these in his lifetime.

In some societies the practical importance of dreams as portents of the future and as phenomena with mysterious healing properties was not only recognized, but also institutions were set up to exploit the fact. In order to achieve both a suitable dream and an explanation of its meaning it was necessary to travel to an oracle and there to sleep on a special bed (from the sound of it, usually particularly uncomfortable), after which any dreams reported would be interpreted. This process of inducing dreaming is called incubation. It was practised in ancient Egypt and Greece, and for ordinary people these special dreams were more important for their curative powers than for their predictive value.

J. G. Frazer, in his monumental work *Folk-lore in the Old Testament* (1918), maintains that the belief that the gods revealed themselves and declared their will to mankind in dreams was widespread in antiquity; and accordingly people resorted to temples and other sacred spots for the purpose of sleeping there and holding converse with the higher powers in visions of the night, for they naturally supposed that the deities or the deified spirits of the dead would be most likely to manifest themselves in places specially dedicated to their worship.

Frazer describes the process of consulting the oracle at a sanctuary dedicated to the soothsayer Ampiaraus of Oropus in Attica. Patients paid a sum of money and presented a sacrificial animal (the skin and shoulders of which would be subsequently kept by the priests), and then slept in male or female dormitories on the hides of their newly killed sacrificial rams. If a cure was achieved then the patients were permitted to drop gold or silver coins into the sacred spring. Similarly, at the Aesculapian sanctuary near Epidaurus dormitories were provided for pilgrims seeking cures. Those who were cured after their night at the sanctuary were permitted to record their dreams and commemorate their recovery on votive tablets, some of which have survived to this day.

Interpretations were not offered by these priests – rather the dreams themselves were thought to be curative. Is there much difference between this sort of arrangement and that prevailing at Lourdes today? Priests have always been regarded as healers of the mind, and their modern equivalents in the psychoanalytic movement are similarly preoccupied with the dreams of their patients.

Frazer further suggests that the story of Jacob's dream (which was deemed so significant that the spot on which it took place was henceforth sanctified in the Jewish religion) 'was probably told to explain the immemorial sanctity of Bethel, which may well have been revered by the aboriginal inhabitants of Canaan long before the Hebrews invaded and conquered the land'. In this case the dream is used as a political device – which is not consistent with the idea of credulous primitives believing in the literal truth of supernatural explanations. At least the politicians who told the story can hardly have believed it, and it seems unlikely that people swallowed everything they were told by their masters in antiquity, any more than they do now.

The Assassins, a Muslim sect founded in the eleventh century, were reputed to reward their devotees with visions of heaven through the use of hashish (from which they are widely assumed to have derived their name). According to Marco Polo's account the sect's leader, the 'Old Man of the Mountain':

used a special 'Paradise' constructed in a secluded valley. Into this Garden of Earthly Delights the selected trainee Assassins were carried while unconscious with drugs ('assassin' is derived from hashashin – 'hashish-eaters'). When they came round in the valley, they were entertained with every delightful variant of wine, women and song promised in the holy scriptures to those who would go to Paradise. Drugged again, they regained consciousness outside the valley in anguish that it had all been a dream. No, they were told, all this will be yours again on completion of your mission (reported in Humble, 1975).

The point of all this was of course to reinforce the belief that the afterlife was a paradise – achievable with certainty only through death in battle – and thus to improve the combativeness of the assassins. This well-known story from Marco Polo dates from two hundred years after the sect had been crushed.

Islamic scholars writing in English have come to regard the story as apocryphal. Even the derivation of the name 'assassin' from 'hashish' is in doubt, according to Bernard Lewis's authoritative historical account of the sect (Lewis, 1980). The term *hashshash* does refer to users of cannabis in Arabic, but *hashish* and *hashishi* originally referred generically to herbage, and only later specifically meant cannabis. In addition, Lewis argues that since *hashishi* is particular to Syria as a term of popular abuse, it was 'in all probability the name that gave rise to the story, rather than the reverse'. Cannabis was widely used in the Middle East during this period, and it seems unlikely that the practice in itself was remarkable enough to cause any comment amongst Arabs.

The sect did use assassination as a highly effective weapon, however, against other Persian groups. Their reputation for fanaticism was widespread amongst the Crusaders, and

> in 1195, when King Richard Coer de Lion was at Chinon, no less than fifteen so-called Assassins were apprehended, and confessed that they had been sent by the King of France to kill him. Before long, such charges became frequent . . . [but] there can be little doubt that these charges are baseless. The chiefs of the Assassins, in Persia or in Syria, had no interest in the plots and intrigues of Western Europe; the European needed no help outside in the various arts of murder (ibid.)

There is no evidence that the Ismaili Assassins ever made contact with the Crusaders in the relatively short history of the sect (they were subdued by the Mongols, who destroyed their castles in 1256).

Speculation about whether the Assassins believed that their experiences in the Alamut garden, fitted out as Paradise, were really a dream, or whether the garden's compliant slaves were all too real is thus academic. This story is apparently an invention of foreigners and does not appear in Arab texts. It seems that fanaticism does not need to be fuelled by credulity about dreams. Indeed the accounts of the feuds between Middle Eastern factions in the eleventh and twelfth centuries read much like the strife between the militias in Beirut during the 1980s, and there is no suggestion that these modern protagonists had particularly mystical views about dreaming.

The conventional Western European view of sleep was as a pleasurable indulgence that, like sex, provided a natural avenue for the temptations of the devil. Nocturnal emissions, or 'wet dreams', were an obvious result of demonic intervention. The Christian requirement for chastity in the clergy and the prohibition against masturbation paradoxically created the conditions most likely to promote these 'pollutions'. St Ambrose accordingly wrote a prayer to guard against them:

Procul recedant somnia
Et noctium phantasmata
Hostemque nostrum comprime,
Ne polluantur corpora.

[Let dreams and nocturnal
Phantasies depart far away,
And suppress our enemy
Lest our bodies be polluted.]

A modern and more finely wrought translation of the prayer, given to me by my colleague John Bernasconi, indicates that this preoccupation has survived its medieval origins:

Suppress our foe's infernal arts,
Lest sensual dreams defile our hearts,
With vain deluding thoughts that creep
On heedless minds disarmed with sleep.

St Augustine similarly asked God to keep him in 'chaste desire' during sleep, and to protect him from dreams that, 'owing to animal images', might lead him 'to pollution'.

Although Tertullian and St Augustine granted dispensations for these 'nocturnal pollutions', dreams were still regarded with deep suspicion. Dream interpretation had been widely practised in the ancient world, but as Christian theologians could establish no way of differentiating between divine and demonic dreams, divination of any sort was pronounced heretical. The clerical domination of Western thought during the Dark and Middle Ages resulted in relative neglect of this subject until the sixteenth century, when the rather trivializing 'dream books' of Artemidorus were rediscovered.

Can we even construe Freudian theory as a nineteenth-century articulation of these ideas about possession? The id, according to Freud, is uncontainable throughout the night, and instinctual pressure periodically forces unacceptable and deeply disturbing ideas into our consciousness. Instead of prayers to protect us from these sources of guilt, shame and terror, Freud suggested that dreams took over, transforming the Gothic horrors into cryptic symbols only interpretable by psychoanalysts, the new priests of nineteenth-century rationalism.

In England, until the sixteenth century it was unremarkable to speak of visitations from incubi and succubi – evil spirits (male and female respectively) that were thought to descend on sleepers, seducing them and perverting them to the ways of the Devil. In particular witches were presumed to consort with incubi. But did this belief encompass the 'normal' dreams that everybody experiences? (Prescientific thinking in Europe is relatively well preserved in the writings of its poets.) The dream poems of Chaucer and the French medieval poets before him make clear that it did not. There is no hint that dreaming, in this context, was any more than a poetic device, with no connotation of the supernatural simply from the fact that it was a dream.

A consideration of two dreams in Shakespeare's plays leads us to a similar conclusion. These are the Duke of Clarence's nightmare in *Richard III*, anticipating his own death, and Caesar's wife's dream in *Julius Caesar*. Both of them seem to involve precognition, predicting dramatic changes in the destiny of great men. The simplest dramatic use of the dream relies on it being ignored or misinterpreted. The audience is thus given a cue as to what is likely to happen, and dramatic tension is created by the characters knowing as much as they do, but carrying on regardless. At a more subtle level, Garber (1974) argues that in both *Richard III* and *Julius Caesar* there is a sense in which disregarding portents is part of a more general characterization – of individuals who have taken their destiny into their own hands, or think they have, in contrast with those who consciously submit to their fate. However, the context in which dreaming is used in the plot has to be constructed to suit the play – the ideology of the culture in which it is set must condition the characters' responses. It is here that we can gain some insight into the assumptions that Shakespeare and his audience made about beliefs in antiquity, compared with more modern medieval beliefs – Richard III reigned a mere century before the play was first performed.

In *Julius Caesar* Calphurnia dreamt that Caesar's statue, 'like a fountain with an hundred spouts, did run pure blood; and many lusty Romans came smiling and did bathe their hands in it'. Portents a plenty are also reported – 'a tempest dripping fire' (St Elmo's fire?), a lion walking sulkily through the city, a bird of the night hooting and shrieking at mid-day, and of course the soothsayer's warning to 'Beware the Ides of March.' In this context the portentious dream is used as another example of the superstition of antiquity, rather than being a statement of current belief.

Incidentally, a character in the play called Artemidorus is described as a teacher of rhetoric, but this is probaby not an anachronistic reference to Artemidorus of Daldis, whose dream books became widely available in printed Latin and Greek on the Continent for the first time in the second half of the sixteenth century. The play was taken from Plutarch's *Lives*, in which Artemidorus is described as a native of the Isle of Guidos and a doctor of rhetoric in the Greek tongue. Artemidorus of Daldis was not born at that time. The first English translation of Artemidorus's *Oneirocritica*, by Robert Woods, was published in 1606. It must have been a popular book as it had gone to five editions by 1656 and 24 editions by 1744. However when the play was written (in 1601) Shakespeare may have been familiar with the Latin or Greek version, but his audience in the main would not.

In *Richard III* Clarence has every reason to fear for his life, since he has been imprisoned in the Tower of London. The reason he offers to Richard for his incarceration is that the king had been 'hearkening after prophecies and dreams ... and suchlike toys as these had moved his highness to commit me now'. Here belief in such portents is presented as being obviously wrongheaded, and it follows that offering such dubious evidence could only be in the interests of dark political ends. Clearly Shakespeare's audience was expected to take a sceptical view of dreams as portents, attributing such beliefs to the ancients.

Clarence's dream is much more closely described than any in *Julius Caesar*, and is a highly believable nightmare of drowning. Clarence has escaped from the Tower and is crossing the Channel with his brother, Gloucester (later to become Richard III). Walking together on the ship's deck, Gloucester stumbles and Clarence, in trying to steady him, is knocked overboard. A graphic description of drowning is followed by his translation to the 'kingdom of perpetual night'. The two abrupt changes of scene – from the deck to the water, and from the water to the next world – are typical of the 'scene shift' phenomenon of dreaming. Even more convincing as an account of a real dream is the idea that Gloucester is somehow was responsible for his death – but only accidentally. This is a truly classic example of dream-work, as described by psychoanalysts. The latent thought is the notion that Gloucester may be plotting to murder Clarence – an idea too horrifying to contemplate. The dream-work process thus thinly disguises this, making Gloucester kill him all the same, but accidentally. 'Gloucester will kill me by accident, though he doesn't want to' (Garber, 1974).

It is my contention here that neither Shakespeare nor his audience believed that dreams predicted the future, although they were certainly prepared to entertain the idea. The interest and subtlety of the plays rely on a considerable degree of scepticism of the infallibility of dreams as guides for the future.

The Grimm brothers, according to Donald Ward (1981), introducing his translation of their legends, described the nightmare as being a traveller in physical form. In one of these stories some shepherds who observed one regularly using a boat to cross a river, and removed the boat, reduced the nightmare to wailing pitifully and threatening them, demanding the return of the boat:

> At night they like to ride horses, and in the morning one can see that they have done so because the horses are exhausted ... They like to tangle their victims' hair into elflocks, or as they are also called, tangle locks, or mare's braids. They do this by sucking on the hair and twisting it.

Are we really expected to believe this? The account hovers on the brink of farce, and must surely have been intended as a spine-chiller more analogous to a modern horror film than a literal description of something that was to be believed. We are invited to thrill to the idea of travelling nightmares, but the essentially humorous style informs us that it is not to be taken entirely seriously.

The upshot of this foray into the literature on beliefs in antiquity seems to be that there was a great deal of credulity but some scepticism, as well as some wonderfully entertaining stories. Much of what went on seems unremarkable in terms of modern beliefs and practices – either in the fringe cults and the established churches or in modern psychotherapy. As today, people liked the idea of weird beliefs about dreaming, but imputed them to foreigners (such as the Assassins) or the ancients.

Modern beliefs about dreaming

The beginnings of modern thought on sleep and dreaming can be traced to the late eighteenth century, the time of the Enlightenment. Scientific writings were read widely by educated people, unlike today, when we are divided into two cultures by the inaccessibility of science to non-experts. In 1794 Erasmus Darwin published *Zoonomia*, which was partly a medical textbook, partly a treatise on biology. Together with his other writings, its profound influence on the Romantic poets illustrates the depth to which scientific ideas that today might remain obscure swiftly penetrated literary and artistic thinking (King-Hele, 1950). His chapters on sleep and reverie, for instance, informed the development of Coleridge's ideas about dramatic illusion, and his evolutionist ideas found expression in Wordsworth's ode 'Intimations of Immortality from Recollections of early Childhood':

> Though inland far we be,
> Our souls have sight of that immortal sea
> Which brought us hither.

Darwin's analysis of the state of consciousness during dreaming is still well worth reading. It was of course self-evident to him as a rationalist that dreams are a product of the imagination, rather than any mystical intervention. The idea prevalent during the 1960s that lack of dreaming might cause madness was anticipated by two hundred years in Darwin's writing. His view was that dreams prevent delirium by allowing trains of ideas to continue in the absence of sensory input:

> if they were to be suspended in sleep like the voluntary motions (which are exerted only by intervals during our waking hours) an accumulation of sensorial power would follow; and on our awakening a delirium would supervene, since these ideas caused by sensation would be produced with such energy, that we should mistake the trains of imagination for ideas excited by irritation; as perpetually happens to people debilitated by fevers on their first wakening; for in these fevers with debility the general quantity of irritation being diminished, that of sensation is increased.

This argument differs from the more modern notion that dreaming is involved in the resolution of conflicts, but similarly ascribes an importance to dreams in preserving sanity.

Central to Darwin's description of dreaming is the suspension of volition, 'and in respect to the mind, we never exercise our reason or recollection in dreams; we may sometimes seem distracted between contending passions, but we never compare their objects, or deliberate about the acquisition of these objects'. This observation, that we remain uncritical observers when dreaming, is an important part of more recent theorizing about dreaming by the psychophysiologist Allan Rechtschaffen, who has described dreams as being 'isolated' and even 'un-imaginative' in the sense that we cannot imagine something else during the action of a dream. (This theory is more fully described in Chapter 5.)

Darwin's work shows just how little scientific thought on dreaming has changed over the intervening centuries, and its popularity and deep influence during his lifetime ensured that these rationalist ideas became an accepted part of literary as well as scientific ideology. However, what can we say with confidence about the beliefs of ordinary people in the nineteenth or even in the late twentieth century?

One approach is to consider the usage of words. A very common modern expression is the dream 'thing' – for instance, a dream kitchen or a dream holiday – implying that dreams are simple wish fulfilments. This usage is now so prevalent that it hardly conveys anything more than the best that can be imagined. When Emerson wrote 'The search after the great is the dream of youth' in 1847, this was a metaphor with considerable impact. The *Oxford English Dictionary* gives no previous examples of this usage, but twentieth-century examples abound, ranging from 'I dream of Jeanie with the light brown hair' and 'I'm dreaming of a White Christmas', to Martin Luther King's dream of a just and non-racist society, the American Dream and every other advertisement for kitchens and holidays in the sun. We can only speculate whether this is yet another example of the pervasive influence of psycho-analytic thinking on our culture.

Since the early 1960s the achievements of physiologists and psychologists in the study of dreaming have received a good deal of attention in the media, much of it sensationalist, so one might expect some of this information to have percolated through to become common knowledge. While much remains to be explained about dreaming, a number of accepted findings have been made. Three of the questions in the Hull survey were designed to assess how well known these findings have become. The statements with which respondents were invited to entirely agree, agree with qualification or disagree were:

- Dreams only occur in the few moments before you wake up;
- Dreaming sleep is commonly accompanied by flaccid (relaxed) paralysis;
- Preventing people from dreaming drives them mad.

We know from experimental evidence that dreams proceed in 'real time' and are just as long as they seem. The flaccid paralysis of rapid eye movement sleep, usually accompanied by dreaming, is also well established. Depriving people of dreaming (rapid eye movement) sleep has been practiced in sleep laboratories and such deprivation drives people no more mad than depriving them of any other sort of sleep, although one highly publicized early report did suggest the reverse.

The responses of those surveyed revealed some ignorance about the first question. Eighteen of the 149 respondents agreed firmly with the statement that 'Dreams occur only in the few moments before you wake up', and a further 23 thought it may be true. The second question, whether dreaming is accompanied by flaccid paralysis, evoked the agreement of a surprising 48 respondents, although these people did not reveal themselves to be well informed about the other questions. There was no evidence of any general consistency in the responses to this group of questions to indicate that the subjects who responded correctly did so out of knowledge of the scientific findings. The large proportion (33 of the 149) who agreed with the statement that preventing dreams can cause madness, however, suggests that some of the publicity may have got through, although this issue may have been con-founded with ideas of brainwashing and the effects of total sleep loss.

Modern beliefs, one might think, ought to be in the rationalist mould of the Enlightenment, but little or nothing is taught about the psychology of consciousness in schools, except in terms of religious studies. Religion has had a decisive influence on thought on dreaming, and it is undergoing a revival in many parts of the world. In particular, fundamentalism is becoming increas-ingly popular in both the East and the West. The UK has been spared so far, but while the majority of the population are religiously inactive in terms of church-going, a large proportion would call themselves Christians, their spiritual beliefs having been informed by Christian teaching. The established Church of England is at one with other Christian churches in upholding the claims of the New Testament while keeping quiet about some of the Old Testament stories. Religious education in schools is of course compulsory in the UK, and is taught using children's versions of the Bible, such as Horton's *Stories of the Early Church* (1963) and Robertson's *The Ladybird New Testament* (1981). The bowdlerizations in these books make it clear that there is little doubt about the credibility of the revelations reported in the New Testament, apart from those which occur to people who are awake. That is, biblical accounts of supernatural visitations during dreams, and dreams fore-telling the future, are presented without comment; however, visitations occur-ring during wakefulness are altered to become visitations during dreams.

The Hull survey included questions on whether spirits visited the body to cause dreams, whether dreams could foretell the future, whether nightmares could be caused by evil spirits, and whether the soul can leave the body during sleep. The respondents were also asked whether the dreams reported in the New Testament could be literally true (Table 1.1).

More than half the respondents considered that dreams could foretell the future, and amongst those who believed in the literal truth of the accounts of dreaming in the New Testament this proportion was much higher. Very few thought that nightmares could be caused by demons, or that the soul leaves the body during sleep. Only two of the 15 believers in the Bible accounts agreed that spirits could visit us during dreams, although it is crucial to the sense of these accounts that God made himself known to individuals during dreams, and actually visited them in their dreams.

Table 1.1   Inconsistencies in beliefs about dreaming

Are the Bible dreams literally true?	Can dreams foretell events?		
	Never	Sometimes	Total
Certainly not	15	11	26
Possibly true	20	21	41
Certainly true	2	13	15
Total respondents	37	45	

This demonstrates that even well educated people can hold mutually contradictory beliefs (a proposition that social psychologists would find quite uncontroversial). In this context it is obvious that we must be careful not to oversimplify the ideology of distant cultures, either in time or in space, simply for our own ease of comprehension. A modern anthropological study of Zulu people in South Africa (Ngubane, 1976) reports that

> ancestral spirits are believed to visit their descendants in their sleep and through dreams make their wishes known. Sleep is *ubuthongo*, and an ancestral spirit is *ithongo*. The etymology here could well indicate the contact during sleep between the living and the dead, in which case sleep may be regarded as a miniature death that takes a person away from the conscious life of the day.

In imputing this degree of credulity to people who live far away in foreign cultures, are anthropologists liable to be careless in the way they ask their questions? The official religion in the UK – Christianity – invokes supernatural dreams; and yet even the most devout Anglicans are most unlikely to interpret their own dreams as messages from a deity. Among the sample of Hull University students over half of those questioned thought that the dreams of Joseph, the Magi and so on were literally true, but it would be naïve to conclude from this that they really believed that communications of this sort were still possible – that is, presumably they happened in Biblical times by unique divine intervention that would never be repeated. A surprising contrast to what any anthropologist would have to report about the religious beliefs of modern Westerners is Turnbull's (1961) authoritative and intimate account of the lives of pigmies in the forests of the Congo – this contains no references to dreaming at all, and offers very little evidence of pigmy mysticism.

Rather than modern Western beliefs being less mystic than those in antiquity or in underdeveloped communities, they seem equally if not more so than some. It could be argued that the very incomprehensibility of the modern world has made us even more credulous. Many of the quite commonplace products of modern technology might as well be magic, for all that any normal person could be expected to understand how they work.

The interpretation of dreams

Lay interpretations

Despots might well take their dreams seriously, just as they would be deeply interested in any of their own bodily functions, as would their courtiers. A pharoah and a modern dictator would share the conundrum that although apparently so similar to their subjects, with their same mortal limitations, they have somehow acquired the privilege of uniquely determining their country's future, and deciding on matters of life and death perhaps every day. The fact that soothsayers were employed by rulers from the pharoahs to Hitler is perhaps unsurprising. The advice given by these advisers would have been guided as much by expediency as by any rules of interpretation, and as such cannot be taken to represent a body of thought on dreaming. In modern life astrology seems to have taken over from dream interpretation as the sooth-sayer's preferred technique.

Fragments of papyri from the second millenium BC seem to be the first writings to deal exclusively with the subject matter of dreams, mainly concerning themselves with incest and bestiality with various animals. The only interpretations offered are 'That is bad' or 'That is good', with no further elaboration. Assyrian cuneiform texts have also been found that give interpretations of dream topics, many of which, again, are taboo behav-iours – eating the flesh of one's penis, killing brothers or sons, eating faeces. According to de Becker (1968), however, others are more mundane:

> To meet a horse was to obtain a saviour. Monkeys, pigs, foxes, mice, cats, birds, snakes and dogs were favourable, indicating posterity and prosperity. But he-goats and sometimes rams were bad omens. Long commentaries were devoted to dreams of flying, even at this period. All, with a few exceptions, signified danger and often death ... The problems of physiological life are not forgotten. Importance is given to teeth-grinding, interpreted in a negative way, together with speaking, groaning or snoring while dreaming.

The most important dream book of this sort was the compilation by Artemidorus in the second century AD, taking material from Middle Eastern, Greek and North African sources. His was not entirely a list of subjects and their meanings, and he preferred to make interpretations by considering a sequence of dreams, and even the personality and circumstances of the dreamer. Quite often a dream was interpreted as an allegory for what was about to happen to the dreamer. The complexity of some of his interpretations and the attention paid to the dreamer have invited comparisons between his methods and those of Freud, centuries later. Charles Rycroft (1979) reports that Artemidorus needed to know at least six facts about a dream before it could be interpreted: 'Whether the events depicted in the dream were plausible or bizarre; whether they were approximately interconnected; whether they were customary for the dreamer; what events prior to the dream could have influenced it; and the dreamer's name and occupation.' His books were not widely circulated, and in one of the last two, which were dedicated to his son (and unpublished), was the assertion that it contains instances 'that will make you a better interpreter of dreams than all, or at least inferior to none; but, if published, they will show you know no more than the rest' – a sentiment that Glover (1909) rather pithily describes as suggesting science declining into profession. While interpretations had previously derived their credibility from divine revelations of one sort or another, from then onwards dream interpretations in Europe drew their authority primarily from their antiquity.

A well developed systematization of dream interpretation apparently existed in China, but was never taken entirely seriously, or at least – being incor-porated into the civil service – lacked the glamour of antiquity or divine revelation. Joseph Needham's only indexed reference to dreaming in ancient China is tantalizingly brief:

Oneiromancy, or prognostication by dreams, was also practised in China, as in most ancient civilisations, though it can hardly be said to have taken a very important place there. The Chou Li says that the interpretation of dreams was in the department of the Grand Augur (Ta Pu), and mentions a special expert of lower grade (Chan Meng) who specialised in it. Here again the chief book was late, the Meng Chan I Chih of Chhen Shih-Yuan, published in +1562 (Ming). How far certain aspects of Chinese dream-interpretation might be considered, as Chinese themselves are sometimes inclined to think, anticipations of Freudian psychology, would be a subject worth investigating. (Needham, 1956)

The invention of printing in Europe in the fifteenth century soon enabled the publication of a number of books offering dream interpretations for ordinary people. These books typically claimed to be the distillation of wisdom handed down from Arab sages through the centuries, and they all drew heavily on Artemidorus's work. They took the form of dictionaries, with lists of subject matter and their associated meanings. As Raymond de Becker (1968) points out, they could have been treated as gospel by the naïve, or turned into parlour games by sceptics. The *Palais du Prince du Sommeil*, written by Celestin de Mirbel in 1667, actually states in the preface that 'The favours of the strictest ladies will be wholly won for you, at the moment when you become the sympathetic interpreter of their dreams' – certainly a pragmatic reason for buying this dream book.

The modern newspaper horoscope has largely taken over from dream books, although the latter are still published and still draw largely on the works of Artimedorus (or claim to). The truth is, few people believe that revelations are going to be made to them in dreams – and even on the rare occasions when an individual really feels that a dream is of overwhelming significance, the so-called dream books only take in the most gullible. Nevertheless, we still tell each other our dreams and look them up in these absurd books, and still read our horoscopes – just for fun.

Psychoanalytic dream interpretation: the lay view

Psychoanalytic thinking has had a deep influence on psychiatry and psychology since the early twentieth century, but this has been by no means decisive and its increasingly fragmented theories have been subjected to continuous criticism. Its influence on Western culture, however, has been pervasive, particularly in literature, theatre and the cinema. Its historical importance to the development of modern ideology has come from its unique claim to explain experience, however eccentrically. That is to say, there was – or at least in the first quarter of the twentieth century – no well developed rationalist alternative to theology or a simplistic materialism to explain mental life. Rejection of official religion drove people to magical or spiritualistic fringe cults and rationalism. While psychoanalysis itself probably had little to do with the decline in accepted religious belief, its early popularizers only benefited from it. As Geoffrey Gorer (1966) has remarked, their books for the lay public implied that psychoanalytic theory offered an insight into matters of general concern of a depth and quality simply not available to the uninitiated, to people without qualifications. The authority of medicine finally ousted Artemidorus's invocations of antiquity, and the increasingly muted references to the supernatural by the clergy, to explain life's ordinary ecstasies and tribulations.

The early splintering of the psychoanalytic movement and independent developments by neo-Freudians such as Alfred Adler in the US undermined the coherence of Freud's original formulations. To the outsider psychoanalysis appears a pretty broad church, at least as far as dream interpretation is concerned. One idea from the psychoanalytic approach that can be said to have made a firm impression is that dreams come from within the mind, rather than from outside (although in the case of Jung's psychology even this is not clear). Many dreams are so bizarre that they seem inexplicable and it follows that only a medically qualified expert could penetrate the machinations of the subconscious mind that produced them. The second psychoanalytic preoccupation that has come through to the public is sex. The idea that dream objects have sexual symbolism, however, can degenerate into a sort of post-Artemidorian dream-book formula, where anything elongated is a phallic symbol, and anything with a hole is a vaginal symbol. This is the layperson's view of psychoanalytic dream interpretation – how any more subtle understanding is achieved is obscure. This obscurity has not detracted from the approach's popularity, and many widely held notions about psychology have originated in the cinema, magazines or novels, based on interpretations of psychoanalytic thought.

To sum up this chapter's survey of what people believe about sleep and dreaming – what seem to be self-evident truths – it appears there is very little consensus. Most people would probably agree that sleep is necessary and provides rest from exertion, and perhaps has some restorative function as well. As far as dreaming is concerned, it seems that the most striking difference between modern Western culture and prescientific cultures is not any decrease in mysticism or informal supernatural beliefs, but an explosion in the number of alternative explanations of dreaming. The scientific explanation (to be developed in the rest of this book) seems to be just one, along with religious, medical or psychoanalytic and superstitious ones. While recent scientific findings on sleep patterns receive regular exposure in popular TV science programmes and magazines, there is little evidence from the results of the Hull survey that they have made any impression on the public mind.

2
Studying Sleep in the Laboratory

The study of sleep was revolutionized in the early 1960s by the systematization of the previously *ad hoc* methods of estimating sleep depth and quality, using EEG (brainwave) and other measures. These new methods of recording and scoring sleep stages in human beings were based on the use of a piece of equipment available in most hospitals and many university departments of psychology – the clinical EEG machine, or electroencephalograph, a device for detecting and recording the electrical activity of the brain. The ready availability of recording devices contributed to the explosion of research into sleep and dreaming during the late 1960s.

Much of the evidence discussed in the next few chapters relies on EEG and other electrophysiological information, and some understanding of the basis of these measures is essential to understanding how we know what we do know about sleep. The next few pages contain an explanation of the history and workings of the EEG, written in a non-technical way.

The story of the electroencephalograph (EEG)

The principles of electromagnetism were established by the late eighteenth century, but it was not until the mid-nineteenth century that measurements could be made of the small currents produced by living tissue. However there had been one or two early attempts to investigate the relationship between electricity and living organisms during the eighteenth century, long before the technology existed to do so properly. According to Grey Walter in his book *The Living Brain* (1953) informal experiments on executed criminals had shown that electric shocks caused muscles to contract and twitch, and Louis XV had 'caused an electric shock from a battery of Leyden jars to be administered to 700 Carthusian monks joined hand to hand, with prodigious effect'. The Leyden jar had simply been a primitive condenser, capable of storing static electricity for short periods of time, and more refined experiments had to await the invention of reliable sources of electric current.

Electrical stimulation could produce dramatic effects, but the proper study of electrophysiology was prevented by the impossibility of recording small electrical potentials. The gold leaf electroscope, available early in the nineteenth century, was too insensitive to register the tiny changes in potential difference associated with nervous and muscular activity.

The first workable device for recording small potentials was the string galvanometer. Although totally obsolete in today's laboratories, a description of this simple device is useful in making clear what is being recorded, and illustrating some of the problems that still confront modern electroencephalographers. Essentially the string galvanometer consisted of a coil of copper wire, connected at either end to two electrodes with string hanging down within the coil, to which was attached a small magnetized mirror. A difference in the electrical potential between the two electrodes caused a current flow through the coil, creating a magnetic field within. The mirror would then rotate in proportion the strength of the current. A light – shone onto the mirror and reflected onto a fairly distant surface – provided an initial doubling in amplification of the movement of the mirror, and the further the light was projected, the greater the subsequent amplification of the change in potential difference. An improvement on this basic design was to mount the magnet and mirror on a lightweight but rigid rotating rod, and to attach a coil spring at one end so that when a change in potential difference was registered the mirror swung back to its original position.

One way of obtaining a permanent record of this in the nineteenth century was for one observer to watch the galvanometer mirror through a telescope and to work a key with his finger that operated a signal pen on a smoked drum kymograph. The magnitude of the excursion of the mirror was read aloud by a second observer (watching the projected light) to an assistant, who wrote it on the drum next to the appropriate signal.

An apparently apocryphal account is of two Prussian medical officers, Fritsch and Hitzig, who in 1870 took advantage of the opportunity offered by the Franco-Prussian War to study the exposed brains of soldiers struck down on the battlefield. What is certain is that they discovered that electrical stimulation of some parts of the cortex caused movements in the limbs on the opposite side of the body from the part of the brain that had been stimulated. Animal experiments showed that these movements could be repeatedly elicited by stimulation of the same areas. This made it possible to map what we now know as the motor cortex (the part of the brain controlling muscle function) in terms of the musculature each section controlled.

The procedure, incidentally, can and has been performed on patients undergoing brain surgery. The surface of the brain is totally insensitive, and operations on the brain in humans commonly involve only a local anaesthetic. The patient is conscious and can even report to the surgeon any experiences he or she has as the operation progresses.

It was now obvious that with sufficiently sensitive recording techniques it should be possible to map the parts of the brain responsible for perception – the sensory cortex – in a similar way. This was the task that Richard Caton (1875) set himself. Using a Thomson reflecting galvanometer and Du Bois-Reymond's coated, non-polarizable electrodes, Caton repeated some earlier experiments on the electrophysiology of nerve and muscle preparations, and then set about recording from the exposed surface of the brain. When doing so he discovered that potentials were spontaneously generated (the EEG) and that it was indeed possible to detect electrical brain responses to stimuli. He succeeded in establishing that the visual cortex was located in the occiput, or rear of the head, but he was unable to find any location specifically responsive to

Figure 2.1   The first recorded electroencephalogram, by Hans Berger. The lower line is a 10 cycles per second sine wave for use as a time marker, the upper line is the recording made from Berger's young son in 1925

sound stimulation. The observation that there was spontaneous electrical activity on the surface of the cortex seemed relatively insignificant at the time, but it did herald the discovery of the electroencephalogram.

Mary Brazier (1961) has described the work of the German psychiatrist Hans Berger as the triumph of a man working with equipment that was inadequate even by the standards of his day. Like Caton, Berger attempted to record electrical responses to sensory stimuli in animals, although it seems that the work he did between 1902 and 1910 was in general unsuccessful. In 1924 he turned to the measurement of human electrical potentials but delayed publication of his results until 1929, when the first recorded electroencephalogram (of his young son) appeared in *Archiv forschung Psychiatrie* (Figure 2.1).

Berger discovered the alpha rhythm, running at 10 cycles per second (hertz, or Hz). He found that this disappeared if the eyes were opened, with mental effort such as doing mental arithmetic (with the eyes closed) and with loud noises or painful stimuli. Berger's work was disregarded by physiologists, partly because it was published in psychiatric journals, and perhaps because of his reputation for eccentricity, seclusiveness and his outstanding belief in psychic phenomena such as telepathy. Only after his work was replicated by Adrian and Matthews in Cambridge did he get the credit he deserved for laying the foundations of human electroencephalography. Brazier's (1961) history of the EEG cannot be recommended too highly for readers interested in a full and authoritative account of the early days.

Modern EEG techniques

The modern electroencephalogram

The modern clinical EEG machine is a far cry from the simple galvanometer devices used by Berger and the other pioneers. Electronic amplifiers are arranged in banks, and between eight and 16 channels of EEG are transmitted to a bank of galvanometers. The use of multiple recordings has allowed the development of a series of techniques to localize sources of electrical activity within the cranium. These have been clinically very useful, for instance in localizing sources of abnormal activity in the head, caused by tumours or foreign objects. Only one EEG channel is necessary for the scoring of sleep stages, although two or more are sometimes used. The other channels are used to record electrical activity generated by movements of the eyes or from the neck muscles under the chin.

The differential amplifiers in EEG machines take the difference between the voltages offered by the two inputs, which is normally less than 200 microvolts (200 millionths of a volt), and amplify this difference to a voltage sufficient to drive the galvanometer pens – perhaps 0.5 volts. In addition there is a selection of electronic high-frequency filters and low-frequency filters.

Modern EEGs work on the same principle as the sprung mirror galvanometer – that is, they are capable of measuring very fast changes in potential difference between the electrodes but are relatively insensitive to slow changes. After a shift in the level of voltage difference between the electrodes has taken place, the output from the amplifier gradually returns to the midline. The rate at which it does this is measured as a 'time constant' – defined as the time it takes for the output to return 63 per cent of the way to baseline after a shift in the input voltage level. The shorter the time constant, the more attenuated the slow activity. To pursue an analogy with the sprung mirror galvanometer, the more powerful the spring, the faster the mirror swings back to its original position.

Recording montages for sleeping subjects

The definitive *Manual of Standardized Terminology, Techniques and Scoring System for Sleep Stages of Human Subjects* (Rechtschaffen and Kales, 1968) gives a detailed account of the internationally agreed system of recording of sleep stages. EEG (electroencephalographic, or brainwave), EOG (electro-oculographic, or eye movement) and EMG (electromyographic, or muscle activity) recordings are taken simultaneously to provide a composite picture of activity throughout the night. The stages themselves are defined in terms of patterns or syndromes of EEG, EOG and EMG activity.

The EEG, according to the manual, should be recorded from an electrode placed centrally on the scalp and one behind the ear. In practice many laboratories use two electrodes on the scalp, one at the vertex (centrally midway between the bridge of the nose and the inion, or bony bump at the base of the cranium), and one frontally, about two centimetres behind the hairline. The EEG is recorded as the difference between these two electrode placements.

Eye movements are recorded from electrodes taped above each eyebrow and electrodes taped over the opposite cheekbone (Figure 2.2), giving two EOG channels. These do not reflect activity from the eyes individually, but between them the two channels record an eye movement in any direction. What is being recorded here is not the electrical activity associated with the muscles controlling the movements of the eyes, but the change in electrical field caused by the rotation of the eyeballs in their sockets. This is caused by the corneoretinal potential – a standing potential across the retina of about one tenth of a volt. EOG changes are of the same order as EEG changes – up to 150 microvolts – and are typically recorded using the same time constants and level of amplification as the EEG channel. An important point to remember about EOG recordings made with EEG amplifiers is that they never give direct information on the direction of gaze – only changes in direction – and the rate at which the galvanometer pens return to the midline of the paper chart is

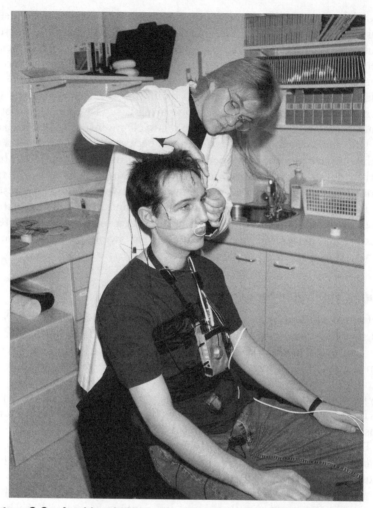

Figure 2.2 A subject being prepared for all-night EEG/EOG monitoring in
St Thomas' Hospital Sleep Clinic. Electrode leads are attached to a box, which are
then plugged into a terminal on the headboard

determined by the time-constant setting. In the early 1960s misunderstandings
about the nature of the recordings contributed to some confusion about
whether the eye movements in dreaming sleep did or did not follow the action
of the dream.

EMG recordings from under the chin reflect the activity of the muscles in the
neck. These muscles are under the control of postural reflexes, which ensure
a level of tonic (continuing) activity almost all the time (unlike, for instance,
the large muscles in the arms and legs). This measure gives a good index of the
tonic level of muscular relaxation in light sleep, identifies periods of movement
that may contribute to outside interference in the EEG and EOG channels, and
is crucial for determining the presence of REM (rapid eye movement) sleep,
when there is little or no EMG activity.

The EEG during sleep

EEG observations

Early work in the 1930s and 1940s (Loomis *et al.*, 1937) established that there are systematic changes in brainwaves during sleep, in that large slow waves develop within 15 minutes of a subject falling asleep at night, and during the night the amplitude of these waves waxes and wanes. A convention was established of sleep stages, indicated by the numbers 1 to 6, with 6 being the 'deepest' (the biggest slow waves). Rather puzzlingly the EEG would sometimes revert to low voltage while the subject was still plainly asleep. These periods of low-voltage sleep were called 'emergent stage 1' because subjects were not as easily roused as from ordinary 'sleep onset stage 1' sleep, and because, being contiguous with deeper stages of sleep, these periods of light sleep were obviously not a transition between wakefulness and sleep, in the way that sleep onset stage 1 seemed to be.

In the 1950s Aserinsky and Kleitman (1953) reported rapid saccadic eye movements that were similar in appearance to waking eye movements and were associated with reports of dreaming. Four years later Dement and Kleitman (1957) identified 'emergent stage 1' sleep as a completely distinct stage of sleep from other light sleep stages, always accompanied by rapid eye movements and frequently by reports of dreaming. Subsequently Ralph Berger (1961) discovered the loss of neck muscle tone that accompanies REM sleep. The latter two findings, linking EEG patterns with eye movement and neck and throat muscle activity, formed the basis of the recording and scoring methods for humans now in use all over the world. Psychophysiological measures are today used to define sleep states, rather than merely to describe them. Figure 2.3 provides good examples of the psychophysiology associated with relaxed wakefulness and five internationally recognized stages of sleep – four slow-wave sleep stages, numbered 1 to 4, and stage REM (rapid eye movement) sleep, which is associated with dreaming.

When subjects arrive at the sleep laboratory for a night's recording they prepare themselves for bed in the normal way. When they are in their pyjamas, or dressing gown if they wear nothing in bed, the electrodes are applied to their faces and heads. It is possible to record from more than one subject at a time on a single EEG machine, so it is common to have two bedrooms equipped with headboards, into which the electrodes are plugged – as at, for instance, the Department of Human Sciences at Loughborough University. The modern hospital-based system at St Thomas' Hospital in London allows up to four patients to be monitored simultaneously. There they have dispensed with pen and paper polygraphic records (which, with four subjects and a standard 16-channel encephalograph, would limit each subject to four channels). Instead, all the EEG/EOG data are digitized and stored on computer, along with ECG (electrocardiograph) data, information on oral/nasal airflow, respiratory effort and oxygen saturation, and a microphone to monitor snoring.

Scoring is initially conducted automatically, and then confirmed by eye (Figure 2.4). According to Simone de Lacy, the sleep services manager at the

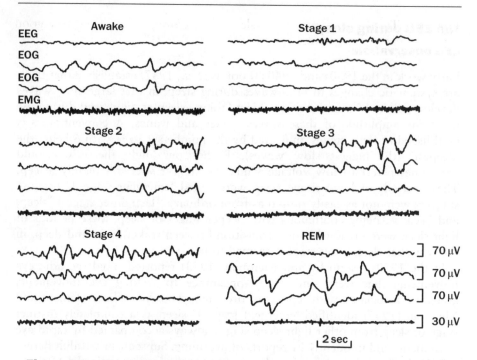

Figure 2.3 Sleep stages. The slow-wave sleep stages 1–4 are characterized by increasing high-voltage, low-frequency EEG. REM sleep is characterized by low-voltage, desynchronized EEG, rapid eye movements and very low EMG in the neck

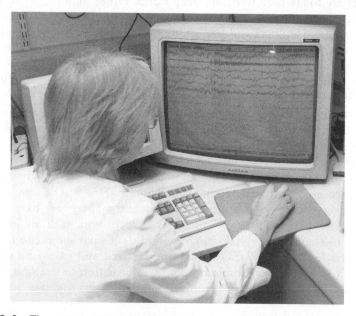

Figure 2.4 The automated sleep stage analysis is checked by eye at St Thomas' Hospital Sleep Clinic

unit at St Thomas' the automated sleep-stage scoring systems are very good but still tend to underestimate sleep and to confuse REM sleep with wakefulness. At Hull University we were fortunate to have a custom-converted suite, with three single bedrooms, electromagnetically screened, soundproofed, environmentally controlled and linked to a control room by hidden cables, but were limited to a paper and pen recording system, like many other university-based facilities.

When the experimenter has ensured that good signals are being recorded from all the subjects he or she will say good night and turn out the lights. Most people find the environment of the laboratory unusual, and on their first night they typically take longer to get to sleep than usual. On the second and subsequent nights subjects remain indubitably awake – showing alpha rhythm (originally known as the 'Berger rhythm' after Hans Berger, who first reported it) at 10 cycles per second (Hz) in the EEG and periodic blinks in the EOG – less than ten minutes. Drowsiness (Figure 2.5) is first indicated by a reduction in the frequency of alpha rhythm (from about 10 Hz to 8.5 Hz or so in a young adult) and a reduction of its amplitude, and then by its disappearance. It is replaced by a low-voltage (relatively flat) record with slow activity in the range 2–7 Hz. At the same time, the blinks typical of wakefulness are replaced by slow rolling movements of the eyes, easily seen in the EOG, as the subject drifts into stage 1 sleep.

Stage 1 sleep is defined in terms of the EEG and EOG records as consisting of a low-voltage EEG with some slow activity and occasional vertex sharp waves, and slow rolling eye movements. Subjects do not usually stay in stage 1 for long – between one and 10 minutes. The less settled subject may alternate for a while between stage 1 sleep and wakefulness, but once sleep takes over there is usually a fairly rapid transition from this stage to the deeper sleep stages.

The onset of stage 2 sleep is taken to be the first sleep spindle or K complex, and this is conventionally regarded as the beginning of sleep proper. Sleep spindles are bursts of fast (13–15 Hz) EEG activity that last about two seconds, increase in amplitude to about 50 microvolts and then decline, giving them their spindle-shaped envelope. K complexes are phasic events (isolated occurrences) in which there is a sudden increase in negativity on the scalp,

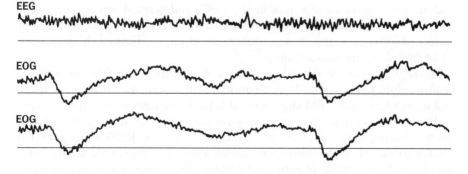

Figure 2.5   EEG/EOG signs of sleep onset

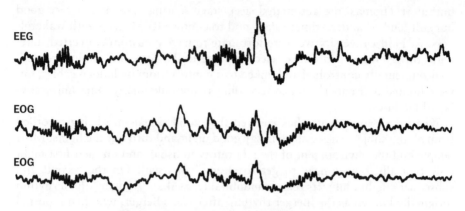

EEG

EOG

EOG

Figure 2.6 Sleep spindle and K complex

followed by a corresponding positive wave. They last between 0.5 and 2.0 seconds, and while their amplitude may only be in the region of 50 microvolts, they may be as large as 250 microvolts from peak to trough (Figure 2.6). Stage 2 sleep is defined as low-voltage EEG with mixed, slow frequencies and periodic sleep spindles and/or K complexes.

More or less as soon as the subject has settled into stage 2 sleep at the beginning of the night, larger slow waves with a frequency of less than 2 Hz begin to appear in the EEG. These increase in amplitude and persistence, and when they occupy 20 per cent or more of the record the requirements for the scoring of stage 3 sleep are satisfied. Sleep spindles and K complexes may continue during stage 3 sleep. A healthy young adult will typically have reached this stage of sleep within 20 minutes of going to bed, and sleep now continues to deepen, with larger and more persistent slow waves dominating the EEG record. These slow waves pervade the head to the extent that they are also picked up by the EOG electrodes, just as K complexes are. When the slow waves occupy 50 per cent or more of the record the subject is judged to be in stage 4 sleep.

As far as the deep slow-wave sleep stages are concerned, therefore, the greater the amplitude and the slower the frequency of the EEG slow waves, the deeper the sleep. Stage 3 is defined as comprising between 20 per cent and 50 per cent of slow waves in the EEG, and stage 4 sleep as comprising over 50 per cent of the record dominated by slow waves. It is conventional to regard all sleep stages 1–4 as slow-wave sleep, to distinguish them from REM (rapid eye movement) sleep.

Figure 2.7 shows a typical pattern of sleep throughout the night for a healthy adult. On going to sleep, all normal people start with slow-wave sleep, and do not have any REM sleep until at least 45 minutes have elapsed. There is then an alternation between slow-wave sleep and REM sleep, with REM sleep recurring about every hour and a half. The first REM sleep period is usually shorter than the subsequent ones – about 15 minutes for adults, compared with later periods of about half an hour. Deep slow-wave sleep (stages 3 and 4) predominates in the first half of the night.

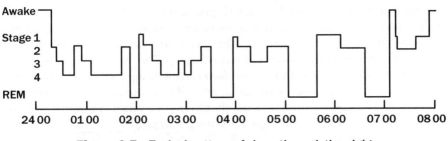

Figure 2.7 Typical pattern of sleep through the night

The pattern of sleep in Figure 2.7 is not only typical, it is also universal. No matter how much people vary in their lifestyles during the day, their sleep proceeds in the same regular pattern, obeying the same rules. While it is unremarkable for some people eat three meals a day while others skip breakfast and lunch altogether, taking all their food in the evening, there is no such difference during sleep – for instance no normal people have been found to take all their REM sleep in one session of 90 minutes at the beginning of the night, or save it all up for a session in the early hours of the morning. We are all slaves to the same mechanism, which proceeds every night to control our sleeping brains according to a complex set of rules that are only now becoming apparent.

It has also been very difficult to detect any reliable differences between the sleep profiles of different sorts of people – men versus women, the extraverted versus the introverted, the intelligent versus the unintelligent. While there are considerable differences between babies, young children, young adults and the aged, which will be dealt with later, the most striking thing about sleep patterns within a broad age group is how remarkably uniform they are.

Actigraphs, and other low-cost systems

The full panoply of EEG/EOG recording, plus other psychophysiological measures, is now highly developed, but it remains an extremely expensive procedure, requiring all-night monitoring in specialized facilities. For many purposes a simple record of movement (for instance, recorded at the wrist) provides enough information to estimate sleep length and sleep stability. Monk *et al.* (1999) were able to compare conventional polysomnographic (PSG) recordings of sleep and wakefulness with actigraph records for four astronauts during a space shuttle mission lasting three weeks. They found a very high correlation between PSG actigraphic estimates of sleep duration (r = 0.96) and sleep efficiency (r = 0.88). (Sleep efficiency is a derived measure – simply the proportion of the sleep period spent asleep.) This high correlation is typical of a number of studies comparing PSG with actigraph estimates of sleep length. Actigraphy is an excellent detector of the time spent asleep, and of sleep restlessness. It has found applications in the study of circadian activity rhythms in shiftworkers and airline workers (Daurat *et al.*, 2000), in assessments of the treatment of insomnia (Friedman *et al.*, 2000), and in assessing sleep among hospital inpatients (Krahn *et al.*, 1997).

A number of systems have been developed to replicate the full PSG montage in the home, with miniaturized recording and storage systems. An interesting half-way house is afforded by the 'nightcap' system, combining only eye-movement and body-movement recordings. Ajilore *et al.* (1995) report an 87 per cent concordance with PSG on *sleep stage* scoring (not merely sleep and wakefulness, as in the case of the actigraph). They commend this system for researchers 'wishing to study the psychophysiology and pathophysiology of sleep in more naturalistic and cost-effective paradigms'.

The first-night effect

Looking at the paraphernalia attached to a subject wired up for a night's recording, one might legitimately ask whether anybody could reasonably be expected to feel natural and to get to sleep in the usual way. Might not the electrodes, the constraining wires and the very fact of being observed in a laboratory not only delay sleep but also change the normal quality of sleep?

Experiments assessing the difference between the sleep achieved during successive nights in the laboratory have indeed revealed some evidence of difficulty getting to sleep on the first night (Agnew *et al.*, 1966). The time between lights-out and getting to sleep (the so-called 'sleep onset time') is increased, as is the amount of time first spent in light sleep before the transition to deep slow-wave sleep (stage 4) and the first REM sleep period. During the second and subsequent nights in the laboratory no progressive changes are observable in young adult volunteer subjects. Most experimental studies of sleep now allow subjects a night of acclimatization to the laboratory conditions – on the first night they are wired up in the usual way, but whatever recordings made are discarded, and the experiments proper begin on the second night. While most all-night recording experiments are conducted over brief periods (up to a week), some very extended studies have been done and there is no evidence that the patterns of sleep observed over short periods (after the first night) are in any way peculiar to the unfamiliar environment of the laboratory.

Brainwaves and the experience of being asleep

If sleeping people are shaken and asked if they were in fact asleep they usually have a definite answer. Everybody is familiar with their own experience of being asleep, and feel they can give a uniquely informed reply. As we shall see in the chapter on sleep problems, sometimes the 'insomniac' who complains of never sleeping is, in fact, by psychophysiological criteria, achieving normal amounts of sleep but his or her experience is of staying awake. What determines whether people feel they are asleep or awake? In a laboratory study using the old (Loomis) classification of sleep stages, subjects lying in bed and getting to sleep were asked to squeeze a bulb to indicate when they were 'drifting' or 'floating' (Davis *et al.*, 1937). Subjects who characteristically had dominant alpha EEG rhythms when awake were most suitable for this task as a low level of alpha rhythm then acted as a good indicator of alertness. (Some people produce few or no alpha rhythms, even when completely relaxed.) These subjects tended to squeeze their bulbs when their alpha rhythms had attenuated, which is consistent with the idea that drifting occurs when cortical arousal drops.

If the hypnagogic sensation of drifting can be identified with the attenuation of alpha rhythm, should we also define this as sleep onset, or should that be defined behaviourally? That is, should sleep onset be defined as non-responsiveness to quiet stimuli rather than on the basis of EEG activity? A study at the MRC Applied Psychology Research Unit in Cambridge compared a behavioural index (response to a faint auditory stimulus by pressing a button) with subjective and physiological indices of sleep onset (Ogilvie et al., 1989). While responses became fewer as subjects passed into stages 1 and 2, they only disappeared in stages 3 and 4 and REM sleep. The authors suggest that the behavioural evidence is of a gradual transition between wakefulness and sleep during what they term the 'sleep onset period', despite clearly notice-able psychophysiological changes between wakefulness and stages 1 and 2.

The lack of any reliable (in EEG/EOG terms) subjective sense of when sleep onset occurs is shown by comparisons between reports from 'good' sleepers and 'poor' sleepers. When normally good sleepers are woken from stage 1 or stage 2 sleep and asked whether they were awake or asleep, they tend to report definitely feeling asleep only in stage 2 sleep (Hauri and Olmstead, 1983), although this is not necessarily true for poor sleepers, who may deny they were asleep even when the EEG traces show clear signs of stage 2 sleep.

Sleep norms

Individual variations

You do not have to record brainwaves in order to know how long people sleep. Surveys have shown that adults sleep for an average of 7.5 hours, with a standard deviation of about one hour. That is, 68 per cent of the population can be expected to sleep for 6.5–8.5 hours per night, about 16 per cent regularly sleep for more than 8.5 hours, and another 16 per cent sleep for less than 6.5 hours (Figure 2.8).

Healthy individuals who regularly sleep for less than five hours a day are rare, but represent a sizable minority. These people are typically described as highly active individuals, as personified by the successful businessman or former British Prime Minister Margaret Thatcher. Jones and Oswald (1968), in a laboratory study of two 'short' sleepers, found that their sleep pattern was not that of the 'normal' sleeper during the first half of the night. Rather, while they showed the normal pattern of alternating between slow-wave sleep and REM sleep about every 90 minutes, the proportion of light sleep stages (1, 2 and 3) was low. Almost all their time asleep was spent in either stage 4 sleep or REM sleep, giving them a near normal total amount of these two sleep stages, and very low levels of light sleep. In another study of an elderly lady in poor health who slept very little, Ray Meddis et al. (1973) found that her sleep was

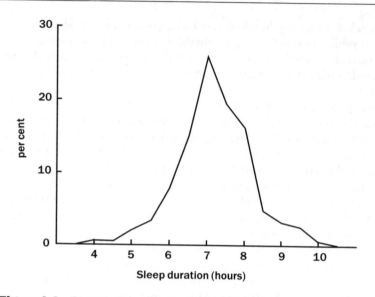

Figure 2.8   Distribution of sleep length by percentage of respondents (from Browman et al., 1977)

light and fitful, and over a period of a week she only achieved one night of proper sleep. During that night her sleep-stage pattern was more similar to that of a normal sleeper than a short sleeper.

There are occasional reports in medical journals of people not sleeping for extended periods of time when suffering from illnesses that interfere with brain function. A very interesting case is that of a 53-year-old man in Italy who suddenly began to sleep less and less (Lugaresi et al., 1986). His habitual amount of sleep had been five to seven hours per night, with a half-hour siesta in the afternoon. As his sleep problem developed he could only manage two or three hours of sleep, frequently disturbed by vivid dreams. Three months after his symptoms started he could not sleep at all, and suffered from waking dreams. The last six months of his life were spent in hospital, where he rarely slept, suffered from disorientation and an inability to concentrate enough to do the simplest task, and was totally unintelligible. After his death an autopsy established that he had suffered from a very rare brain condition in which the thalamus progressively degenerates. Two of his sisters and many of his relatives over three generations had died in the same way, indicating that the condition might have been inherited.

A follow-up study of five more cases from the same family and a study of 28 affected members of the family from four generations (Manetto et al., 1992) confirmed that this syndrome is determined genetically. Postmortems of the five revealed the same pattern of damage to the anterior ventral and medio-dorsal nuclei of the thalamus. The age of onset varied between 37 and 61, and death ensued after seven to 25 months, during which time the same pattern of sleep reduction followed by complete insomnia was accompanied by waking dreams, hallucinations and finally stupor and coma.

Did lack of sleep alone kill this man and his relatives? We cannot be sure, since the thalamus is a very important structure and damage to it may be lethal for a variety of reasons. In these cases, however, it seems that the nature of the disease was systematically to destroy nerve cells essential to the control of sleep, and these unfortunate people are probably the closest that we can expect to find in the way of subjects of a natural experiment on the long-term effects of the denial of sleep in human beings.

A total of 25 apparently unrelated families suffering from this inherited disorder have been identified since the first findings in Italy: five Italian, two French, four American, one Japanese, two Australian, eight German, one Austrian and two British (Gambetti and Lugaresi, 1998).

Periodically there are press reports of otherwise healthy individuals who need no sleep at all. These people rarely volunteer to be investigated in controlled EEG studies. One person who did submit to continuous observation is reported by Oswald and Adam (1980). This was a middle-aged man who had been involved in a road accident, after which he had suffered from headaches, difficulty walking and a total lack of sleep. After repeated medical examinations and seven years of litigation he was awarded £12 000 compensation, and 'aided by continuous benefits, he stayed off work, exhausted through lack of sleep'.

After an initial two nights in the sleep laboratory, when it was confirmed that he was continuously awake, he returned with his wife for a five-night stay. During the first three days he was watched increasingly closely, as it appeared that he may have been sleeping during the early evening when no recordings were being made, and during the nights his wife seemed to be doing her best to keep him awake. By the fourth day he had become obviously very sleepy. His speech was slurred, he was making visual misinterpretations, looking very dishevelled and seemed scarcely able to keep his eyes open. On the fifth night he finally fell asleep when the electrodes were on and recordings were being made. He stayed asleep for two and a half hours, at which point his wife woke him. 'He appeared disoriented, begged to be allowed to sleep, and said he must have been cured by an injection. The EEG appearances of slow-wave sleep and rapid eye movement (REM) sleep had been normal' (ibid). Despite this demonstration of habitual need for normal sleep, even if only for a few hours a night, this same individual appeared on television a few years later, again claiming never to sleep. Whatever the explanation of this case, it is obvious that such claims must be treated with the greatest scepticism. Nobody has yet been discovered who can maintain any semblance of normal health without sleeping.

What constitutes a normal amount of sleep, or precisely how long does each of us need to sleep? Apart from calculating the average amount of sleep taken, and the range in variation between people, it might seem that little more can be done to answer these questions. However, it has periodically been suggested that the demands of the modern world result in us typically sleeping less than optimally. Webb and Agnew (1975b) argue this case, pointing out that archival sources show that between 1910 and 1970 there was a reduction of sleep time in the US of about 90 minutes.

People commonly sleep longer at weekends than during the week, again indicating an unnatural restriction of sleep length on weeknights. In a study of this problem, Harrison and Horne (1996) investigated mood, performance and sleep latency over 26 nights: seven nights of baseline sleep, 14 nights of extended sleep (up to 10 hours per night) and five nights of recovery sleep. They found that over the 14-night period of extended sleep, subjects could indeed sleep for an additional hour, but that this extra sleep did not improve their self-rated mood or alertness levels during the day. There was a slight improvement in performance on a vigilance task, and sleep onset time on the multiple sleep latency test (MSLT) showed a reduction of about one minute. (The MSLT involves subjects' repeated attempts to go to sleep, with EEG/ EOG monitoring, and being reawakened whenever they achieve stage 2 sleep.)

These results show some gains for increased sleep, but fairly unimpressive ones in the context of an increase in sleep time of about 90 minutes. They contradict earlier work in the US that revealed better improvements in mood and performance following extended sleep (Levine *et al.*, 1988; Roehrs *et al.*, 1989; Wehr *et al.*, 1993). Harrison and Horne (1996) provide a number of explanations for these differences, some of them rather technical. What is clear is that the advantage of sleeping longer is marginal (and may be counter-productive as excessive sleep can produce a sort of lethargy of its own – see Chapter 7 on the 'Rip Van Winkle effect'). Also, the ability to sleep longer clearly does not necessarily indicate a greater need for sleep.

Sleep patterns in normal babies

Newborn infants' behavioural repertoire is somewhat limited, and there is, of course, no question of their reporting whether they are awake or asleep. A systematic description of neonatal 'states' was first suggested by Wolff (1959). Avoiding any 'anthropomorphic' assumptions, observations of the regularity of respiration, open or closed eyes, movements and vocalizations resulted in the definition of five mutually exclusive syndromes or states that are now widely accepted. Two of these states can be identified with sleep states that show a continuity of development to maturity in the form of REM sleep and deep slow-wave sleep. In neonates (newborn infants) REM sleep is termed 'active' sleep, and the neonatal equivalent of slow-wave sleep is 'quiet' sleep. The greatest changes in sleep in humans take place during the first year of life, with the normal one-year-old showing essentially the same patterns of sleep as an adult, although in different proportions of stages and with a recognizably different EEG.

As any parent knows, the neonate makes no distinction between night and day. His or her pattern of sleep and wakefulness is determined by an intrinsic cyclical pattern of alternating behavioural activity and sleep states, modulated by the demands of hunger and thirst, which commonly resolves into a four-hour 'day' by the end of the first month. By the age of two months, while some infants pass the night uncomplainingly and without demanding food, they do not spend the whole time asleep. Observations show that they wake periodically and the establishment of uninterrupted night-time sleep is uncommon before three months of age.

A neonatal infant's EEG during quiet sleep has few slow waves and no sleep spindles. Slow waves appear in bursts, separated by periods of low-voltage activity of about 10 seconds. In the first month after full term these slow-wave bursts increase in length until the low-voltage periods of quiet sleep are entirely displaced (Parmelee et al., 1967). Sleep spindles develop during the first two months of life, varying in frequency between 10 Hz and 14 Hz although showing no systematic tendency to increase in frequency with age (as is the case with the waking alpha rhythm, which becomes progressively faster with age to reach a maximum of 10–11 Hz) (Ellingson, 1964).

While there has been some disagreement about the incidence of EEG spindling in neonates, the consensus is that the development of spindles in the EEG of normal sleeping infants occurs between the end of the second month and end of the fourth, and the appearance of persistent spindling earlier or later than this period tends to be associated with clinical abnormalities (Monod and Guidasci, 1976). Normal sleep patterns at this age have, however, been reported for a group with known severe brain abnormalities (Williams et al., 1974). There are also large individual differences between normal infants that are not always obviously related to maturational age, so the timing of the appearance of EEG spindling during sleep cannot be taken as a reliable indication of abnormality.

Sleep patterns in the first three months of life are difficult to categorize and, compared with the remarkable uniformity of adult sleep, show a high degree of idiosyncrasy. Despite this, some consistent patterns have been established. The typical full-term infant sleeps for about 17 hours out of the 24. Active sleep is easily identifiable with adult REM sleep, and the neonate spends 60–80 per cent of sleeping time in active (REM) sleep (10–13 hours). Unlike adults, infants may show very short delays between sleep onset and active sleep onset, and sometimes go straight into active sleep. The time between sleep onset and active sleep onset thus tends to be either very short indeed – less than 10 minutes – or more than 50 minutes, as the period of alternation between active and quiet sleep is of the order of 60 minutes. Active or REM sleep onset persists for the first twelve months of life in normal infants.

Developmental sleep norms

The definitive work on sleep norms at different ages (Williams et al., 1974) reports on the sleep patterns of more than 200 subjects aged between three and 70 plus in a study conducted over a period of 15 years at the Florida Sleep Laboratory. The descriptions of sleep norms that follow derive largely from this study, with the exception of the norms for infants. Many other studies have been conducted on the development of sleep but their results do not contradict the norms established in Florida, and the principle advantage of the work of Williams' group is that their sample sizes were suitably large – at least 20 in each of 13 age groups – and a consistent system of recording and scoring was used for all the subjects. Prechtl's (1974) norms for infant sleep are similarly uncontroversial and based on recordings from 20 babies.

The considerable differences between infants' sleep and children's sleep are undeniable, even if there is some lack of unanimity about the precise relative amounts of active sleep, intermediate sleep and quiet sleep. (The sleep of new-born infants is quite different from the sleep of humans with fully developed brains so the techniques developed for recording and scoring adult sleep are inappropriate for infants.) The common system of techniques and norms published by Anders *et al.* (1971) was developed in association with a dozen other leading researchers. During childhood, adolescence, adulthood and middle age we can be confident of the consistency of evaluation of sleep. In old age there is a problem with assessing the amount of deep slow-wave sleep (stages 3 and 4). When scoring sleep stages in young and middle-aged adults one encounters individual differences in the amplitude of the slow waves of stage 4 sleep, and there is an understandable tendency to categorize the periods of sleep with the biggest slow waves in any individual as his or her stage 4 sleep. Typically, the amplitude of slow waves in deep sleep becomes smaller with aging. When applied to the elderly, this shifting criterion for scoring stages 3 and 4 may tend to inflate the actual amount of deep slow-wave sleep actually scored.

Another progressive change in sleeping patterns with age is the number of awakenings during the night. The 20-year-old sleeps with fewer interruptions than the 36-year-old (Feinberg *et al.*, 1967), and there is evidence that this increasing fitfulness in sleep continues throughout the lifespan, with 66-year-olds sleeping more soundly than 95-year-olds (Kahn and Fisher, 1969). These brief awakenings do not result in a reduction in total quantity of sleep, since we tend to stay in bed slightly longer as we get older. There is some evidence that sleep disturbance in normal elderly men is more frequent than in normal elderly women. It is possible that the increase in the number of awakenings during the night is related to attenuation of the 24-hour (circadian) rhythm of

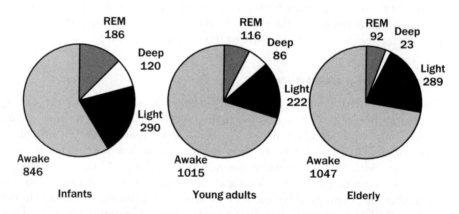

The three pie charts show the amount of time (in minutes) spent in wakefulness and sleep by groups of 3–5-year-olds, 20–29-year-olds and 70–79-year-olds, respectively. In these charts light sleep comprises stages 1 and 2, and deep sleep comprises stages 3 and 4

Figure 2.9   Quantities of sleep at three ages (from Williams *et al.*, 1974)

body temperature and other physiological functions with age. Figure 2.9 illustrates the major changes in proportions of sleep states at different ages.

Comparisons between quantities of neonatal quiet sleep and deep slow-wave sleep stages (3 and 4) in older children and adults are improper, since quiet sleep develops into the whole range of slow-wave sleep stages. However, when well established – as in the three-year-old toddler – stage 3 and 4 slow-wave sleep occupies about three sleeping hours, reducing with age in the same way as REM sleep. Unlike REM sleep, these sleep stages continue to reduce in the middle-aged and elderly, so that in the over-70s very little stage 3 or 4 sleep is taken. Typically, people over 70 take half as much REM sleep as a toddler and about the same as a 20-year-old. Their deep slow-wave sleep, however, is a quarter of that taken by a toddler and about half that of a 20-year-old. However, even this short period spent in stages 3 and 4 may be an over-estimate, as pointed out above.

Part II
The Experience
of Sleep

3

The Dreams of Rapid Eye Movement Sleep

In this preliminary chapter on dreaming and REM sleep, some basic laboratory findings on dreaming sleep will be discussed. The identification of particular EEG/EOG signs with a sleep state in which people are likely to be dreaming, has made it feasible to answer a number of questions that had previously been a matter of speculation but were, and still are, perennially asked by ordinary people. How long do dreams last? Do they really go on for as long as they seem to, or are they, as some people have suggested, fleeting sensations before waking up? Does everybody dream, and what determines whether a dream is remembered? Does everybody really dream in colour? Is dreaming necessary to maintain sanity? If rapid eye movements accompany dreaming, does it mean that our eyes are following the action of the dream?

Answers to most of these questions were provided in the 15 years between 1960 and 1975. There are, of course, still mysteries about dreaming, and for some of them perhaps the technology of the dream laboratory on its own will never provide a solution. As Ian Oswald once remarked to me, we know very little about the function of everyday, waking consciousness, so perhaps it is overoptimistic to believe that we can achieve a complete understanding of sleeping consciousness merely because we have reliable physiological indices of when dreams are likely to occur.

The natural history of dreaming

How long do dreams last?

The idea that time may be dramatically distorted when dreaming, or even reversed, was given support in 1861 in Maury's book *Sleep and Dreams*. Maury gave an account of a dream he had about the French Revolution, and the reign of terror that followed it. In the dream he was a participant, as a prisoner, of a revolutionary tribunal whose judges included Marat and Robespierre. After being tried and sentenced to death he was taken to be guillotined in front of a large crowd. He dreamt of the actual execution, including his head being separated from his body, and then abruptly woke to find that the headboard of his bed had fallen and struck him on the back of the neck in the same place as the guillotine in the dream. The only rational explanation was that the stimulus of being struck must have initiated the whole dream sequence, which although apparently very lengthy must have proceeded fast enough to fit in between the blow on the neck and waking up.

The notion that dreams are fleeting impressions formed immediately before waking is still fairly prevalent. In the Hull survey, one of the statements that respondents were invited to comment on was 'Dreams occur only in the few moments before you wake up'. Of the 149 respondents, 18 endorsed this statement and 23 thought it may be true. Some of those who thought the statement was true may have had very few experiences of extended dreams, and for them dreaming may actually have consisted of recollections of thoughts or images that had occurred immediately before waking up. Others may genuinely have believed that even lengthy dreams had been compressed into a brief period.

In the 1950s, William Dement conducted a number of experiments to establish the extent to which subjects lost track of time during REM sleep (Dement and Kleitman, 1957; Dement and Wolpert, 1958). In the first of these, reports of dreams were elicited from subjects woken from REM sleep on a total of 126 occasions. As a rough estimate of the amount of dreaming that had been going on, they counted the number of words used by subjects to describe their dream. The longer the REM sleep period before the awakening, the larger the number of words the subjects tended to use. In another experiment, the subjects were woken either five minutes or 15 minutes after REM sleep had started and asked to estimate which of the two periods applied in their case. They were correct 92 times out of 111, indicating very good awareness of the amount of time that had elapsed.

A third, and crucially important, experiment involved the use of external stimuli to influence the content of dreams. Dement and Wolpert (1958) used a pure tone stimulus, light flashes and a water spray on an exposed part of the body, and found that the water spray was most effective in influencing the content of dreams (although this stimulus also tended to wake the subjects up!) Here is one of their examples:

> S was sleeping on his back. It was a hot summer night, and he was completely uncovered. An eye-movement period started, and after 5 min. cold water was sprayed on his feet and legs. One minute later he was awakened. The first part of the dream involved being in a room talking to some friends. Then, 'two children came into the room and came over to me asking for water. I had a glass of ice water and I tipped the glass to give it to them. I was sitting, and I spilled the water on myself. The children wanted the ice and tried to grab it, but it slipped away. I got mad, because they were so greedy, and tried to shove them away from the chair. Then I got out of the chair and was going to change my pants. As I left the room I seemed to be in a school and I saw many children in the hall and I seemed to be late for a class. I was starting to climb up some stairs when the bell rang'. (Ibid.)

They sprayed the subjects with cold water when they were undoubtedly in REM sleep, and then woke them after varying intervals of a few minutes. Ten of the subjects (like the one above) had unambiguous accounts of cold water in their dreams, and these subjects' dream reports showed a very good correlation (in terms of the time that the action in the dream would have taken since the cold water spray) with the actual time that had elapsed.

Despite Maury's odd experience with his French revolution dream, it seems that dreams proceed at a normal temporal pace. Perhaps Maury had not been completely woken up by the falling headboard, and had dreamt some of his dream with the headboard lying on him. It seems likely that our dreams are attempts to make sense of experiences that are vivid but inconsequential (as suggested by John Hughlings Jackson in his perceptual release theory, developed by J. L. West (1962) to account for the generation of hallucinations and dreams), and this will be dealt with later in the chapter. Maury's dream could be a good example of an attempt at comprehending a series of striking but unconnected images and sensations, a form of the 'effort after meaning' that the Cambridge psychologist, Sir Frederick Bartlett, ascribed to normal waking memory processes, in the first half of the twentieth century.

Does everybody dream?

While most of us can recall dreams at least occasionally, there is a sizeable minority of people who claim never to dream, and who understandably have some difficulty understanding what everybody else is talking about. Laboratory experiments, comparing dreamers with non-dreamers, have shown that there is little difference between these groups in respect of EEG/EOG patterns while asleep (Antrobus et al., 1964; Goodenough et al., 1959). In all subjects there is the same orderly sequence of sleep stages, with REM sleep periods recurring at about 90-minute intervals throughout the night. Non-dreamers, however, tend to spend slightly less time in REM sleep than dreamers. Does their failure to recall dreams upon waking up in the morning mean that they really do not dream, or do they merely fail to remember having them?

In order to address this issue, Goodenough et al. (1959) scored 60 subjects on the frequency with which they remembered dreaming. They then persuaded the eight highest scorers, who 'dreamed every night', and the eight lowest scorers, who dreamt less than once a month, to submit to laboratory recordings and awakenings during the night. When woken from REM sleep, the self-reported dreamers reported dreams on almost every occasion (44 of the 49 awakenings), and also reported dreams on about half the occasions when they were woken from non-REM sleep. The non-dreamers reported dreams on less than half the occasions when woken from REM sleep (19 out of 42), and only seven times in 43 awakenings from non-REM sleep. REM sleep is thus even more clearly associated with dreaming in so-called 'non-dreamers' than in regular dreamers, who tend to report dreaming whenever they are woken up!

Experiments have also revealed that, while awakening people from REM sleep regularly produces reports of dreaming, delaying the awakening until after the end of the REM sleep period produces a dramatic drop in the number of dreams recalled. Even while asleep, we tend to forget our dreams as soon as they are over. People who claim that they generally do not dream, when woken from REM sleep do in fact report dreams, but they are particularly prone to forgetting them – if woken after the REM period is over, they recall even fewer instances of dreaming than those who claim regularly to recall dreams in the morning (Antrobus et al., 1964).

The Goodenough study described above generally supported these findings, and it was also noticed that non-dreamers tended to report that they had already been awake and thinking when woken from REM sleep (Goodenough et al., 1959). When their reports of what they had been thinking about were examined, it was found that these were frequently bizarre, commonly involved complex stories with visual imagery and, as far as the experimenters were concerned, were indistinguishable from dream reports. These subjects may therefore have been having the same sorts of experience as dreamers, but did not label their REM sleep experiences as 'dreams', but as 'thinking'. It seems that while everybody does dream during REM sleep, most dreams are forgotten and some people forget more readily than others.

Why are so many dreams forgotten?

The poet Emerson (1884) expressed the difficulty of remembering dreams most eloquently:

> Dreams are jealous of being remembered; they dissipate instantly and angrily if you try to hold them. When newly awakened from lively dreams, we are so near them, still agitated by them, still in their sphere – give us one syllable, one feature, one hint, and we should repossess the whole; hours of this strange entertainment would come trooping back to us; but we cannot get our hand on the first link or fibre, and the whole is lost. There is a strange wistfulness in the speed with which it disperses and baffles our grasp.

The experiments discussed in the previous section make it clear that most of the dreams that can be recalled if people are woken up during the night are not normally remembered in the morning. Even people who claim to remember dreams every morning only recall their most recent dream, and any dreams they may have had during the two or three REM periods earlier in the night, or even during non-REM sleep, are completely lost.

While we are all familiar with (and resigned to) a certain amount of forgetfulness during the day, being unable to remember breakfast or lunch by three o'clock in the afternoon would definitely put one in the category of suffering from a severe case of amnesic syndrome. The evidence, however, clearly shows that this sort of wholesale forgetting is normal while we are asleep.

Something about the experience of dreaming makes dreams peculiarly difficult to remember, even in ideal circumstances. A common method of collecting dream reports is to ask people to keep dream diaries – to write down, as soon as they wake up in the morning, any dreams they can remember. Cohen and Wolfe (1973) asked their subjects to telephone the local weather information service upon awakening, and to record a few details of the weather forecast at the top of their diary sheet before writing down their accounts of their dreams. A control group were instructed to lie quietly in bed for a few moments before writing down what they could recall of their dreams. The experimental subjects, distracted for a moment by having to make a telephone call and record the predicted temperature for the day, recalled very few dreams indeed, compared with the control group. Again, while distraction can cause forgetting during the day, this is normally confined to very recent memories that have no obvious meaning (such as unfamiliar telephone numbers that have just been looked up). If briefly distracted from watching a film or television programme, we would be very surprised not to be able to remember anything about it afterwards.

Dreams are, therefore, peculiarly unmemorable – unless remembered! There are two possible explanations for the difficulty we have in recalling dreams: there is something about the dream itself (its illogicality perhaps) that makes it difficult to remember; or there is something about our physiological state when we first wake up that makes remembering difficult.

There is a problem with investigating the first of these hypotheses, in that the dreams that are remembered are presumably the ones that have a more logical structure. The most chaotic experiences are forgotten. However, of the dreams that are reported, some are more structured – have more coherent themes and plots – than others, and waking subjects do not have any more difficulty remembering the more chaotic dreams than the most coherent (Barber, 1966). Incoherence *per se* therefore should not make a dream impossible to recall. Another hypothesis is that dreams are forgotten because they are repressed. That is, their content arouses anxiety, causing their recall to become unacceptably upsetting. Freud expressed the view that some dreams, but not all, may be forgotten for this reason. (It would of course be inconsistent with his theory, if dreams that have already been rendered 'harmless' by the dream-work during dreaming remain potent sources of anxiety upon awakening.) Goodenough (1978), in a scholarly review of the very technical evidence on this issue, comparing the recall of dreams by different personality types, concludes that while repression may be responsible for the forgetting of some dreams, it is not feasible that it could account for the majority. This is very much in line with the evidence on repression in everyday life – while convincing anecdotal accounts certainly exist, as does some good experimental evidence of repression in the laboratory, the theory remains unconvincing as an explanation of most of what we forget. One obvious example is looking up a telephone number, closing the directory and then being distracted for a moment by someone asking the time. Merely looking at one's watch and giving the right time is usually enough to prevent the accurate recall of an unfamiliar telephone number. Nobody would suggest that repression was at work here.

It seems likely that there is something about the state that we are in while asleep, that prevents memories from being stored in the normal way. In Chapter 4, which deals with experiments on sleep learning, amongst other things, the evidence for this proposition will be discussed more fully. The findings indicate that, as might be suspected from common experience, impressions formed during sleep are not retained. Even if people are woken up and asked to learn something, if they go straight back to sleep they are likely to forget the whole episode. Material presented to people during sleep is not remembered unless they are woken up by it, and remain awake for some time. A minimum period of time filled by waking cortical arousal seems essential for the retention of memories.

Do we dream in colour?

Just as some people claim never to dream, while others say they dream every night, there are those who rarely remember having dreams in colour and those who always do. A survey of college students found that 51 per cent of men never dreamt in colour, compared with only 31 per cent of women (Middleton, 1942). In Hall's (1951) monumentally large survey of dream content, only about a third of the total number of dreams reported contained references to colour. In a more systematic study, the subjects were asked to match the colours they could recall with colours on a standard colour chart – only about half the dreams contained colour, and many of these were in pastel shades. Interestingly, fully saturated colours tended to be at the red end of the spectrum for the six subjects involved in this study, and only rarely were saturated blues, purples or blue-greens reported (Padgam, 1975).

When the subjects in another study were woken from REM sleep and questioned about their dreams, the incidence of reporting colours was 70 per cent (Kahn *et al.*, 1962). Another 13 per cent of the reports were of 'vaguely coloured' dreams. Of the 61 dreams in which colour was reported, it was spontaneously mentioned in only 22 instances and was elicited by further questioning in the other 39. As the authors point out, colour is not usually the most important aspect of a dream, and similarly might not be mentioned in accounts of events in everyday life. When dreams are recalled during the day, it is, therefore, the most salient points that will be recalled, and the colour detail that would have been available if the dreamer had been questioned about it upon awakening will have been forgotten. In support of this argument (that colours are not well remembered in comparison with plot), Berger (1963) found that subjects woken from REM sleep reported colour in their dreams far more frequently than did people asked about their dreams during the day – even subjects who claimed never to dream in colour.

Hence a simple answer to the question 'Do we dream in colour?' is that we generally do, but this aspect of the dream tends to be forgotten.

Experimental investigations

Looking at dreams

Watching the eye movements of subjects during REM sleep and then obtaining reports from them of intense visual imagery, it seems only natural to assume that one has something to do with the other. That is, the intense visual experiences of dreaming during REM sleep are signalled by eye movements, because the eyes are actually scanning the images generated by the dream. However, it has proved extremely difficult to establish the truth or falsehood of this apparently simple statement.

Some dreams are more visually intense than others, and some REM sleep periods have a great many more eye movements than others. (As explained in the previous chapter, REM sleep may be scored as such when hardly any rapid eye movements are occurring, as long as the record of low-voltage EEG and reduced EMG continues uninterruptedly.) Berger and Oswald (1962b) have established that REM sleep periods characterized by few and small eye movements are accompanied by what they call 'passive' dreaming, with few reports to indicate that a subject might have been scanning. 'Active' dreams are accompanied by profuse and rapid eye movements. Even within a period of REM sleep there are phases of intense eye movement separated by intervals of ocular quiescence. Molinari and Foulkes (1969) have found that subjects woken up after bursts of eye movement, report more vivid imagery than when woken up after intervals of REM sleep in which the eyes have been still.

The high correlation of bursts of rapid eye movements with intense visual imagery tended to encourage early investigators' impression that the eyes were following the actions in 70–80 per cent of vivid dreams (Roffwarg et al., 1962). However, when blind matches of EOG records with dream narratives have been made simply on the basis of written evidence and the polygraphic record, the odds on matching reports to records have been no better than chance (Moscovitz and Berger, 1969).

Second, while adults who have been blind all their lives report no visual dreams and have no measurable rapid eye movements (using EOG measures), they do have periods of low-voltage EEG with reduced muscle tone, which is consistent with REM sleep (Berger et al., 1962), and if mechanical sensors are used to assess eye movement, it appears that their eyes do indeed wiggle about during these sleep phases (Gross et al., 1965). The lack of evidence of movement using standard EOG measures can be attributed to retinal degeneration in these subjects. This commonly results in the loss of the corneo-retinal potential, a standing potential difference to the order of one tenth of a volt across the back of the eyeball, which contributes largely to the measurable changes in potential on the face resulting from eye movements in normally sighted people.

Third, attempts to map eye movements directly onto reported dreams (in terms of direction of gaze and so on) have been dogged by the problem of measuring the position of the eyes using standard EEG equipment. (EEG amplifiers record changes in potential, but because they automatically filter out slow changes they are unable to provide information on the actual position of the eyes. They are not direct coupled – DC – amplifiers.) When Jacobs et al. (1972) made recordings using DC amplifiers it became apparent that during REM sleep the eyes of the subjects were almost constantly in motion, making slow, roving movements that could not be picked up by the standard (AC) amplifying equipment. Bursts of fast eye movement were superimposed on these slow movements. This study also found that fast eye movements were associated with passages of vivid dreaming that involved tracking moving images, but the measured direction of eye movement did not correspond very well with the reported direction of movement of the objects in the dream.

Waking saccadic (scanning) eye movements are faster when the eye has further to travel, with the effect that an eye movement over five degrees and one over 10 degrees are both completed in about 60 milliseconds. These movements are preprogrammed 'ballistic' responses whose velocities are determined by the anticipated distance of travel, ensuring that the eye arrives at the right place after a fixed period of time. Aserinsky et al. (1985) discovered that the fast eye movements of REM sleep tend to be consistently slower than waking saccadic movements. In addition there is no difference in acceleration or final velocity between movements that are long and movements that are short. They checked on the possibility that saccadic movements made with the eyes closed, or in the dark, might be slowed, and that velocity may then be independent of length of saccade, and found that they were not. That is, waking eye movements with the eyes closed, or in the dark, are the same as with the eyes open and in the light. The pattern of velocity of eye movements in REM sleep is quite unlike that of waking eye movements, and seems inconsistent with the idea that they reflect scanning responses.

Finally, it can be pointed out that newborn babies have profuse eye movements during REM sleep, even though their vision is not good. The weight of evidence against the scanning hypothesis for REMs is very great. It seems likely that these eye movements are involuntary symptoms of neurophysiological events taking place during REM sleep and have no direct relation to the images generated during dreaming.

However, the debate is by no means over. Positron emission tomography (PET) techniques can be used to measure and visualize, in scans that last about 15 minutes at a time, the oxygen uptake of localized areas of the brain during different attentional states. Hong *et al.* (1995) have observed increased local cerebral glucose metabolism in association with REM sleep in the same cortical areas that control waking eye movement and attention. In a preliminary study on one subject, the same group investigated the possible correlation between the number of eye movements during REM sleep and the amount of visual imagery reported on subsequent awakening (Hong *et al.*, 1997). They found that REM sleep eye movement counts were positively and significantly correlated with the reported intensity of visual imagery when dreaming, particularly when the eye movement counts were taken over shorter periods before awakening.

A close association between eye movements in REM sleep and the content of dreams is a vital assumption of some of the most influential theories on the generation of dreaming (discussed in Chapter 5), so this issue is of some importance. It is clear that in the 1960s and 1970s there was overhasty acceptance of the relationship, on the basis of rather weak evidence, and there has been general scepticism about the issue ever since. In terms of science, one must conclude that we do not yet know whether or not this relationship is a causal one (based on actual scanning of the contents of dreams). However, evidence is now acccumulating to support the relationship, rather than refute it.

'Lose your dreams and you will lose your mind' (Rolling Stones, 'Ruby Tuesday')

The idea that dreaming is essential for sanity has been prevalent in popular science since the eighteenth century. The modern story of this notion is a good example of the way in which the media and the public at large love to cite scientific evidence, however slender, to justify what they think, ignoring any evidence to the contrary.

The discovery of a practicable way not only of monitoring dreaming sleep but perhaps also of controlling it presented a great challenge. Normal subjects always begin a sleep period with slow-wave sleep and do not start their first REM sleep period for at least 45 minutes, sometimes as long as two hours. They never begin the sleep period with REM sleep. If they are woken during the night at the beginning of each REM sleep period and then allowed to return to sleep, do they pick up where they left off, starting REM sleep, or start the night all over again? What is the psychological effect of preventing the dreams of REM sleep?

Dement (1960) woke six subjects in this systematic way over a period of six nights, and found that on the first night they did seem to 'start all over again' whenever properly woken, so that by the end of the night they had had a good deal of slow-wave sleep and very little REM sleep. On subsequent nights it became more difficult to prevent REM sleep, especially in the early hours, and the number of awakenings that were necessary increased night by night. By the fifth or sixth nights the subjects were hardly getting any sleep at all. On recovery nights, when the subjects were allowed to sleep undisturbed, they took more REM sleep than usual, as if they were making up to some extent for the amount lost. These findings are consistent with the idea that REM sleep, and perhaps the dreaming associated with it, is especially important and perhaps the most important function of sleep.

Dement (ibid.) also found that his subjects tended to become paranoid when deprived of REM sleep – ascribing sinister motives to the experimenter and developing all sorts of unreasonable suspicions, as well as having bizarre experiences such as hallucinations (seeing or hearing things that were not there). Therefore, not only did the subjects' sleep mechanisms rebel against the regime by making more more and more attempts to initiate REM sleep during the period of deprivation, and to some extent made up for the amount lost when allowed to do so, but the subjects also showed signs of psychological distress when it was prevented.

However, Dement subsequently established that these psychiatric symptoms were not reliably elicited by REM sleep deprivation (Dement, 1965). Rather, they were probably the consequence of the expectations of the experimenters – the so-called 'experimenter effect'. In this instance the experimenters' expectations were communicated to the subjects through genuine concern for their well-being. Not only were the subjects told of what Dement thought might be the probable results of the regime, but they were also provided with the full-time services of a psychiatrist, to whom they could report any unusual sensations. After the third day of REM sleep deprivation, little sleep at all was being achieved, and the symptoms that the subjects showed were a combination of the effects of total sleep deprivation and suggestion.

Despite the fact that Dement performed subsequent experiments in which his subjects showed no psychiatric symptoms after REM sleep deprivation, and that he himself stressed that his early observations about the effects of REM sleep deprivation were probably misleading, the idea that dreaming preserved sanity had been strongly reinforced. It is not uncommon even now to read in works of popular science that this notion has firm scientific support. It has not.

Many of the American psychiatrists who did much of the important pioneering empirical work on dreaming during the 1960s were deeply influenced by psychoanalysis. While strict Freudian interpretations of the function of dreaming do not necessarily imply that it preserves sanity, neo-Freudians have developed the notion that conflicts are resolved during dreams, giving dreams a purpose in maintaining psychic equilibrium. Freud himself did not think that dreaming preserved sanity – on the contrary, as we shall see in the next chapter, his view was that the function of dreaming was to allow sleep to continue uninterrupted, despite a number of unacceptable ideas being expressed. Dreaming, or the dreamwork, allowed ideas that would otherwise be too upsetting to be compatible with sleep, to be dressed up in symbolism, defused of their obviously sexual or aggressive meanings. As it stands, classical Freudian theory should therefore predict that sleep might be disturbed by the prevention of dreaming, but that any untoward effects will be from the prevention of restorative sleep, rather than the prevention of dreaming *per se*.

On the other hand, dreaming can be seen as having a function in resolving emotional conflicts by a process of emotional integration. This neo-Freudian theory has been articulated by Breger (1967) and others, and represents the sort of thinking underlying Dement's original hypothesis that the prevention of dreaming causes emotional difficulties. The effects of total sleep deprivation and of both REM sleep and deep slow-wave sleep deprivation on subsequent sleep and performance will be discussed in Chapter 7.

4

The Quality of the
Sleeping Experience

The experience of sleep

When I go to bed, the experience is oddly similar to getting into a swimming pool. It takes a few moments to adjust – one moment one is dry, wearing dry swimming trunks and walking about, and the next moment one is getting progressively wetter (including the swimming trunks, which somehow seems particularly inappropriate) – and it is only when half a length or so has been swum that the whole thing seems ordinary again. Similarly, one minute I am a busy, wide-awake person, and the next, when the decision has been made to go to sleep, I am a wide-awake person lying down in bed. It requires a period of adjustment, before the normal daytime mode of thinking changes to that of drowsiness, and is finally displaced by the onset of sleep.

During this rather curious period when our thoughts are free to wander, we are sometimes aware that the quality of the sensations that we are used to when awake has changed. These odd experiences, typical of getting to sleep or periods of drowsiness during the day, are not uncommon. We accept our experience of waking consciousness as being normal, and for the most part only professional philosophers spend much time thinking about its significance. For the rest of us, it seems commonplace and obvious that we should be able to think, imagine, perceive and remember in the ways that we do, and we tend to take it for granted that the rest of the world has the same sort of experience of everyday life that we do. Our experiences while asleep, or under the influence of drugs, sometimes seem inexplicable in terms of this rather humdrum awareness, much more personal and therefore more interesting. Some aspects of drowsiness fit this mould.

Early sleep stages and experiences

In the period of drowsiness preceding the oblivion of sleep, the quality of thinking changes, becoming less logical and sometimes bizarre. The incidents that are reported the following day are necessarily the more memorable ones – memorable for their oddity. While much of the thinking during drowsiness may be humdrum, as shown by experiments involving waking people up during this state, there are undoubtedly some unusual styles of thinking and dreamlike imagery during drowsiness. The psychologist Clark Hull (1962) reports the following sequence of thoughts:

> 'Bill Hambra – Ju (sic) know him?'
>   Note: A moment ago while passing in mild lapse of attention, the above came into my mind with great distinctness. It seemed almost as if I were speaking it ... I have noticed this just as clearly as the above many times while half asleep in bed but never had paper handy and so never wrote it down ...
>   Question: Where in the world could that name have come from? I haven't the slightest recollection of anything like it.
>   This human machine is a queer thing!

Apart from thinking of this sort, a large proportion of people report odd perceptual experiences – not dreams, strictly speaking, but quite different from the ordinariness of waking consciousness. Hypnogogic experiences, as they are called, are characterized by a series of relatively disconnected but vivid images. In a survey of Aberdeen University students, about two thirds stated that they had experienced such sensations, which were slightly more often auditory than visual (McKellar, 1957). When asked to describe their auditory sensations, many of McKellar's subjects reported hearing snatches of music, which could be recurrent:

> as is illustrated by a subject who recurrently imaged the last movement of Rachmaninov's Second Piano Concerto. This subject added: 'Occasionally I hear the first movement of his Third Concerto, which I do not know well enough to construct in my mind when I am fully conscious.' (Ibid.)

Voices are also very commonly heard in this drowsy state; for instance, calling the sleeper's name. These experiences are easily confused with reality, and sometimes result in the sleeper waking up and attempting to answer the voice.

Visual hypnagogic sensations may be either isolated images or a series of images. Very commonly, people see static landscapes, moving faces or a sequence of pictures or geometric shapes. McKellar's subjects 'quite frequently likened the images to lantern slides', and their unrelatedness, both to current preoccupations and to each other, made them seem like a series of lecturer's slides that had not only 'been mixed up but were really intended for some other lecture'. There have been suggestions that some of these experiences, especially the sequences of geometrical shapes, or flashes, may be the result of discharges from the retina occuring in the absence of stimulation – the so-called entoptic phenomenon, which can also be observed when the eyes are open in the pitch dark (Schacter, 1976).

Hypnagogic experiences can also consist of after-images of activities protrac-tedly engaged in during the preceding day. When going to sleep after spending a night watching the EEG traces of sleeping subjects, for instance, I sometimes have hypnagogic images of the traces (moving backwards) made when falling asleep. Incidentally, these images of traces sometimes persist into my dreams, appearing in the sky above the action of the dream, giving me the impression that I can actually monitor my own sleep stages while dreaming. Canadian psychologist Donald Hebb (1968) reports:

A day in the woods or a day-long car trip after a sedentary winter sometimes has an extraordinarily vivid aftereffect. As I go to bed and shut my eyes – but not till then, though it may be hours since the conclusion of the special visual stimulation – a path through the bush or a winding highway begins to flow past me and continues to do so till sleep intervenes.

One explanation of how random entoptic discharges and after-images become fully developed perceptions – the perceptual release theory – was proposed by the neurologist John Hughlings Jackson (1874), and was later developed as a general theory to account for hallucinations and dreams (West, 1962). Simply put, during waking consciousness there is a demand by the alert cortex for perceptual information from the senses and the senses provide an abundance, but most of this is disregarded as only topically relevant information is attended to. In the drowsy state there is very little coming in and yet the cortex is still relatively alert and demanding something to work on, although not alert enough to inhibit effectively any nonsense being offered by the senses. Perceptions are constructed or formed from what would normally be inhibited (such as low-level random discharges from the retina). According to this theory, half-formed thoughts, memories and low-quality visual and auditory inputs now become grist to the perceptual mill, combining to give hypnagogic images.

Estimates of the proportion of people who experience hypnagogic imagery vary considerably, depending partly on exactly how they are asked. McKellar (1972) argues that while over 70 per cent of people who answer a questionnaire report at least one hypnagogic experience the actual incidence may be even higher, as 'it can be overlooked for a very long time even by those who subsequently realize that they have the experience frequently. ... False negatives seem to occur by a process of ignoring what one is not alerted to notice, as well as from emotional blockage.' McKellar's work is in the tradition of Francis Galton's (1883) inquiries into the considerable variations between individuals in respect of quality of imagery. One might expect that those who report intense imagery when awake would also report more hypnagogic experiences; however, the evidence suggests that subjects who are weak imagers in the waking state are just as likely to report hypnagogic images as those who are strong imagers (Holt, 1972). (Readers wishing to pursue the phenomenological approach to hypnagogic experience should consult the excellent book, *Hypnagogia*, 1987, by Andreas Mavromatis.)

Physiological correlates of hypnagogic experiences

When subjects are interrupted upon falling asleep and asked to report on any mental activity that might have been taking place, they usually have something to say about what was going on in their mind. Foulkes and Vogel (1966) describe a laboratory study in which standard EEG/EOG recordings were made and the subjects were questioned after periods of wakefulness, stage 1 sleep and stage 2 sleep. There was no clear relation between depth of sleep, as indicated by these measures, and the incidence of reports. Subjects came up with well-organized fantasy sequences after being roused from periods with high levels of EEG alpha and saccadic eye movements, consistent with relaxed wakefulness, but it was difficult to distinguish these reports from those which were more dreamlike and elicited from subjects roused from deeper levels of sleep.

The experimenters categorized the experiences in relation to the sensory modality principally involved and the connectedness of the plot. One example, of a 'dream' in the state of relaxed wakefulness, reads more like a fantasy of wish-fulfilment than a sleeping dream account, although others were remarkably dreamlike. Reports of thinking and directed imagery were also elicited from subjects woken from light stage 2 sleep.

There were, however, consistent differences in the quality of experience as wakefulness gave way to sleep. The subjects began to feel a loss of control over the course of their thinking. Their awareness of being in a laboratory declined, and similarly their awareness that they were under instruction to observe their own sensations became less strong.

Thinking and fantasizing seem to have constituted the majority of Foulkes and Vogel's subjects' reports, but while it was possible to make fine distinctions between degrees of sleep depth, using EEG/EOG measures, these did not seem to be very predictive of the quality of experience reported. Most surprising, perhaps, were the number of reports of 'everyday' thinking from subjects who were undoubtedly asleep, according to psychophysiological criteria. In addition, there were some reports of dreaming during wakefulness and light slow-wave sleep that were bizarre, quite well organized in terms of plot and involving unusual visual imagery – just like the fully fledged dreams of REM sleep.

Any hope of a unique syndrome of EEG/EOG patterns that might be associated with the odd experiences reported by McKellar's (1972) subjects must be abandoned. As we fall asleep our mental state becomes somewhat unpredictable and immune to such gross measures. Sometimes we appear to ourselves to be making sense, sometimes we seem to be obviously deranged and sometimes our thoughts are driven by the vivid imagery of dreams. The psychophysiologist cannot as yet match the experiences of going to sleep with the measures of brain function that are currently available. While the majority of us, if not all, probably have hypnagogic experiences of the sort reported by McKellar, they were by no means typical of Foulkes and Vogel's drowsy subjects, and must represent the more memorable events in most people's half-sleeps, rather than the most common.

Are dreams confined to REM sleep?

In the 1950s Aserinsky and Kleitman (1953) and Dement and Kleitman (1957) stated that 74 per cent and 79 per cent of their subjects reported dreams after REM sleep awakenings, respectively, and only 7 per cent after non-REM sleep awakenings, indicating a virtually perfect isomerism between the experience of dreaming and a well-defined psychophysiological pattern. In the first flush of enthusiasm following these unprecedented claims, there was a very strong tendency to identify dreaming exclusively with REM sleep, presuming that any lack of identification of dreaming with eye movements could be put down to experimental error. Some researchers, such as Ernest Hartmann, even called it D sleep (for dreaming) to distinguish it from non-dreaming, slow-wave sleep. However, it was not long before other researchers were reporting dream recalls after non-REM sleep awakenings, and a lively controversy began on the question of whether night-time dreaming was confined to REM sleep, or whether it might be continuous through all sleep stages.

A thorough review of the literature on this topic by Herman *et al.* (1978) found that reports of dreaming varied between studies from 74–100 per cent for REM sleep awakenings, and from 0–75 per cent for non-REM sleep awakenings. There were no obvious differences between the ways in which the studies had been conducted, to account for the wide range of rates for non-REM sleep. The studies only agreed on a consistently high rate of dream reports for REM sleep. While sleep stages are well defined in terms of psycho-physiology, the same is not true of what constitutes a dream, and the reviewers suggest that the predisposition of the experimenter was an important determinant of the number of non-REM dreams collected. That is, the reports made by subjects woken from non-REM sleep were ambiguous and open to interpretation as either thinking or dreaming, while reports from REM sleep awakenings tended to be indubitably of dreams.

What is clear is that mental life does not cease during non-REM sleep, and REM sleep is not a necessary condition for dreaming. Primary process thinking, dream 'logic' and the construction of generally illogical stories all seem to take place throughout the night's sleep. What sets the experience of REM sleep apart is the vividness of the visual imagery and the generally more compelling quality of the dreams associated with it.

The incorporation of stimuli into dreams, and dreamwork

Almost everybody has a story to tell about dream incorporation – for instance, dreaming about Arctic exploration only to wake up to find that the covers have slipped off and they are freezing cold, or dreaming of bells ringing only to wake up to find that the alarm clock has been clattering for the last few minutes. Are these dreams really triggered by outside stimuli, or are such reports only the outcome of rather memorable coincidences? How frequently are dreams influenced by such stimuli? As we saw in the previous chapter, Dement and Wolpert (1958) verified that external stimuli could indeed be incorporated into dreams during REM sleep. One example they gave is as follows:

> S was sleeping on his stomach. His back was uncovered. An eye movement period started and after it had persisted for 10 minutes, cold water was sprayed on his back. Exactly 30 seconds later he was awakened. The first part of the dream involved a rather complex description of acting in a play. Then, 'I was walking behind the leading lady when she suddenly collapsed and water was dripping on her face. I ran over to her and felt water dripping on my back and head. The roof was leaking. I was very puzzled why she fell down and decided some plaster must have fallen on her. I looked up and there was a hole in the roof. I dragged her over to the side of the stage and began pulling the curtains. Just then I woke up.'

Dement and his students played recordings of a variety of sound stimuli, such as bugles, as soon as an REM period started. They found that more than 50 per cent of the dreams reported by their subjects had been noticeably affected by the stimuli. The incorporation of stimuli is thus extremely common if not invariable (given that on many occasions the effects of stimulation on dreaming are so idiosyncratic that they are not recognized by the experimenters).

Berger (1963) assessed the effects of meaningful verbal stimuli on dreaming. These stimuli were the names of the subjects' friends (provided by the subjects) that when presented while the subjects were awake had elicited the largest galvanic skin responses (GSRs). Dream incorporation was judged to have taken place on about half of the occasions. Of the 48 dreams that were judged to have been affected by the stimuli there had been 31 incorporations on the basis of assonance alone – for instance, 'Gillian' had been voiced as 'Chilean', 'Jenny' as 'Jemmy', and 'Mike' as 'like'. Only on three occasions had the named individual actually appeared in the dream as themselves.

The orthodox psychoanalytic view of the processes underlying dream incorporation is that they maintain sleep. The all-important notion of 'dream-work' involves an assumption about the function of dreaming (and possibly of consciousness in general) – that is, that the dream is controlling the subject's psychological state, and not the other way round. Thus, internally generated ideas that would otherwise cause the subject to wake up blushing with shame or racked with guilt are transformed by the dream-work into a symbolic code. In the same way, external stimuli become incorporated into dreams in order to reduce their arousing effect.

The experimental evidence does not contradict this view, but nor does it support it very strongly. While dream incorporations can be explained by the psychoanalytic model, it could also be that only stimuli that fail to arouse the brain sufficiently to tip it into wakefulness result in dream incorporation, rather than that the dream incorporation resulting in continued sleeping. Experimental evidence from Bradley and Meddis (1974) shows that the incorporation of stimuli into dreaming is indeed associated with continued sleep rather than awakening. It remains unclear whether the incorporation actually protects sleep, as the Freudian theory would predict, or whether incorporation is the consequence of delayed arousal.

Internally generated stimuli (such as feelings of hunger, thirst or sexual arousal) might also be expected to have an effect on dream content. If dreams are wish fulfilments, then thirsty subjects should dream of quenching their thirst and hungry subjects should dream of eating. Primo Levi, who spent a year in Auschwitz, reported widespread dreaming of food amongst the inmates:

> One can hear the sleepers breathing and snoring; some groan and speak. Many lick their lips and move their jaws. They are dreaming of eating; this is also a collective dream. It is a pitiless dream which the creator of the Tantalus myth must have known. You not only see the food, you feel it in your hands, distinct and concrete, you are aware of its rich and striking smell; someone in the dream even holds it up to your lips, but every time a different circumstance intervenes to prevent the consum-mation of the act. Then the dream dissolves and breaks up into its elements, but it

re-forms itself immediately after and begins again, similar, yet changed; and this without pause, for all of us, every night and for the whole of our sleep (Levi, 1960).

Volunteers in an experiment on the effects of prolonged starvation, conducted by Ansel Keys in the 1950s, did not report an increase in dreams about food, although their food intake was very low indeed, low enough to match the deprivation suffered by people in places such as Auschwitz (Keys, 1950). Clues to explain this discrepancy have been provided by some laboratory studies.

Bokert (1968) increased the degree of thirst in his subjects by not only depriving them of water for 24 hours but also giving them a salty meal before going to bed. Their dream reports included more water-related imagery, such as lakes or snow, as well as some explicitly thirst-satisfying objects, such as Pepsi Cola, than on control nights when they had been allowed fluids *ad-lib*. Subjects who reported gratifying dreams of eating and drinking during the course of the night drank less in the morning and rated themselves as less thirsty than those who had not.

Thus, while drive-related dreams and even simple dreams of wish fulfilment can occur, they are not reliably elicited by the mere existence of an unsatisfied appetite. In this context Primo Levi's (1960) account of his recovery from his Auschwitz ordeal may be relevant. Liberated by Soviet troops, he and his fellow inmates spent a year in the Soviet Union. While well-intentioned, the wartime Russian authorities were somewhat unreliable about providing supplies, especially in any variety, and the story of these twelve months is one of a continuous preoccupation with food and with foraging. However, there are no more reports of dreaming about food. Thus, with liberty and the opportunity to cope realistically with the problem of getting enough to eat, the dream process was no longer invoked. Keys' (1986) subjects knew they were not going to be starved to death, being part of a controlled experiment under constant medical supervision, so in their case hunger was not life-threatening. The dream process, perhaps not surprisingly, appears to be invoked in response to the meaning of hunger rather than the level of deprivation. Thirst is a more imperative drive, intruding into dreams even when the subjects know full well that they are merely taking part in an experiment, and that water will be available in the morning.

People who give up cigarettes very commonly report explicit (and guilty) dreams about smoking during the first few weeks, even though there is every reason to believe that sleep actually becomes less disturbed after withdrawing from nicotine. (Withdrawal from other drugs is typically associated with increased REM sleep, disturbed sleep and vivid dreaming.) Again the strength of craving in itself can be sufficient to induce dreams of wish fulfilment, even when the dreamers have no intention of smoking again.

Presleep stimulation and dreaming

It is very well known that dreams often contain elements – visual or idealizational – that can be identified as part of the previous day's experience. Much of our dream content is not so easily traced, but the incorporation of 'day residues' into dreams is very well established. In a systematic study of his own dream life, Freud tried to relate all his dreams to feelings and thoughts experienced the previous day. It is not possible to do this without assuming that dream-work transformations have taken place. That is, the 'manifest dream's' apparently irrelevant and unpredictable content is deemed to have been systematically arrived at from a 'latent dream', whose implicit content has been the subject of some extensive dream-work. With sufficient ingenuity, an analyst can therefore trace any reported dream back to certain themes that he or she believes are preoccupying the dreamer. If we could be sure that all dream content is determined in this way, then this would not be an unreasonable thing to do.

Experimental studies relating presleep stimulation to dream content are not encouraging in this respect. Foulkes and Rechtschaffen (1964) showed either an amusing or a violent TV western to adult subjects before bedtime and found that direct incorporation of the content of either film was very rare indeed, although the violent film reliably induced more vivid, emotional dreams. A similar study, using 7–11 year-old children as subjects (Foulkes *et al.*, 1967), compared the subjects' dream reports after viewing a violent western and a bland film about baseball. Fourteen out of the 179 dream reports were judged to contain elements from the films. There was no difference in the frequency of incorporation of scenes from the two films – the more violent film was not followed by any more intense or hostile dreams than the bland one, perhaps indicating how accustomed these young subjects were to watching violent westerns!

Goodenough *et al.* (1975) later confirmed that the emotional content of dreams could be affected by presleep stimulation, in this case a film entitled *Subcision* explicitly showed a series of operations carried out on the penis as part of a tribal aboriginal initiation rite. They found that the dreams reported after the screening of the stress-inducing film were more anxious than those reported after a neutral film.

A third study of the effects of films on dreaming demonstrated the limitations of this technique and indicated some important determinants of what is incorporated into a spontaneous dream. Cartwright (1977) showed a pornographic film to a group of conventional male medical students and a group of young homosexual men (members of a university chapter of a national American gay group). The film included a suggestive 10-minute scene set in an eighteenth-century brothel, in which a male customer chose a female prostitute, helped her to undress in a bedroom and then got into bed with her; and an explicit 10-minute scene of a newly wed bride and groom in a hotel bedroom. Both groups of subjects showed signs of sexual arousal during the screening of the film, indicated by penile strain gauges. However, there were marked differences between the groups' dreams, perhaps unexpectedly, in that the homosexual men experienced a great many explicit sexual dreams while the medical students tended, when scenes of nudity were included in their dreams, to interpret these in terms of clinical practice, maintaining their professional role. (One might have expected the heterosexual young men to be more influenced by what were, after all, exclusively heterosexual scenes.)

Were the gay group's 'control' dreams also more sexually charged than those of the the medical students? Were their dreams after seeing the films more sexually explicit than on control nights? Neither Cartwright's book nor the more detailed published experimental reports answer these questions. It is likely that the pornographic film provided a potent stimulus for both groups of young men, yet the effect it had on their dreams was only explicable in terms of their ideology, particularly in terms of how they viewed sexuality in relation to their own lives. The homosexual men were deeply preoccupied with their own sexuality and with proselytizing a liberated view of sexual practices. The medical students, having decided to enter a traditionally conservative profession, were obliged to subscribe to conventionally repressive attitudes. Just as in waking life they had to adopt a clinical attitude towards human activities, many of which are taboo in Western society, their dreaming interpretations of their own sexuality were also in terms of the medical model.

Both these experiments, and the studies on the effects of hunger and thirst on dreaming, demonstrate the unpredictability of dreaming, explicable only in terms of semantics. All the evidence points to dreaming being a highly complex cognitive activity. Whatever the limitations of the psychoanalytic approach to dream analysis, it does at least attempt to take this into account, and the procedure of showing films, however vivid and disturbing, and then recording spontaneous dream reports is intrinsically limited by the construction the individual puts on the film and the experiment itself.

Two laboratory studies that attempted to assess the effects of real-life stresses on dreams used patients who were either awaiting major surgery or were undergoing group therapy sessions in which each patient had to prepare her or himself for a session devoted entirely to her or his own problems (Breger et al., 1971). The major findings of this combination of case study and experimental method in the surgery patients were that (1) the preoperative dreams of the surgery subjects incorporated stress-related material both directly and symbolically; (2) the degree of incorporation was quite marked when the personal meaning of surgery and the individual modes of preparation were taken into account; and (3) the content of the dreams was more repetitious and constricted before than after surgery.

Similarly, for the patients anticipating and then undergoing a psychotherapeutic focus session devoted entirely to their own problems, there was clear evidence that this traumatic event affected dream content. One explanation is that dreaming is an essential part of our adaptation to the demands of the world we live in. Not only does dreaming perhaps help in the storage of new memories, but it is actively helping us to solve our emotional problems. The dream process is thus a way not only of rehearsing new experiences, but also of commenting on them and resolving conflicts. A problem with this idea is, of course, that most dreams are not remembered; so that even if solutions to problems are achieved during dreams they cannot be regarded as adaptive, unless we are to believe that these solutions are somehow incorporated unconsciously. Some more recent theories on dreaming will be discussed in Chapter 5.

Why do we remember our dreams?

Incubation has, of course, a long and reputable history in antiquity. In the modern world, the reasons for wanting to remember dreams have changed – nobody believes any more that an appropriate dream will cure physical illness, or perhaps predict the future. Rather, the influence of psychoanalysis has encouraged the belief that the analysis of dreams will help cure mental ills. While psychoanalysis is very expensive, time-consuming and not available on the National Health Service in the UK, and is therefore practised on only a small number of wealthy neurotics living in larger cities, its influence has by no means been confined to those directly benefiting from treatment. Especially in the US, there is a widespread belief that people should actively seek ways of developing themselves. Meditation, yoga and psychotherapy have all been taken up by Westerners as ways of helping them to cope and give meaning to their lives. One prevalent notion is that this self-improvement can be achieved by encouraging less rational, more intuitive styles of thinking, and that dreams represent this ideal.

Modern exponents of this ideal include Anne Faraday (1972, 1975) and Paul Garfield (1974), whose books encourage the reader not only to keep dream diaries but also to attempt to alter their dreams. Griffin and Foulkes (1977) report an experimental study of the ability of subjects to influence their own dreams. Twenty-nine subjects were selected who claimed to have already successfully controlled what they were going to dream, and who were strongly motivated to prove that this was indeed possible. They prepared lists of their intended dream topics, and kept daily records of their efforts at control and the dreams they recalled. Four judges then tried to match the reported dreams with the topics, identifying between five and nine of the 29 target suggestions, barely more than a chance rate. This disappointing result indicates that control over ones own dreams is much more difficult than Garfield and Faraday suggest.

Some memorable dream themes

While dreaming is inevitably idiosyncratic and personal, a number of scenarios regularly recur for many people. Particular sensations, such as of falling or immobility, are occasional but almost universal. Dreams of being chased and of flying are also more frequent than one might expect, given that neither of these events happen frequently, or at all, in real life. The dream topics discussed here are by no means representative of the dreams reported from laboratory awakenings, some of which are quite uncommon. In fact, one study found that 'typical dreams' (for example of loss of teeth, nudity, death, flying, examinations) constituted less than 1 per cent of dreams collected from REM sleep awakenings (Snyder, 1970).

However, these dreams represent the more interesting and memorable products of our sleeping minds, and it would be churlish not to say anything about them simply because they rarely surface in the laboratory.

Asking people whether they have ever dreamt of a special topic (Griffith et al., 1958) gives a different picture. Table 4.1 shows the responses of American and Japanese college students in respect of a variety of dream topics. This survey, conducted in the mid-1950s when the differences between the US and Japanese cultures were even greater than they are now, produced a

Table 4.1   Dreams reported by Japanese and American students (per cent) (from Griffith et al., 1958)

	American (n = 250)	Japanese (n = 223)	Total (n = 473)*
Have you ever dreamed of:			
1. Being attacked or pursued	77.2	91.0	83.5 (J)
2. Falling	82.8	74.4	78.9
3. Trying again and again to do something	71.2	87.0	78.6 (J)
4. School, teachers, studying	71.2	86.1	78.2 (J)
5. Being frozen with fright	58.0	87.0	71.7 (J)
6. Sexual experiences	66.4	68.2	67.2 (J)
7. Eating delicious food	61.6	68.2	64.7
8. Falling, with fear	67.6	59.2	63.6
9. Arriving too late, e.g. missing train	63.6	48.9	56.7 (A)
10. Fire	40.8	65.9	52.6 (J)
11. Swimming	52.0	52.5	52.2
12. Dead people as though alive	46.0	57.4	51.4
13. Being locked up	56.4	43.5	50.3 (A)
14. Loved person to be dead	57.2	42.2	50.1 (A)
15. Snakes	48.8	49.8	49.3
16. Being on verge of falling	46.8	45.3	46.1
17. Finding money	56.0	25.6	41.6 (A)
18. Failing an examination	38.8	41.3	40.0
19. Flying or soaring through the air	33.6	45.7	39.3 (J)
20. Being smothered, unable to breathe	44.4	33.2	39.1
21. Falling, without fear	33.2	39.9	36.4
22. Wild, violent beasts	30.0	42.2	35.7 (J)
23. Being inappropriately dressed	46.0	23.3	35.3 (A)
24. Seeing self as dead	33.2	35.0	34.0
25. Being nude	42.8	17.5	30.9 (A)
26. Killing someone	25.6	27.8	26.6
27. Being tied, unable to move	30.4	20.6	25.8
28. Having superior knowledge or mental ability	25.6	25.1	25.4
29. Lunatics or insane people	25.6	13.5	19.9 (A)
30. Your teeth falling out	20.8	16.1	18.6
31. Creatures, part animal, part human	14.8	15.7	15.2
32. Being buried alive	14.8	15.2	15.0
33. Seeing self in mirror	12.4	11.7	12.1
34. Being hanged by neck	2.8	4.0	3.4

* 'J' indicates that the frequency amongst the Japanese was statistically significantly greater than amongst the Americans. 'A' indicates the opposite.

positive correlation coefficient of 0.87 between these two samples' dream rates for 34 topics – accounting for over 75 per cent of the variance. (This correlation is somewhat inflated by the number of topics that hardly anybody in either group dreamt about, but using only the 15 topics dreamt about by at least half of one of the groups still gives a fairly high correlation of 0.63 between the groups.) Some differences were explicable only in terms of cultural factors, as indicated in the table, but the most remarkable thing about these data is the general similarity between the rates for two groups of people living thousands of miles apart.

Reflective dreams

Some dreams apparently offer a comment on life, and these are what I call reflective dreams. The absurdest dreams are probably some of the most difficult to remember, but some are great fun, as with one recalled by the Irish poet Louis MacNeice, who had just returned from a visit in 1937 to the government's fighting front in Spain:

> I had a dream at this time that I was caught by the Nazis. They took me to an enormous wall built of Pelasgian blocks. In this wall was a great wrought-iron gate of eighteenth-century workmanship. They unlocked this gate and thrust me through it, locked it behind me. I found myself in the Alps with a narrow pass before me, began to ascend the rough and desolate track. Plodding upwards, looking straight ahead of me or hardly looking at all, I was conscious suddenly of something on either side, looked to the right and the left. On the right and the left of my track, padding along in parallel silence were bears. Bears of every size and colour, going inexorably forward, but looking at me sideways. I had the feeling they were 'not quite right', steeled myself to go on, careful not to annoy them. Then ahead of me, higher up the pass, I saw a woman, with a stab of joy in my diaphragm hurried to overtake her. Overtook her; she looked straight out of Bond Street, tall and blonde, the height of elegance. She too had been caught by the Nazis, I walked along beside her and the bears walked on each side of us. But everything was all right now. 'Who are you?' I said at last. 'Oh,' she said suavely, 'I am the Czar's governess.' (MacNeice, 1982)

What more can one say? It brilliantly combines a legitimate trepidation about the Nazis with a certain ambivalence (perhaps typical of those on the bourgeois left in Britain at the time) about the Russian bears who may or may not have been rescuing him, resolved in the end by the arrival of the charming governess – better keep a hold on nurse, just in case of something worse!

A reflective dream of my own occurred when I was in the midst of writing my doctorate on the role of REM sleep in the consolidation of memories. One of the hypotheses I was considering was that during REM sleep (and therefore during REM sleep dreams) the entire memory system is accessible – none of the inhibitions present during wakeful life are active, and new memories can be fitted into the appropriate cognitive structures during REM sleep.

Habitually a somewhat forgetful person, for a couple of days I had been trying to remember the name of the director of the film *Such Good Friends*.

In my dream I was alone on an empty road, trying to remember the director's name, when a large open-topped car drove up, full of laughing passengers who seemed to be sharing a joke in a foreign language. The actor Robert Mitchum was in the back seat, and before they drove off I attracted his attention and said, 'Mr Mitchum, please help me. You starred in a film called *River of No Return* with Marilyn Monroe. Please can you tell me the name of the director, because he also directed *Such Good Friends*, and I haven't been able to remember his name?' Mr Mitchum leaned back, extremely relaxed, and said, 'Very sorry, but I can't remember either.' The car then drove off, but suddenly I set off running after it, shouting, 'Otto Preminger! Otto Preminger!' and woke myself up shouting out loud.

Was my hypothesis correct? Even my dream about it was ambivalent!

Falling

The sensation of falling typically occurs at the beginning of the night during stage 1 sleep. It is associated with a muscular spasm of the arms, legs or whole body and is known as a 'myoclonic jerk', which is common to many mammals. Like yawning and hiccupping, it is involuntary, and yet undeniably under the control of the brain. Oswald (1959a) suggests that these jerks may be the outcome of an arousal response, since they can be elicited by sounds heard while dropping off to sleep, and are associated with small K complexes in the EEG. These events are not normally associated with any coherent dream sequence, although they may be preceded by a feeling of floating (reminiscent of the 'aura' often experienced by people suffering from epilepsy, giving warning of an imminent convulsive fit). While analogous, in this sense, to an epileptic seizure, there is no evidence that these jerks have anything else in common with epilepsy. It seems likely that the sensation of falling is the outcome of cortical interpretation of the production of this innate response, rather than being intrinsic to its generation.

Falling in dreams is quite common: surveys have found that between 50 per cent and 80 per cent of subjects report at least one falling dream (Saul and Curtis, 1967). These dreams tend not to be about sudden drops or stumbles, but of long drops from high buildings or down deep holes, ending in collision with the ground, or perhaps with a miraculously soft landing.

Flying

In *The Interpretation of Dreams* Freud (1932) related how a patient regularly dreamt of floating a couple of feet off the ground. His interpretation was that this fulfilled her wish to avoid contamination from other human beings, and to achieve greater stature. (She was a very short woman.) More generally, he attempted to relate the sensation of flying during a dream to sensations from the ventilation of the lungs during sleep, or to childhood memories of being thrown in the air. At the age of nine, my son told me of dreaming of swinging violently in the hammock (something he did frequently during the summer) and falling out (again a frequent occurence), but instead of landing on the ground he floated effortlessly around the garden, suspended above the ground. Although the hammock part of the dream is explicable in terms of actual experience, the subsequent floating cannot reasonably be related to my son's usual fate when falling out of the hammock; such dreams, which are not uncommon, seem uniquely detached from any experience in real life. For Artemidorus all dreams were classified as either theorematic or allegorical. The former describes events that are possible if not mundane, while the latter are metaphors. In these terms, flying dreams qualify as more allegorical than most.

From personal experience and from reports from her subjects, Ann Faraday (1972) describes two types of flying dream: floaters, like the ones above, and ones in which the dreamer is at tree-top height. Flying dreams seem to be distinct from recollections of flying in an aeroplane – few people have flown in an aeroplane at roof-top height, and in any case the experience would be quite different from the drifting and soaring of the typical flying dream. If they are as divorced from experience as they seem, the only explanation for their regular occurrence in a variety of people must be either, following Jung, that they are archetypal dreams with some allegorical significance, or that they represent an attempt to make sense out of experiences that are really occurring during dreaming sleep – an attempt to make a coherent story out of some or other pattern from the highly active discharges from the hindbrain that are a feature of REM sleep. This argument will be developed at greater length in Chapter 5. An unusual aspect of these dreams is the cautious attitude that dreamers tend to adopt towards flying – a rare example of commentary within a dream, of insight or lucidity. This is perhaps an indication of the forced nature of the experience – forced by a combination of the sensation of immobility of REM sleep and the rich visual experience offered by the overactive hindbrain.

When I conducted a phone-in on sleep and dreaming on a local radio station a few years ago somebody called in to ask what I had to say about flying dreams.

'Do you have them?' I asked.

'Yes.'

'Oh, so do I, aren't they fun?' I said.

'Yes, but how do you get the height?' he replied, 'Most of the time I just float two feet off the ground, and hardly ever get to fly at any decent height.'

This struck me very forcibly, as I too had had both sorts of flying dream, and while floating was quite enjoyable, flying at tree-top level was much more satisfactory. I could not think of any suitable advice at the time. That night I had a floating flying dream. Hovering in an upright position two feet or so above the ground I remembered the caller's problem and immediately found a solution. In my right hand was a small tray, and by tilting it in the breeze I found that I could obtain enough lift to get to any height I wanted, and was soon soaring into the air and travelling at will. When I woke up it was with the certainty that I had solved an extremely important problem, and was eager to try it out at once. It seemed incautious to attempt it indoors, and I was halfway out of bed to get a tray to take out into the garden before I realized the ridiculous nature of the enterprise.

Another solution to the problem of gaining height was told to me by one of my respondents, who had dreamt of climbing a high flagpole. When at the top he had been disappointed to find no flag, but with some cautious experimentation had discovered that he did not need to hold on to the pole – he could float. Once confident in his new power he had flown at flagpole height with the greatest of ease.

Revelation

A 'feeling of knowing' sometimes accompanies an aspect of a dream that is carried over into wakefulness (for instance, the certainty that I could fly when I had my flying dream). This feeling is familiar to heavy drinkers – *in vino veritas* – inspiring William James's (1896) comment: 'Sobriety diminishes, discriminates and says no; drunkenness expands, unites and says yes.' This phenomenon is also well known to people who take nitrous oxide or mescaline (McKellar, 1957). A revelation experienced by William James when taking nitrous oxide took the form of doggerel, which he genuinely believed to be of enormous significance while he was under the influence of the drug:

> Higamous hogamous, women are monogamous,
> Hogamous higamous, men are polygamous. (James, 1896)

A curious example of the converse situation, in which an accurate perception arises but the subject cannot acknowledge its veracity, is found in patients suffering from Capgras' Syndrome. This syndrome consists of the delusion that familiar people have been replaced by imposters. Ellis and Young (1990) have sought neuropsychological explanations for this syndrome, as well as for other disorders of face recognition. They suggest that, normally, there is more than one route to the recognition of faces, and that emotional recognition, mediated by different but parallel neurological pathways, may have to take place at the same time for a normal feeling of knowing. That is, our normal experience of recognition involves the integration of at least two sources of analysis. Patients suffering from Capgras' syndrome have an intact intellectual route for recognition, but a damaged emotional one. Patients suffering from a related condition of being unable to identify faces of people very familiar to them (prosopagnosia) are presumed to have the reverse form of damage. Possibly the same pathways, permanently damaged in these unfortunates, also fail to be coordinated during sleep, and the feeling of knowing becomes all too easily invoked by less than adequate intellectual perceptions.

There are a few instances when genuinely creative thinking has been documented as taking place during dreams. Most popular books on dreaming include Kekulé's discovery of the benzene ring and Coleridge's 'Kubla Khan' as examples.

Inspiration without effort is an attractive idea. The psychedelic movement of the 1960s promised increased understanding with the use of drugs. The Romantic movement of the early nineteenth century also celebrated personal revelation and inspirational creation, and opium, like cannabis in the 1960s, was a fashionable drug (freely available over the counter in all sorts of remedies). Samuel Taylor Coleridge had been reading Purchas's *His Pilgrimage* after taking some opium:

> In Xamdu did Cublai Can build a stately palace, encompassing sixteene miles of plaine ground with a wall, wherein are fertile Meddowes, pleasant Springs, delightful Streames, and all sorts of beasts of chase and game, and in the middest thereof a sumptuous house of pleasure.

Almost twenty years after the incident, Coleridge was persuaded by Byron to publish 'Kubla Khan'. At that time, he made the sensational claim that he had been able to remember 200 to 300 lines of perfect poetry when he had awoken from a drug-induced sleep, and had been busy writing them down when he had been interrupted by somebody from Porlock insisting on seeing him on business, and that when the visitor had left an hour later he had been able to remember nothing of the rest – hence the incomplete nature of the 54 lines of verse with which we are left. Some literary critics (Lefebure, 1974; Schneider, 1975) suggest that this account is probably a gross exaggeration – that is, while Coleridge may have dreamt about Kubla Khan, the poem had not been provided in the dream in its complete form, but had required years of revision. All the evidence seems to indicate that the account of the dream grew in the interval, in accordance with the Romantic ideal of the autonomy of the creative process. As William Empson (1964) comments, 'I find it a completely achieved poem; probably Coleridge was lying when he told the story of the person from Porlock, nearly twenty years later'. Coleridge's other drug-induced efforts are sheer doggerel in comparison, and like many drug addicts he was famous for frequently taking great liberties with the truth – especially where his drug habit was involved.

The other frequently cited example of creation during a dream is that of F. A. Kekulé, a nineteenth-century chemist. It was known that each molecule of benzene consisted of six atoms each of carbon and hydrogen, and Kekulé attempted to construct a model of the molecule. Because of the valencies of these two elements there was no obvious way that the twelve atoms could be arranged into a conventional chain, and he wrestled with the problem for some years. One evening he was dozing in front of a fire when he had a hypnagogic vision:

> this time the smaller groups [of atoms] kept modestly in the background. My mental eye, rendered more acute by repeated visions of this kind, could now distinguish larger structures, of manifold conformation; long rows, sometimes more closely fitted together; all twining and twisting in snakelike motion. But look! What was that? One of the snakes had seized hold of its own tail and the form whirled mockingly before my eyes ... I awoke as if struck by lightning; this time again I spent the rest of the night working out the consequences.

Arranging the carbon atoms in a ring, or hexagon, satisfied the laws of valency, since each of them could share a double bond with one of its neighbours and a single bond with the other, leaving the final one to attach to the hydrogen atoms arranged around the outside. This insight opened up the whole world of aromatic organic chemistry. (This account of creative inspiration during dreaming has been the subject of some controversy, of which Strunz (1993) has provided a carefully researched historical account.)

A less well known example is that of H. V. Hilprecht, an archeologist at Pennsylvania University. In 1893 Hilprecht was given drawings of fragments of agate excavated from the Babylonian temple of Bal at Nippur. He thought they might be finger rings, but was not sure. In a dream, a tall thin priest informed him that the two pieces had come from the same votive cylinder and had been cut in two to make earrings for a statue of the god Ninib. Later in the year he visited the museum in Istanbul where the fragments were kept and demonstrated their exact fit.

These two examples of successful problem solving when dozing or dreaming are typical only in that they were accompanied by a feeling of certainty – what is unusual is that they were realistic solutions. Just how often is inspiration misguided? Arthur Koestler (1966) comments:

> every original thinker who relies, as he must, on his unconscious hunches, incurs much greater risks to his career and sanity than his more pedestrian colleagues. 'The world little knows', wrote Faraday, 'how many of the thoughts and theories which have passed through the mind of a scientific investigator have been crushed in silence and secrecy; that in the most successful instances not a tenth of the suggestions, the hopes, the wishes, the preliminary conclusions have been realized'. Darwin, Huxley, and Planck, among many others, made similar confessions; Einstein lost 'two years of hard work' owing to a false inspiration. 'The imagination', wrote Beveridge, 'merely enables us to wander into the darkness of the unknown where, by the dim light of the knowledge that we carry, we may glimpse something that seems of interest. But when we bring it out and examine it more closely it usually proves to be only trash whose glitter had caught our attention. Imagination is at once the source of all hope and inspiration but also of frustration. To forget this is to court despair.'

As with all creative activity, the final synthesis of ideas represents the endpoint of a great deal of thinking, of preoccupation with some problem. A nineteenth-century physiologist, physicist and psychologist, von Helmholtz, who contributed substantially to every discipline he engaged in, described the process thus:

> It was always necessary, first of all, that I should have turned my problem over on all sides to such an extent that I had all its angles and complexities 'in my head' and could run through them freely without writing ... To bring the matter to that point is usually impossible without long preliminary labour. (Quoted in McKellar, 1957)

While Helmholtz did not report solving problems in dreams, apparently he did rely to some extent on autonomous process, so that once he had done the groundwork on a problem he sometimes achieved his insights spontaneously, for instance, when out walking. The role of dreaming in this very important process must be regarded as slight. The 'feeling of knowing' offered either when drunk, drugged, drowsy or asleep is no reliable indication of having achieved a real solution to a problem: unfortunately there are no short cuts in that direction.

Exposure – dreams of shame

Freud commented on dreams of exposure in his early essay, *Project for a Scientific Psychology*:

> the dream of nakedness demands our attention only when shame and embarrassment are felt in it, when one wishes to escape or to hide, and when one feels the strange inhibition of being unable to stir from the spot, and of being utterly powerless to alter the painful situation. ... The essential point is that one has a painful feeling of shame, and is anxious to hide one's nakedness, usually by means of locomotion, but is absolutely unable to do so. (Freud, 1966)

Freud's observation that such dreams are fueled by a sense of shame seems uncontroversial. Interestingly, in the survey referred to earlier (Griffith *et al.*, 1958) twice as many Americans as Japanese reported dreams of being inappropriately dressed or nude. An explanation for this may lie in the way that children are brought up in these two cultures. Western conditioning tends to be based on the idea of guilt. Telling children that they are bad when they have behaved wrongly is common in the West, but as Susan Sontag (1969) has observed, it is unheard of in the East, where children are instead told to be ashamed of themselves. For Westerners, the sense of shame and embarrass-ment has become strongly associated with nakedness and the proprieties of dress and attitudes towards nudity (especially among conventional Protes-tants). They are also peculiarly prudish and voyeuristic. For the Japanese students in the survey, shameful dreams may not have been confined to these topics – for instance, many of their dreams about failing examinations or their schooling in general may have been intrinsically shameful, and they reported both of these more often than the Americans.

Immobility

The sensation of being unable to move is common in many dreams, including some nightmares. Sometimes one can move only excruciatingly slowly, how-ever pressing it seems to move quickly. It is well established that we are, in fact, in a state of muscular flaccid paralysis during REM sleep, with the exception of the muscles controlling respiration and the eyes. In some species, this inhibi-tion of motor discharge at the level of the pons (a structure at the top of the spinal cord) is more general than others. Dogs in REM sleep sometimes move their legs as if running, and in monkeys the entire face may writhe and twitch.

At any rate, it is reasonable to interpret this very common experience during dreaming as a response to awareness, at some level, of the inability to move. Interestingly, Freud anticipated the discovery of motor paralysis during REM sleep by more than 60 years when, in his *Project for a Scientific Psychology* (1966), he asserted that there is no motor discharge during dreaming. He later addressed the question of why this awareness only arises occasionally (in *The*

Interpretation of Dreams, 1932), saying that it is an expression of conflict about the will. That is, if we do attempt to make a movement during dreaming it is certain to fail, and this provides an opportunity to express the idea that our intentions are being thwarted – anticipating, in a way, the neuropsychological explanations for dreaming, such as the activation-synthesis hypothesis described in Chapter 5. One could also argue that imperative, strenuous movements are rarely dreamed – one tends to be an observer, paying little attention to how one gets about. Only when the dream focuses on the attempt to make a movement is the problem apparent.

Nightmares – dreams of fear

Nightmares can perhaps better be defined in terms of the emotions they evoke, rather than any particular subject matter. These emotions are primarily fear, guilt and horror, in various proportions, and the dream ends with the subject waking up. While they might be regarded as disorders of sleep, and will be discussed in the chapters on sleep problems, they are so prevalent, so much a part of normal life that, like sleepwalking, they deserve a place in any account of normal sleep and dreaming.

Sheer terror in a nightmare can be the result of an unseen, hidden menace – for instance, a menace lurking behind a closed door. Unusually for dreaming, the plot is not in this case driven by the visual imagery, rather it is almost as if the feeling of terror is primary, and the purpose of dreaming is to present the somewhat mundane imagery to accommodate the emotion. While some nightmares like this are consummated by the monster making an actual appearance, it is not necessary – the terror may never be actualized.

It is necessary to distinguish 'night terrors' from dreaming nightmares. The former, which are relatively common amongst children, occur during deep, slow-wave (stage 4) sleep and are not accompanied by visual imagery or a coherent dream (Broughton, 1968). Nightmares occurring during REM sleep may be equally frightening, but they take the form of a story with vivid visual imagery.

The purely guilty nightmare can be illustrated in terms of sexual repression and guilt by Mary Baker Eddy's dream of being assaulted by a strange man while she was attending a Christian Science meeting (Shulman, 1979). She managed to disengage herself from this unwanted lover and ran into a house, which unfortunately turned out to be one of ill-repute. The man followed, locked the door, and laughed. Only when Mrs Eddy understood her predicament did the nightmare dissolve.

Nightmares of pure horror can involve cannabalism, gory death and graveyard ghouls. The author Gustave Flaubert once dreamed of

> lying in a curtained bed. He was aware of footsteps on the stairs and, at the same time, a breath of foul-smelling air wafted into his room. Then seven or eight black-bearded fellows entered with daggers held between their teeth. They approached the bed; their teeth made gnashing sounds. Each finger left a tell-tale bloodstain on the white bed curtains. For a long while seven or eight pairs of lidless eyes gazed

down at Flaubert. The typical prisoner of nightmare, he could neither shout nor move. When at last they drew back, he saw that one side of their faces was skinless and bleeding. They lifted all his clothes, leaving blood on every item, and sat down to eat. As they broke bread it spurted and dripped blood, and their mirth was the rattle in a dying man's throat. The apparitions vanished to leave the whole room smeared with blood. Flaubert knew a choking sensation and felt as if he had swallowed flesh. Then he heard a long cry. (Ibid.)

As in a Hammer horror film, the anticipation of something dreadful was the engine of this dream – for instance, the seven bearded men's appalling appearance was not immediately apparent, and even though they removed Flaubert's clothes and started to eat, there was no explicit imagery of being eaten. In the somewhat incoherent climax, Flaubert was himself implicated in the cannabalistic orgy – tasting flesh, presumably his own. Again, it seems that the emotion of horror comes first and the dream is constructed to accommodate it. How else could the dreamer know at the beginning of a nightmare (as he or she always does) that something horrific is going to happen? There are no screen credits at the beginning of dreams to tell you what sort of dream you are going to have, but they might as well be in the nightmares because the terror, horror or guilt is excruciatingly present before the first scenes have even been played.

5
What is a Dream?

A description of dreaming

While a great deal has been discovered about the physiology of sleep, and psychologists have developed reliable techniques for establishing when people are likely to be dreaming, there has not been equivalent progress in understanding the nature of dreams. A starting point for any analysis of this nature must be to establish clearly how dreaming differs from waking consciousness.

Dreams happen to us, rather than being the products of conscious control in the way that fantasies are. When dreaming, we are the spectators of an unfolding drama, and only rarely do we have the impression of being in control. 'Lucid' dreaming, when the dreamer knows that he or she is dreaming and makes decisions about how the dream plot should develop, is rare. More typically, things happen and we observe. While there may be a coherent plot, events do not unfold in any steady progression; rather, there are sudden changes in scenario, or scene shifts, which are sometimes baffling. Ordinary logic is suspended. One can fly. People can turn into animals. We encounter people who have been dead for years, or improbably have conversations with film stars or royalty.

The dreams that subjects report in the laboratory tend to be mundane and lack the bizarre quality of dreams reported in the morning. This is probably because only the strangest experiences are remembered by people waking normally after a night's sleep, and the more everyday the dream content, the less memorable it is. Faraday (1972) offers some evidence that the last dreams of the night tend to be more vivid than those earlier in the night. The oddness of the dreaming experience is, however, undeniable. One feature of this oddness that has perhaps been overlooked is pointed out by Rechtschaffen (1978) – what he calls the single-mindedness of dreams. When awake, we normally reflect on the stream of consciousness as it goes on. Furthermore, we can be aware that we are in one place, for instance, seated at a desk, and at the same time imagine something else. Rechtschaffen claims that during dreaming this is not possible: 'I cannot remember a dream report which took the form, "Well, I was dreaming of such and such, but as I was dreaming this I was imagining a different scene which was completely unrelated".' The imagery of the dream totally dominates consciousness. Paradoxically, while dreaming, we are without imagination, and we are not aware that we are dreaming. Instances of 'lucid' dreaming, when dreamers are aware that they are dreaming, are rare, even amongst those who claim frequently to experience it. This is totally different from the state of affairs when we are awake but have taken an hallucinatory drug – in this case, however compelling the hallucination, we are well aware that the experience is drug-induced and not real.

Conscious control of our attention between the reflective, evaluative stream of thought and the thinking essential to the task in hand, is vital to our normal process of registering memories. We form intentions to remember, categorize and order what we are going to remember in terms of our past experience. The massive forgetting of dreams can be explained in terms of the straitjacket of a single thought stream, preventing the formation of any such intention and preventing dream events from being brought into perspective or made sense of. As Erasmus Darwin commented in 1794, 'we never exercise our reason or recollection in dreams' (see Chapter 1). Rechtschaffen's (1978) work provides a lucid, insightful account of the phenomenology of dreaming, which despite the many advances made in understanding the natural history of sleep and dreaming, remains unusual in attempting to deal directly with the experience of dreaming. Of course, the phenomenological approach has been with us for a long time, and has been the primary source of evidence in the psychoanalytic tradition.

The psychoanalytic approach

Freud's analysis of dreaming remains the most influential account we have. He and other psychoanalysts have relied on dreams recollected during therapy sessions, or those they could recall themselves. The goal of psychoanalysis was to develop a new set of techniques for use in psychiatry, and in this context dreams tended to be treated as neurotic symptoms rather than as a normal aspect of experience. Dreams seemed to provide a royal road to the understanding of the patients' subconscious. For Freud (1922), 'dreams are the fulfilment of wishes'. He asserted that there are two distinct forms of thinking – primary process thinking, as exemplified in dreaming, and secondary process thinking, as exemplified in logical reasoning. Primary process thinking is driven by what he called the pleasure principle, whereby the instant gratification of infantile desires is immediately achieved by making use of a number of irrational but personally satisfying mental tricks (mechanisms he called condensation, displacement, substitution and symbolization). During childhood, primary process thinking is gradually displaced by secondary process thinking, but in the adult it remains as a neurotic symptom, most clearly during dreaming but also at a subconscious level to influence waking behaviour.

Most dreams are not obviously simple wish fulfilments – dreams of personal glory, gratifying sexual encounters ending in orgasm, or the confounding of enemies. In order to accommodate this fact Freud did not abandon the idea of all dreams being wish fulfilments, but hypothesized a mechanism, the dreamwork, whereby dreams are censored. The manifest dream that is available for recall is thus a compromise, whereby the wish fulfilments have been disguised. The latent dream, only accessible through extensive analysis of the manifest dream, is the 'true' dream – the expression in wish fulfilment of strongly felt desires. Sleep is physiologically necessary, and while asleep there are periodic surges of instinctual energy that give rise to unacceptable, anxiety-provoking thoughts. Manifest dreams are the outcome of a process that allows the expression of these thoughts, preserving sleep by preventing them from being overtly explicit.

Freudian dream analysis starts with the patient lying down on the couch and attaining as relaxed a frame of mind as possible. The patient then recounts his or her dream and, considering each dream image in turn, provides free associations to the object represented. This technique of free association, in which the patient is encouraged to say the first thing that comes to mind, reveals connotations of the dream image that might otherwise not become obvious. In practice, the analyst will direct the patient towards those connotations which seem most pertinent – in Freud's case, sexual connotations. An analysis may go on for years, so the free associations and the dreams recalled become conditioned by the analytic process itself, the patient's contribution increasingly representing the assumptions of the analyst.

Modern psychoanalysts still make extensive use of dream analysis, but are not necessarily interested in uncovering the 'latent dream' – the simple wish fulfilment of erotic urges. Rather, they use patients' dreams to explore the latter's current preoccupations. One British psychoanalyst went so far as to reject entirely the Freudian theory of the origin and function of dreaming (Rycroft, 1979). He argued that as everybody dreams, dreams cannot be regarded as a neurotic symptom – unless everybody is neurotic. Describing everybody as neurotic makes any distinction between normality and neurosis impossible. In addition, the idea that infants are born with a totally maladaptive nervous system – capable only of primary process thinking – is biological and evolutionary nonsense. As he says, when quoting from Freud's *Introductory Lectures on Psycho-analysis* (1922):

> If we started life as 'a chaos, a cauldron full of seething excitations', with 'no organization' and given to satisfying our wishes by hallucination, it is hard to imagine how we could begin to experience the external world in such a way as to learn adaptation from it. This difficulty does not arise if one assumes that both processes co-exist from the beginning of life, that they both have adaptive functions, and they are not necessarily in conflict with one another – even though they may on occasion be. (Rycroft, 1979)

Imagination and artistic creation are also, according to the strict interpretation of Freudian theory, neurotic symptoms. Rycroft argues against relegating so much of our mental life to the status of pathology, preferring to liken dreams to waking imaginative activity, such as creative writing. Metaphor and symbolism are intrinsic to both, and it seems only reasonable to him to treat dreaming as normal and creative unless good evidence emerges that it is indeed pathological.

Freud was a pioneer in taking dreams seriously, and in recognizing that the quality of logic in dreams, while sometimes bizarre, may follow certain rules. His psychological theorizing was developed during the course of his life, but many of his assumptions can be traced to an early work, *Project for a Scientific Psychology* (1966, first published in 1895). This essay is, incidentally, unusually accessible for the lay reader as it does not rely on any familiarity with the technical terminology he developed later. As well as addressing psychiatric issues it deals, very insightfully in most instances, with topics of general psychology, such as primary memory and forgetting. As Freud was a trained neurologist, his psychological theory was essentially based on the neurophysiological thinking of his time. McCarley and Hobson (1977), in an analysis of Freud's psychological theory, have pointed out just how deeply his psychology was informed by these neurological assumptions, which subsequent science has frequently shown to be wrong.

Freud's theory on dreaming has similarly been overtaken by the evidence. REM sleep – during which our most vivid dreams almost invariably occur – is universal amongst mammals, which makes it unlikely that its primary role is as a neurotic defence mechanism, unless gorillas, dogs, cats and skunks are all credited with repressive superegos! Neurophysiological studies have shown that REM sleep is an essential part of brain function – not an optional extra invoked to deal with unacceptable thoughts that emerge during sleep.

Some recent ideas

Rather than devoting any more space to criticizing a theory based on nineteenth-century science, it seems more profitable to follow Freud's example and look to our current knowledge of the biological basis of sleep in order to build a psychological model of what dreaming really is. Hobson and McCarley (1977) followed up their work on the dated neurophysiological underpinnings of Freudian theory in general with an analysis of current knowledge of the neurophysiology of sleep, as applied to dreaming. In the spirit of Freud's belief in the isomorphism of mind and body, they set out to do what he did, but in the light of modern findings about the physiology of sleep mechanisms. Rather than dreaming primarily being psychologically necessary – a mechanism to deal with occasional neurotic erotic impulses during sleep – they argued that it is in fact the outcome of automatic, preprogrammed neural processes. Like most good theories, theirs integrates a large body of evidence, which – when presented in a single context – makes the theory seem almost self-evident.

As it relies largely on neurophysiological evidence, the argument for the theory is inevitably rather technical and could be seen as following more in the tradition of Hughlings Jackson, a nineteenth-century neurologist, than that of Freud. Jackson's perceptual release theory addressed the notion of the brain struggling to make sense of perceptual input, some of which may have been generated within the perceptual system rather than by the outside world. This idea was developed by West (1962) to account for hypnagogic phenomena in terms of the integration of sensations generated in the retina – the random ectopic discharges and after-images we experience when we close our eyes.

There is every indication that the cortex is highly active during REM sleep, although little external sensory stimulation is received by it. In addition, although the motor cortex is highly active and generates impulses that would normally result in movement, the commands do not reach the muscles controlling the limbs but are 'switched off' at a relay station at the top of the spinal column, so that we are effectively paralyzed during REM sleep. This explains the loss of tone in the neck muscles under the chin, which is one of the defining characteristics of REM sleep.

Not only is the cortex unable to control the musculature, but there is also an inhibition of incoming signals generated by the sensory system. That is, perceptions of the 'real' world are selectively attenuated. The hindbrain and midbrain structures, normally associated with relaying sensory information to the cortex spontaneously, generate signals that are responsible for cortical activation, and these are indistinguishable from the signals that would normally be relayed from the eyes and ears. This activity is under the control of a periodic triggering mechanism in a structure at the top of the spinal column/base of the brain known as the pontine brainstem. Activity in giant cells in the pontine brainstem has been shown to precede eye movements in REM sleep in animals (or paradoxical sleep as it is called in rodents and cats) and there is no evidence that cortical activity can influence these cells' discharges. During REM sleep, Hobson and McCarley (1977) argue, the cortex is largely under the control of these random discharges from the hindbrain. The interaction between stimulation from hindbrain structures normally associated with the transmission of sensory information and cortical structures normally devoted to integrating sensory input of this sort gives rise to dreaming. They call this the activation–synthesis hypothesis of the dream process, and suggest that dreaming sleep may have a functional role in some aspect of the learning process.

This theory has been elaborated by Crick and Mitchison (1983). REM sleep, or paradoxical sleep, is universal amongst mammals. In people, cats and rats the prevention of REM sleep by selective awakenings results in increased amounts of this sleep stage upon recovery, as if what had been 'missed' was then 'made up for', suggesting that this sleep stage not only has its own drive mechanism but may also have an important function. Since most dreams are not remembered, this function must either have nothing whatever to do with dreaming, or, if dreaming is essential to the process, forgetting must be a necessary part of it. According to Crick and Mitchison, the random pontine activity stimulating the cortex during REM sleep therefore has the function of erasing memories, which in their terms have become 'parasitic' – interpretations that whatever their origin have no place in our latest view of the world, and are redundant but persistent. This accumulation of nonsense is expressed in dreams that are created only in order to be forgotten. Those which are remembered are later repeated, so that frightening dreams that wake people up, and are remembered, tend to become recurrent. The theory is supported by a mathematical model ('the Hopfield net') of the effects of random stimulation on very complex interactive systems (neural nets), accounting for both bizarre and repetitive dreams.

In a subsequent paper, Crick and Mitchison (1986) defend their theory against a number of criticisms, and develop it further with new evidence. As they point out, selective forgetting of parasitic traces will have the opposite effect – on the memory system as a whole – of simply losing memories. 'The process of reverse learning is designed to make the storage in an associative net more efficient.' In a system as complex as human memory, the result of erasing what they call parasitic connections will thus have the effect of sharpening and making more accessible those cognitive structures which represent our world. As such this theory, in practical terms, has no quarrels with Hobson and McCarley's (1977) hypothesis that REM or dreaming sleep has a positive function in the learning process.

When a neural net, as described by Hopfield *et al.* (1983), becomes overloaded, memories or concepts that share some simple feature are liable to become conflated – linked together by 'parasitic associations'. Crick and Mitchison (1986) argue that the phenomenon of condensation in dreaming, first described by Freud, is specifically predicted by their theory. While most of what Freud has to say about the 'latent content' of dreams is at best arguable, the phenomenon of condensation as part of the 'manifest content' has been well established by Foulkes (1985), even in children's dreams, and of course, as neural net theory would predict, 'in condensation the objects or events brought together always turn out to have some feature in common'.

Additional evidence presented by Crick and Mitchison (1986) in support of their theory comes from what they call 'nature's experiments' – relating in this case to the few species of mammals that have no REM sleep. They had previously noted that the echidna, an Australian monotreme, lacks REM sleep. It also has, in relation to its size, a very large neocortex, and Crick and Mitchison had attributed the large size of the cortex to the lack of system for 'reverse learning'. They subsequently learned of Mukhametov's work on the sleep of cetaceans (described in Chapter 10), showing that two species of bottle-nosed dolphin and porpoise experience non-REM sleep but no REM sleep. As is well known, cetaceans have very large neocortices in relation to their size, and in the past this was taken as a potential indication of great intelligence. However, Crick and Mitchison argue that these animals are not particularly intelligent, but rather that REM sleep did not need to develop in them because there was no evolutionary pressure for them to have small heads (being constantly supported by water). Seals, on the other hand, while also sea mammals, do have to support their heads out of water, and have in fact been shown to have normal REM sleep. Thus, the 'function of REM sleep is to make advanced brains more efficient and, in particular, to allow these brains to have a smaller size than they would otherwise have'.

Hobson and McCarley's (1977) thesis has also been developed by Seligman and Yellen (1987). The latter took the theory further by mapping the psychological reality of dreaming onto contemporary neurophysiological evidence of brain functioning during sleep, accounting for the emotional quality of dreaming as well as its visual content. They invoke three pieces of evidence, closely following Hobson and McCarley's arguments to start with. First, the neurophysiological evidence suggests that the hindbrain is in control of the generation and maintenance of REM sleep.

Second, rapid eye movements are not continuous during REM sleep, but come in periodic bursts, typically lasting between two and 10 seconds, and are separated by periods of sleep lasting up to three minutes with low-voltage, mixed-frequency EEG and muscle atonia. Subjects woken during a REM burst report highly vivid visual experiences much more frequently than when woken from periods of REM 'quiescence' (Molinari and Foulkes, 1969). Categorizing these reports as either 'primary visual experiences' (PVEs) or 'secondary cognitive elaborations' (SCEs), Seligman and Yellen (1987) found that 82 per cent of reports of mental activity when woken from REM bursts were PVEs, and 12 per cent were SCEs; 80 per cent of reports after awakenings from REM quiescence were SCEs, while only 20 per cent were PVEs. Subsequent work (Bosinelli *et al.*, 1974; Foulkes and Pope, 1973) has shown that the very striking differences between the experiences during REM bursts and those during REM quiescence are not as great when subjects are questioned at any length, rather than being allowed to make spontaneous reports of what has been going on in their minds. That is, there is something to report from REM-quiescent periods when the subjects are carefully prompted. However, it is undeniable that there is a great difference in the quality of experience during REM bursts and REM quiescence, with visual and auditory hallucinatory sensations characterizing the REM bursts, even if the difference is not quite as striking as was first thought.

Given the evidence outlined above, it would not seem unreasonable to conclude that discharges from the pontine brainstem are causing the dreams. How is it that what seem like random discharges from a part of the brain that we share with the humblest reptiles can end up as the elaborate, coherent cognitive activity we know as dreaming? The third piece of evidence invoked by Seligman and Yellen (1987) shows how adept the cortex is at making sense out of chaos. Like John Hughlings Jackson's (1874) perceptual release theory in the context of hypnagogic hallucinations, they argue that dreaming is the outcome of the cortex integrating sensory inputs over which it has no control. Following a survey of university students' dreams, they concluded that dream images that are highly vivid also tend to be 'surprising', and at the centre of the visual field:

> These results suggest the existence of two different kinds of visual events during dreaming as we predicted. One kind is vivid, detailed, colorful, large, and in the center of the visual field. The other kind is less vivid, less detailed, less colorful, smaller, and in the periphery of the visual field. The detailed are more constrained and continuous with the plot. We suggest that this is so because the vivid events are hallucinatory bursts whose content is unconstrained by the previous visual events, the ongoing emotion, or the ongoing integration; whereas the less vivid events are visual material generated by the cognitive integration, and as such, are constrained in content. (Ibid.)

Seligman and Yellen also compared the coherence of subjects' dream reports with their ability, when awake, to construct dream plots when shown a series of unconnected slides. They predicted that those who integrated random visual events well in the waking state would also be those whose dream images were very constrained by the dream plot. Those who integrated random visual events inadequately when awake would be those whose dreams images fitted least well into their dream plots. Strong positive correlations were indeed found between measures of the integration of images into dream plots, with the integration of the unrelated slides into dream stories made up while awake, showing that their subjects had a consistent characteristic style of integration while awake and asleep:

> We suggest that the same process by which individuals make coherent the externally generated visual episodes of daily life is at work during dreaming; when an individual encounters the internally generated visual episodes in REM sleep, he deploys this ability (in whatever measure he possesses it) to make this encounter coherent. (Ibid.)

A couple of obvious doubts could be expressed. First, if there is such continuity between waking skill in integrating visual material and the coherence of dream reports, why is it that 'dream logic' follows rules of its own, characteristic of Bleuler's 'A-thinking' or Freud's primary process thinking? Second, would waking subjects really respond to dream images in the same way as when asleep? Nonetheless, this approach to the nature of dreaming is highly compelling. Because it relies on continuing cognitive synthesis as a mechanism for the construction of dreams, it explains the apparently dream-like quality of many experiences reported to happen during non-REM sleep, including hypnagogic imagery. This could be described in terms of Freud's dream-work as a sort of cortical rearguard action in the face of incoherent but highly active discharges from the hindbrain. In the previous chapter, dreams of exposure were described as dreams of shame, nightmares as dreams of fear, guilt or horror. Is it similarly possible that these emotions are not a consequence of the dream but of the apparently haphazard interaction between midbrain and hindbrain activity during REM sleep? That is, just as cognitive synthesis is required to make sense of the input from the visual cortex, so it is needed to comprehend the intense emotions being offered to the cortex by overstimulated midbrain limbic structures.

In addition to these developments of the activation–synthesis model (by Crick and Mitchison, and Seligman and Yellen), Hobson (1990, 1992) has developed a psychological underpinning for his theory. A three-dimensional psychological model of conscious states (the AIM model) shows them to be a product of activation (A), information flow (I: internal versus external) and mode of information processing (M). Activation refers simply to general cortical activation. Information flow refers to 'input source', which is the outside world (via the senses, mainly vision) when we are awake. This source of stimulation is actively attenuated during REM sleep, so all 'input' during REM sleep is internally generated. Mode of information processing is described by Hobson (1990) as the 'most speculative and original component of the model ..., the estimated ratio of aminergic to cholinergic neurotransmitter concentration, which measures the mode of information processing manifested by the brain-mind'. Thus, dreaming during REM sleep is characterized by high activation and low external information flow (with inhibition of sensory input), and the specific mode of dreaming consciousness is triggered by cholinoceptive and/or cholinergic 'REM-on' cells and terminated by aminergic (noradrenergic and serotonergic) inhibitory 'REM-off' cells. There is ample physiological evidence to demonstrate the control of REM sleep processes by the hindbrain in the way required by Hobson's model (Figure 5.1).

Hobson *et al.* (2000) has restated and elaborated the AIM model in a special issue of *Behavioral and Brain Sciences*. This journal specializes in peer review, whereby a substantial theoretical position set out by one author is publicly commented on by a large number of others. In this article Hobson reiterated his strongly held belief in isomorphism between the phenomenology and physiology of dreaming, restated his case that REM sleep is a product of pontine stimulation, and replied to a number of criticisms of the theory.

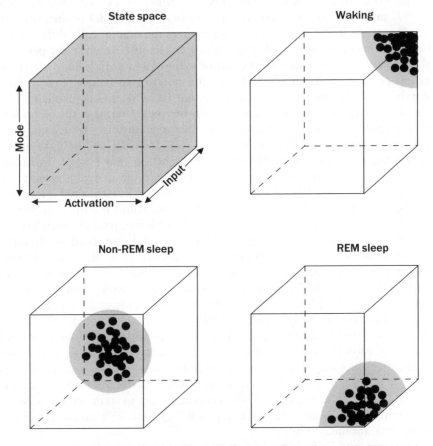

Figure 5.1 Hobson's AIM model. Three-dimensional state space defined by the values for brain activation (A), input source and strength (I) and mode of processing (M) (after Hobson, 1990)

Two major problems, which are highlighted in the *Behavioral and Brain Sciences* issue on sleep and dreaming mentioned above, confront both Hobson's theory of dreaming and all others that are based on a physiological if not psychophysiological approach. One is the imperfect correlation between the REM sleep state and the experience of dreaming. That is, as noted in Chapter 4, a person may be in REM sleep but does not have a dream (or rather, does not remember one when woken), and similarly may report a dream when woken from non-REM sleep (typically, light sleep at the end of the sleep period or at sleep onset). Nielsen (2000) addressed this problem and came up with the solution of 'covert dreaming', whereby some REM processes may occur in non-REM sleep, stimulating dreaming. This is in fact similar to Hobson's explanation of the same problem, that some cholinergic pontine activity may go on during non-REM sleep that initiates dreamlike experiences even outside REM sleep.

A second problem, probably more damaging to Hobson's theory, is that presented by Solms (1997, 2000), who cites evidence from human and animal brain lesion studies. In his book *The Neuropsychology of Dreams*, Solms (1997) puts forward an alternative psychobiological model of dreaming consciousness. As in the AIM model, it recognizes the dramatically different ways in which information flows during waking consciousness, with low perceptual thresholds and full control of the motor system, and during REM sleep, with raised perceptual thresholds and a motor system that is in a state of flaccid paralysis. While Solms does not dispute that REM sleep is controlled by pontine brainstem activity, he disagrees with the thesis that it is this stimulation that directly causes the experience of dreaming through its effects on the primary visual cortex. Rather, dreaming is a construct of forebrain activity. As evidence he cites the well-known phenomenon that loss of dreaming is typical of lesions in the forebrain (known since the end of the nineteenth century), while these lesions have no direct effect on REM sleep. Lesions in the pontine brainstem will eradicate REM sleep, but Solms reports that they may not eliminate the experience of dreaming. In addition, patients with lesions in the primary sensori-motor areas of the cortex (with concomitant disabilities in respect of movement and sensation when awake) typically report dreams in which movement and sensation are normal, which is not compatible with Hobson's thesis that dream imagery is isomorphic with cortical activation. While agreeing that REM sleep and dreaming normally occur together, Solms argues that this is simply because REM sleep, controlled by the pontine brainstem, provides a sufficient level of brain activation and inhibition of external stimulation to enable the forebrain to generate the experience of dreaming. Thus, dreaming may also occur during light non-REM sleep, when a similar level of brain activation prevails. Solms also cites evidence from a number of functional imaging studies of the sleeping brain to support the case that 'dreaming involves concerted activity in a *highly specific* group of forebrain structures' (Solms, 2000).

Hobson's and Solms's models attempt to explain how the consciousness of dreaming is generated during sleep explicitly in terms of the interactions between different structures in the brain, and between different neurochemical systems. Since the early 1980s a number of purely psychological models have been developed. These may have been stimulated by the psychobiological approach, but they attempt to explain dreaming and REM sleep in purely psychological terms. (Some of the older ideas also refuse to go away – Solms, for instance, has argued for revival of the Freudian approach to interpreting dream content and explaining dreams as the guardian of sleep.) One problem that remains is explaining the recurring dream – if the stimulation from the hindbrain pontine structures is truly random, how is it that people repeatedly have the same dreams? Such questions must remain unanswered, but this strategy for understanding the nature of dreaming is the most promising yet suggested. Our knowledge of the neurophysiology of sleep is highly advanced, but our psychological understanding of dreaming is very limited. If we accept the existence of isomorphism between brain states and mental functioning, taking some account of neurophysiological evidence must be the best approach to understanding dreaming at this stage in the state of the art.

Antrobus (1986, 1990, 1991) has proposed an explanation of dreaming in terms similar to Hobson's AIM model, but instead of three dimensions he has restricted himself to two – activation and input, with the mode of consciousness (determined neurochemically in the Hobson's model) being determined by the interaction of these two factors alone. Thus, during REM sleep, when sensory thresholds are raised and there is heightened cortical activation, dreaming naturally occurs as the response of a complex, parallel neural network system, which the brain is. During wakefulness, when sensory thresholds are low and cortical activation is high, the contents of consciousness are naturally dominated by the stream of information coming into the brain. During deep non-REM sleep cortical activation is low, and sensory thresholds are also low, so little conscious activity is generated. While explicitly psychological, this model is obviously considerably informed by new understandings of the neurobiology of REM sleep.

Foulkes (1982) has developed a purely cognitive model of dream production, in which dreams result from the release of diffuse and more or less random items in the memory system, including memories inhibited during wakefulness. The process of dream generation is one in which these more or less random memories are organized within a coherent scenario, normally related to the recent or distant past of the dreamer. However, Foulkes attributes no important function to dreaming: 'Since it seems that the activation of mnemonic elements during dreaming and their selection for dream processing *is* random and arbitrary, it's not likely that *particular contents of our dreams –* in and of themselves – serve any adaptive functions' (Foulkes, 1985, p. 200).

At the moment, Hobson's psychobiological theory, and variations such as that by Solms, seem to offer the best way forward in understanding dreaming. However, psychology has a chequered and sometimes unhappy history of combining physiology with psychological explanation, as seen in the enthusiastic reception of physiological explanations of arousal mechanisms during the 1960s and 1970s. (It now seems that arousal is not controlled by the ascending reticular activating system in the simple way that physiologists thought in the 1950s.) Perhaps a little scepticism is in order, plus the maintenance of a tradition of psychological explanation that is free from any reference to mechanism.

It may be appropriate to allow the poet W. H. Auden to have the last word on the subject:

> James Watt
> Was the hard-boiled kind of Scot:
> He thought any dream
> Sheer waste of steam.

Part III
The Physiology and Natural History of Sleep

6

The Physiology of Sleep

Biological rhythms and sleep

Circadian rhythms and zeitgebers

The nineteenth-century 'classical' account of physiology, typified in the work of the great French scientist Claude Bernard, held that physiology functions to maintain a constancy of the internal environment, and that all physiological control consists, in modern terms, of a series of negative feedback systems responding to changes produced either internally, by other systems, or in the external environment. It is certainly true that many biological systems do respond like this, for instance pupils dilate in the dark, and perspiration increases in the heat. However, since life began one of the great certainties on this planet, in all habitable zones, has been that there has been a regular alternation of light and dark, warm and cold on a 24-hour basis. Despite so much uncertainty confronting organisms, the sun has remained uniquely and totally predictable. It is, therefore, perhaps unsurprising that physiological systems should have evolved to rely on, and in many cases to anticipate, such a regular routine. That is, rather than simply reacting to changes when they occur, they behave proactively, preparing the organism for changes that are known to be about to occur.

For example, it was known over a hundred years ago that body temperature varied with time of day in a regular way. However, it did not become clear until the middle of this century that variations such as this, and the control of the timing of wakefulness and sleep, were largely under the influence of biological clocks that were relatively independent of external cues. Two facts forced scientists to this conclusion. First, when animals were removed from all external cues as to the time of day, they continued to show pronounced rhythmicity in behaviour (alternating wakefulness and sleep) on a 24-hour basis. Second, to bring home the point that this 24-hour rhythmicity was in no way a response to minimal cues that the experimenters had not been able to exclude from the animals' environment, it was usual for the free-running rhythms to deviate slightly from the exact 24 hours.

An important paper reviewing the evidence for the new science of chronobiology in the mid-1960s (Aschoff, 1965) shows the activity of a chaffinch in an isolated environment (Figure 6.1). The horizontal bars in the figure denote times of activity. The first four days were under normal illumination (LD 12:12, with lights on for 12 hours and off for 12). The next four weeks were under continuous illumination at a low level (0.4 lux),

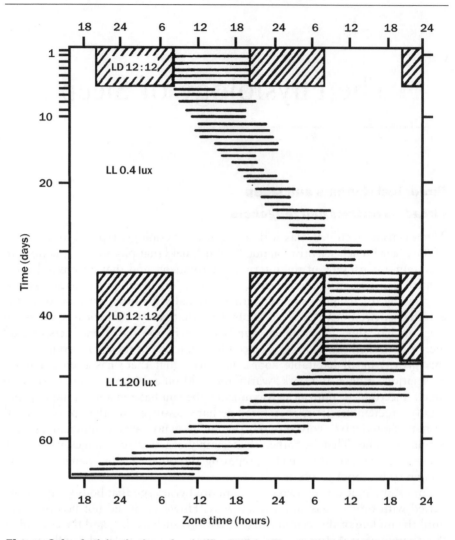

Figure 6.1 Activity rhythm of a chaffinch (*Fringilla coelebs*) in a light–dark cycle with 12 hours of light and 12 hours of darkness (LD 12:12) and in continuous illumination (LL) with an intensity of 0.4 lux and of 120 lux. Black bars denote activity time; shaded area denotes darkness (from Aschoff, 1965)

followed by two weeks of LD 12:12, and then a period of continuous and relatively bright light (120 lux). When under continuous low illumination the animal's pattern of behaviour was governed by a 'day' that was slightly longer than 24 hours, and while under continuous brighter illumination its day was shorter than 24 hours. Aschoff went on to experiment on human volunteers isolated in an underground bunker for three or four weeks. Like the chaffinch, these volunteers maintained a more or less regular routine of wakefulness and sleep, although the human rhythms were almost all longer than 24 hours, whatever the level of illumination. Their rhythms of body temperature and urine excretion followed the same pattern as that of the chaffinch in response to continuous light, with the spontaneously generated day becoming longer the dimmer the continuous light.

In short, both chaffinches and human beings (and virtually every other animal species) seem to have an independent (endogenous) biological clock ticking away somewhere inside them, and this clock is instrumental in controlling some of our most important physiological functions, including preparing us for wakefulness and making sleep possible.

The study of biological rhythms necessitated the integration of knowledge from a number of disciplines, ranging from mathematics to biology, and generated a specialized vocabulary of its own. Some useful terms are listed below.

General oscillator terms:

- **Amplitude:** the peak to trough difference in biological oscillation;
- **Frequency:** the reciprocal of the period of a rhythm, for example 10 cycles per second, or once per 24 hours;
- **Period:** the time it takes to complete one cycle of a rhythm;
- **Phase:** a particular reference point in the cycle of a rhythm; for example, sleep onset time.

Biological rhythm terms:

- **Circadian periodicity:** rhythms of about 24 hours. Halberg (1969) first introduced the word 'circadian' to describe this imprecise but highly regular rhythmicity;
- **Endogenous periodicity:** an innate rhythm, apparent in the absence of any time-giving external cues;
- **Exogenous periodicity:** rhythmic activity derived mainly from external cues; for example, some flowers opening in response to sunlight (but not the heliotrope, famous since 1729 for opening its flowers on a circadian basis even if kept in the dark);
- **Entrainment:** the coupling of an organism's endogenous rhythm with time-giving external cues (*zeitgebers*);
- **Ultradian periodicity:** rhythms with a period of less than 24 hours, for example 90-minute cycles of REM–non-REM sleep;
- **Zeitgeber:** literally, 'time-giver': a forcing oscillation in the environment.

The role of daylight in controlling the timing of the *circadian rhythm* – its *phase* and *period* – is absolutely crucial, and constitutes an example of *entrainment*. Biological clocks share many of the properties of mechanical clocks. A surprising property of even the simplest mechanical oscillators at the heart of clocks is the tendency towards entrainment. The Dutch scientist Christiaan Huygens, working in the seventeenth century, was one of the first to build reliable pendulum clocks. He noticed that when these clocks were in close proximity they tended to tick in synchrony, keeping the same time even if they did not do so when restarted in isolation from each other. This tendency for the frequency of oscillators to adjust in accordance with quite weak rhythmic stimulation is known as *entrainment*. In the example of the pendulum clocks, the vibration generated by each activation of the escapement – the tick – was transmitted through the wooden case of one timepiece to the one in contact with it. Similarly, while biological clocks drive physiological functions at a variety of time periods close to 24 hours when isolated from external cues, all relevant physiological functions settle into an exact 24-hour routine in the presence of natural *zeitgebers*, or time-giving cues such as sunlight.

The suprachiasmatic nucleus, circadian rhythms, sleepiness and bright light

It is obvious from isolation studies that biological clocks exist, controlling biological rhythms in almost every important physiological function. Given the phenomenon of entrainment, it is logically possible for any organism to have one biological clock governing all functions, a small number governing important functions, or indeed a clock in every cell in the body, since they would normally all be entrained upon one another. Experiments like those conducted by Aschoff (1980), on human beings isolated from time cues have shown that, given time, different physiological functions commonly become dissociated in phase, even though they still exhibit circadian periodicity (Figure 6.2). A group at Harvard University report that during extended studies in their isolation facility, every single subject had developed a dissociation between temperature rhythm and the sleep–wake cycle by the end of two months' isolation (Kronauer *et al.*, 1982). On the basis of this finding

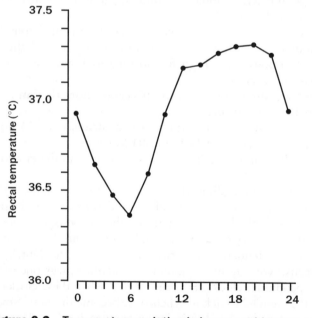

Figure 6.2 Temperature variation in human subjects over 24 hours (from Aschoff, 1980)

they constructed a mathematical model involving two major circadian oscillators, one directly governing body temperature and the other governing rest–activity. According to the model, interactions between these oscillators (and their respective entrainment) normally resolve into a coherent circadian pattern governing all physiological functions.

Neurophysiological evidence is crucial to Kronauer *et al.*'s argument. Experiments on the rat indicate that in this animal at least there is only one biological clock governing circadian activity, and that it is located in the suprachiasmatic nucleus (SCN) of the hypothalamus. (In humans the hypothalamus lies at the base of the brain, under the thalamus, below and anterior to the third ventricle. The pituitary gland is attached to the base of the hypothalamus.) Moore and Eichler (1972) and Stephan and Zucker (1972) simultaneously reported experiments showing that lesions in this area of the brain abolish any noticeable circadian periodicity in activity, hormone secretion, drinking and sleep. Their laboratory animals continued to eat and sleep in normal amounts, but not at regular times. The question remains whether the clock is really located in this structure, or whether the SCN is simply a vital coordination centre.

Subsequent experiments have shown that even when all nerve connections between the SCN and the rest of the brain have been severed, this structure still produces a circadian pattern of discharges, as monitored by microelectrodes (Inouye and Kawamura, 1979). (Not suprisingly, animals show no circadian patterns in wakefulness and sleep at this stage.) Finally, there is further evidence that the SCN exerts its control over the rest of the brain largely through the medium of neuromodulators, or local brain hormones (Fuller *et al.*, 1981). If an animal's SCN is destroyed and then replaced with nuclei obtained from donor animals, circadian rhythms are re-established, even though the grafts have very few neural connections with surrounding nervous tissue (Lehman *et al.*, 1987). Such grafts can re-establish circadian rhythms in as short a time as a week (De Andres *et al.*, 1976).

To return to Kronauer *et al.*'s (1982) mathematical model, they argue that the SCN controls the human sleep–wake cycle, while the temperature cycle is relatively independent and governed by a different oscillator. It is obviously impossible to make direct electrophysiological recordings from the human brain to establish whether our SCN is comparable to the rat's. However anatomical studies show that we do have such a structure (Lydic *et al.*, 1980), and experiments on squirrel monkeys show that their SCN is implicated in the control of the sleep–wake cycle, but not the temperature cycle.

Additional evidence for this two-oscillator model comes from studies of jet lag. Fast transmeridian travel (across time zones) results in passengers arriving at destinations whose local time is very different from that of the zone they left, often on the same day. Body rhythms, including temperature rhythms, take time to adjust to the new environment. That is, while the sleep–wake routine may change within 48 hours to adjust to the new time zone, body temperature rhythms take much longer. According to the Kronauer model the SCN responds immediately to zeitgebers provided by light – particularly bright sunlight – and the sleep–wake oscillator therefore adjusts quickly.

It then forces the second oscillator, controlling body temperature amongst other functions, to entrain to the new phase of the 24-hour cycle. Kronauer's group studied body temperature recordings from individuals in an isolation chamber, where they were exposed to phase shifts in lighting and the temporal displacement of regular activities were announced by gongs (simulating travel between time zones). In one condition (with a 'weaker' regime) these subjects were given control over reading lamps. In the regime with a stronger artificial zeitgeber, the subjects had no control over lighting. For both these regimes the researchers found a very good match between the predictions of their mathematical model for the rates of resynchronization of body temperature. In addition to these laboratory studies, they obtained temperature recordings from four NASA scientists who regularly made international flights involving time zone changes. Again, good matches were obtained between the temperature adjustments predicted by the model and those actually recorded from these scientists (Gander *et al.*, 1985).

While mathematical models of continuously variable oscillators can naturally be used to predict continuous variables such as body temperature, it is less clear how they can predict all-or-nothing changes such as the transition between wakefulness and sleep. It is necessary to postulate a threshold in the circadian oscillation for propensity for sleep, above which one remains awake (or wakes up) and below which one stays asleep (or falls asleep). The Kronauer model is excellent for explaining changes in body temperature, but seems less useful in predicting sleep behaviour itself.

Borbely and Tobler (1989) have developed an alternative model that aims to explain and predict the circadian sleep–wake cycle and other circadian variations. They propose a single 'sleep-regulating variable', which is basically a propensity to sleep, or sleepiness (S). Sleep onset is only possible when this is at a high level, and spontaneous awakening from sleep occurs when it is at a low level. Two factors control the level of propensity to sleep: an endogenous circadian sinusoidal oscillation; and the degree of prior wakefulness.

Factor S, or sleepiness, is reduced by deep slow-wave sleep and increased by wakefulness. (REM sleep is assumed to be independently controlled, and its occurrence is basically determined by the circadian cycle.) A person with a normal regime of regular sleep at night will have the cycle of propensity to sleep shown in Figure 6.3. The endogenous sinusoidal circadian rhythm (C) summates with the relaxation oscillation described by the 'prior sleep factor' (PSF) to produce a pattern of sleep propensity, S, over the 24 hours. Figure 6.3 assumes that the circadian cycle is sinusoidal, peaking in sleepiness at 6 a.m., and that the subject normally goes to sleep at 11 p.m. and wakes at 7 a.m. It also assumes that the amplitude of the variation in S over every 24 hours is influenced equally by circadian and prior sleep factors, although Borbely and Tobler estimate that the amplitude of variation contributed by circadian factors is somewhat less than that contributed by the homeostatic effects of prior wakefulness. All the same, the illustration shows how the concatenation of these two simple but different oscillations produces a plausible pattern of sleep propensity. That is, sleepiness does not simply increase progressively with time since the last sleep period – rather, alertness is maintained or

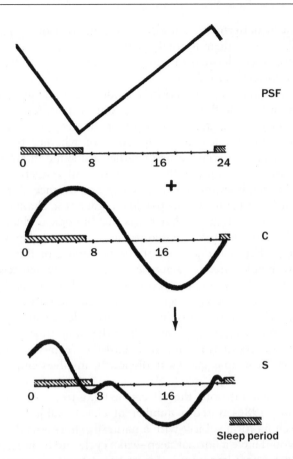

Figure 6.3   Borbely's model. Prior sleep factor (PSF) summates with the circadian factor (C) to give propensity for sleep (S) over a typical 24-hour period (from Borbely and Tobler, 1989)

increased over the day and into the evening, and sleepiness rather suddenly descends as bedtime approaches.

This model has been tested by comparing its predictions for the effects of sleep deprivation (when S, as determined by the homeostatic function, would monotonically increase, although modulated by circadian factors) and the effects of bed rest with the effects of shift-work regimes on sleep length. A major virtue of the model is that it addresses the problem of predicting changes in state from underlying factors that are continuously variable. In the researcher's terms, 'a model containing only a single circadian pacemaker that gates a noncircadian homeostatic sleep–wake process is sufficient to explain in the quantitative detail the major phenomena of human sleep timing'. Borbely's model has been improved upon by others in respect of quantification of the variables involved, with a view to making ever more precise predictions of sleepiness after varying amounts of sleep loss at different times of the day. Akerstedt and Folkard (1996), for instance, have applied their version to predicting sleep patterns both under conditions of isolation and using shift-workers adhering to their normal regimes. The regression analysis of sleep latency on predicted alertness obtained a maximum R^2 of 88 per cent – a very high level of correlation indeed.

Both the Kronauer and the Borbely models give adequate accounts of the nature of circadian rhythms in humans, but with different emphases – one emphasizes body temperature and the other the sleep–wake cycle. The differences between them, such as the question of whether there is one major oscillator or two, may seem to be of rather academic interest. However, the question of which constitutes the most powerful zeitgeber in resetting our cycles is undoubtedly of immediate practical importance. After transmeridian flights, is it the change in the sleep–wake regime, the change in mealtimes or simply the change in lighting that resets our biological clocks to local time? How should the traveller be advised to ensure speedy adaptation?

As with the chaffinch discussed at the beginning of this chapter, lighting schedules are highly effective zeitgebers in humans when tested in isolation facilities. This could be because people go to bed when the lights are turned off, and their rhythms are then reset by the activity of sleeping. Early experiments on human rhythms during isolation demonstrated that social cues (for instance, receiving a telephone call at the same time every day) are very important zeitgebers. It is natural to regard the sleep–wake cycle as a highly significant synchronizing cue as it obviously involves important aspects of brain function.

In order to separate out the effects of light from the sleep–wake cycle, Czeisler *et al.* (1986) tested a number of elderly subjects in their isolation facility, searching for a subject with a naturally short circadian cycle. Such an individual would have a normal sleep–wake cycle and be normally entrained in every respect to circadian cues in his or her natural environment, but would swiftly demonstrate a phase advance in body temperature when such cues were removed. The researchers found a person, who showed a pronounced phase advance in body temperature after as little as 24 hours' isolation, and then proceeded to test her in the isolation facility on a 12:12 LD lighting routine with normal room lighting. Even under these conditions her body temperature and cortisol cycles tended to drift, advancing to become out of phase with her sleep–wake cycle. However, when exposed every evening for four hours to bright light her temperature cycle was reset on the first day. (The levels used were 7000–12 000 lux, equivalent to the ambient outdoor light intensity that prevails just after dawn, and over ten times dimmer than midday sunlight.)

In a subsequent experiment, Czeisler's group subjected 14 younger subjects (aged 18–24) to a total of 45 'resetting trials' in their isolation facility. That is, after three baseline days on 'normal' time the clocks were put forward or back by up to 12 hours, and a variety timings of bright light exposure were employed. The researchers confirmed that exposure to bright light, particularly in the evenings, speeds adaptation, and that their subjects' body temperature, urine output and plasma cortisol cycles were all completely adapted after three days (Czeisler *et al.*, 1989). (Normally, people might take as much as nine days to adjust completely to a phase advance of six hours, such as a winter flight from the east of the US – for example, Boston or New York – to the UK).

From a practical point of view, this research highlights the importance of going out into the sunshine during the first two or three days after a time zone shift, particularly in the afternoons and evenings. Obviously this advice also applies to shiftworkers going back onto a daytime shift, and the Czeisler group duly tested the application of their recommendations on shiftworkers (Czeisler *et al.*, 1990). The experimental group were exposed to bright light at night (7000–12 000 lux) and to complete darkness during the day, while the control group were exposed to normal levels of artificial light during the night and allowed to sleep at home during the day, with only their own bedroom curtains to keep out the sunlight. Comparisons made between the first and sixth days on the regime showed that the experimental group had completely adapted to the new regime, with pronounced phase shifts in plasma cortisol, urine production, body temperature, subjective alertness and performance on a simple task. As in many previous studies of the circadian rhythms of shiftworkers over this length of time, the control group showed little or no adaptation at all.

Czeisler *et al.* argue that nightworkers can substantially improve their adaptation to shifts by making use of commonly available heavy or blackout curtains during their sleep periods, and by seeking out, rather than avoiding, bright light during the night. As many shift rotation sequences are too short to allow workers any adaptation at all, it remains unclear how generally useful this advice is. Two other, less contentious, applications of the effects of exposure to bright light are the treatment of early awakenings in the elderly and the reinforcement of circadian rhythmicity in people living in the Arctic circle.

Circadian rhythms are all-pervasive and highly physiologically significant for sleep-related processes. Other biological oscillators also exist, however, with both long periods and short ones. Those with periods longer than 24 hours are known as infradian rhythms, while those with periods shorter than 24 hours are called ultradian rhythms.

Ultradian rhythms

Superimposed on the circadian rhythm is the human 90–100 minute cycle of REM sleep alternating with slow-wave sleep – an important ultradian rhythm. The deep slow-wave sleep stages predominate in the first two or three hours, and light slow-wave sleep alternating with relatively long periods of REM sleep is characteristic of the second half of the night.

Is this pattern the result of processes intrinsic to sleep, or do the sleep stages 'belong' to different periods of the 24 hours? Systematic studies in which subjects have been allowed to go to sleep at various times of the day and night have shown that stage 4 sleep can occur at any time, almost always appearing early in a sleep period, whenever it starts. Consequently, sleep during the day may start well, with some deep slow-wave sleep, but then tends to be fitful, as REM sleep fails to sustain itself later in the sleep period (Hume and Mills,

1977). It loses out in competition with stage 4 at the beginning of the sleep period (in the morning when it would otherwise be at its most abundant) and then the drive for REM sleep appears to dissipate later in the sleep period, during the early afternoon. The amount of deep slow-wave sleep seems to be determined simply by the amount of prior wakefulness, while REM sleep periods are short and relatively unstable at all hours of the day, apart from the hours between 2 a.m. and noon (Webb and Agnew, 1964).

This evidence has been invoked to suggest that the deep slow-wave sleep stages are somehow more important than REM sleep as they seem to be independent of circadian entrainment, displacing REM sleep even when it ought to appear. Normally, as we have seen, body temperature and the sleep–wake cycle are in phase, and it is extremely difficult to disentangle the web of cause and effect between sleep processes, arousal, time of day and temperature.

Hume (1986), reporting an experiment conducted in an isolation bunker, states that when dissociation between temperature and the sleep–wake cycle occurs, and the onset of sleep coincides with low body temperature, REM sleep can indeed displace the deep slow-wave sleep stages in the early part of the sleeping period. When these rhythms are operating normally and a person goes to sleep in the early hours of the morning when the body temperature is at a minimum, deep slow-wave sleep dominates the first few hours of the sleeping period. Hume's work suggests that while deep slow-wave sleep mechanisms normally override considerations of time of day, they do not simply reflect an imperative need that is more urgent than that of other sleep stages, determined simply by the amount of time that has elapsed since stage 4 sleep was last enjoyed. Rather, these preliminary results suggest that stage 4 sleep occurs either when the temperature is high, or when cortical (behavioural) arousal is low, but when sleep is achieved with a combination of high arousal and low temperature, stage 4 is displaced by REM sleep early in the sleep period. The interpretation, referred to above, that deep slow-wave sleep is more important than REM sleep is thus an oversimplification.

Incidentally, body temperature has been shown to affect sleep directly in both crocodiles and humans. Higher temperatures (induced by sunbathing for reptiles and hot baths for humans) are followed by unusually persistent high-amplitude slow waves in the EEG during sleep (see Chapter 9). We can only speculate whether crocodiles given a hot bath would produce as much slow-wave sleep as after sunbathing! More seriously, these results illustrate how although studies of sleep patterns over the day may indicate an apparently simple relationship between pressure for stage 4 sleep and the time since it was last taken, the actual drive mechanisms are considerably more complex. Any imputation of functions from drive mechanisms is also hazardous, as we shall see in Chapter 11.

The 90-minute cycle – does it run all day?

The alternation between slow-wave sleep and REM sleep during the night has been described by Kleitman (1969) as the expression of a basic rest–activity cycle (BRAC), which he suggests continues during the day and on which the sleep–wake cycle is superimposed. An alternative explanation is that the cycle is the outcome of a homeostatic interplay between the mechanisms that control REM and non-REM sleep. Ephron and Carrington (1966) were among the first to suggest this, explaining that the periodic REM sleep phases could be a method of maintaining arousal in an otherwise increasingly unresponsive brain. If this were true, we would expect the timing and quantity of REM sleep to be determined principally by the amount and depth of prior slow-wave sleep. The evidence for this is equivocal. Globus *et al.* (1969) have found that the timing of REM sleep periods is to some extent preprogrammed, so that they occur at the same times of the night, regardless of when people go to sleep or whether they have missed an REM period. While the entrainment of 90-minute cycles into the 24-hour day has not always been observed in subsequent studies, Globus *et al.*'s work stimulated the study of periodicity during the day, as well as the study of sleeping cycles.

An elegant and ingenious experiment reported by Carskadon and Dement (1975) has resolved the question of whether sleep mechanisms for the main sleep states are interdependent in the literal way suggested by Ephron and Carrington (1966). Carskadon and Dement's five subjects lived on a regime of successive 90-minute 'days' for almost a week, being allowed sleep for 30-minute periods with waking intervals of 60 minutes. If the Ephron–Carrington model were right, the subjects would experience no REM sleep since slow-wave sleep could not 'accumulate'. In the event all the subjects showed all the normal sleep stages, but frequently went straight from waking to REM sleep (REM sleep occurred within ten minutes of sleep onset in 79 of the 110 sleep periods containing REM sleep). They typically alternated the type of sleep between successive sleep periods, although REM sleep was primarily between 7.30 a.m. and 2 p.m.

Sleep mechanisms are therefore normally entrained to their own internal clock with a period of about 90 minutes, which may itself be entrained to the ubiquitous circadian cycle. It follows from this that the 90-minute clock is also ticking during the day (and some of Globus *et al.*'s 1969 work on the timing of REM sleep periods during afternoon naps supports this idea). If so, does it affect waking behaviour? Two American psychiatrists, Friedman and Fisher (1967), observed a group of psychiatric patients over periods of six hours and counted the number and timing of eating, drinking and other oral behaviours. Deeply committed to Freudian theory, they devised a scoring system that awarded 10 points for a drink of milk (because of its symbolic importance) and only one point for a sandwich. A clear 90-minute cycle in oral behaviour was evident, which they interpreted as a manifestation of the sublimated outcome of fluctuations in erotic drive level.

This experiment suffered from two major flaws. First, the subjects were observed as a group, so that interactions between the patients may have led to them eat and drink cyclically at the same times. Second, the food and drink provided was nutritious, and thus certainly directly affected the subjects' appetite level: the study becomes much less interesting if the results merely reflect the timing of digestive processes. Oswald *et al.* (1970) repeated the experiment using non-nutritious food and drink, and the six subjects were

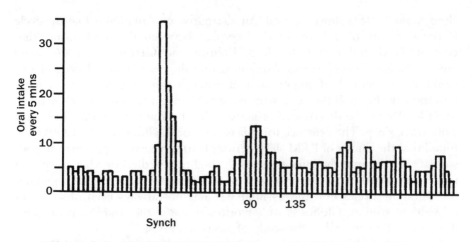

Figure 6.4 Distribution of oral intake scores when peak intakes are synchronized for the period 30 minutes to two hours from start (from Oswald *et al.*, 1970)

isolated from one another. A simple count of the timing of feeding and drinking (with no complicated points system) confirmed that there was a 90-minute cycle (Figure 6.4).

If the 90-minute cycle (BRAC) persists during the day, how does it affect cognitive processing and performance? There is EEG evidence of relative activation of the right hemisphere during REM sleep with respect to the left, and we know from a variety of sources that there is some specialization of function between the hemispheres. In most right-handed people, for instance, linguistic skills seem to be a function of the left hemisphere, while skills that demand the analysis of patterns (for instance, the recognition of faces) are performed better by the right hemisphere. One could argue that the times of day that contain REM sleep should also be characterized by right hemisphere activation, resulting in improved performance on tasks that tap spatial abilities and worse performance on tasks that tap verbal ability. Tests on eight subjects over a period of eight hours using verbal and spatial tasks revealed that performance on both showed periodicity, with a peak of 96 minutes. What is more, these cycles in efficiency were 180 degrees out of phase, just as the experimenters had predicted (Klein and Armitage, 1979). If the two sides of the brain are indeed activated on a 90-minute cycle, then this should be reflected in power in the EEG. Further experiments have confirmed that there is a significant cycling in EEG power at periods of 72–120 minutes (during one day of isolation for eight subjects), although there are no differences between the hemispheres (Manseau and Broughton, 1984).

While these experiments have provided good evidence of 90-minute periodicity in daytime behaviour, and it is reasonable to assume that this is related to the 90-minute sleep cycle, it remains to be positively demonstrated that daytime fluctuations in performance are determined by the REM–non-REM sleep cycle of the previous night. (Readers wishing to follow this up are referred to the recent models of the REM–non-REM cycle provided by Achermann and Borbely, 1990, and McCarley and Massaquoi, 1986.)

Infradian rhythms

After the alternation of day and night, the next most noticeable cosmological changes we experience are the seasons. In past times, people got up with the lark and went to bed soon after it got dark. In the northern hemisphere this naturally meant that they slept longer in the winter than in the summer. This pattern still prevails among people living in the Arctic circle, for instance, in Spitzbergen, where it is very difficult indeed to get children to go to bed during the summer in constant, 24-hour sunshine. In the modern world, one might assume that city dwellers would be relatively unaffected by the seasons as far as their sleep was concerned, with the sleep–wake cycle under voluntary control with the help of electric lighting. However, a study conducted at Hokkaido University has shown that the sleep–wake cycle is phase-delayed by 90 minutes in winter compared with summer – a surprisingly large difference but one that is explicable by photoperiodic time cues (Kohsaka et al., 1992). More surprisingly, in the winter stage 4 sleep duration decreases by 16 minutes and REM sleep duration increases by 20 minutes compared with the summer. During the study, the temperature in the recording facility was strictly controlled at 20–24°C at all times, so ambient temperature cannot be invoked as an explanation of the findings, except insofar as the subjects were exposed to seasonal temperatures during the day.

The most pronounced single infradian rhythm is of course the female menstrual cycle. This is not governed by an oscillator, but by the interaction of the parts of the endocrine system that regulate oestrus. Sleep is not greatly affected by this cycle, except when it ceases with the menopause.

More mysterious in many ways than the female's rhythms are those of the male, which are much less pronounced and without a well-understood physiology, although there is some evidence of periodic (20-day) changes in urinary 17-ketosteroid excretion and in plasma testosterone, and of a 20-day cycle in pitch perception. A study on body temperature, conducted at Hull University, arose from my own work on the 90-minute REM–non-REM cycle, using skin temperature as a measure of the penile erections that normally accompany REM sleep (Empson, 1977). (Unlike the EEG and other usual psychophysiological parameters, temperature is easily measured using a simple portable pen recorder that can be accommodated in the subject's own bedroom.) Although recordings of the single subject did not show stable patterns of REM sleep over 17 weeks, analysis of the average temperature values per night did show signs of periodicity at 21 days. Subsequently, 21 male subjects took part in a study of temperature and mood over periods varying from 49 to 102 days. This study confirmed that there is a weak but reliably detectable periodicity at about 20 days, not only in body temperature but also in subjective ratings of alertness in the morning. It would be curious indeed if there were a stable intrinsic rhythm to this frequency, since there are no equivalent natural zeitgebers. Simon Folkard suggests that these findings may reflect the interaction between the intrinsic 25-hour circadian rhythm in humans and entrained 24-hour zeitgebers.

Hormonal changes correlated with sleep and circadian rhythm

Growth hormone

Probably the most physiologically spectacular hormonal change associated with sleep is the surge in human growth hormone (hGH) during the first three hours of the night. Takahashi *et al.* (1968) have demonstrated that this is associated specifically with deep slow-wave sleep (Figure 6.5), and Sassin *et al.* (1969) have shown that deep slow-wave sleep deprivation actually prevents the release of hGH. Hence, it seems that the regulation of hGH is intimately connected with sleep mechanisms (Mendelson *et al.*, 1983).

Adrenaline and noradrenaline

Adrenaline and noradrenaline are secreted by the adrenal medulla, which is a gland under the control of the sympathetic nervous system. They increase blood flow to the muscles and promote the breakdown of stored nutrients into glucose in muscle tissue, making energy available. These two hormones both exhibit clear circadian rhythms during a normal sleep–wake regime. Unlike hGH, however, the rhythmic patterns of secretion of these hormones are almost entirely dependent on physical activity (Gillberg *et al.*, 1986).

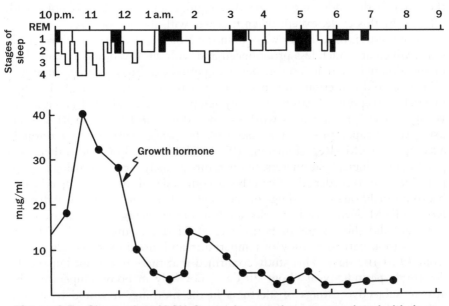

Figure 6.5   Sleep-related hGH. Surges in secretion are associated with deep slow-wave sleep (from Takahashi *et al.*, 1968)

Cortisol

Like growth hormone, cortisol has a very marked, high-amplitude circadian rhythm in its secretion. It is at its highest upon awakening and declines over the course of the waking day, reaching its minimum about an hour after sleep onset, whereupon it begins to rise again (Aschoff, 1979). The regular relationship between cortisol secretion and circadian phase has made it a useful indicator of circadian activity, for instance, in the assessment of circadian rhythm disorders in the blind (Lockley et al., 2000).

Melatonin

Melatonin is secreted by the pineal gland in a marked circadian rhythm. It is produced during the night, and daylight has the effect of suppressing secretion and entraining its production at night. Arendt et al. (1999) summarize its primary function in mammals as a whole as conveying information about the length of daylight, so that seasonally varying functions can be controlled (such as the growth of mammals' winter coats, which vary in colour and density from summer growth, and, in some animals, the reproductive phase). In humans it may have a role in the entrainment of other physiological functions to the solar day, and therefore may play a part in, for instance, the adjustment to jet lag caused by transmeridian flights. While its physiology is still imperfectly understood, it has been used to aid jet flight adjustment (see Chapter 9) and to control particular sleep disturbances associated with blindness, caused by the failure of daylight to entrain circadian rhythms in the patients in question (see Chapter 13).

Gonadotropin releasing hormone (GnRH), luteinizing hormone (LH) and follicle stimulating hormone (FSH)

In males, LH secretion shows sleep dependency during puberty (Boyar, 1978), but this relationship disappears in adulthood, when daytime levels rise to match the night-time levels (Parker et al., 1980). In females, there is less evidence of sleep-dependent secretion during either puberty or adulthood (Akerstedt, 1984). Akerstedt has also demonstrated that in adults sleep deprivation for 64 hours does not affect LH secretion (Akerstedt et al., 1980). Secretion of both these gonadotrophins from the pituitary is, of course, contingent on hypothalamic GnRH, and this is reported to be at high levels in the neonate (Hayes and Crowley, 1998) and then at low levels until puberty, when it is sleep entrained. In the adult, GnRH pulsatile secretion in the male takes place approximately every two hours, and in the female it varies with the stage of the menstrual cycle.

Prolactin (PRL)

Sassin et al. (1972) were the first to demonstrate that PRL is at a low level in blood during waking hours but rapidly increases between 60 and 90 minutes after sleep onset, reaching its maximum in the early morning between 5 a.m.

and 7 a.m. Parker et al. (1974) suggest that its relation to deep slow-wave sleep (stages 3 and 4) is as close as that of growth hormone, whose release is actually triggered by slow-wave sleep onset, but the evidence for this is equivocal (Rubin et al., 1975). However, there is clear evidence from studies on sleep–wake reversal and daytime naps that PRL activity is sleep-related, not circadian (Boyar, 1978). Akerstedt (1984) has found that, in general, prolactin and growth hormone secretion have rather similar relations to the sleep–wake pattern.

The amplitude of the circadian variation in PRL is reportedly greater in women than in men, during enforced wakefulness over a 24-hour period (Waldstreicher et al., 1996). A more recent study compared the diurnal characteristics of PRL pulsatile secretion between menopausal women (mean age 56), young males (mean age 25) and young women (mean age 28) at three phases of the menstrual cycle (Katznelson et al., 1998). Serum PRL levels and pulse frequency were significantly higher during the night than in the day for all groups, but were highest in the cycling women. Essentially, pulsatile PRL secretion was similar for the postmenopausal women and the men.

Testosterone

Testosterone secretion, expressed as the 24-hour average for young male subjects, follows a near cosine waveform, with the maximum value occurring towards the end of the sleep period. Data from individuals do not necessarily show this pattern, since secretion typically takes place in two or more large and slow (three to five hours long) peaks per day, the largest and most consistent of these being during the latter part of sleep (Parker et al., 1980).

Testosterone secretion also varies over a 20-day cycle (Doering et al., 1975). As described above, Empson (1977) reports a 20-day cycle in body temperature and self-reported alertness in male subjects, but does not offer any evidence of specific effects on sleep.

The menstrual cycle and sleep

Manber and Bootzin (1997) note that 'what little we do know about the relationship between the menstrual cycle and sleep in healthy women comes primarily from the control groups in studies that were designed to identify sleep markers of late luteal phase dysphoric disorder or premenstrual syndrome'. In their own diary study of 32 healthy women over two menstrual cycles, they found evidence of a significant increase in sleep onset latency and a significant decrease in sleep efficiency and sleep quality during the late luteal phase, as assessed by self-report.

Findings from sleep laboratory studies are not consistent with these results. Sleep onset time and sleep efficiency have not been found to differ significantly across the phases of the menstrual cycle when all-night polysomnographic measures are taken (Parry et al., 1989). However, systematic changes in the frequency of sleep spindles (characterized by EEG phasic activity in the band

12–15 Hz) have been noted in a study of five women (Ishizuka *et al.*, 1994), where spindle frequency was lowest about 18 days before the onset of menses and highest three days before menses. No other sleep stage parameters differed significantly. This finding was confirmed by a study of nine women by Driver *et al.* (1996), in which EEG power density was objectively assessed. It was found that, in non-REM sleep, EEG power density in the 14.25–15.0 Hz band (at the upper end of the frequencies defining sleep spindles) reached its maximum in the luteal phase. Core body temperature was invoked as an important covariant of sleep spindle frequency. As in the other studies, no other regular changes in standard sleep parameters were noted with respect to menstrual phase.

The menopause and sleep: evidence from self-reports

The menopause is defined by the cessation of menstruation, after which the ovaries become smaller and the Graafian follicles disappear. Oestradiol and progesterone are no longer secreted by the ovaries in the cyclical manner characteristic of the younger, cycling woman, despite an increase in the pituitary gonadotrophins FSH and LH. Studies of self-reported symptoms have established that the menopause is often associated with daytime hot flushes, night-time sweats, vaginal dryness and disturbed sleep. It is widely assumed that the disturbed sleep is a consequence of arousals triggered by night sweats (Ravnikar *et al.*, 1983).

Night-time menopausal hot sweats: laboratory studies

The hot flush (or in the US, 'hot flash') of the menopause has been studied since the 1970s in psychophysiological laboratories, beginning with Molnar's (1975) work. It has been established that this reflex is not simply a response to warming but is a distinct, centrally generated psychophysiological response. It is invariably accompanied by a short-lived cardiac acceleration of about 10 beats per minute (Sturdee *et al.*, 1978), and when it occurs during sleep the peripheral vasomotor manifestations are *preceded* by cortical arousal and awakening (Erlik *et al.*, 1981).

This vasomotor instability is commonly attributed to oestrogen deficiency (Rebar and Spitzer, 1987). Hot flushes are not confined to the climacteric, but are frequently observed in postpartum women whose circulating oestrogen is low, and also in men with testicular insufficiency (Feldman *et al.*, 1976). Oestrogen replacement therapy has been shown to reduce the incidence of hot flushes (see next section).

Hot flushes are invariably accompanied by pulses of LH secretion (Casper *et al.*, 1979; Meldrun *et al.*, 1980; Tataryn *et al.*, 1979), but there is no simple causative link between these two events as hot flushes also occur in the absence of LH secretions in women after hypophysectomy (Meldrun *et al.*, 1981) and when a godadotrophin-releasing hormone agonist has abolished the pulsatile release of LH (Casper and Yen 1981; DeFazio *et al.*, 1983).

From this combined evidence, Rebar and Spitzer (1987) conclude that hot flushes apparently originate in the central nervous system, in close proximity to gonadotrophin-releasing hormone-secreting neurons within the anterior hypothalamus.

The effect of these phasic events on sleep is to induce awakenings during the night, resulting in total wakefulness of up to 60 minutes per night in women who are badly affected (Thomson and Oswald, 1977). Hot flushes that occur before sleep onset, on the other hand, have the paradoxical effect of improving slow-wave sleep depth, possibly because they increase the core temperature (Woodward and Freedman, 1994). (It is known that a slight elevation in core temperature – achieved, for example, by lying in a warm bath for 30 minutes – increases the depth and amount of deep-sleep stages 3 and 4 – Horne and Reid, 1985.)

Sleep and hormone replacement therapy (HRT)

Campbell (1977), in a double-blind crossover study, found that (self-report) insomnia was oestrogen-sensitive in that it consistently responded to hormone replacement but not to a placebo. This finding was confirmed by Polo-Kantona et al. (1998).

The effects of HRT on sleep architecture were first assessed in three polysomnographic studies (Erlik et al., 1981; Schiff et al., 1979; Thomson and Oswald, 1977). Erlik et al. found that nine post-menopausal women had, on average, five episodes of hot sweats associated with wakefulness per night, whereas four oestrogen-treated women had fewer than one per night. In a crossover study Schiff et al. found a significantly shorter sleep onset time and more REM sleep during treatment with ethinyl oestradiol than with a placebo. A small-scale laboratory study of seven women also confirmed that hot flushes reduced in number and sleep efficiency improved with oestrogen replacement therapy over a four-week period (Scharf et al., 1997). Thomson and Oswald (1977) also observed more REM sleep – as well as reduced wakefulness and fewer arousals – during eight weeks of oestrogen treatment compared with baseline measures, while untreated control patients showed no such improvements. Measures of mood showed some evidence of improvement with oestrogen, but not statistically significantly when compared with control patients.

Work in Hull (Purdie et al., 1995) was designed to confirm Thomson and Oswald's findings on sleep quality, assessed polysomnographically. The study was also to be extended over a longer period of time to allow any placebo effects affecting self-reported mood to dissipate. In the event, however, the change in prescribing patterns meant that HRT was virtually available on demand, and it was very difficult to recruit women with serious sleep disturbance who had either not tried HRT already or who had never taken it but had no contraindications. Although our sample reported significant menopausal symptoms, night-time recordings at baseline revealed a very low level of wakefulness (about 10 minutes compared with Thomson and Oswald's 60 minutes) and only about one hot sweat per night. Over 12 weeks HRT produced a significant improvement in self-reported menopausal symptoms such as hot flushes, hot sweats and vaginal dryness, but there was no measurable improvement in sleep quality, assessed polysomnographically. Interestingly, there was a highly statistically significant decrease in free-floating anxiety, somatic anxiety and depression, assessed using the Crown–Crisp experiental index (Crown and Crisp, 1979). It had commonly been assumed that the changes in mood and other psychological symptoms accompanying the menopause (irritability, emotional lability and persistent lapse of attention) were a consequence of protracted sleep disturbance. Although our measure of absent-mindedness showed no improvement with HRT, the mood scales certainly did, and this, in the absence of any improvement in sleep, implying a direct humoral action on the brain. Oestrogen receptors have been found in the hypothalamus and the preoptic nuclei (Pfaff and McEwen, 1983), as well as in the hippo-campus (Frankfurt *et al.*, 1973), indicating a range of central nervous system activities for these sex steroids that are not yet completely understood.

The effects of hot sweats on sleep are most unwelcome, and are one of the most frequently reported complaints about the menopause. However, even with wakefulness of 60 minutes a night, women usually achieve a reasonable total amount of sleep. Indeed, a normative polysomnographic study on sleep at different ages has shown that men in late middle age sleep slightly worse than women (Williams *et al.*, 1974). It is possible that the long-term psychological effects of menopausal sleep disturbance were overestimated in the past, and any changes in mood may be a direct result of hormonal events rather than chronic sleep disruption.

Sex steroids and sleep apnea

The discovery of obstructive sleep apnea (OSA) syndrome at Stanford University (Guilleminault *et al.*, 1973) was one of the major successes of the sleep laboratory clinic movement that sprang up in the US in the wake of the establishment of polysomnographic indices of sleep quality during the early 1970s. Some patients suffering from daytime somnolence were discovered, upon polysomnographic assessment, to be having over 30 apneic episodes during the sleeping period, each lasting at least 10 seconds and resulting in cortical arousal, awakening and chronic sleep disturbance. Male sufferers were found to outnumber females by ratios ranging from 6 : 1 to 15 : 1 (Guilleminault *et al.*, 1976). A typical sufferer is male, overweight and a drinker. The overall prevalence of this syndrome has been estimated at 1–2 per cent (Nasser and Rees, 1992).

OSA is more common in men than in women. However, in postmenopausal women the incidence of OSA increases, suggesting that reproductive hormones may have a role in its aetiology. Treatment with testosterone has been shown to induce OSA in the male (Cistulli *et al.*, 1994). A recent clinical report that a woman with a benign testosterone-producing ovarian tumour was also suffering from OSA supports this relationship. Removal of the tumour resulted in the normalization of the patient's testosterone levels and resolution of the OSA (Dexter and Dovre, 1998). Progesterone has been found to be effective in relieving some patients' symptoms of sleep apnea (Strohl *et al.*, 1981), which returns when the treatment is withdrawn. This treatment was previously found to be effective for some patients suffering from Pickwickian syndrome (Sutton *et al.*, 1975). Strohl *et al.* (1981) suggest that OSA sufferers may be a heterogeneous group, and that those who benefit from progesterone treatment have a particular problem with maintaining activity in the upper airway muscles during sleep.

Conclusions

Many hormones are secreted in a circadian pattern, and for some of them, there is a close link between secretion and the sleep pattern, hinting at some causal relationship if not a functional one. The relationships between human growth hormone and sex steroids and sleep are yet to be completely understood. Growth hormone obviously has different roles in the growing child than in the adult, where its function is still obscure. Similarly, the sex steroids must have different roles in men and women. (Despite their names, and although they are found in the male, LH and FSH cannot have the same target organs in the male as they do in the female.) However, it is clear that the gonadotrophins, testosterone, oestradiol and progesterone are all implicated in sleep and thermoregulatory processes, although we cannot yet define their precise roles.

Physiological mechanisms of sleep and waking

Neurophysiology has a specialized vocabulary that is as large, or larger, than that used in biological rhythms research. The following list of terms and definitions is a selection of those used in the sections that follow that may need some explanation for some readers. Many of the definitions are taken from Carlson's authoritative text, *Physiology of Behavior* (1991).

- **Acetylcholine:** a neurotransmitter found in the brain and spinal cord;
- **Afferent:** towards a structure – all neurons afferent to the central nervous system convey sensory information;
- **Agonistic drugs:** drugs that facilitate the effects of a particular neurotransmitter;
- **Axon:** a thin, elongated process (outgrowth) of a neuron that transmits nerve impulses towards its terminal buttons, from where impulses are relayed across the synapse to other neurons, gland cells or muscle cells;
- **Basic rest–activity cycle (BRAC):** a 90-minute cycle (in humans) of waxing and waning alertness, controlled by a biological clock in the caudal brain stem; during sleep it controls cycles of REM sleep and slow-wave sleep;
- **Brain stem:** the 'stem' of the brain, from the medulla to the midbrain, excluding the cerebellum;
- **Caudal:** literally, of the tail – towards the posterior (opposite of rostral);
- **Central nervous system (CNS):** the brain and spinal cord;

- Cerebrospinal fluid (CSF): a clear fluid, similar to blood plasma, that fills the ventricular system of the brain and the subarachnoid space surrounding the brain and spinal cord;
- Decerebrate: an animal whose brain stem has been transected;
- Dopamine (DA): a neurotransmitter; one of the catecholamines;
- Efferent: away from a structure; the efferent axons of the central nervous system control the muscles and glands;
- Hindbrain: those parts of the brain immediately above (in humans) the spinal cord; comprising the medulla oblongata, the pons and the cerebellum;
- Hypothalamus: a central region of the brain that is implicated in the control of temperature, hunger and thirst;
- Locus coeruleus: a dark-coloured group of noradrenergic cell bodies located in the pons near the rostral end of the floor of the fourth ventricle;
- Medulla oblongata (usually just medulla): the most caudal portion of the brain, immediately rostral to the spinal cord;
- Microelectrode: a very fine electrode, generally used to record the activity of individual neurons;
- Midbrain: that part of the brain (in humans) directly above the pons and in front of the cerebellum;
- Norepinephrine: a neurotransmitter, also referred to as noradrenalin;
- Neuromodulator: a naturally secreted substance that acts like a neurotransmitter except that it is not restricted to the synaptic cleft but diffuses through the interstitial fluid. Presumably it activates receptors on neurons that are not located at synapses;
- PGO waves: bursts of phasic electrical activity originating in the pons, followed by activity in the lateral geniculate nucleus and visual cortex; a characteristic of REM sleep;
- Pons: a region of the brain rostral to the medulla and caudal to the midbrain;
- Projection: the efferent connection between neurons in one specific region of the brain and those in another region;
- Raphe: a group of nuclei located in the reticular formation of the medulla, pons and midbrain, situated along the midline;
- Reticular formation: a large network of neural tissue located in the central region of the brain stem, from the medulla to the diencephalon;
- Rostral: nearer the nose and mouth (opposite of caudal);
- Serotonin: a neurotransmitter, also known as 5-hydroxytryptamine (5-HT);
- Somatosensory cortex: the gyrus (brain convolution) caudal to the central sulcus (groove), which receives many projection fibres from the somatosensory system;
- Synapse: the junction between the terminal button of an axon and the membrane of another neuron.

Humoral systems for controlling sleep and waking

Brain function is easily influenced by drugs, either activating or depressing cortical activity, promoting wakefulness or inducing sleep. It would, therefore, seem reasonable to think of natural sleep normally being induced and maintained by endogenous soporifics, perhaps produced within the brain itself. These would build up during wakefulness, and would also be under the influence of the circadian rhythm (rather like Borbely's factor S – Borbely and Tobler, 1989), inducing sleep when in great enough concentration, only to become dissipated during sleep itself. If this were the case, and if such substances could be identified and manufactured, they could become the basis for ideal sleep-inducing drugs, or hypnotics – acting directly on sleep mechanisms without side effects.

Unfortunately, the evidence is against any blood-borne substances having a substantial role in controlling sleep: attaching a second head to a dog does not result in both heads sleeping simultaneously (De Andres *et al.*, 1976). Early this century Pieron (1913) tested the hypothesis that the cerebrospinal fluid (CSF) contained a sleep-inducing factor by extracting CSF from dogs deprived of sleep and injecting it into the ventricles of animals that were not sleepy. While these experiments appeared to be successful in inducing sleep, it now seems that injecting any fluid into the ventricles is enough to induce apparent sleep. Crucial evidence comes from the dolphin, only half whose brain sleeps at a time (see Chapter 10 for further details of this animal's sleep). Such an orderly alternation of sleep by the two halves of the brain would be impossible if sleep were controlled by chemicals circulating in either the blood or the CSF.

The search for endogenous sleep-promoting substances has been intense – so much so that a major review in 1989 cited over 400 papers on the subject (Borbely and Tobler, 1989). While some highly effective soporific substances have been found, it remains unclear whether they normally have an important role in the physiology of sleep. However, as Neil Carlson comments in the *Physiology of Behavior* (1991), it is difficult to imagine a sleep control system not involving such chemicals, particularly to keep track of sleep debt. Possibly, the mysterious chemicals accumulate inside neurons rather than in the interstitial fluids.

Neural control of arousal

It is clear from the discussion on biological rhythms in the first half of this chapter that the brain is not only aroused by external stimulation – the sleep–wake cycle is controlled by circadian rhythms as much as by alarm clocks. The brain mechanisms governing arousal must therefore be proactive and capable of causing awakening, or increasing alertness, in the absence of stimuli that act on the senses. Many decades ago Moruzzi and Magoun (1949), reporting a pioneering series of experiments, announced that when an area in the brain stem – the reticular formation – was stimulated electrically, the level of an animal's alertness increased.

Ascending afferent neurons carrying signals from the senses (for example, the surface of the skin) project to the thalamus, and then – in the case of somatosensory neurons – to the somatosensory cortex. There are, however, also collateral axons from these axons that go to the reticular formation. Lindsley *et al.* (1950) discovered that if the main sensory pathways were disrupted by lesions, animals could still be aroused by touch, presumably via the collateral projections through the reticular formation. On the other hand, if the reticular formation was destroyed, touch stimuli only briefly roused the animals from torpor, even though the main afferent pathways were intact. Microelectrode recordings from the reticular formation also showed it to be highly active when an animal was alert, less so when it was drowsy. The reticular formation, with its *ascending reticular activation system*, was identified as the major neurological mechanism subserving the functions of arousal and the direction of attention in the brain.

Almost all the experiments that drew physiologists to this conclusion involved immobilized, decerebrated, or anaesthetized rats or cats. More recent studies on freely-moving cats, using recordings from single units in the brain stem, have thrown considerable doubt on this interpretation. It now appears that the activity of individual neurons in the reticular formation is closely related to specific movements, and not to general levels of arousal. The increases in general activity in the brain stem reported in earlier experiments were interpreted in terms of increases in arousal, or the direction of attention. However, these patterns of activity could equally have been in anticipation of punishment or reward, and related to preparations for movement, or attempts at movement (Siegel, 1985; Siegel and McGinty, 1977).

A specific structure in the hindbrain, the *locus coeruleus*, is now thought to serve many of the functions previously attributed to the reticular formation as a whole. This structure, which contains predominantly noradrenergic neurons, has only two inputs, one excitatory and one inhibitory, but its axons send messages throughout the brain (Aston-Jones *et al.*, 1986). Aston-Jones (1985) took recordings from unrestrained rats and found that the rate of activity in this area correlated very well indeed with behavioural arousal. Oddly, when the animals were grooming or drinking, activities that require a relatively high state of arousal, the locus coeruleus was quiet. Aston-Jones suggests that the function of this nucleus is to increase the animal's sensitivity to environmental stimuli – that is, to modulate its level of *vigilance*, rather than arousal *per se*.

Neurophysiology of the sleep states

The control mechanisms governing arousal, described in the previous section, have proved extremely elusive. Although our understanding seemed almost complete 30 or so years ago, the more that was discovered about the reticular formation and its functions using single unit recordings in intact animals in the subsequent years, the less certain we became about its precise role. In the same way, our understanding of the mechanisms that control the initiation of non-REM and REM sleep, and their maintenance, is now less certain than it was in the late 1960s.

Slow-wave sleep

The neurophysiology of slow-wave sleep has proved a very slippery matter for physiologists. A number of brain structures have been identified as good candidates for control sites, and it now seems that non-REM sleep is normally generated by interactions between them. Oddly, however, it is also true that non-REM sleep can be generated in either half of a brain that has been transected across the axis, implying that multiple generators in the brainstem and forebrain are capable of independently maintaining non-REM sleep (Siegel, 1990). In the following paragraphs a number of structures will be described, as will the evidence linking them to non-REM sleep.

The *raphe nuclei*, situated in the hindbrain, are two long columns that extend from the medulla to the pons in the midline and contain the majority of the serotonin-containing neurones in the brain stem. During the mid-1960s a group in Lyons discovered that destruction of the raphe nuclei caused total insomnia in the cat (Jouvet and Renault, 1966). It was also shown that (1) the pharmacological suppression of serotonin production (using p-chlorphenylalanine, PCPA) causes insomnia, which could be reversed by the serotonin precursor 5-HTP, and (2) the critical site for the action of serotonin in reversing insomnia induced by PCPA was the anterior hypothalamus. This evidence might lead one to think that serotonin, produced in the raphe nuclei, somehow initiates and maintains sleep through the interaction of these nuclei with structures in the hypothalamus. However, it seems that the raphe nuclei are more active during wakefulness than during sleep (McGinty and Harper, 1976), making any such simple interpretation impossible.

The *nucleus of the solitary tract*, located caudal to the raphe nuclei, has been shown to receive inputs from neurons that relay information about taste, and from the viscera. Electrical stimulation of the nucleus causes EEG signs of sleep (synchronized slow waves) in the cat, which continues after the stimulation is turned off (Magnes *et al.*, 1961). It is well known that feeding promotes sleep (see Chapter 9), so it is perhaps unsurprising that the same structure that relays information from the gut is involved with the promotion of sleep. However, single unit recordings by Eguchi and Sato (1980a) have revealed that while about half the neurons in this nucleus are more active during non-REM sleep than during wakefulness, they only become active after non-REM sleep has already become established, ruling them out as important instigators of sleep initiation.

The *basal forebrain region*, which is rostral to the hypothalamus, has also been implicated in the control of slow-wave sleep. Lesions in this area cause insomnia in rats and cats. Single neuron recordings by Szymusiak and McGinty (1986, 1989) have confirmed a correlation between activity changes in this area and sleep. It has also been found that the neurons in this region are thermosensitive, being more active when warmer. In Chapter 9, evidence is discussed that links body warming in humans to an increase in deep slow-wave sleep levels (as well as evidence showing that reptiles may sleep more deeply when warmer). The links between sleep and temperature are at least as strong as those between sleep and feeding.

While these neurophysiological findings from animals seem to suggest strongly that the basal forebrain region is an important sleep centre, human clinical evidence points to another structure – the thalamus. Recent post-mortem studies of seven unfortunate members of an Italian family who suffered from a syndrome of fatal familial insomnia found that they all had a common pathology – an atrophy of the anterior ventral and mediodorsal thalamic nuclei (Lugaresi *et al.*, 1986).

To summarize, it is clear from animal studies that the basal forebrain and the nucleus of the solitary tract are both important in the control of non-REM sleep, and from human clinical evidence that the thalamus is also involved, but the neural circuits through which these structures exert their control have yet to be mapped and their precise roles have yet to be established.

REM sleep

As discussed in Chapter 2, REM sleep is characterized by a lowering of muscle tone; low-voltage, desynchronized EEG and bursts of rapid eye movements. Intracranial electrophysiological recordings have shown that other typical events – called ponto-geniculo-occipital (PGO) waves – are associated with REM sleep. As Michel Jouvet (1967) reported some decades ago, these waves are generated in the pons and travel through the lateral geniculate nuclei to the visual cortex. They typically occur in bursts, starting a little before the other signs of REM sleep in the cat and continuing throughout the REM sleep period (see Steriade *et al.*, 1989). They often seem to precede individual eye movements, and a major theory of the neurophysiology of dreaming (the activation–synthesis theory, described in Chapter 5) suggests that their activity is the prime source of the dreaming experience.

The total loss of muscle tone during REM sleep (muscle tone is normally kept up to a minimum level by antigravity or postural reflexes even when we are perfectly relaxed) is general to all mammals, although it is more complete in some than in others. The motoneurons are hyperpolarized during REM sleep and incapable of discharge. It is clear the specific inhibition of almost all these post-synaptic neurons comes from the lower brainstem, leaving only respiratory and oculomotor motoneurons unaffected, but it has not yet been ascertained which structures in the lower brainstem are responsible. When a lesion is made caudal of the pons of a cat the muscle atonia of REM sleep may sometimes be lifted, and the animal apparently acts out its 'dreams'. According to Jouvet (1972) 'There are orienting movements of the head or eyes toward imaginary stimuli, although the animal does not respond to visual or auditory stimuli.'

A similar syndrome can occur naturally in human beings, typically as a result of withdrawal from alcohol dependence, giving rise to the apocryphal pink elephants of delerium tremens, and also to waking dreams accompanied by movement. Mahowald and Schenck (1989) of the University of Minnesota have studied more than 20 such cases, using EEG/EOG recordings of REM sleep to confirm that it is accompanied by high levels of tonic EMG and movement artefacts. Sufferers complain of vigorous and often dangerous behaviour during sleep, accompanied by vivid, striking dreams. They are almost invariably older men, often with a history of drug use – either alcohol or other sedatives.

The control of REM sleep is better understood than that of slow-wave sleep. Experiments on cats involving transections have given a good indication of localization of function in REM sleep control, as distinct from control of wakefulness and non-REM sleep. Figure 6.6 shows the sites of three different transections of the brain of the cat. When the cuts are made at levels A or B, all the signs of REM sleep are caudal to the cut, and these reappear in a regular ultradian cycle (Jouvet, 1967). The brain left rostral to these two cuts (in front of them) alternates between periods of synchronized EEG and desynchronized EEG.

During the synchronized EEG periods, cats seem not to be in REM sleep, but in a state more resembling wakefulness, as eye movements are not spontaneous but occur in response to visual stimuli. Thus, following Siegel (1990), we can conclude that 'structures rostral to the midbrain are not required for REM sleep and that structures caudal to the midbrain contain neurons that are sufficient to generate REM sleep'. Transection at point C in the figure allows both REM and non-REM sleep in the brain rostral to it, showing that the spinal cord is not necessary for the development or maintenance of these states.

In a series of experiments involving transections between these sites, Siegel and others have established that the area of the hindbrain that is crucial to the generation of REM sleep in the cat is quite small, and is located ventrally to the locus ceruleus (Figure 6.6). Intracranial, single unit recordings have confirmed that the activity of cells in this region is uniquely associated with REM sleep. Hence all the evidence points to this area of the hindbrain being essential for the generation and maintenance of REM sleep, including the production of PGO waves and rapid eye movements. As Siegel (ibid.) points out, it is unlikely that this also means that this small part of the hindbrain is

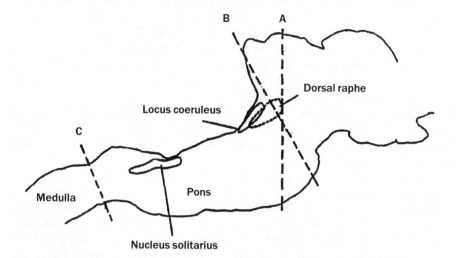

Figure 6.6   Sagittal section of a cat's brain, displaying five structures that are important in sleep regulation: the medulla, pons, nucleus solitarius, locus coeruleus and dorsal raphe. The dotted lines (A, B and C) are the planes of sections whose behavioural consequences are discussed in the text (from Siegel, 1990)

sufficient for the complete control of REM sleep, which doubtless requires the interaction of many structures in the brain, some of them quite remote from the hindbrain. Siegel suggests that studies of decerebrate animals may give a misleading impression of an active hindbrain (during REM sleep) bombarding the relatively passive cortex with PGO waves. The patterns of PGO waves in these preparations appear in regular bursts rather than in the irregular patterns normally seen in the intact animal. The amplitudes of the PGO waves are also very strongly affected. The generation and maintenance of REM sleep is probably the result of a dynamic interaction between cortex and hindbrain, and while the structures that Siegel and others have identified in the pons are necessary for REM sleep, they are not sufficient in themselves to produce it.

7

Sleep Disturbance

The effects of sleep deprivation

The experience of sleep loss: heroic experiments

Oliver Goldsmith, writing in 1811, described the effects of sleep loss thus:

> But man is more feeble; he requires its [sleep's] due return; and if it fails to pay the accustomed visit, his whole frame is in a short time thrown into disorder; his appetite ceases; his spirits are dejected; his pulse becomes quicker and harder; and his mind, abridged of its slumbering visions, begins to adopt waking dreams. A thousand strange phantoms arise, which come and go without his will: these, which are transient in the beginning, at last take firm possession of the mind, which yields to their dominion, and, after a long struggle, runs into continued madness. In that horrid state, the mind may be considered as a city without walls, open to every insult, and paying homage to every invader; every idea that then starts with any force, becomes a reality; and the reason, over fatigued with its former importunities, makes no head against the tyrannical invasion, but submits to it from mere imbecility.

This extract sums up what many people might expect to be the consequences of going without sleep for any length of time, but it is a pity that Goldsmith, in his characteristically journalistic style, does not cite any source for this assertion. Floridly psychotic episodes in people's lives, when they experience hallucinations of the sort Goldsmith describes, are often preceded by periods of sleeplessness, or at least of gross sleep disturbance, and this is perhaps why the association between sleep loss and madness has been made. It does not necessarily follow that sleep loss will cause these symptoms in otherwise normal individuals.

Relatively few controlled observations of the effects of sleep loss have continued for longer than 48 hours. When they have, disorders of perception, including hallucinations, have sometimes been reported, but by no means invariably. A not untypical pattern of distortion of sensation was reported after the first documented vigil of this sort:

> The first subject, J.A.G., is a young man of 28 years, assistant professor in the University. He is unmarried, of perfect health, of nervous temperament, of very great vitality and activity. He is accustomed to about 8 hours of sound sleep from 10 p.m. to 6 a.m. He awoke at his usual time Wednesday morning, November 27, and remained awake until 12 o'clock Saturday night. The second night he did not feel well and suffered severely from sleepiness. The third night he suffered less. The

fourth day and the evening following he felt well and was able to pass his time in his usual occupations. During the last 50 hours, however, he had to be watched closely, and could not be allowed to sit down unoccupied, as he showed a tendency to fall asleep immediately, his own will to keep awake being of no avail. The daily rhythm was well marked. During the afternoon and evening the subject was less troubled with sleepiness. The sleepy period was from midnight until noon, of which the worst part was about dawn. The most marked effect of the abstinence from sleep with this subject was the presence of hallucinations of sight. These were persistent after the second night. The subject complained that the floor was covered with a greasy-looking, molecular layer of rapidly moving or oscillating particles. Often this layer was a foot above the floor and parallel with it and this caused the subject trouble walking, as he would try to step up on it. Later the air was full of these dancing particles which developed into swarms of little bodies like gnats, but colored red, purple or black. The subject would climb upon a chair to brush them from about the gas jet or stealthily try to touch an imaginary fly on the table with his finger. These phenomena did not move with movements of the eye and appeared to be true hallucinations, centrally caused, but due no doubt to the long and unusual strain put upon the eyes. Meanwhile the subject's sharpness of vision was not impaired. At no other time has he had hallucinations of sight and they entirely disappeared after sleeping' (Patrick and Gilbert, 1896).

Two more subjects then underwent the 90-hour procedure, and similarly became extremely sleepy, especially during the hours between midnight and noon, reviving somewhat during the afternoons. They did not experience any of the hallucinations experienced by J.A.G.

In a later experiment, four volunteers underwent 205 hours (eight days) of sleeplessness (Pasnau et al., 1968). They became increasingly sleepy over the first four days and it became almost impossible for the experimenters to keep them awake. Making them responsible for keeping each other awake at this stage restored the sense of group cohesion and common purpose, although from then onwards some serious changes in behaviour occurred, marked by emotional outbursts, grossly impolite eating habits and what the authors of the report describe as an 'infantilization of personal habits, . . . including toilet and bathing activities'. At one point one of the subjects went berserk during a psychomotor tracking task, screaming in terror and pulling off his electrodes, falling to floor and sobbing and muttering incoherently about a gorilla. Oddly enough, at the end of the 205 hours the subjects claimed that they could go on longer, that after the fifth day things had got easier, and, indeed, they offered to stay awake for another day if paid at the ninth day's rate.

In the forty-odd experimental studies that have been reported to date on periods of sleep loss lasting longer than two days, hallucinations have been uncommon, tending to affect solitary individuals rather than those in groups. Similarly, other frankly psychiatric symptoms, such as paranoia, have affected lone volunteers more than those in groups.

A study, in which the majority of the subjects suffered from mental aberrations of one sort or another, required them to perform tasks continuously and in isolation for 42 hours (Mullaney et al., 1983). Three of these 10 subjects experienced actual hallucinations, and seven suffered perceptual distortions or illusions. Two other groups of 10 subjects were allowed either six one-hour naps or one six-hour sleep during the experiment, and they both managed to maintain a high level of performance on the tasks. Even in these groups, however, a minority had hallucinations. It is well known that isolation in itself, with no sleep loss, can induce hallucinatory experiences, and it seems that in this experiment the effects of sleep loss potentiated the relatively mild levels of isolation imposed on the subjects.

In such experiments, the subjects have invariably found it most difficult to remain awake in the hours between midnight and noon, with a period of revival every afternoon. In addition, it typically becomes very difficult indeed to keep people continually awake without keeping them moving, and this naturally confounds the effects of physical fatigue with those of sleep deprivation *per se*. Curiously, however, deliberately increasing exercise levels during a vigil does not seem to increase or decrease the impairments attributable to sleep loss (Angus *et al.*, 1985).

After about 72 hours of sleep loss it is impossible to prevent subjects from obtaining brief 'microsleeps', which (when EEG measures are made) have been shown to be indistinguishable from brief periods of natural sleep (Williams *et al.*, 1959). Using Dement's analogy, rather than taking their sleep in one meal, subjects may obtain enough to keep them going by snatching 'snacks'. Such heroic experiments are therefore diminished as a source of insight into the effects of loss of sleep, although they have demonstrated that it is an intensely stressful experience, taxing the psychological resources of individuals to their utmost.

Effects on performance and psychophysiology

The sleep-deprived person may feel terrible and look pretty ragged but is typically capable of achieving the same levels of performance on psychological tests as when rested. Many common tests of perceptual functioning, memory or skilled performance seem insensitive to the effects of sleep loss. Despite the good number of studies that were undertaken in the first half of the twentieth century, it was not until the late 1950s that the particular decrements in the performance of sleepy subjects were established. Researchers at the Walter Reed Army Institute of Research in the US (Williams *et al.*, 1959) and at the Medical Research Council Unit for Applied Psychology in Cambridge (Wilkinson, 1959) simultaneously identified that tasks sensitive to the effects of even one night's loss of sleep were those which were not self-timed, went on for at least 10 minutes and were not intrinsically motivating. While a sleep-deprived subject at the Walter Reed Institute was able to respond as quickly in a simple reaction-time task as when rested, his pattern of responses over an extended series of trials, with the experimenter determining when stimuli were presented, included an increasing number of very slow responses.

The Cambridge subjects were faced with the five-choice serial reaction task, where a subject responds to one of five lights coming on by pressing one of five buttons on a continuous basis (every time a response is made the relevant light goes out, but another one immediately comes on). Average response latency tended to increase over a period of 20 minutes in the sleep-deprived subjects, unlike in the rested controls. However, their best (fastest) responses were just as fast as when rested, although the number of slow responses (or gaps in responding) increased dramatically after the first five minutes. Ascertaining the effects of sleep deprivation was therefore not simple; for instance, one could not say that the nervous system had simply slowed down, as on occasion the subjects responded as quickly as when they were rested.

The theory developed to account for these findings, lapse theory, proposes that the special effect of sleep loss is to increase the number of lapses in attention, possibly through 'microsleeps'. This attentional failure may be caused by a lowering of the arousal level, which may be temporarily counteracted by the subject making a special effort to remain awake. Evidence supporting the theory has come from experiments on the interaction of sleep loss with other manipulations that are known to increase the arousal level, such as incentives and noise.

Giving the subject immediate knowledge of the results of a monotonous task provides an intrinsic incentive, which can be sufficient to overcome completely the effects of one night's sleep loss for brief periods (Wilkinson, 1961). This improvement is achieved by the subject making an extra compensatory effort, measurable in terms of increased muscle tension (EMG). In such subjects the level of EMG has been shown to be well correlated with their level of performance (Wilkinson, 1962). Offering extra payment for good performance, and 'fines' for missed signals in a vigilance task have similarly led to maintained performance after one night's sleep loss at normal levels. Later work at the Loughborough sleep laboratory found that the protection from the effects of sleep loss provided by incentives was not maintained after the second night, and after the third night without sleep the subjects with incentives performed no better than those without (Horne and Pettit, 1985).

Loud noise impairs performance on the five-choice serial reaction time task in normal, rested subjects. This has been interpreted as arousal being increased to a level that is incompatible with that task. Sleep-deprived subjects, however, improve their performance on the five-choice when subjected to white noise, as if their arousal level has been raised sufficiently to allow them cope with the demands of the task (Corcoran, 1962).

Lapse theory can be invoked to explain all the results described above, but it is unclear whether the lapses in attention induced by lowered arousal are the only important symptoms of sleep loss. For instance, are the fast reaction times of the sleep-deprived subject really as fast as when they are rested, and is the slightly slower average reaction time really just the result of a number of isolated lapses? Analysis of moment-by-moment changes in performance over a ten-minute period has shown that while the sleep-deprived subject may perform well at the beginning, *all* responses are slowed towards the end, as well as frank lapses occurring. That is, in a boring, repetitive task subjects are not only prone to occasional failures to respond, but their 'good' responses are also impaired (Lisper and Kjellberg, 1972). According to Kjellberg (1977), lapses are the most dramatic outcomes of lowered arousal, but when a sleepy subject performs a work-paced task for any length of time, his or her responses become degraded even before the occurrence of frank lapses in attention.

The lowered-arousal explanation of sleep loss effects is further supported by studies on selective attention. Loud noise (usually delivered as 'white noise' – a wide-band mixture of tones, sounding like a monotonous hiss as from a TV set unconnected to an aerial), as we have seen, is a potent arouser, and in rested subjects it has the effect of focusing attention when undertaking a dual component task (Hockey, 1970a). This involves tracking a moving dot as well as monitoring lights that are either centrally or peripherally placed. When performing the same task for 40 minutes after sleep loss, at first the subjects make faster responses to the centrally placed lights than the peripheral ones, as do rested subjects. As the task goes on, they gradually demonstrate more and more signs of a defocusing of attention, which is consistent with the view that although performance is not disrupted by lapses, habituation leads to a marked drop in arousal level (Hockey, 1970b). Similarly, sleep-deprived subjects have been found to be easily distracted by irrelevant stimuli in a card-sorting task, again demonstrating a failure to maintain focused attention on the job in hand (Norton, 1970).

The EEG is probably the best single indicator of cortical arousal at low levels. Recordings of sleep-deprived subjects have shown a reduction in the amplitude of alpha rhythms (Bjerner, 1949). This is consistent with the view that, even when they are successful in remaining awake, subjects do not maintain the levels of cortical arousal that are normal in a rested person. In rested subjects alpha rhythm is indicative of low arousal, but sleep-deprived subjects commonly only achieve this level at best. Alpha rhythm appears when they are performing the most demanding tasks, and disappears altogether when less is demanded of them and their eyes are closed – almost as if they were drifting into a light sleep. EEG recordings made while sleep-deprived subjects are engaged in tasks have disclosed that errors of commission are not associated with EEG patterns that differ from those made during correct performance, while errors of omission (indicating failure to maintain attention) are associated with reduced alpha rhythm (ibid.). In addition, slow waves (consistent with being asleep) may occur during lapses in performance.

The development of an EEG event-related potential measure of error detection in subjects while they are performing tasks has allowed a more fine-grained analysis of the effects of sleep loss on performance. This measure, error-related negativity (ERN), detects increases in negativity on the scalp after an error is made in choice reaction-time tasks, and is said to be associated with the development of realization in the performer that he or she had erred (Falkenstein et al., 1991). Are failures in performance after sleep loss the result of failure to recognize errors as they occur, or of failure to make correction after recognition of the error? Scheffers et al. (1999) present evidence that when subjects begin to make errors in visual search tasks and memory search tasks as they work through the night, these errors are not accompanied by ERN waveforms, suggesting that failure to recognize error is the main cause of decline in performance with increasing sleepiness.

This evidence is again consistent with the lapse theory of sleep loss. Further EEG evidence comes from studies of the contingent negative variation (CNV) – a negative waveform in the EEG that is elicited when a warning stimulus is given, shortly followed by an imperative stimulus that requires the subject to make a response. For instance, a buzzer will sound, followed one second later by a series of flashes of light, which the subject has to turn off by pressing a button. Sleep-deprived subjects have been shown to have lower-amplitude CNVs (Gauthier and Gottesmann, 1983; Naitoh *et al.*, 1971), and it could be assumed that this is associated with inattention or poor preparation for making a response. In rested subjects the relationship between response speed and CNV amplitude is not simple (Papakostopoulos and Fenelon, 1975), but one might assume that if lapses of attention are responsible for the generally lowered CNV with sleep loss, these should be associated with slow responses when the subjects are ill-prepared for the second, imperative stimulus, having failed to notice the warning stimulus. According to a simple application of lapse theory, slow responses ought to be preceded by low-voltage CNVs, while fast responses (as quick as when rested) should be preceded by high-voltage CNVs similar to those recorded from rested subjects.

Studies carried out in Hull (Giannocorou, 1984; Kluvitse, 1984; Lister, 1981) did nothing to confirm this prediction. Response speed was reduced for both fast and slow responses after sleep loss. Paradoxically, while CNV amplitude was on average lower after sleep deprivation, sleep-deprived subjects produced higher voltage CNVs before making the eight slowest responses out of 60 trials than the eight fastest ones. When rested, the same subjects had higher-voltage CNVs before fast responses than before slow ones. These findings reinforce Kjellberg's (1997) contention that the sleep-deprived person is not, as lapse theory would suggest, essentially 'normal' but suffering periodic lapses. Rather, the subject's psychophysiological state undergoes a profound change; the result of compelling sleepiness inducing inertia and sleep, and a determined effort to stay awake. Neither a simple arousal model nor lapse theory is adequate on its own to explain the complex effects of sleep loss.

The effects of sleep loss on subsequent sleep

It is a common observation that if we lose a night's sleep we tend to sleep a bit longer on subsequent nights, as if to repay a 'sleep debt'. Generally speaking, the amount of sleep lost is not made up for entirely on the recovery nights. Recordings of the EEG of recovery sleep have confirmed that the first night's recovery sleep is longer than usual. There is a large increase in percentage terms of stage 3 and 4 sleep, at the expense of the lighter slow-wave sleep stages. While more REM sleep is taken than on control nights in absolute terms, this is not because of any increase in REM sleep as a percentage of total sleep. Only during the second and subsequent recovery nights do subjects typically show a relative elevation of REM sleep percentage levels. Thus, over the course of two or three nights, stage 3 and 4 and REM sleep are almost made up, while stage 2 sleep is not (Berger and Walker, 1972; Kales *et al.*, 1970). Analogous effects have been observed in rats deprived of sleep, when paradoxical sleep recovery is delayed in favour of slow-wave sleep on the first recovery night (Bergmann and Rechtschaffen, 1989).

Schedules of sleep

Reduced sleep in the short term

Once the tasks that are particularly sensitive to the effects of even one night's sleep loss had been identified, it became feasible to attempt to establish how little sleep is enough to prevent any of the effects of sleep loss. Experiments such as those conducted at the MRC Applied Psychology Unit in Cambridge, indicate that even short periods of sleep are enough to prevent any measurable worsening of performance (Wilkinson, 1970). In that experiment, 19 enlisted men were repeatedly tested over a period of six weeks. Every week their sleep was rationed on two nights to between zero and 7.5 hours, and they spent the subsequent days being tested in the laboratory on vigilance and adding tasks. These tasks were repetitive, lengthy and lacked any intrinsic interest. This regime should have been more than adequate to demonstrate any significant short-term effects of reduced sleep. However, performance deficits were only noticeable after two hours' sleep or less for one night, and after five hours or less for two successive nights, showing some evidence of an accumulation of sleep debt potentiating the otherwise rather slight effects of reduced sleep. This finding – that reduced sleep in the short term has little effect on performance on this set of tasks – was confirmed in later work (for example, Hamilton *et al.*, 1972).

The question of whether low levels of sleep deprivation have no effect at all, or an effect in proportion to the amount of sleep that the subjects have enjoyed, has been addressed by Jewett *et al.* (1999). Reporting an analysis of their own previously published work, they show that there is in fact a linear relationship between the amount of sleep allowed (zero, two, five and eight hours) and experienced sleepiness and performance on a psychomotor vigilance task – a simple unprepared reaction-time task. Thus, although the effects of one or two hours of reduced sleep may be slight, they are measurable.

The effect of interrupting sleep after two or three hours is to deny subjects almost all REM sleep, while allowing them much of the deep slow-wave sleep they might be expected to have in a normal night. Only sleep-stage deprivation experiments can answer the question of whether one stage is more restorative than another, and such experiments are discussed next.

Sleep-stage deprivation experiments

Selective deprivation experiments involve highly artificial regimes designed systematically to eliminate one or other of the major sleep stages. These will be discussed again in Chapter 11 in relation to hypothesized functions of sleep, but the effects on subsequent recovery sleep and the consequences for performance will be outlined here. REM sleep deprivation experiments were also discussed in Chapter 3 in the context of beliefs about dreaming – in particular the notion that the prevention of dreaming sleep might cause temporary psychosis. Briefly, William Dement's (1960) early experimental work provided some support for this idea but was subsequently found, both by himself and others, to be unrepeatable. In retrospect, it seems that genuine concern on the part of the experimenters was communicated to the subjects, providing a potent suggestion that they might suffer symptoms of paranoia and hallucinations, and combined with cumulative sleep loss over the six days of the experiment this provided fertile ground for the production of these symptoms. It has also become clear that dreaming is by no means confined to REM sleep (see Chapter 4), so even if the theory were correct, a regime of REM sleep deprivation would not be an adequate test of it.

Well-established aspects of the early findings relate to the behaviour of sleep mechanisms when REM sleep is prevented by repeated awakenings. While it may be virtually abolished on the first night by as few as four or five wakenings, on subsequent nights REM 'pressure' increases and successively more awakenings are required, as the number of times REM sleep is initiated is increased. In addition, on recovery nights the amount of time spent in REM sleep increases. This REM sleep 'rebound' may be of the order of 50 per cent over baseline levels, although the total amount of REM sleep 'lost' during the period of selective deprivation is rarely made up entirely.

It is also possible to prevent subjects from having any stage 4 sleep (or very little) by disturbing their sleep with loud noises, rather than waking them up fully (Agnew *et al.*, 1964). The effects of this regime on subsequent recovery sleep are similar to the effects of REM sleep deprivation, in that a rebound of about 50 per cent occurs on recovery nights. (Figures 7.1 and 7.2).

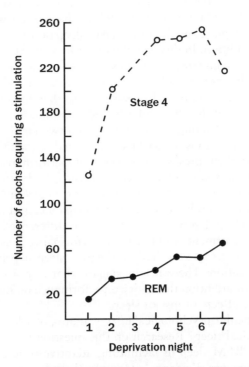

Figure 7.1 Number of epochs requiring a stimulation for deprivation of REM and stage 4 sleep (from Webb, 1969)

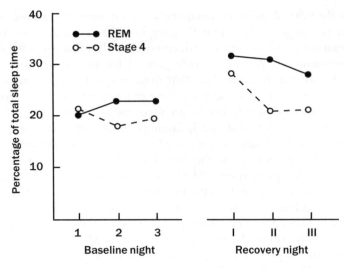

Figure 7.2   REM and stage 4 percentages for baseline and recovery nights
(from Webb, 1969)

Two experiments that combined total sleep deprivation, REM sleep deprivation and stage 4 sleep deprivation, compared the effects of a variety of
regimes of total and selective sleep deprivation on recovery sleep and performance (Johnson *et al.*, 1974; Lubin *et al.*, 1974). The subjects were denied any
sleep for the first two nights, and then allowed to sleep under one or other sleep-
stage deprivation condition. In this way the restorative effects of sleep without
REM sleep could be compared with those of sleep without stage 4 sleep.
Another group of subjects were subjected to REM or stage 4 sleep deprivation
for three nights, and then deprived of sleep altogether for one night, again
allowing a comparison of the effects of a four-day cumulation of stage 4 sleep
loss with REM sleep. Restricting recovery sleep after two night's loss of sleep by
excluding stage 4 sleep or most of REM sleep seemed to make no difference –
subjects returned to their presleep-loss levels of performance regardless of
whether recovery sleep was uninterrupted or selectively deprived.

In the second experiment, selective deprivation of stage 4 or REM sleep over
three nights had no measurable effects on performance, and after the subsequent night of total sleep deprivation there was no difference between groups
in their degree of impairment. In fact, their performance was slightly better
than that of a control group who had one night's sleep deprivation with no
prior selective deprivation. These results suggest that any sleep is enough to
prevent the failures of attention that worsen performance on the tasks that are
most sensitive to the effects of loss of sleep.

What are the particular psychological effects, if any, of selective deprivation
of REM or paradoxical sleep? Research on this question has concentrated on
the possible role of REM sleep in facilitating adaptive processes, and in the
consolidation of memories. Evidence relating to these issues will be discussed
in Chapter 11.

Reduced sleep in the long term

As pointed out in Chapter 2, some people seem to require very little sleep, while others take more. Those who sleep less sometimes claim to do so by choice, self-righteously accusing others of being idle if they spend more than six hours in bed. How much control do we have over our requirement for sleep, and what are the consequences of individuals taking things into their own hands and reducing their sleep?

The effects of deliberately reduced sleep on sleep patterns have been studied in a number of relatively short experiments, and one that went on for two years. The short-term effects can be illustrated by an experiment in which sleep was restricted to five hours for seven days (Carskadon and Dement, 1981). Sleep onset time was reduced from 33 minutes during baseline recordings to less than five minutes by the seventh night, and the time spent awake after preparing for sleep was reduced from about 30 minutes to virtually zero. Sleep efficiency was thus notably improved. While asleep, stage 1 and 2 and REM sleep were reduced at the expense of stage 3 and 4 sleep, which were maintained at base-line levels. There was a tendency for REM sleep time to recover slightly during the week of restriction, and during recovery sleep an increase in REM sleep time over baseline levels (a REM sleep rebound) indicated accumulated pres-sure for REM sleep. The subjects slept like short sleepers insofar as sleep efficiency was improved, and deep slow-wave sleep was maintained at baseline levels. However, their REM sleep time was reduced.

Longer-term effects were studied in four young couples, three who normally slept about 8.0 hours a night and one who slept 6.5 hours a night. The subjects volunteered to attempt progressively to reduce their sleep to 4.5 hours a night over a period of six to eight months (Friedman *et al.*, 1977). They reduced their sleep time by 30 minutes every two weeks until it was down to 6.5 hours, then by 30 minutes every three weeks until it was 5.0 hours, and finally by 30 minutes after four weeks. At the final stage, when they were sleeping only 4.5 hours a night, the subjects complained of falling asleep during the day, and the reductions in sleeping time were discontinued.

The participants' subjective reports on the effects of reduced sleep were that it produced a chronic feeling of sleepiness (as measured by the Stanford sleepiness scale questionnaire) and, perhaps not surprisingly, increased the feeling of needing more sleep. The estimated time needed to get to sleep after going to bed was reduced to a quarter of the baseline levels, and reports of difficulty getting to sleep were reduced to a third of what they had been. The more subtle effects on mood are indicated by a quotation from one of the subjects: 'I get discouraged more easily, slightly depressed about overcoming difficulties, very much like when I am sick with a cold.'

Despite the reports of sleepiness during the day, performance of tasks known to be affected by sleep loss was generally unaffected during this regime (including two tasks developed at the Medical Research Council Applied Psychology Unit, the Wilkinson auditory vigilance task and the Wilkinson addition task). Only one test proved sensitive to the effects of gradually reduced sleep – the rapid alternation test – where an increase in the number of long responses, or lapses, was noticed at the lowest sleep levels. Subjects also reported difficulty maintaining concentration when driving.

After this phase of the experiment was over, the subjects were allowed to sleep as much as they wished, but they continued to keep sleep diaries for a year. The six who had originally slept for about eight hours did not immediately return to their baseline level, and continued to sleep less than they had before, and even a year later they were sleeping 1–1.5 hours less than they had previously. The two subjects who had slept little to start with did not achieve any such permanent reduction in sleep. This experiment is interesting in highlighting how the subjective experience of sleepiness is not necessarily reflected in performance measures, and, more importantly, in demonstrating some long-term if not permanent changes in the sleep patterns of the six 'normal' sleepers.

This study included EEG/EOG recordings during sleep, and it is interesting to compare the sort of sleep that these subjects were getting after months of sleep reduction with that of subjects who reduced their sleep for briefer periods of time (Mullaney et al., 1977). In particular, did the regime permanently change their pattern of sleep, as well as reducing their sleep requirement by over an hour?

Comparing the 8.0-hour with the 5.5-hour sleep regimes for the six subjects who had normally taken 8.0 hours sleep, stage 2 and REM sleep were significantly reduced, while stage 4 sleep actually increased slightly. Although REM sleep time was reduced, its share of the first 5.5 hours' sleep increased in the 5.5 hour sleep condition. See Table 7.1. That is, there was evidence of some compensation, partly due to a shorter time to the onset of REM sleep. On follow-up, when these subjects were sleeping only 6.0 hours and no longer feeling sleepy during the day, the proportions of sleep stages were no different than they had been during the experiment when they were restricted to 6.0 hours sleep and did feel sleepy.

Table 7.1 Sleep characteristics during gradual sleep reduction (minutes) (from Mullaney et al., 1977)

Sleep phase (hours)	Number	Wake	Stage 1	Stage 2	Stage 3	Stage 4	REM	Sleep onset
8.0	6	17	17	228	32	48	116	16
7.5	6	14	13	213	37	40	113	15
7.0	6	10	14	200	40	43	99	14
6.5	6	9	12	163	38	58	101	11
6.0	6	12	15	138	37	54	91	14
5.5	6	4	9	147	31	56	83	9
5.0	4	5	10	111	30	51	80	9
4.5	2	3	11	123	27	35	68	8
Follow-up	6	13	10	155	35	57	88	15

In a less ambitious sleep-reduction study, three pairs of subjects systematically reduced their sleep from eight hours to six over a period of six weeks (Horne and Wilkinson, 1985). Recordings of sleep patterns again showed that this was achieved at the expense of REM and stage 2 sleep, leaving stage 4 sleep levels unaffected. As in the longer experiment, the subjects tended to sleep less during the three month follow-up, indicating that even relatively short periods of training can be sufficient to reduce the sleep requirement by an hour or so in individuals who wish to do so.

How much sleep do we actually need? The two subjects in the eight-month restriction study who had already limited themselves to six hours' sleep did not benefit from the regime, and reverted to their previous norm. Many of us who sleep for seven hours or more may be able to cope with less sleep without feeling sleepy, given training, but this only applies to those of us who are sleeping more than we really need to. On the other hand there is evidence that, given the opportunity of *ad-lib* sleep, most young adults will sleep longer than usual, the extra sleep being composed of stage 1 and 2 and REM sleep (Webb and Agnew, 1975b). Does this imply a chronic sleep debt in these young people? Perhaps not, but while the seven to nine-hour sleeping habit is certainly based on physiological need, it seems to be a socially defined and somewhat procrustean norm imposed on all of us whatever our individual needs, which are probably genetically determined.

Extended sleep, displaced sleep and the Rip Van Winkle effect

Somewhat surprisingly the consequences of sleeping longer than usual are similar to sleeping less, as far as performance decrement is concerned. Taub and Berger (1976) required their subjects to sleep for an hour or more longer than usual, by putting them to bed at either 10 p.m. or 1 a.m. but getting them up at the same time – 9 a.m. They found that this caused increases in the total amount of REM sleep and stage 2 sleep. When tested after two hours' extra sleep the subjects performed worse on a vigilance task, although not significantly worse on a calculation task. In another experiment (Taub *et al.*, 1971), in which sleep was extended by a similar amount, the subjects were tested on a vigilance task, a calculation task and a pinball game. The combined number of omissions and false reports on the vigilance task were 50 per cent greater after extended sleep, and scores on pinball were reduced by 10 per cent. Again there was no significant decrement on a calculation task.

This group of researchers went on to compare the effects of extended sleep with those of reduced sleep (five hours) and displaced sleep (Taub and Berger, 1976). The subjects slept either from 9 p.m. to 5 a.m. or from 3 a.m. to 11 a.m. Both shifting the timing of the sleep period from the habitual midnight to 8 a.m. and either increasing or decreasing the total amount of sleep had similar effects in restricting accuracy and speed of response on a vigilance task. These effects were attributed to physiological changes resulting from the disruption of the habitual circadian cycle of sleep and wakefulness, rather than any direct effects by the regimes on sleep itself – correlations between the actual amounts of sleep achieved and the performance and mood measures were poor.

The consequences of sleep loss and sleep reduction, therefore, cannot be simply interpreted in terms of denial of sleep, but must be regarded as the outcome of a combination of sleep loss, causing sleepiness, and the subversion of the normally well-ordered physiological cycles that substantially control our states of arousal. The implications of this conclusion will be explored further in the section on shiftworking.

Practical implications of sleep disturbance

Apart from the implications for theories of sleep function in physiology, the findings of experiments on the effects of sleep deprivation have some practical importance. All of us lose sleep at some time in our lives, and many individuals lose sleep as part of their jobs, which may be extremely responsible and demanding. Shiftworkers progressively lose sleep when working night or morning shifts, and may be employed in nursing, in controlling power stations or chemical plants, as well as in manufacturing industries. Airline pilots commonly have difficulty sleeping properly after long flights, especially when there have been time zone changes. Young babies substantially disrupt their mother's sleep during their first three months of life, when they are at their most dependent and when the mother's judgment and good temper are most important. Junior hospital doctors may be on call for extended periods and sometimes have to manage with little or no sleep. It is commonplace for soldiers to get very little sleep indeed during a battle. In all these contexts there are high demands on individuals for effective and responsible behaviour, and it is crucial to know the precise effects that sleep loss has on their normal functioning.

Overwork

When a group of junior hospital doctors were asked whether their efficiency was impaired by their long hours of duty, over a third replied 'often' and almost half replied 'occasionally' (Wilkinson *et al.*, 1975). Junior doctors frequently have sole responsibility for assessing the needs of patients who are brought to hospitals in the middle of the night, for instance, to casualty wards. Tests of efficiency in detecting abnormalities in the electro-cardiogram have shown that after a night of reduced sleep doctors' performance is considerably worse (Friedman *et al.*, 1971).

When taking a patient's history, the doctor has to listen carefully to what the patient says, which may be incoherent, and extract from this account the elements that are medically relevant. This very important task involves a high memory load, as items mentioned by a patient early in the interview may turn out to be significant later on. Tests of resident doctors after a night spent on emergency admissions (when they got an average of 1.5 hours sleep) showed them to be significantly worse at a memory task designed to tap these skills than after a night off duty (Deary and Tait, 1987). The differences between the doctors were great, not only in respect of their general level of performance but also in the degree to which their level of performance was affected by the lack of sleep. Referring to recent studies indicating that some people are particularly vulnerable to the effects of sleep disruption, Deary and Tait (ibid.) suggest that work should be done to identify doctors who are most at risk so that they can be assigned to other duties.

How does sleep loss affect soldiers? A study carried out at the Army Personnel Research Establishment (APRE) in Farnborough simulated wartime conditions for 10 soldiers, who were required to defend a position during a tactical exercise lasting 10 days (Haslam, 1981). Military staff ensured that they had no sleep for the first three days, after which short periods of sleep (four hours) were permitted every 24 hours. As well as being kept extremely busy with military duties (digging trenches, receiving signals, countering surprise attacks by 'enemy' troops), the men were tested three times a day on logical reasoning, a decoding task and marksmanship. Logical reasoning and decoding had deteriorated by the end of the first three days but recovered significantly, almost to baseline levels, when four hours' sleep per night were allowed. Marksmanship was relatively unaffected when the soldiers were allowed to shoot at a target in their own time, but when shooting was combined with a vigilance task (with the target appearing briefly at unpredictable times) the number of hits dramatically reduced.

In a larger study assessing endurance over nine days with different amounts of sleep loss, the APRE found that with no sleep at all soldiers could only operate effectively for four days, while with 1.5 hours sleep per day 50 per cent of a platoon lasted nine days in the field, and nearly all of a platoon who were allowed three hours' sleep completed the nine-day exercise (Haslam, 1982). The same pattern of performance decrement in cognitive and shooting tasks was observed as in the smaller experiment. This combination of good marksmanship with poor reasoning ability can only be viewed as alarming – particularly when so many military duties are concerned with public order, as in Northern Ireland, the Balkans and the Middle East, where the rules of engagement require soldiers to make decisions on the basis of evidence that is often ambiguous. To quote the Duke of Wellington, 'I don't know what effect these men will have upon the enemy, but, by God, they terrify me.'

Shiftwork

Shiftworkers commonly complain of not being able to get enough sleep and feeling chronically sleepy. This problem is not confined to nightworkers, it also affects those on early shifts (for example 6 a.m. to 2 p.m.), who may have to allow an hour to get to work (Knauth et al., 1980). Summarizing the results of a number of studies, Tilley and Wilkinson (1982) describe the effects of shiftwork on sleep as being:

- A one- to two-hour reduction in the duration of the main sleep period for the night shift and a reduction of about one hour for a morning or early shift;
- An increase in the total amount of sleep per 24 hours compared with that of non-shift workers. This increase, however, can be attributed to long naps

taken outside the main sleep period and increased sleep time on rest days. Both effects suggest a compensatory response to the shorter main periods;
• A change in the quality of sleep (that is, more time awake, increased stage 1 sleep and sometimes reduced REM sleep) and a disruption of the normal temporal organization of the sleep stages during daytime sleep.

In their own study (ibid.), which involved the use of a portable tape recorder to record EEG/EOG measures of sleeping shiftworkers in their own homes, they found that sleep during the day was generally shorter than night-time sleep, and more frequently interrupted by awakenings. The consequences for the performance of simple tasks was that simple and choice reaction times were worse at night than during the day, and that as the period spent on the night shift went by, simple reaction-time tasks took longer. Circadian (24-hour) fluctuations in performance thus seem to combine with the effects of cumulative sleep loss in a cycle of degradation of efficiency on the night shift.

Some individuals take to shiftwork with no problems, while others find the regime intolerable. Folkard and Monk (1981) suggested that it may be individuals whose rhythms *do* adjust to the regime who experience the most difficulty. After recording body temperatures throughout the day of groups of well-adjusted shiftworkers, intolerant shiftworkers and dayworkers who had given up shiftwork because they could not tolerate it, Reinberg *et al.* (1984) indeed found that it was the best-adjusted group whose circadian rhythm was most immutable. Intolerant workers tended to exhibit cycles that were longer or shorter than 24 hours when they were on shifts, although they resumed normal 24-hour cycles when they returned to daywork.

As with the effects of sleep reduction, sleep displacement and increased sleep, the effects of shiftworking on performance and mood are a consequence of the interaction of innate biological rhythms with sleep and arousal mechanisms. The implication of Reinberg *et al.*'s work is that rapidly rotating shifts, where no adjustment is made in terms of body rhythms, are preferable to longer cycling systems. Monitoring the body temperatures of shiftworkers might also give early warning of shiftwork intolerance, allowing transfer to daywork before performance deteriorates.

Sleepiness and driving

It is widely accepted that a fairly large proportion of road accidents are caused by drivers falling asleep at the wheel. What is surprising is that this general acceptance did not come about until the early 1990s, although there was awareness of the phenomenon amongst road traffic police. Evidence came from single-vehicle accidents in which cars left the road and collided with objects but left to no skid-marks to indicate an attempt to slow down or stop. Such accidents have been found to occur disproportionately in the early hours of the morning and during the early afternoon, times of day when one might expect sleepiness to be at its peak (Akerstedt *et al.*, 1994). A short nap of under 20 minutes has been found, paradoxically, to reduce sleepiness more than a longer one of over an hour (Naitoh, 1992). Applying this finding to the driving situation, it was found in two studies using a driving simulator that ingesting a significant amount of caffeine (150 milligrams, equivalent to about two cups of coffee) and taking a 15 minute nap (before the caffeine has been absorbed in the gut) is effective in reducing signs of sleepiness, but that on their own the caffeine or the nap are much less effective (Horne and Reyner, 1996; Reyner and Horne, 1997).

To compare the effects of lack of sleep with the effects of drinking alcohol, Lamond and Dawson (1999) systematically compared the effects on performance of up to 28 hours of wakefulness with those of blood alcohol levels of up to 0.10 per cent. About '20–25 hours of wakefulness produced performance decrements equivalent to those observed at a blood alcohol concentration of 0.10%'.

In a survey of commercial truck drivers in Finland, 40 per cent of the 148 long-haul drivers questioned reported having difficulty staying alert on at least 20 per cent of journeys, and 20 per cent of short-haul drivers reported the same. Of the long-haul drivers, over 20 per cent had dozed off at least twice while driving (Hakkanen and Summala, 2000). Drivers are invariably aware that they are sleepy well before they become dangerously so, and have been reported to take various measures to wake themselves up – stretching at the wheel, winding down windows, and even driving faster. The issuing of public information about the best course of action – taking a break, a coffee and a nap – may significantly reduce the number of road accident casualties in the future.

8

The Psychology of Sleep

Perception and memory in sleep

While asleep we do not, in general, respond when spoken to, or initiate coherent actions. We also have very little to report about our sleep after waking up. Just how oblivious are we when asleep? Our inertia during sleep poses severe practical problems to answering this question, but clues are provided by some common observations. Sleepers can easily be woken by being spoken to loudly, and yet they can sleep uninterruptedly through loud noises. People who fall asleep in a moving car or on a train are surrounded by a very high level of noise, but it is often relatively quiet sounds – somebody mentioning they have arrived, or an announcement on a railway station tannoy system in the distance – that wake them up. It follows that since they seem to be able to choose what will wake them, they must be continuously monitoring what they are hearing while asleep. In psychological terms, it is obvious that attentional and perceptual processes are functioning at some or other level.

Oswald *et al.* (1960) took advantage of the fact that during stage 2 sleep it is commonplace to elicit very large EEG potentials ('K complexes') of about 150 microvolts from peak to trough with even fairly quiet sounds (although K complexes also occur spontaneously, with no stimulation). They instructed their subjects to listen out for particular names, and then played a variety of names to them when they were asleep, including their own. The K complex responses to the target names were larger and more reliable than the responses to control names, and the subjects also almost invariably responded to their own name with a large K complex – another example of the so-called 'cocktail party effect', where from a medley of sounds one unerringly picks out fragments of conversation relating to oneself.

Langford *et al.* (1974) have shown that speed of awakening is faster when a subject's own name is played forwards than it is when played backwards, thus confirming this finding. Anecdotal accounts of being able to listen out when asleep for babies' cries, or other particular sounds, are of course ubiquitous. Not surprisingly, the empirical evidence confirms this universal experience. It could be argued that this behaviour is supported by attentional mechanisms at a simpler level than the more complex processing that goes on during wakefulness. That is, it is one thing to remain vigilant to one of a small number of predetermined sounds, but another to make qualitative judgments about all the sounds that might be heard in the night. The overwhelmingly large EEG slow waves of stages 3 and 4 make it impracticable to record K complexes, and K complexes are absent during REM sleep, so K complex evidence cannot be used to assess perceptual processing during deep slow-wave sleep or REM sleep.

Macdonald *et al.* (1975) extended Oswald *et al.*'s (1960) work in two experiments. They first confirmed that K complexes were more reliably elicited by a subject's own name in stage 2 sleep, and further showed that this effect was measurable in heart rate (HR) and finger plethysmograph (FP – measuring the blood supply to the skin, which is normally reduced by alerting or alarming stimuli). Using these autonomic measures, it was also shown that perceptual discriminations were being made in REM sleep but not in stage 3 and 4 sleep.

In the second experiment, the subjects were conditioned when awake to associate a highly unpleasant blast of noise (produced by 'two pairs of dual freon boat horns') with either a low-pitch or a high-pitch tone of relatively low intensity (40 dB). The conditioned signal elicited FP and HR responses in all stages of slow-wave sleep, including stages 3 and 4, and K complexes in stage 2. Interestingly, these conditioned stimuli (undoubtedly well-established, since responses were made to them in the other sleep stages) did not produce any response during REM sleep. Since the authors had already established that meaningful stimuli can be processed during REM sleep, they argue that these findings support the notion that only cognitively meaningful material is dealt with in this sleep stage. The results could also be interpreted as evidence that the mental activity engaged in during REM sleep is peculiarly efficient at coping with stimuli denoting unpleasant consequences. This is, in essence, the Freudian view of what dreamwork does – rendering potentially upsetting internally generated ideas harmless by transforming them into symbolic codes.

Neither of these studies has thrown much light on the actual level of perceptual processing going on, however, since only particular stimuli, previously defined during wakefulness, were used. The subjects did not have to do more than set up 'templates' to recognize these particular sounds. Nonetheless, the experiments have confirmed that some monitoring of the outside world does go on throughout sleep, so that only signals previously defined as 'important' cause us to wake up.

Shanon (1979) has gone some way towards answering this question. In one experiment, tape-recorded words were played to subjects throughout the night. As in Oswald *et al.*'s experiment the subjects were instructed to listen out for target words (two) and to respond, if they could, by pressing a key taped to their right hand. In addition to non-target English words, the tape recording contained an equal number of words in French, including translations of the target words. As in other experiments, the target words evoked K complexes more frequently than non-target words. Interestingly, more K complexes were produced in response to English words than to French words, indicating that some selection of stimuli on the basis of language was taking place, rather than simply the sound of the particular target words chosen for the subject. This work thus suggests that auditory perceptual analysis continues at a high level of semantic complexity even in stage 2 sleep, even though most sounds are then studiously ignored in the interests of staying asleep.

ESP during sleep

Many of us have a story to tell of happenings that seem totally inexplicable unless we resort to a parapsychological explanation. That is, individuals somehow become aware of facts that are inaccessible to their senses (clairvoyance), have a vision of the future (precognition) or receive a communication from another person with whom there is no physical contact (telepathy). It would be wonderful indeed if we had all these powers, and even the most hardened sceptic is more readily disposed to believe in them than some other equally fatuous proposition, which, if necessary, could be readily disproved.

However, there is a good case to be made for treating apparently impossible claims with some respect – even if they seem impossible to test empirically. Darwin's theory of natural selection and J. J. Thomson's discovery of electrons are examples of advances that were initially treated with almost universal disbelief by the scientists of the time. The empirical investigation of paranormal phenomena began in 1882 with the foundation of the Society for Psychical Research by Henry Sidgwick and Frederick Myers. Despite over a century of effort to establish the validity of such phenomena, an unbiased assessment must be that no clear conclusion can yet be reached.

The credulity of many parapsychologists and their generally sloppy use of scientific control is well documented by David Marks, among others, in a splendid book debunking particular claims about clairvoyance and other psychic powers (Frazier, 1986). The most extraordinary story in this context is that of Project Alpha. In 1979 James S. McDonnell, chairman of the board of the McDonnell-Douglas Aircraft Corporation, granted $500 000 for paranormal research at Washington University. The grant holder announced that he was going to investigate psychokinetic metal bending by children, and advertised for subjects. James Randi, a professional magician, asked two young conjurers he knew to volunteer, and they were the only subjects chosen out of 300 applicants. For three years they were at the McDonnell laboratory, astounding the parapsychologists with their tricks. Throughout this period Randi wrote to the grant holder and offered to attend experimental sessions as a consultant, but with no response. The two conjurers were under strict instructions to answer honestly if they were ever directly asked whether they were cheating. They were not asked. The account of the simple manoeuvres that were sufficient to delude the team of parapsychologists makes hilarious if somewhat chilling reading.

Hansel's (1980) book on ESP provides an excellent account of the total failure of scientists and scientific method in the investigation of ESP and other paranormal phenomena, showing (1) how easily otherwise brilliant scientists can be hoodwinked by charlatans, and (2) how difficult it is to deal with outright fraud by investigators themselves. Science crucially depends on honesty and goodwill and can be subverted all too easily into a spurious scientism, relying on the authority of science more than its methodology. In the twentieth century 'racial theory' and genetics were both exposed to this sort of treatment, with catastrophic political consequences. The consequences of people believing psychic flim-flam are of little importance to anyone other than themselves. Fringe science tends not to be good science, and of course bad science is not science at all. Whatever one's own beliefs, it is therefore essential to consider evidence that is presented as 'scientific' with a certain degree of scepticism.

Clairvoyance and precognition have both been claimed to take place in dreams. Accounts of prophesies in dreams are common to the scriptures of many religions and may also be invoked in more secular epic legends, particularly to establish the divinity, or at least the supernatural authority, of great kings. Even as modern a tyrant as Adolf Hitler ascribed such significance to one of his dreams when serving as a soldier in the trenches during the First World War. This dream (of an explosion and the collapse of the trench) woke him up, and by leaving the shelter of the trench and retreating into the night he saved himself from an actual direct hit that killed most of his comrades. Soldiers might be expected to dream frequently about explosions, and direct hits on trenches were regular occurrences. It is not reported how often Hitler used to flee his trench during the night, but this may also have been a regular habit. As with many anecdotal accounts of prophetic dreams, pure coincidence begins to seem less unlikely the more one considers the matter.

Commoners and humble worshippers are not conventionally expected to presume to prophesy in their dreams. J. W. Dunne's *An Experiment with Time* (1927) rekindled the interest of psychical researchers in the topic. Dunne claimed that in his own dreams he had as much access to future events as to actual memories. Besterman (1933) tested this proposition by asking subjects to keep dream diaries and to send him carbon copies every morning so that a check could be kept on any events predicted by the dreams. The results were very disappointing, and even when Dunne himself served as a subject he only recorded 17 dreams in a four-month period, and these were inconclusively prophetic. Precognition is difficult to deal with in the sleep laboratory because it occurs so rarely (if at all), and no attempts have been made to collect precognitive dreams from REM awakenings.

Telepathic dreams are, however, more amenable to investigation, and a famous series of experiments conducted by Ullman, Krippner and Vaughan – reported in their book *Dream Telepathy* (1973) – comprise the core of evidence on this subject. The procedure in these experiments was to employ two subjects, one as a 'receiver' who would sleep in the laboratory, and the other chosen by the receiver from amongst the members of the laboratory staff as the 'sender', who would remain awake throughout the night. The sender was alerted by the experimenter when the receiver had started a period of REM sleep, and then concentrated on a stimulus picture provided by the experimenter. When the REM sleep period was ending the experimenter awakened the receiver through an intercom, obtained an account of any dreams and asked questions to clarify the imagery of the dreams. In the morning, further questioning took place to establish the precise nature of the images in the dreams that had been interrupted during the night. Tape recordings of a number of such dream reports and interviews were then

matched with the stimulus pictures by an outside judge, who had no knowledge of which stimulus related to which REM sleep episode, nor did the
receivers themselves.

The most spectacular results were obtained when the receiver was Robert
Van de Castle, a well-known parapsychologist, whose dreams matched the
stimuli looked at by the sender on every occasion over eight nights of
recording – a highly statistically significant score. Subsequent attempts to
repeat this feat, in which other experimenters who were well known in sleep
and dream research collaborated, failed to achieve better than chance results
(Belvedere and Foulkes, 1971).

Hansel (1980) has analysed the possible reasons for this failure and
concludes that the original experiments were flawed, in that the experimenter
knew which stimuli were being telepathically transmitted to the receiver. When
questioning the receiver, the experimenter may have even unwittingly provided
cues that facilitated the subsequent matching of tape recordings to pictures.
The experimental conditions were tightened in the subsequent experiments,
and it was therefore not surprising that the results could not be repeated.
(In the later studies it was ensured that experimenters were unaware of which
stimuli were being transmitted, and the choice of sender was limited to three
candidates previously chosen by the investigators.) Adrian Parker (1980)
argues that the less friendly atmosphere in the laboratory when sceptical
scientists were present may have put the receiver off his task during his
dreams: the more rigorous the methodology, the greater the connotation of
suspicion of fraud. The idea that science may be intrinsically inimical to ESP is
understandably invoked by established charlatans, but many investigating
parapsychologists also seem to share a certain ambivalence in their attitude
towards science as a testing ground for their deeply held beliefs. As with all the
other work on parapsychological phenomena, in the case of dream telepathy
one has to return a verdict of 'not proven'.

Sleep learning

One of the earliest applications of the EEG in assessing perceptual and
memory functioning during sleep was directed at 'sleep learning' – the rather
attractive notion that instead of students having to work hard at learning
material during the day, it could be painlessly drilled into them when fast
asleep. In order to test this idea, Emmons and Simon (1956) used EEG
recordings to present material *only* when the subjects were indubitably asleep.
The next day the subjects had no recollection of the material presented to them
during sleep. Despite this clear finding, the idea that sleep learning was
possible persisted in the public mind, popularized, for instance, by Aldous
Huxley's *Brave New World*.

An earlier source for the notion, as mentioned in Emmons and Simon's
paper, was Hugo Gernsbach – whose work I was unable to find in any library.
Eventually, I got in touch with Dr Simon himself and he was kind enough to
provide the following answer:

Hugo Gernsbach wrote to me after our sleep work was published and sent me material he had prepared for his ego-battle with Aldous Huxley. Gernsbach wanted the world to know that he, not Huxley – hypnopedia in *Brave New World* – had been the first to conceive of learning during sleep ...

[Th]ere were many attempts by many types of people to use learning during sleep. The adjunct stories in this regard are in many ways more interesting than the experiments. Various national newspapers and magazines carried stories about it. There were many large, elaborate commercial ventures selling learning-during-sleep machines and tapes – to learn languages, to quiet the mentally disturbed, to modify attitudes, to stop bed-wetting and thumb-sucking, to learn how to be healthy, wealthy, and wise, to learn to play the piano, etc.etc.etc. and to learn these (quoting the ads) 'while you sleep'. There were con men and sincere people selling the idea ... One man tried to con a rich woman out of some money to support his machine which he claimed worked because unlike everyone else's, it sent messages to the sleeping subject above the audio range. One of the largest commercial companies in Los Angeles worked with many of the popular TV shows of the time to get them to make 'learning during sleep' a part of their plot. When people saw Lucy make Desi lose his Cuban accent while he slept (and then change it back when she missed it), that was reality to the viewer and it probably sold lots of machines.

I had better stop. I haven't thought about this for years and it brings back pleasant memories.

Although it seems that nothing is remembered of material presented during sleep, there is evidence that it is heard, and that fairly subtle perceptual processing goes on. Evans *et al.* (1970) told sleeping subjects that their left or right leg would become cramped and uncomfortable when they heard a particular word. The subjects duly moved the appropriate leg as though it was indeed uncomfortable. This 'sleep learning' was retained very well for over a week, and one of the subjects, when retested after six months, again moved the leg in response to the word learnt all those months earlier. No recollection of the cue words could be elicited from the subjects when awake, either by direct questioning or with the use of indirect free-associative techniques.

This result intriguingly suggests a dissociation between waking and sleeping life, reminding one of the dilemma of Chuang-tzu, the Chinese philosopher who posed the following conundrum in the third century BC:

> One night I dreamed that I was a butterfly, fluttering hither and thither, content with my lot. Suddenly, I awoke and I was Chuang-tzu again. Who am I in reality? cfA butterfly dreaming that I am Chuang-tzu or Chuang-tzu imagining he was a butterfly?

To return to the issue of whether learning can take place during a sleep period, Portnoff *et al.* (1968) woke subjects during the night and presented them with lists of words to remember. They were then either allowed to go back to sleep immediately or kept awake for five minutes. The next day, the subjects could not recall many of the words they had seen before immediately returning to sleep, but recalled many more from the trials in which they had been kept awake for a while, although they had shown just as much evidence of learning in both conditions. Similarly Koukkou and Lehmann (1968) found that sentences read out to sleeping subjects were not recalled the next day unless the subjects had both been woken by the presentation and stayed awake (with measurable alpha in EEG) for at least 25 seconds. Awakenings with low-frequency alpha rhythm were associated with poorer subsequent recall than those with high-frequency alpha rhythm (indicating higher cortical arousal). These researchers went on to confirm this finding in a later study, which also showed that the level of cortical activation during the presentation of the stimulus sentences (which were to be learned) was not as crucial in deter-mining their retention in the memory as the level of activation afterwards (Lehman and Koukkou, 1974). Taken together, these experiments suggest that while perceptual processing may go on during sleep, the immediate consolidation of memory in a retrievable form only properly occurs during wakefulness, and is prevented by sleep, or disrupted by going to sleep.

When we are awake, a novel stimulus almost always gains our attention, and may elicit a range of physiological responses that are controlled by the auto-nomic nervous system. Autonomically controlled events, such as changes in heart rate, the constriction of peripheral blood vessels and galvanic skin response, all form part of a pattern of responses known as the orienting response (OR). The gradual diminution of these responses with repeated stimuli (such as, for instance, the ticking of a clock) is called habituation. Habituation is probably the simplest form of learning in our repertoire, although experiments in the former Soviet Union established that habituation of the OR can be in response to the meaning of a stimulus, as well as its physical characteristics (Sokolov, 1963). Conventional methods of assessing whether learning has taken place demand voluntary responses from subjects (for instance, in repeat-ing back lists of words or numbers) and these are obviously inappropriate when the subject is asleep. The physiological methods used to measure the orienting response and its habituation make no such demands, and any learn-ing through habituation should be evident in a sleeper as much as in a waking subject. K complex responses during stage 2 sleep and alpha responses (brief bursts of EEG alpha rhythm) during REM sleep are similarly involuntary responses that may be sensitive to the effects of habituation.

The Russian work established that an OR habituated during wakefulness returns with full force (is dishabituated) if sleep onset intervenes (Sokolov and Paramanova, 1961). However, it is a common observation that we can become accustomed to sleeping in a noisy environment, implying that habituation during sleep does occur. During stage 2 sleep auditory stimuli commonly elicit EEG K complexes – the easily recognized excursions of up to 150 microvolts that also occur spontaneously, and form one of the defining characteristics of this sleep stage. Studying the way in which responses habituate to sounds should cast light on the general issue of how accustomed sounds, whether cocks crowing, traffic noise or nearby church bells, lose their power to disturb our sleep. Unfortunately, despite much experimental work on this subject no simple answer has emerged.

The evidence for habituation during sleep is contradictory. A number of studies have shown that K complexes do not habituate. If stimuli are regularly but infrequently presented during stage 2 sleep they elicit arousal responses as much at the end of the night as they did at the beginning, with little evidence of reduction even during particular phases of stage 2 sleep (Johnson and Lubin, 1967). On the other hand, Firth (1973) has reported successful habituation during sleep: while a novel stimulus almost invariably elicits a K complex, when repeated promptly the rate of responding drops to about 50 per cent within three presentations, and this level of responding persists for as long as that particular stimulus is presented. (The level of spontaneous responding, when no stimuli are presented, is about 20 per cent.) If the interstimulus intervals are long, and the trials are averaged over periods of ten minutes or more (as, for instance, in Johnson and Lubin's 1973 study) no evidence of K complex habituation can be found, while if the intervals between the stimuli are short and regular there is clear evidence of habituation. (This very fast habituation to trains of stimuli with short interstimulus intervals has been confirmed by Caekebeke et al., 1990.)

Swift habituation may or may not have any bearing on how we become accustomed to particular noises over a period of days or weeks. As we have seen, the evidence on learning during sleep is not encouraging in this respect.

Habituation during sleep is therefore swift but incomplete, in that the rate of K complex responses by the habituated subject is still over twice that when no stimuli are presented. It is also fragile, in that changes in sleep stage may cause dishabituation. In addition, different response systems, indexed by EEG and autonomic measures may habituate independently, and behave differently according to sleep stage and interstimulus interval. In Firth's (1973) experiment, the EEG alpha rhythm responses during REM sleep habituated regardless of the length of the interstimulus interval, as did skin potential and heart rate responses during stages 2 and 4.

Behaviour during sleep

It might seem a contradiction in terms to talk of behaviour while asleep. We tend to think of sleep as a sort of oblivious coma, when all interactions with the outside world are suspended. However, people move about quite a lot while asleep, and if they did not they would soon develop bed sores. Paraplegic patients in hospital who cannot move for themselves need to be turned every two hours. Time lapse photography of sleeping subjects shows them in an apparent frenzy of activity during the night, nothing of which they can remember in the morning. This tossing and turning during the night is obviously adaptive and necessary. Sleepwalking is somewhat unusual, although talking, groaning, crying out and laughing are quite common.

Sleep talking

The idea that we might be speaking in our sleep without remembering it in the morning can be worrying, especially if we have things to hide. In *The Adventures of Tom Sawyer*, Tom and Huckleberry Finn were secret witnesses to a murder:

Tom's fearful secret and gnawing conscience disturbed his sleep for as much as a week after this; and at breakfast one morning, Sid said:

'You pitch around and talk in your sleep so much that you keep me awake about half the time.'

Tom blanched and dropped his eyes.

'It's a bad sign,' said Aunt Polly gravely. 'What you got on your mind, Tom?'

'Nothing. Nothing't I know of.' But the boy's hand shook so that he spilled his coffee.

'And you do talk such stuff,' Sid said. 'Last night you said, "It's blood, it's blood, that's what it is!" You said that over and over. And you said, "Don't torment me so – I'll tell." Tell what? What is it you'll tell?' ...

[A]fter that [Tom] complained of toothache for a week, and tied up his jaws every night. He never knew that Sid lay nightly watching, and frequently slipped the bandage free, and then leaned on his elbow listening a good while at a time, and afterwards slipped the bandage back to its place again. Tom's distress of mind wore off gradually, and the toothache grew irksome and was discarded. If Sid really managed to make anything out of Tom's disjointed mutterings, he kept it to himself. (Twain, 1943)

It is difficult to estimate how many people talk in their sleep, because most are unaware of it unless somebody hears them and tells them about it afterwards. An early survey (Gahagan, 1936) found that about two thirds of college students knew that they had talked in their sleep at least once in their lives, and about half the sample were, by their own accounts, persistent sleep talkers. Since this probably underestimates the actual prevalence of sleep talking, as many who do talk will be unaware of it, this aspect of sleeping behaviour must be regarded as commonplace, and essentially normal.

Some people talk more in their sleep than others, varying from the odd word to long monologues. One individual's utterances, tape recorded by friends while he was asleep, have been collected and published as a book (McGregor, 1964). Arthur Arkin, an American psychologist who has specialized in the study of sleep talking, quotes this example:

Attention! Attention! Let me stand on that table, they can't hear me. Attention! Now this is a scavenger hunt. You all got your slips. First one there; a yellow robin's egg! Second one: a wolf's dream! Third: a Welsh shoelace! Fourth: a dirty napkin used by Garbo! Fifth: a tree trunk! Sixth: Valentino's automobile hubcap! Seventh: one of the swans in Swan Lake! Eighth: a Chattanooga choo-choo! Ninth: a bell from the Bell Song in Lakme! Tenth: Yrma Loy! Eleventh: the Hudson River! Twelfth: a teller from the San Francisco Bank of America! Thirteenth: a witch's tail! Fourteenth: David Susskind's mother! Fifteenth: nobody and his sister: That's it! That's it! Now everybody disperse, disperse. Meet back here – three-quarters of an hour, three-quarters of an hour. Come on, we can win, you know we can. Now first of all – oh, let's see – you get one, three, five, seven, nine and twelve; you get two and four: I'll get the rest! O.K., let's go. O.K., everybody back, three-quarters of an hour are up! IT'S OVER!!!!! Uhhh! Aaaahhhh! Ummmmmmmhhhhh! (McGregor, quoted in Arkin, 1966)

This was the shortest of the published somniloquies by Dion McGregor. According to Arkin (who met him), McGregor, a professional writer of lyrics, seemed perfectly sane when awake, if slightly odd. This individual was simply unusually articulate when asleep, and the somewhat weird ideas expressed may represent the sort of autistic or A-type thinking (as described by Bleuler, 1930) that is typical of dreaming sleep (discussed in Chapter 5.)

In a laboratory study of self-confessed chronic sleep talkers, Arkin (ibid.) confirmed the previous finding that for most people sleep talking occurs mostly during non-REM sleep, although about a quarter of episodes occur during REM sleep. He noted large individual differences between his 13 subjects, one of whom was garrulous enough to account for almost half the total number of utterances collected, mostly during REM sleep. The distribution of talking across sleep stages for the other 12 subjects was 19 per cent during REM sleep, 28 per cent during stage 4, 26 per cent during stage 3, 28 per cent during stage 2 and 1 per cent during stage 1. Sleep talking thus occurred in all sleep stages approximately in proportion to their relative prevalence in the night, apart from in stage 1, when the subjects remained unusually silent. Arkin points out that while sleep talking can be said to be associated with a particular sleep stage, the EEG, EOG and EMG measures tend to be so contaminated with movement artifacts during utterances that precise definition of sleep stage is not usually possible while the utterances are going on.

In a further experiment, Arkin *et al.* (1970) recorded sleep talkers' utterances and then immediately woke them to ask what had been going on in their minds. The waking recollections were then compared with the utterances. Evidence of subject-matter concordance between the utterance and the recollections was clearest after REM awakenings, least clear after stage 3 and 4 awakenings, and intermediate after stage 2 awakenings. Thus REM sleep talking typically provides a commentary on the dream in progress, but there is no obvious relation between what is spoken and what is remembered in the case of stage 3 and 4 sleep talking, possibly because of a failure to recall non-REM sleep mentation in any detail rather than because what was said had no bearing whatsoever on what the subject was thinking about.

Arkin (1978) reports experiments in which he attempted to engage sleep talkers in conversation. Many anecdotal accounts exist of such conversations, which can be quite extensive but are not recalled by the sleep talker the next day. Arkin made verbal responses to sleeping subjects' utterances, and also initiated conversations himself, trying at all times to get into the spirit of what the subjects seemed to be saying. He was generally unsuccessful in maintaining extended dialogues, and attributes this to the lack of intimacy between himself and his subjects – most such dialogues are reported as taking place between husband and wife.

Sleepwalking

Getting up and walking about is not consistent with our definition of sleep, so sleepwalking is an intrinsically paradoxical activity. However, it is not uncommon – a survey in Sweden found that 75 out of 212 children had had at least one episode (Klackenberg, 1987). It can persist into adulthood, and like other disorders of arousal – as somnambulism, enuresis, bruxism and night terrors have been called – it tends to occur during periods of psychological stress and therefore will be discussed in this context in the chapters on sleep disorders. However, a behaviour that is experienced by such a large minority of the population can hardly be called abnormal, so it will also be considered here.

After getting out of bed, sleepwalkers may get dressed and then walk about, often repetitively, but may remain standing still. They typically return to bed spontaneously after as much as 30 minutes of activity, and remember nothing about the incident in the morning, when there may be some puzzlement at finding clothing scattered about, removed or put on. Observations of sleepwalkers from times long before EEG/EOG recordings (for example, Roger, 1932) describe them as being able to avoid obstacles, and even on one occasion to negotiate a dangerous walk along the edge of a roof. They tend to adopt rigid, unnatural postures when not moving about. These can be adjusted by a waking observer, and sleepwalkers passively adopt whatever position is imposed on them. This cataleptic behaviour (typical of some schizophrenic patients) is also exhibited by subjects who have been deprived of sleep for an extended period (Anders and Weinstein, 1972). Sleepwalkers respond to verbal suggestions, but do not engage in coherent conversation.

EEG recordings have shown that sleepwalking episodes always begin during stage 3 or 4 sleep (Broughton, 1968). While walking about, the delta waves may attenuate in the adult, to be replaced by faster frequencies, and when returning to bed, the subject normally enters stage 2 sleep. EEG recordings of sleepwalkers naturally tend to be confounded by signals produced by actual physical movement, but careful analysis of recordings of children has shown that the episodes are preceded by an unusual pattern of high-voltage delta rhythms that are in synchrony on both sides of the head. These persist during somnambulism. Sleepwalking is therefore unlikely to have anything to do with dreaming. Rather, it is a condition in which sleep and arousal mechanisms seem to have become locked into an unresolved conflict, with the sleeping victim behaving with the inappropriateness of a malfunctioning automaton.

There is good evidence of a genetic basis to sleepwalking. Monozygotic (identical) twins show a 47 per cent concordance for this behaviour, while dizygotic (non-identical) twins only show a 7 per cent concordance (Bakin, 1970). There are many anecdotal accounts of families whose members all walk in their sleep. For instance, a student who consulted me about the problems caused by her sleepwalking in her hall of residence said that the whole of her family had once woken up in the early hours of the morning to find themselves seated around the kitchen table, where they had all congregated in their sleep.

Waking up

The ending of sleep is as much a function of sleep mechanisms as its initiation. What normally determines when we wake up? The answer to this question depends to a great extent on factors determined by the circadian (24-hour) rhythms that crucially affect sleep, as discussed in Chapter 6. Assuming, however, that sleep has not been displaced from its proper time (at night), what is it that wakes us up in the morning?

Arousal thresholds

We are all exposed to some level of noise during the night, whether living in the depths of the countryside, next to a busy urban thoroughfare or under an approach flight path to a nearby airport. It is of some practical importance to know what levels of noise disturb sleep.

Even before EEG measures of sleep depth were available, a number of experiments were done to estimate arousal thresholds through the night, beginning in 1862, when a student of the psychophysicist Fechner established that there was an early maximum threshold followed by a progressive reduction through the night (Kohlschutter, 1862). Michelson (1897) illustrates the methods used in those early days. He varied the amount of noise by dropping steel balls onto a metal surface from different heights, progressively increasing the length of drop until the subject woke. He did this every half hour throughout the night. Figure (8.1) shows a general decrease in threshold towards the early hours, superimposed on what looks like a 90 minute cycle.

The relation between sleep depth and EEG was first assessed in the 1930s by Blake and Gerard (1937), who applied a constant tone stimulus and then asked their subjects whether they were awake. The nineteenth-century findings

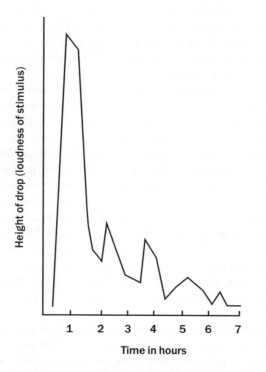

Figure 8.1 Awakening threshold during the night (from Michelson, 1897)

on the decline in depth of sleep over the course of the night were confirmed. Awakening thresholds were also found to be highly correlated with the amplitude and prevalence of delta waves in the EEG. Later, Bonnet (1982) established that slow-wave sleep depth, defined in terms of awakening threshold, is best predicted simply by the number and size of slow waves in the EEG. Estimates of sleep depth during REM sleep vary somewhat, but it seems to be roughly similar to that of stage 2 sleep. Estimates of the absolute magnitude of the stimulus intensity required to awaken people also vary, from around 40 dB to over 90 dB in stage 4 sleep. However, the rank order of slow-wave sleep stages in terms of sleep depth has been consistently confirmed.

The elderly seem particularly sensitive to noise at night, despite their propensity for hearing loss. Sounds that merely cause sleep-stage changes in middle-aged and young subjects will wake up people in their seventies. In one study (Lukas and Kryter, 1970), 70-year-olds were shown to be particularly sensitive to sudden loud noises (a sonic boom) compared with 45-year-olds and eight-year-olds. Such noises almost invariably woke them from REM or stage 2 sleep, and about half the time from stage 4, while younger subjects almost always slept through, whatever their sleep stage. Flyover noise – lower in volume but sustained for longer – woke the elderly on about one third of occasions, compared with about one tenth for the younger subjects.

Waking at a particular time

While most of us rely on an alarm clock if we have to get up at a particular time, there are many individuals who claim to be able to wake up whenever they wish. They may have a ritual such as banging their head on the pillow as many times as the time at which they plan to wake – 'seven times before going to sleep, you'll wake at seven o'clock in the morning'.

How reliably can we estimate time during sleep? People who claim to be able to do it have been shown to be remarkably accurate in their times of awakening (Omwake and Loranz, 1933), and it seems that they do not achieve their punctuality by periodically waking up and looking at the bedside clock. Those who claim not to be able to wake at a specific time are much worse at waking on time than those who claim to be able to do it. An experimental study using EEG/EOG recordings involved a randomly selected group of 22 subjects who had made no particular claims about being able to wake up at a particular time. They were required to wake up at a prearranged time between 2 a.m. and 5 a.m., and were promised extra payment for their services as subjects if they managed to ring a bell within 10 minutes of their allotted time. They were only allowed one response, and had no clocks available to them in the laboratory bedroom, which was windowless, air-conditioned and sound-proofed, so no clues about the time could be picked up from the outside world (Zung and Wilson, 1971).

There was no evidence that sleep patterns differed on experimental nights from those on the two adaptation nights as far as the proportion of sleep stages was concerned, but there were 33 awakenings with bell responses during the 44 experimental nights, and 14 of these were within 10 minutes of the target times. While this level of accuracy is not as good as 'reliable wakers' describe theirs to be, it is strongly statistically significant, indicating that most of us have some ability to assess the passage of time while asleep, and have some control over waking up. (It may have been instructive to perform the same experiment on subjects while awake, without access to a clock and in a featureless environment for between two and five hours – I suspect that people would perform little better when awake, and perhaps worse.)

9

Determinants of Sleep Quality

This chapter is concerned with the effects of various regimes on sleep itself, rather than any behavioural consequences or the influence of biological rhythms on sleep patterns. It is normally very difficult to observe spontaneous behaviour in adults as the mere presence of the observer has a strong effect on behaviour. However, when sleep mechanisms take over there is little scope for self-consciousness, and psychophysiological recordings allow direct measurement of the sleeping brain's free-running rhythms. Its response to experimental manipulation – including for instance changes in the times available for sleep, the deprivation of food or the effects of exercise – not only inform our knowledge of sleep mechanisms but also provide clues about the function of sleep itself.

Food, exercise and sleep

Food and sleep

People frequently ascribe the quality of their sleep (or lack of it) to the previous night's food intake. It is undoubtedly true that indigestion can disturb sleep, but does food have any more subtle effects? The efficacy of Horlicks as a night-time, sleep-inducing drink was tested among a young adult group (mean age 22 years) and an older group (mean age 55 years) (Brezinova and Oswald, 1972). While Horlicks (or another malted milk drink) had little effect on sleep onset time for either group, restlessness during the night was reduced in both, and in the older subjects the advantage conferred by this nourishing drink was greatest in the second half of the night, reducing restlessness and increasing total sleep time.

Crisp and Stonehill (1977) describe a series of studies on the effect on sleep of drastic reductions in food intake. Patients suffering from anorexia nervosa experienced very poor sleep, but when they began to put on weight they slept more, and with fewer interruptions. There was also a change in the proportion of the various stages of sleep during remission, with a massive increase in the amount of deep slow-wave sleep at the expense of light slow-wave sleep. These findings are consistent with the idea that slow-wave sleep is concerned with bodily anabolic (growth) processes, which will be discussed more fully in Chapter 11 in the context of sleep function.

Exercise and sleep

As with food, folklore has much to say about exercise and its effects on sleep – the claim that a good night's sleep is the result of strenuous exercise the preceding day is entirely uncontroversial. However, the experimental evidence on the subject is by no means unambiguous. A number of studies have found that human sleep is unaffected by large amounts of exercise during the day (Hauri, 1966; Baekeland and Laski, 1966; Zir et al., 1971), although experiments on rats have shown that prolonged exercise increases the amount of slow-wave sleep.

Other researchers have compared the effects of exercise on trained and untrained subjects. Some could find no effects (Walker et al., 1978), while others found some increase in slow-wave (stage 3) sleep, but only in trained subjects (Griffin and Trinder, 1978). The large number of studies addressing this issue have varied considerably in the amount of exercise used, the physical fitness of the subjects, the length of time over which they were monitored and the scoring system for slow-wave sleep. Horne (1981) has conducted a comprehensive review of the evidence. (His own work indicated that exercise produces an increase in stage 3 sleep in the first half of the night.) He concludes that, in general, untrained subjects show little, if any, sleep EEG effects after daytime exercise, while trained subjects have increases in stage 3 and 4 sleep in the first recovery night after raised exercise rate. That is, the deep slow-wave sleep stages are elevated if the rate of energy expenditure during the day is increased, rather than merely the total amount.

This conclusion was followed up in an experiment in which subjects' rate of energy expenditure (REE) was elevated to high level, but not for long enough to have a significant effect total energy expenditure (TEE) for the day (Bunnell et al., 1983). The increase in stages 3 and 4 sleep before the first REM sleep period of the night was of the same order as had been found in other experiments where both REE and TEE had been increased (for instance, Griffin and Trinder, 1978). The idea that exercise might increase the need for bodily restitution because of its heavy energy demands, and that deep slow-wave sleep will increase to accommodate this requirement is unsupported by this evidence. Rather, the effects are probably mediated by some other change brought about by exercise, such as increased body temperature.

Horne and Moore (1985) report that athletes who exercise strenuously in their tracksuits, with no cooling, show elevations in rectal temperature of over 2°C and elevated levels of stage 4 sleep the ensuing night. When exercising in light, damp clothing under cooling fans the same athletes show an increase of rectal temperature of only 1°C and no change in sleep from the baseline levels. In a further study, Horne and Reid (1985) demonstrated that passive heating (by lying in a warm bath for 90 minutes) also causes increases in stage 4 sleep. Body temperature clearly affects sleep, in reptiles as well as mammals: in one study on crocodiles, warming the animals produced evidence of slow waves in the sleeping EEG that had not hitherto been observed in reptiles (Warner and Huggins, 1978). Since the total amount of exercise taken does less to determine sleep quality than does the rate achieved, it is unlikely that this effect is mediated through the effect on metabolic rate over the day. It is still unclear whether the changes in human sleep are caused by the effects of warming on the musculature, or whether brain temperature itself can be altered by these procedures and affect the quality of sleep directly. These findings are interesting in suggesting a common sleep mechanism between reptiles and ourselves, and it will be discussed further in Chapter 11, where the functions of sleep are considered.

The effects of drugs on sleep

The most widely used drugs in our society are nicotine, alcohol, caffeine and the benzodiazepines, or minor tranquillizers, some of which are marketed as hypnotic, or sleep-inducing, medicines. All these drugs are taken regularly over long periods of time by a large proportion of the population, so their effects on sleep, if any, must be assessed carefully. Prescribed drugs that affect sleep include antidepressants, major tranquillisers, barbiturates and opiates, and while the numbers of people involved are small (compared, for instance, with smoking) some of these drugs' effects on sleep are considerable. Other 'recreational' drugs such as cannabis, amphetamines, cocaine and LSD are for the most part taken only periodically, except by a few.

Smoking

Soldatos *et al.*, (1980) compared 50 smokers with 50 non-smokers and found that the smokers took longer to get to sleep than the controls, although other sleep parameters were unaffected. Of course, comparing self-selected groups like this may tell us less about the effects of smoking on sleep than about the differences between people who take up smoking and those who choose not to. For instance, the smokers generally drank more coffee than the non-smokers (although the two groups did not differ in their regular consumption of alcohol or other drugs). However, within the smoking group those who drank more than three cups of coffee a day did not take any longer to get to sleep than those who drank less than three cups a day, suggesting that coffee consumption was not an important factor in how long these people took to get to sleep.

Crucial evidence on the effects of smoking on sleep came from eight heavy smokers (consuming an average of two packets a day for over two years) who abruptly stopped smoking. The time spent awake during the sleep period and sleep onset latency were immediately reduced, with the time taken to get to sleep dropping from an average of 52 minutes when smoking to 18 minutes on the first two nights after giving it up. This improvement in sleep quality was maintained by the four subjects who continued to abstain for two weeks.

While smokers adapt to some of the effects of nicotine, such as nausea, studies have shown that it continues to elevate heart rate, blood pressure and general psychophysiological arousal in even the most dedicated addicts. These immediate effects of nicotine are probably sufficient to explain the delay of sleep onset by an average of half an hour.

Alcohol

Much attention has been focused on REM sleep following drinking, as alcohol is essentially a sedative, or a cortical-depressant drug like the barbiturates, which are known to suppress REM sleep. The effect of 1 gram per kilogram body weight (equivalent to about a quarter of a bottle of spirit for an average-sized man) taken on one occasion only has been reported to inhibit REM sleep to some extent during the ensuing night (Yules *et al.*, 1966). When this regime was continued for five days, however, REM sleep time recovered, and, in fact, exceeded the baseline levels. Over a four-day recovery period the REM sleep time declined to baseline values. This finding was in general confirmed by another study using a slightly lower dosage (0.9 grams per kilogram) and appreciably more subjects (Rundell *et al.*, 1972). There was also some evidence that the reduction in REM sleep was confined to the first half of the first night after drinking. In those subjects, the REM sleep levels in the second half of the night were elevated, as if in compensation for the REM sleep lost during the first half. On the second and third nights after the same dose, there was no reduction in REM sleep time, and no REM 'rebound' was noticeable on recovery nights.

Sleep onset latency was subsequently found to be reduced with moderately high doses (Stone, 1980), and while objective measures with lower doses (0.32 and 0.64 grams per kilogram) did not reveal statistically significant effects on latency, the subjects reported that they felt they had fallen asleep more quickly.

Alcohol is metabolized relatively quickly, and of a dose of 1 gram per kilogram body weight taken before bedtime, about 50 per cent is eliminated in the first four hours. Consequently, its effects on sleep are not simple even within one night, and over extended periods of regular drinking sleep patterns may also undergo progressive changes. Evidence from young healthy volunteers suggests that moderate drinking does no harm to sleep, and a nightcap may actually help them get to sleep. If it were being assessed as a hypnotic drug, alcohol would come out as being moderately effective and relatively harmless (compared for instance with barbiturates).

A possibly serious side effect of drinking, however, has been reported amongst elderly patients suffering from chronic emphysema, a chronic obstructive pulmonary disease (Easton *et al.*, 1987). In these patients, 1 gram of alcohol per kilo of body weight reduced total REM sleep time from about one hour to about 25 minutes and reduced total sleep time by almost an hour. In addition, the oxygen levels in the patients' arterial blood, estimated from analyses of expired air, were found to be significantly lower than on control nights, and was accompanied by some elevation in heart rate. Oxygen desaturation was especially marked during REM sleep. Although alcohol does not seem to be a direct cause of cardiac arrhythmia, as Easton *et al.* point out, failure to maintain adequate levels of oxygen in the blood provides an additional challenge to the cardiovascular system. Some widely advertised palliatives for bronchial conditions (such as Night Nurse in the UK) contain an appreciable amount of alcohol which, when added to a moderate alcohol intake earlier in the evening, could be enough to disturb and reduce patients' sleep, rather than improve it.

Caffeine

Caffeine does not simply keep you awake – that is, increases sleep latency – it also reduces the amount of deep slow-wave sleep, increases the number of arousals and, at high doses (300 milligrams), causes early waking after only three hours or so of sleep (Gaillard *et al.*, 1989). A cup of strong coffee contains about 100 milligrams of caffeine.

Anxiolytics

The minor tranquillizers, or anxiolytics (anxiety-reducing drugs), first became available in the early 1960s after the discovery and patenting of chlordiazep-oxide (Librium) and diazepam (Valium). While many different benzodiaze-pines have now been developed, these two remain typical and are still brand leaders. Their usage increased consistently over 15 years, reaching a peak in the mid-1970s. The prescribing level in England, according to data collected annually by the Department of Health, stood at 12.3 million in 1980 and reached its lowest in the early 1990s (for example 5.1 million in 1993), staying at about that level until 1999. Diazepam was by far the most commonly prescribed anxiolytic.

While chlordiazepoxide is widely prescribed as an anxiolytic, like some of the other benzodiazepines, it has frequently been prescribed to patients who present themselves with sleep problems. Hartmann (1968) reports that it increases the time spent asleep without reducing REM sleep, but that it reduces the amount of deep slow-wave sleep (stage 4) and over long periods REM sleep may be reduced. After a month of drugged sleep there is no strong evidence of REM rebound in a recovery month. Diazepam's effects on sleep seem to be similar in most respects (Hartmann, 1978).

Hypnotics

Barbiturates used to be widely prescribed as hypnotics, but non-barbiturate alternatives, developed from benzodiazepines, have now almost entirely re-placed them. This change took place in the late 1960s and was a response not only to a surge in deaths through overdose and the availability of relatively non-toxic alternatives, but also to advances in knowledge about the effects of barbiturates on sleep, and of their addictiveness, as revealed by EEG studies. Among others, Oswald and Priest (1965) showed that barbiturates reduced the amount of REM sleep when first taken, like many other drugs. Tolerance developed over a few days and the level of REM sleep returned to normal, but on withdrawal the habitual user experienced vivid dreams and nightmares, with frequent night-time awakenings caused by a massive REM sleep rebound, with double the usual amount of REM sleep for a period of five or six weeks. These effects often caused patients to return to their doctors to ask for repeat prescriptions, ensuring drug dependency amongst otherwise healthy people.

The benzodiazepine-derived hypnotics (such as nitrazepam and Mogadon) appeared to be innocuous in comparison, and by the mid-1970s they had become the drugs of choice for doctors treating sleep disorders. It subsequently became apparent that some patients were becoming very dependent on these drugs, and that the effects of withdrawal could be extremely severe. Hence there was a marked reduction in the number of prescriptions for benzodiazepines to treat anxiety, falling from about 16 million in 1976 and levelling off at about five million between 1991 and 1999. The number of prescriptions for hypnotics (largely benzodiazepines) did not undergo the same dramatic reduction over this period. (See Figure 12.1 on page 181 for the prescribing trend in England over the period 1981–99.)

There have been a good number of EEG studies of the effects of various hypnotics on sleep, but not all of them have been as extensive as they ought to have been, or have not used appropriate subjects. Hypnotics are usually prescribed for a fortnight or a month, but repeat prescriptions may be issued many times. The time course of drug use and recovery is normally of the order of weeks rather than days. However, most empirical studies of the psycho-physiological effects of these drugs only take recordings for a week or so – typically two nights of baseline recordings, three nights on medication and three nights' recovery. This may be sufficient to give an indication of the pharmacological action of the preparation, but cannot provide valid data on the effects of the drug in the real world. An honourable exception to the snapshot approach is the work of Ernest Hartmann (1976), who studied the effects of a variety of drugs on sleep in a series of extended experiments, taking periods of drug use of three weeks, rather than three days, and conducting follow-up investigations for up to six weeks after withdrawal. (More recent studies of the long-term effects of these drugs and the effects of their withdrawal, as well as the short-term effects of drugs with short half-lives in the body, will be discussed in Chapter 12.)

Another flaw in many laboratory studies on the effects of hypnotics on sleep is that they usually involve healthy volunteers in their early twenties – typically university students. The majority of patients receiving medication for sleep problems are over 40, and many are quite elderly. It is admittedly quite difficult to recruit older people for sleep laboratory experiments, but perhaps the development of home recording systems will facilitate this sort of research in the future.

Nitrazepam (marketed as Mogadon in the UK) is widely prescribed as a hypnotic in the UK and Australasia. Flurazepam, a similar drug, is more often the drug of choice in the US. Like Valium and Librium they are both benzodiazepine derivatives. Unlike barbiturates, they do not suppress REM sleep when used in normal clinical doses (Haider and Oswald, 1971; Johns and Masterton, 1974). Benzodiazepines vary somewhat in their particular effects on sleep; for instance, flunitrazepam tends to suppress the first REM sleep period of the night, thus increasing REM onset latency, although it does not depress the total amount of REM sleep in the night by very much (Belyavin and Nicholson, 1987). With the first dose, stage 4 sleep is increased in the first half of the night but decreases later. With repeated doses, stage 4 sleep may be abolished altogether. Growth hormone is normally released in the early part of the sleep period, at the same time as the first episodes of stage 4 sleep. Flurazepam, a drug with similar effects on slow-wave sleep (like flunitraze-pam, this has not been prescribed in the UK since the mid 1980s), has been shown not to interfere with the timing of growth hormone release, despite the fact that it abolishes stage 4 sleep (Weitzman and Pollak, 1982). It has also been reported that the amplitude of slow waves is reduced by benzodiazepines, but not the actual number, making the scoring of stage 4 sleep particularly difficult (Feinberg et al., 1979; Gaillard and Blois, 1989). Possibly, therefore, the effects of flunitrazepam and flurazepam may not be as disruptive to slow-wave sleep as a reading of the stage changes might suggest: that is, while the drug modifies the EEG signs of deep slow-wave sleep, it may not interfere with sleep's essential physiological functions.

Chloral hydrate, like the barbiturates, initially suppresses REM sleep, but causes a massive rebound on withdrawal (Hartmann, 1978). However, it is rapidly metabolized, unlike the barbiturates and many benzodiazepines, whose half-lives in the body extend to 14–30 hours. Most hypnotics have a long half-life in blood, so their effects are not confined to the night, when taken in the evening. Experiments have shown that both benzodiazepines and barbiturates can depress performance on simple psychomotor tasks the day after administration. This is perhaps not surprising in the case of barbiturates, but it is somewhat unexpected in the case of benzodiazepine, which is normally credited with tranquillizing without sedating (Walters and Lader, 1970). Benzodiazepines with short half-lives (three to five hours), such as temazepam, have received increasingly enthusiastic medical approval, with prescriptions for temazepam in England now running at over double those for nitrazepam, while 20 years ago 10 times more nitrazepam was prescribed than temazepam. Nitrazepam's long half-life means that it steadily builds up in the blood if it is consistently taken each night, and therefore it also tends to cause daytime drowsiness. None of these drugs are ideal, but the benzo-diazepines have certainly proved preferable to the barbiturates they replaced, and are still the hypnotics most likely to be prescribed by doctors in the UK. It is perhaps the case that they have become overprescribed, especially in respect of repeat prescriptions. Like other benzodiazepines, they are habit-forming in some people when taken over extended periods of time. The Com-mittee for the Safety of Medicines in the UK warned in 1983 that as many as 40 per cent of patients who were regularly taking benzodiazepines may have become physiologically dependent on them. That is, they would suffer with-drawal symptoms, including anxiety attacks and sleeplessness, if they stopped taking them.

Zopiclone is one of a group of newly developed drugs that are similar to the benzodiazepines in their pharmacological action but have different receptor sites in the brain. Zopiclone first appeared in the UK in 1989 and has become a common treatment for insomnia. It acts rapidly and typically induces sleep within 30 minutes. It is also claimed that while it has many of the desirable properties of the benzodiazepines, the development of tolerance is less marked than with the benzodiazepines, the withdrawal effects are less and the interactions with other drugs, such as alcohol and other sedatives, are also less (Schneerson, 1999). Zolpidem, another new hypnotic, has similar pharmaco-logical effects but a very short half-life (2.5 hours in young adults, 3.0 hours in the elderly), so there are few residual effects the next day. An analysis of over 50 clinical trials has established its efficacy in inducing sleep and preserving normal sleep architecture, including deep slow-wave sleep (Priest *et al.*, 1997). It is not yet widely prescribed in the UK, although since its introduction in 1994 the rate of increase in prescriptions in England has closely paralleled the rate for zopiclone between 1989 and 1994.

Melatonin

Melatonin is a naturally occuring hormone that is secreted by the pineal gland, as described in Chapter 6. Although its physiological effects are not completely understood, it has been used as a drug, particularly in the US, where it is classed as a dietary supplement and is therefore not controlled by the Food and Drugs Administration. Preparations sold in the US as containing melatonin vary widely in quality, with some containing no melatonin at all (Schneerson, 1999).

Its major advocated use has been to control jet lag, as it is considered to be capable of resetting the circadian cycle. Taken in the evenings when travelling eastward, it should cause a phase advance, and taken in the mornings when travelling westward, it should help delay sleep onset.

Another application of melatonin's ability to reset the sleep-phase cycle in humans has been in blind patients, who have disturbed circadian rhythms as a result of the failure of daylight to entrain these rhythms. Lockley *et al.* (2000) have assessed the efficacy of this treatment in seven blind subjects whose circadian cycles, estimated by measuring urinary cortisol and 6-sulphatoxy-melatonin (aMT6s), were free running. They found that melatonin could indeed entrain the phase and period of the circadian cycle, but only if it was administered at the right time of day.

Tricyclic antidepressants

Amitryptyline, a typical tricyclic antidepressant (TCA), is regularly prescribed to relieve depression, and to treat elderly patients with sleep problems. It has been shown to cause a slight increase in total sleep time and a reduction in REM sleep (with no adaptation over a 30-day period), with a relatively short-lived REM sleep rebound upon withdrawal (Dunleavy and Oswald, 1973).

In the UK, the number of prescriptions for this drug fell from about three million in 1975 to less than one million by 1985, and the number has re-mained relatively low ever since. This does not indicate that fewer people are complaining of depression, but more probably that doctors are increasingly tending to prescribe non-barbiturate hypnotics for patients to whom they might have given tricyclics in the past.

A more recently developed group of drugs – the selective seratonin reuptake inhibitors (SSRIs) – have been described as stablemates of the TCAs and have specific effects on brain chemistry. While a number of studies have assessed their effects on sleep over brief periods of time, it is only at the Psycho-pharmacology Unit of Bristol University that ecologically valid, long-term trials have been conducted. Wilson *et al.* (1995) report a study with home-based sleep assessments at baseline, three weeks after drug treatment onset and twelve weeks after drug treatment onset. The 12 patients who completed the trial showed an initial reduction in total sleep time, recovering by week three. REM latency increased early in treatment, but had recovered towards baseline by week 12. The suppression of REM sleep that typifies TCAs was evident throughout the trial, but there was evidence of adaptation by week twelve. This study again demonstrates the importance of measuring the effects of drugs over long periods of time, thus allowing the adaptation process to take place – particularly when, as with antidepressants, the patients who take them are likely to be taking them for months if not years.

Monoamine oxidase inhibitory antidepressants

Monoamine oxidase inhibitors (antidepressants that act directly on brain metabolism) actually abolish REM sleep as they take effect on the patient's mood, and it has even been proposed that it is the removal of REM sleep that causes the therapeutic effect (Dunleavy and Oswald, 1973; Vogel *et al.*, 1975). While this is the most marked effect of these drugs on sleep, it is misleading to state that it is their only effect. Phenelzine also reduces the amount of slow-wave activity in the EEG in slow-wave sleep, virtually abolishing stage 3 and 4 sleep just as it does REM sleep. Another, shorter-acting monoamine oxidase inhibitory drug, brofaremine, similarly suppresses REM sleep and reduces deep slow-wave sleep (Steiger *et al.*, 1987). Surprisingly enough, patients seem to cope without these stages of sleep, and even become less depressed.

EEG/EOG measures of sleep processes seem to be so stereotyped in the population as a whole, following such formal rules, and so successful in predicting mental states such as dreaming that one might identify them not only as indexing normal sleep processes but also as an inevitable consequence of them. Evidence such as this may suggest that they are merely the epiphenomena of (or signs normally accompanying) processes that can, in certain circum-stances, carry on without them. Otherwise, we would have to conclude that the benefits normally conferred by deep slow-wave sleep and REM sleep were in fact unnecessary in patients suffering from depression. If this were true, what would it say about the function of these sleep stages for the rest of us?

Beta blockers

Beta blockers block the beta adrenergic receptors and are normally prescribed to control the cardiovascular system by reducing heart rate and blood pres-sure. Another of their effects is to reduce muscular tremor, and they have been used by musicians and sportsmen (such as shooters and snooker players) to control anxiety-related tremors during public performances and competitions.

Patients who take these drugs to control hypertension, angina or cardiac arrhythmia often complain to their doctors that vivid dreams and nightmares are disrupting their sleep. These drugs achieve their desired effect peripherally and have no need to cross the blood–brain barrier into the central nervous system. Some beta blockers (the hydrophilic group, including atenolol) do not have any effect on sleep parameters or produce dream disturbance (Betts and Alford, 1985). The hydrophilic drugs do not cross the blood–brain barrier very effectively, unlike the lipipholic drugs (for example, propanalol and meto-prolol) (Wood, 1984), which seem to be the ones responsible for dream disturbances. In high doses they can also suppress REM sleep, and have even been used in the treatment of narcolepsy (Meier-Ewart *et al.*, 1985).

10

The Sleep of Animals

All animals sleep for at least part of the 24 hours. The majority of species sleep at night, when in most places the temperature drops and it is dark and cool, if not cold. Others have evolved to take advantage of prey, or the absence of daytime predators, by being active at night. Nocturnal animals either sleep during the day or take naps at night, or both. In this chapter some general points will be made about sleep in animals, and the sleep habits of a selection of species will be described, using both observational and electrophysiological evidence.

Goal-directed (appetitive) behaviours before settling down to sleep consist, at their simplest, of finding an appropriate place and adopting a sleeping posture. More complex 'sleep rituals' are displayed by some animals. Borbely (1986) describes how the fox begins by digging a shallow hole in the ground, and then walks around it in ever tighter circles until its nose is almost touching the tip of its tail. When it eventually lies down it lifts it head to look around before burying it under its tail. Dogs display a similar circling behaviour, although less obsessively. Only narcoleptics (animal or human) drop down asleep from a standing position without some preparatory activity.

The postures adopted by sleeping animals are also highly predictable. It is unclear whether this is the result of instinct or an aspect of synergy – the inevitable outcome of anatomy. An adult giraffe cannot curl up like a kitten, and is obliged by its anatomy to sleep in a sitting position. Bats, on the other hand, could presumably sleep lying down, but always choose to roost hanging upside down. Sleep habits can be among the most stereotyped behaviours that animals display, and it would not be unjustifiable to describe them as instinctive, in the same sense that courtship rituals and nest-building in birds are described as instinctive.

Appetitive instinctual activity usually leads to active consummatory behaviour such as feeding, copulation or egg-laying following foraging, courtship or nest-building, respectively. In many animals, appetitive behaviour is composed of a series of highly specific sequences of action, triggered by appropriate cues in the environment, normally offered by other animals. For instance, courtship behaviour in the male stickleback is triggered ('released') by the sight of a female with an abdomen bulging with eggs to be fertilized. Sleep is much less socially determined. It could perhaps be thought of as a function that is as inevitable as defecation (which also involves stereotypical behaviour in some animals). However, the ethologist Niko Tinbergen (1951) argues that

152

behaviours that are followed by sleep or rest ought to be described as goal-directed, appetitive activities, and despite the inactive nature of sleep it can still be regarded as a consummatory activity so far as ethology is concerned.

Mammals

Electrophysiological studies have shown that the sleep of mammals is strikingly similar to that of humans, in that slow-wave sleep alternates with REM sleep (or paradoxical sleep as it is more usually called in animals). The only exception is the echidna, or spiny anteater, a burrowing, egg-laying Australian monotreme that sleeps more than eight hours a day without showing any signs of paradoxical (REM) sleep (Allison and Goff, 1968). During sleep, the changes in brain state in animals, as measured by EEG/EOG recordings, are just as predictable as in human beings.

Inevitably, what we know about animal sleep either comes from detailed laboratory studies (including EEG/EOG recordings) or from less well-controlled observations in the wild, of the amount of time that animals spend resting, together with more or less anecdotal accounts of the behaviours animals engage in before they sleep. However, estimates of sleep from laboratory studies can be misleading, and may under- or overestimate sleep duration in the free-living animal. A frightened or distressed animal may not sleep, and one report on the sleep of cattle actually claimed that they do not sleep at all because the two animals studied did not sleep during a 24-hour period (Merrick and Sharp, 1971). On the other hand, animals that have become accustomed to the laboratory environment may sleep considerably more than usual. Estimates of the amounts of sleep taken by rabbits and cats, for instance, can vary considerably, depending presumably on how tame the individuals are and the amount of environmental stimulation to which they are exposed in the laboratory. The amounts of reported sleep per 24 hours range from less than three hours in some grazing animals to almost 20 hours in bats and opossums.

Both sleep quantity and quality vary enormously amongst mammals, but some coherence is apparent when living habits are taken into account. Animals that normally rest underground or in a den are 'secure' sleepers, and sleep longer and more soundly than those which sleep in the open. In addition, animals that spend a good deal of their time feeding (such as the grazing ungulates) sleep less than, and differently from, animals that have less demand on their time, such as omnivorous pigs or rats. Predators with little to fear, such as lions, sleep differently from animals that are regularly preyed upon.

From an analysis of known sleep habits and ecological variables such as safety of sleeping place and severity of predation, Allison and Cicchetti (1976) conclude that precariousness of lifestyle tends to be associated with reduced levels of paradoxical sleep, while the amount of slow-wave sleep is best predicted by overall body size. That is, larger species have less slow-wave sleep. The significance of correlations such as these will be discussed more fully in the next chapter. In this descriptive chapter, it is only necessary to indicate the importance of customary living habits in determining sleep habits.

Figure 10.1   Rats sleeping in the light (left) curl up with their eyes closed, while in the dark (right) they stretch out and their eyes remain open (from Chenen *et al.*, 1983)

The rat

The laboratory rat is one of the most thoroughly studied animals in terms of sleep. It sleeps 'polyphasically' – that is, periods of sleep lasting 10 minutes or so are interspersed with short periods of wakefulness throughout the day (the rat is also nocturnal). About 13 hours in every 24 may be spent asleep. Each sleep period begins with slow-wave sleep, as in humans. The rat's EEG changes from a low-voltage pattern with theta rhythms (about seven cycles per second) to large slow waves (Borbely and Neuhaus, 1979). Muscle tone drops, and then drops further when the animal enters paradoxical (REM) sleep, when the EEG is again low voltage (although not as low as when awake), with rapid, regular, fast activity. Not only are there rapid eye movements during this sleep stage, but also the paws and whiskers twitch and quiver.

When sleeping in the light, the rat keeps its eyes closed and typically curls up, but light-sensitive camera observations have shown that in the dark the animals go into paradoxical sleep stretched out and with their eyes open (Chenen *et al.*, 1983) (Figure 10.1) Periods of slow-wave sleep prior to paradoxical sleep onset are very short indeed, and rats occasionally even go straight into paradoxical sleep (with open eyes) from wakefulness. Although laboratory rats sleep mainly in the light, it is likely that wild rats withdraw to dark places to do so, when their sleep must follow the rather paradoxical pattern observed by Chenen *et al*. Despite years of study by humans, until recently the rat seems to have preserved some of its secrets of sleep!

The rabbit

Rabbits differ from rats in that they sleep less – about eight hours – and have less paradoxical (REM) sleep (just under an hour in all). During paradoxical sleep they do not show the suppression of muscle tone that is typical of REM sleep in humans and paradoxical sleep in other mammals (Pivik *et al.*, 1986). Rather, they flatten their ears against their necks during paradoxical sleep, as though there is some relaxation of the muscles controlling the ears. Like rats, rabbits sleep polyphasically. In the wild they are active at dawn and dusk, and rest during the day.

The cat

Cats usually lie down to sleep, but sometimes fall asleep crouching. Unlike rats and rabbits, they may sleep continuously for hours on end, and have no clear circadian cycle, taking naps at any time of day or night. Cats in the laboratory sleep for up to 16 hours a day (Delorme *et al.*, 1964).

Reidun Ursin (1968) has devised a classificatory system for the scoring of feline EEG that gives two distinct slow-wave sleep stages as well as para-doxical (REM) sleep. Most other animals (except primates and humans) have only been credited with a single, undifferentiated stage of slow-wave sleep. According to Ursin, the EEG in alert cats is low voltage with fast activity (above 16 cycles per second), while in the resting animal there are occasional bursts of waves of four to eight cycles per second. During light slow-wave sleep, cats' EEGs show signs of spindles of 12–14 cycles per second, not unlike the human sleep spindles in stage 2 sleep. There is also some higher-voltage activity at one to four cycles per second. During deep slow-wave sleep the EEG is dominated by high-voltage slow waves of one to four cycles per second, together with sleep spindles. In paradoxical sleep there is low-voltage, fast activity in the EEG, with frequent eye movements and a lack of muscle tone in the neck.

As in normal human beings, paradoxical sleep never made an appearance in Ursin's cats at sleep onset, and a period of slow-wave sleep invariably preceded the first paradoxical sleep episode. The feline cycle length (between successive periods of paradoxical sleep) appeared to be relatively constant at about 30 minutes. In Ursin's study the cats that slept soundest (with the most deep slow-wave sleep) also had the most paradoxical sleep, and light slow-wave sleep appeared to replace deep slow-wave sleep in the lighter sleepers, which slept just as long as the deep sleepers. These differences between indi-viduals may reflect the degrees of tameness among these animals, which were recruited from Norwegian farms.

Farm animals

Yves Ruckebusch and his associates have studied a variety of farm animals' sleep patterns – horses, cattle, sheep and pigs (Ruckebusch, 1972a). Cattle, they found, spend about 12 hours out of every 24 lying down, and about a third of this time is spent asleep, according to EEG criteria. During para-doxical sleep the cow's muzzle, which is otherwise kept cool and moist if not wet, suddenly becomes dry, causing the surface temperature to rise by as much as 4°C. This temperature rises in spite of a general reduction in blood flow to the snout and the peripheral blood vessels in the cow's head, and is a direct consequence of the lack of regular cooling by the evaporation of nasal fluids (Toutain and Ruckebusch, 1972).

The other two thirds of lying down time is characterized by a drowsy state that varies in depth but seems to be intermediate between wakefulness and slow-wave sleep in terms of EEG. In humans, drowsiness normally very quickly resolves into deeper sleep or is terminated by an awakening, but in all four of the farm animals considered here it seems to be a stable, distinct state.

Table 10.1 The sleep of ungulates (hours and minutes per 24 hours)*

	Awake	Drowsy	Slow-wave sleep	Paradoxical sleep	Standing
Horse	19.13	1.55	2.05	0.47	22.01
Cow	12.33	7.29	3.13	0.45	9.55
Sheep	15.57	4.12	3.17	0.34	16.50
Pig	11.07	5.04	6.04	1.45	5.10

* Measured over two to three days for three animals from each species (from Ruckebusch, 1972a)

In Ruckebusch's laboratory, horses spent relatively little time in this state (two hours) while sheep, pigs and cows drowsed for four, five, and seven hours respectively (Table 10.1). Ruckebusch (1972a) acknowledges that animals in the field may spend less time asleep than these creatures – chosen for their docility – did in the laboratory, but what remains important about this study was the discovery of a stable drowsy state that is distinct from sleep, and the charting of broad patterns of sleep in these different species.

Drowsiness in the cow is a time of rumination. When Ruckebusch (ibid.) changed the cows' feed from long hay to pelleted ground grass their need to ruminate was greatly decreased, and consequently the time spent in drowsiness reduced from 30 per cent of the 24 hours to a mere 5 per cent, with increases in slow-wave sleep and wakefulness. Observations of free-ranging cows and horses have revealed that the amount of time spent lying is less variable than the time spent resting and standing (which depends largely on the amount of time spent standing and feeding) (Arnold, 1985), although the weather has an effect on the amount of time spent lying, with cows tending to stand in the shade on hot (above 24°C) and humid days. On cold and windy days cows tend to lie down when resting, while on milder winter days they stand more than in the summer, perhaps in order to minimize the heat loss (and discomfort) incurred when lying on cold wet ground.

Free-ranging horses similarly vary somewhat in the amount of time they spend lying down, and observations of the wild horses of the Carmargue have shown that stallions spend twice as long lying down as mares (Ruckebusch et al., 1970). The reason for this is obscure.

Ruckebush (1972b) has also studied sleep in the fetal and newborn lamb. Of course, lambs are born at a much later stage of development than human babies, and are able to stand up almost straight away and to run about on their first day of life. Gestation in the sheep is 150 days. Two weeks before parturition the fetus has fully developed sleep patterns, alternating between slow-wave sleep, paradoxical sleep and wakefulness, with short periods of drowsiness. It enjoys more than twice as much slow-wave sleep as an adult sheep and about 10 times as much paradoxical sleep. During the first day of life the amount of wakefulness increases dramatically, mainly at the expense of paradoxical sleep (which is still four to five times as much as in the adult). Drowsiness in the lamb does not seem to have the stability it has in adult sheep, with most episodes lasting less than 10 minutes.

The giraffe

This beautiful and improbable animal feeds and ruminates almost constantly, and sleeps very little. It is also an extremely timid creature, which makes systematic observation difficult. Studies at Frankfurt Zoo (Immelman and Gebbing, 1962) and Buffalo Zoo in New York (Kristal and Noonan, 1979) indicate that sleep is polyphasic, with three to eight reclining episodes per night, lasting between one or two and 75 minutes. The animals hold their heads and necks erect most of the time while on the ground, sometimes with their eyes open. The one or two episodes of paradoxical sleep per night begin with the animal lowering its head, either along its back, like a swan, or onto the ground facing its tail, or in front. There is some evidence that younger animals favour the swan posture. The photograph in Figure 10.2, which was taken by myself and Kelvin Murray at Regents Park Zoo in London, is of a seven-month-old giraffe. Taken with infrared film with a four-second exposure, this picture shows the typical reclining posture, with head and neck erect.

Figure 10.2   The giraffe sleeps with its head erect most of the time

The eyes are in fact shut. (The lids are light-coloured, and comparisons with photographs taken during the day show that when the eyes are open they appear dark on infrared film.)

It would take a chapter by itself to give an account of the taking of this photograph, which is one of a series taken by time-lapse (every ten minutes). This not only presented considerable technical difficulties photographically, but was also made extremely difficult by the timidity of the animals. Even after a month of regular visits, most of the five giraffes – all zoo-bred and handled daily by their keeper – avoided the camera by retiring to the pen next door.

A more systematic study of eight giraffes at Emmen Zoo in Zurich (Tobler and Schwierin, 1996) found that adults sleep standing as well as recumbent, and during paradoxical sleep their heads rest on the ground. Total sleep time in the adults studied was 4.6 hours, with paradoxical sleep taking up about 15 minutes of this. The youngest animal (two months old) had about 30 minutes' paradoxical sleep, but no more total sleep than the adults. Short naps were also taken in the afternoons.

Dolphins and porpoises

These animals, as improbable in their own way as the giraffe, spend most of their lives in deep water that is rarely calm enough to rest on the surface without continuing to swim. However, EEG recordings of Black Sea porpoises and dolphins have shown that they do sleep regularly (Mukhametov *et al.*, 1977; Mukhametov and Polyakova, 1981). The most surprising aspect of their sleep is that it is normally hemispherically independent. That is, one half of the brain shows all the EEG signs of slow-wave sleep while the other remains alert, with low-voltage, mixed-frequency EEG patterns. Over an eight-hour period the two halves of the brain take turns to sleep, showing both light and deep slow-wave sleep. Muscle tone is always high, and there are no rapid eye movements to indicate paradoxical (REM) sleep. In fact, one or other eye is commonly open all the time. In these animals, each eye's neural output is entirely connected to the opposite hemisphere. It seems, however, that the opening and closing of the eyes is unrelated to which hemisphere is asleep at the time.

It is possible that the cortical arousal in the 'non-sleeping' hemisphere reflects some sort of paradoxical sleep, or that the functions of paradoxical sleep are served during this state in a way that is as yet unclear. This odd arrangement has obviously evolved to make it possible for these air-breathing animals to maintain respiration in the water while sleeping. Interestingly, there is never any point at which these animals are completely immobile. (Some theories of sleep function argue that the primary purpose of sleep is to conserve energy by maintaining immobility.)

Primates

The sleep of the chimpanzee is very similar to human sleep. According to Freemon *et al.*, 1971), it is even possible to apply directly the criteria for human sleep stages, using the standardized scoring system for human sleep stages (Rechtschaffen and Kales, 1968). The only difference is that EMG (neck muscle tone) is not very helpful in discriminating REM sleep in the chimpanzee. Freemon *et al.*'s two four-year-olds slept for about 10.5 hours per night. The proportions of the four slow-wave sleep stages and REM sleep were in the normal range for human subjects, although stage 4 (at 10 per cent) was slightly less than might be expected in an adolescent. Another study using adult chimpanzees (Bert *et al.*, 1970) had similar findings, except that the proportion of REM sleep was only 15 per cent compared with the four-year-olds' 23 per cent, and the total time spent asleep was about an hour shorter. These differences could be entirely due to the age differences between the animals in the two studies.

Birds and reptiles

Birds

In many ways, birds sleep rather like mammals. That is, EEG recordings show periods of high-voltage, slow-wave sleep alternating with periods of low-voltage EEG, associated with rapid eye movements. As with mammals, para-doxical (REM) sleep always follows a period of slow-wave sleep, although in birds the length of time spent in paradoxical sleep is very short, varying between one and 30 seconds. While muscle tone is not completely lost in roosting birds during paradoxical sleep, their heads do show signs of drooping (Key and Marley, 1962). Young chickens, for instance, sleep perching, with their heads bent forwards and wings drooping. More rarely they sit down to sleep, with their legs folded under the body. Older birds tuck their heads under their wings, whether sitting or perching. Periods of paradoxical sleep in the chicken are typically very brief, often less than four seconds, but they increase in frequency throughout the night. While in human beings, the preponderance of REM sleep in the second half of the night is achieved by a lengthening of the REM sleep periods, in the chicken, as in other birds, the periods remain short but more episodes of REM sleep occur in the second half of the night (Schlehuber *et al.*, 1974).

Owls, which do not move their eyes when awake, do not exhibit rapid eye movements when asleep, although they do show EEG signs of paradoxical sleep. These animals are also unusual in maintaining a tonic level of muscle activity in the neck that is as great during paradoxical sleep as during slow-wave sleep. However, their increased arousal threshold during these periods (when they are harder to wake up) indicates that, despite the lack of eye movements and loss of muscle tone, this is a true variety of paradoxical sleep rather than lighter sleep or dozing (Berger and Walker, 1972).

The similarities between avian sleep and mammalian sleep are great, and are all the more remarkable because of the tenuous evolutionary link between birds and mammals. The implications of this will be discussed in the next chapter.

Reptiles

Reptiles are typically inactive for much of the time, but EEG studies have produced conflicting results in respect of whether this represents a true sleeping state. Crocodilians, for instance, the American alligator, have been reported not to sleep at all as they show no EEG signs of sleep (Van Twyver, 1973). Other researchers have reported that the waking EEG of the crocodile *Caiman sclerops* shows large amplitude waves, which reduce during sleep and are replaced by large spike-like waves (Flanigan *et al.*, 1973). Two other studies have reported that crocodiles have periods of sleep marked by high-voltage slow waves associated with increased arousal threshold, which is consistent with all the signs of slow-wave sleep (Meglasson and Huggins, 1979; Warner and Huggins, 1978). These authors argue that previous workers may have neglected to ensure that the animals were at their preferred (high) temperature when they were given the opportunity to sleep.

During wakefulness, the EEGs of the desert iguana and the red-footed tortoise are dominated by high-voltage sharp waves and spikes. During behavioural sleep these high-voltage waves diminish in frequency and amplitude, and arousal thresholds are demonstrably higher. There are no signs of slow-wave sleep stages or paradoxical sleep (Flanigan, 1973; Huntley and Cohen, 1980). This is contrary to the findings of earlier observations of paradoxical sleep in two species of lizard, where there was almost complete muscle atonia, arousal thresholds were very high and electrophysiological recordings showed rapid eye movements and bursts of 5–10 Hz activity in the EEG (Tauber *et al.*, 1968).

Sleep in reptiles remains something of a mystery. There appear to be greater differences between species of reptile, in terms of sleep pattern, than even between mammals and birds. One thing that is clear is that their neurophysiological state is highly temperature-dependent, and, as far as crocodiles are concerned, it seems that a high temperature is necessary if they are to sleep soundly enough to show high-voltage EEG slow-wave sleep. Inconsistencies between the results of studies on the same species involve not only crocodiles, and one wonders whether the recordings reported in some studies are of natural sleep at all. It is less than 20 years since it was asserted in a serious scientific journal that cattle never sleep. Perhaps many reptiles are less stoical than they appear to be, and despite their inert, ponderous and sometimes fearsome appearance, their natural timidity sometimes prevents normal rest and sleep in the laboratory. It is possible that careful and sensitive experimentation will uncover regularities in the psychophysiological state of these creatures.

Animal hypnosis

More than 200 years ago the Seminole Indians in the swamps of Florida discovered a peculiarity of alligator behaviour that is now demonstrated daily in parks such as Busch Gardens in Florida. It is not possible to tame these creatures, and every care has to be taken when handling them. However, when an alligator is caught in a noose it can be dragged onto a table in order to demonstrate its behavioural peculiarity to the audience. When it has been placed on its back, with its mouth held shut and its tail held still, the keeper slowly strokes its belly two or three times. When the hold on it is released, more often than not it remains completely motionless until it is touched again, whereupon it springs into writhing activity. (The alligator's jaw exerts enormous force when closing, but the muscles controlling its opening are not at all strong, and even a fully grown alligator's jaw can be held shut with one hand.)

This sort of 'freezing' behaviour is common to many animals, ranging from spiders to rabbits, although it is most commonly associated with birds and reptiles. It is induced primarily by physical restriction, although a sudden and violent stimulus can produce the same result. Drawing a chalk line in front of a chicken is reputed to 'hypnotize' it, but of course the chicken first has to be immobilized to ensure that it is looking at the line. Freezing or 'death feigning' is not accompanied by muscle relaxation, and is sometimes referred to as a state of 'tonic immobility'. It is quite distinct from the catalepsy shown by narcoleptic patients, who fall down and go immediately into REM sleep when overstimulated, and there is no evidence that it is mediated through the mechanisms that normally control sleep.

Hibernation

One might assume that the hibernating dormouse, bear or squirrel simply sleeps through the winter. The truly hibernating animal, however, is more than merely asleep. Its body temperature is lowered and its metabolic rate is reduced, and some metabolic processes may be drastically altered. For instance, the polar bear gives birth to cubs and feeds them during the winter months.

Figure 10.3 The somnolent dormouse in Alice in Wonderland (probably the hazel 'mouse' – *Muscardinus avellanarius* – according to one authority) (from Lyman, 1982)

During these three months it neither eats nor drinks, and urea, instead of being concentrated in urine, is either not produced or is recycled within the body (Nelson *et al.*, 1973).

Hibernation in some animals (such as the dormouse, weasel, ground squirrel and hamster) is a state of complete inactivity coupled with lowered body temperature, and it lasts for months. Other groups of animals (such as squirrels and brown bears) become torpid, but periodically make foraging expeditions in fine weather, and are relatively easily roused from their winter sleep.

James Walker, Ralph Berger and their colleagues in California have conducted a number of studies of hibernation and torpor. Electrophysiological measures of the sleep of American ground squirrels show that during the summer they sleep for about 16 hours per day, with 80 per cent slow-wave sleep and 20 per cent paradoxical (REM) sleep. The animals enter hibernation from slow-wave sleep. When hibernating at body temperatures of 25–35°C, they sleep almost 90 per cent of the time, of which 90 per cent is slow-wave sleep and a mere 10 per cent paradoxical sleep, so paradoxical sleep actually reduces during light hibernation in real terms. When the body temperature drops below 25°C, EEG amplitude is reduced to such an extent that slow-wave sleep can no longer be measured, and there are no signs of paradoxical sleep (Walker *et al.*, 1977).

Desert-living round-tailed squirrels withdraw into a torpor when food is scarce – a response called 'estivation'. Walker and Berger (1980) were able to induce this state in the laboratory by withdrawing food, and found that as the animals entered this torpid state their body temperature dropped every night by as much as 10°C, returning to normal in the two hours before daylight. Sleep time increased somewhat, but paradoxical sleep, as during true hibernation, was reduced in both percentage and real terms. The authors argue that hibernation and the torpor of estivation are both energy-conserving processes, allowing great reductions in the expenditure of energy during periods of privation and enabling the animal, effectively, to close up shop and wait for more favourable conditions. They further argue that normal sleep (and slow-wave sleep in particular) has evolved as an adaptive mechanism of the same sort, and that its primary function is to reduce energy expenditure.

11

The Evolution and Functions of Sleep

It must be admitted straight away that the function of sleep remains a mystery, and its evolution is still a matter of conjecture. Although predictably affected by age and to some extent by drugs, diet and exercise, sleep is a largely autonomous process that is relatively impervious to the vicissitudes of life. The parallel between sleep and processes essential to metabolism, such as respiration and digestion, is obvious. The difference is that we understand the role these play in metabolism, as well as the mechanisms or drives that regulate breathing, eating and drinking, while the functions of sleep remain opaque. In order to establish the physiological function of a process such as this it is necessary to understand its role in fulfilling physiological needs, which may not always be obvious and may be somewhat obscurely related to drive mechanisms.

It might appear that understanding the physiology that regulates sleep drives will give a unique insight into its function. However, while physiologists have made great strides in understanding sleep mechanisms, this has not greatly helped our understanding of what sleep is for. Only a larger understanding of the role of sleep in human functioning (including its psychology) can give us the answer to this.

It is important here to distinguish needs from their related drive mechanisms. The control of breathing, providing a supply of oxygen essential for life, is a good example. The drive mechanism that regulates the ventilation of the lungs is (somewhat unexpectedly) unaffected by oxygen levels in the blood, but is very sensitive indeed to its acidity – normally determined by carbon dioxide dissolved as carbonic acid. This system works very well when we are breathing the mixture of gases present in natural air. Breathing artificial mixtures of gases with no carbon dioxide can however result in a catastrophic failure to breathe, even when adequate oxygen is available. Understanding the mechanism of this vital drive mechanism would give us little clue, in itself, of the nature of the need. A mere understanding of the drive system might lead one to argue that the system is designed to regulate the constancy of the internal environment (slavishly following the insight of the great physiologist, Claude Bernard) and maintain blood acidity at a constant level by invoking changes in gaseous exchange. Of course, this would be a fatuous explanation, but where sleep is concerned we are at a level of ignorance that is much greater than in the nineteenth century when physiologists were dealing with gross metabolism. The rather more subtle functions of sleep will probably be suggested even more obliquely by their drive mechanisms than those driving respiration.

The consequences of preventing sleep are well known. Generally speaking, people become increasingly sleepy as sleep is denied, and decrements in performance related to sleep loss can largely be explained in terms of the involuntary lowering of arousal and 'microsleeps'. It is unclear whether this is merely a consequence of the operation of the drive mechanism, or whether it reflects some real physiological need. Similarly, selective deprivation experiments, in which either REM sleep or slow-wave (stages 3 and 4) sleep are prevented, have shown that when sleep is allowed *ad lib*, subjects experience 'rebounds' of the sleep stage that was previously denied (see Chapter 7). This may reflect a genuine physiological need, or simply a peculiarity of the operation of the drive mechanism responding to very artificial conditions.

In the absence of any definitive answer to the question of why we sleep, this chapter will describe and assess the three main suggestions that have been made: that sleep serves an essential recuperative function; that it may serve no physiological purpose at all; and finally (and not in any way as an alternative to the other two) that its function may best be established by considering the way in which sleep has evolved in life forms on this planet.

Restorative theories

Theories that relate sleep functions to processes of growth and bodily restoration have the advantage of making intuitive sense: we all feel the need to sleep, so it must be doing us good, and we all know that sleep is essential for growth in children. Why should it not have a similar role in adults?

Metabolic processes can be broadly divided into two categories: anabolic, in which complex substances are formed from simpler ones, energy is stored and body tissues are built up; and catabolic, in which energy is made available by the conversion of complex substances into simpler products. Both processes occur simultaneously in the body, and over a lifetime they must, of course, balance out exactly. On the 24-hour time scale it makes sense to think of the expenditure of energy during periods of activity, and of the conservation of energy and regrouping of resources during sleep. Ian Oswald (1969) articulated a coherent theory incorporating these ideas thirty-odd years ago.

Oswald's theory of REM sleep function was informed by his observations of the course of recovery of normal sleep after drug overdoses and drug withdrawal, and other brain insults such as intensive ECT. He found that all these traumatic insults to the central nervous system were followed by prolonged elevations in the quantity of REM sleep. The time scales involved were also very consistent with the estimated times for the half-life of amino acids in the brain. (While brain nerve cells are not replaced if they die, there is a constant turnover of protein in brain tissue, so that in a six week period, about half the total protein in the brain is replaced.) He suggested that the increases in REM sleep time that occur after drug withdrawal or drug overdose are a manifestation of recovery processes going on in the brain, involving intensive neuronal protein synthesis. REM sleep quantity also seems to be well correlated with brain weight increase in the early years across a range of species. Large amounts of REM sleep in the very young could thus be explained in terms of brain growth, and adult anabolic and recovery processes in the brain are similarly seen to require REM sleep.

Stage 4 sleep does not develop until about six months post-partum, but thereafter the quantity taken is well correlated with bodily growth in the juvenile. The nocturnal secretion of growth hormone (which stimulates somatic protein synthesis in the growing animal) is actually dependent on uninterrupted stage 4 sleep (Sassin *et al.*, 1969). In adulthood, a chronic lack of normal stage 4 sleep is found in sufferers from fibrositis, whose EEG during deep sleep is characterized by 'alpha–delta' patterns – a mixture of sleeping and waking EEG that typically results in fitful, 'unrestorative' sleep, leaving patients feeling as tired the next day as they had before going to bed. (See Chapter 12 for more details of the syndrome of alpha-delta sleep.) Not only do these sufferers exhibit aberrations in stage 4 sleep, but the disturbance of stage 4 sleep in healthy volunteers actually causes the symptoms of fibrositis to appear (Moldofsky *et al.*, 1975). All this evidence is consistent with a general anabolic function for sleep: REM sleep subserving brain growth, repair and memory functions, and slow-wave (stage 4) sleep promoting bodily growth and repair.

People suffering from disorders that affect the secretion of thyroxine from the thyroid gland are of great interest with respect to this theory, as this hormone directly regulates metabolism and promotes anabolic processes. Dunleavy *et al.* (1974) have found that hyperthyroid patients (with overactive thyroid glands) have an excess of stage 3 and 4 sleep, which is associated with increased plasma growth hormone levels. Thus, the increased demands made on tissue reserves by hyperthyroidism are compensated by a matching increase in anabolic processes. Moreover, as the theory would predict, as treatment normalizes their thyroid gland activity the patients' stage 3 and 4 sleep gradually reduces to normal levels. In the same way, patients with underactive thyroid glands (suffering from hypothyroidism) have little or no deep slow-wave sleep, but this is restored as they respond to treatment (Kales *et al.*, 1967).

Studies of patients suffering from anorexia nervosa have provided direct evidence of the effects on sleep of prolonged starvation (Crisp and Stonehill, 1977). Such patients sleep little and fitfully. However, when putting on weight they sleep more, and with fewer interruptions. Also, as the theory would predict, there is a change in the proportion of sleep stages, with a massive increase in the amount of deep slow-wave sleep at the expense of light slow-wave sleep. While these findings support the anabolic theory of sleep function, some caution needs to be exercised when interpreting them as sleep disorders frequently accompanying psychiatric problems, and as patients get better they might naturally sleep more soundly, given an accumulated sleep debt. In fact, normal people who go on starvation diets for short periods of time undergo increases in slow-wave sleep – an apparent paradox until one considers that metabolic turnover has to increase during starvation to accommodate the utilization of bodily food stores (Shapiro, 1982).

Studies of sleep during periods of illness, whether psychiatric or physical, may be confounded by factors associated with the conditions involved, unrelated to sleep functions themselves. A series of studies of normal people, carried out by Colin Shapiro and others, in collaboration with two psychologists, have provided some interesting confirmatory evidence of the close relation between sleep and metabolism (Shapiro *et al.*, 1981). In these studies, lean body mass was estimated by a novel technique developed at the Scottish Universities, Research and Reactor Centre at East Kilbride, in which total body potassium can be estimated from the amount present of a potassium isotope – potassium 40 – measured using a whole body counter. The amount of potassium in the body is a very good indication of lean body mass, and has been found to be highly correlated with metabolic rate. When comparing the sleep patterns of individuals that differed in body weight and composition, the researchers found that lean body mass consistently correlated positively with the amount of non-REM sleep.

The effects of exercise on sleep are not straightforward. The evidence, discussed in Chapter 9, appears to show that an elevation in deep slow-wave sleep can be caused by increased energy expenditure, but that this need not be very great. It seems that sleep mechanisms are more sensitive to increases in the rate of expenditure than to the total amount of energy expended, and also that changes in body temperature crucially determine subsequent sleep quality. That is, increased body temperature can elevate deep slow-wave sleep. The evidence is therefore mixed, and somewhat difficult to interpret.

Direct measurement of cell division or protein synthesis in man is impractical, but there have been a number of studies on animals, as reviewed by Adam and Oswald (1983). In nocturnal animals, the peak period of cell division (in almost every tissue studied) occurs when the animal is asleep, and during sleep cells may divide in half the time taken during the waking period. Likewise, measurements of the rate of protein synthesis show that this peaks during during the sleep period.

This account of sleep function, the Oswald theory, is an expression of what many non-specialists would consider to be the commonsensical view that sleep is good for you, especially in the case of growing children. While the theory is supported by a good deal of evidence, it is highly correlational and there is no conclusive evidence linking sleep to restorative processes. The correlation of periods of growth in the young with high levels of REM sleep could of course be fortuitous, and need not indicate that REM sleep is essential to brain growth. The net increase in anabolism during sleep may not be a consequence of anything more than inactivity, reducing catabolic processes. This sceptical view of the evidence on the restorative benefits of sleep has been expressed by theorists who believe that sleep has no function at all, and this will be critically assessed in the entitled section 'Is sleep a waste of time'.

Indeed, the theory has already undergone some revision. For instance, Adam (1980) has pointed out that, in some small mammals, the time required for protein synthesis in the brain is too long to allow for the completion of significant amounts during the short REM periods, so if REM sleep has any particular significance for brain protein synthesis in these animals, it must be to do with influencing the quality of protein production rather than simply accelerating the rate. Nevertheless, the view that sleep has a restorative function remains a compelling explanation and, despite years of accumulation of evidence, nothing has emerged to discredit it.

Implications for memory

Restorative theories (e.g. Oswald, 1969) imply that memory processes are affected by the amount of REM sleep during the night, since it is indisputable that the consolidation of memories involves protein changes of some sort in the brain. Thirty or so years ago I set out to test this hypothesis directly, depriving subjects of REM sleep and measuring the effects of the regime on the retention of material learned the day before (Empson and Clarke, 1970). The tests involved 10 pairs of yoked subjects who had learned the same material the evening before and were woken up whenever the experimental subject was roused from REM sleep. The retention of complex material (stories) was greatly reduced by REM deprivation, while the retention of lists of words was not. The retention of syntactically correct but meaningless sentences was intermediate.

Others later confirmed that REM sleep deprivation has little effect on the retention of meaningless material (Fowler *et al.*, 1973). Following up on this, Tilley and Empson (1978) showed that REM sleep deprivation is more disruptive of memory consolidation in human subjects than stage 4 sleep deprivation, so it is unlikely that the effects observed were non-specific consequences of a stressful regime. In this context, a fascinating study of three-month-old babies found that babies who had apparently forgotten about a kickable overhead mobile and were reminded of its existence showed reminiscence (improved evidence of memory retention) in proportion to the amount of sleep intervening between the reminder and the test (Fagen and Rovee-Collier, 1983). Of course, there is no direct evidence that REM sleep was implicated, but it is very tempting to speculate, given that babies' quiet sleep is largely REM, that the reactivation of old memories could be a function of REM sleep, as much as the consolidation of new ones.

Further behavioural evidence from Empson *et al.*, (1981) suggests that the advantage given to the retention of memories by REM sleep relies on an orderly sequence of REM sleep periods, in that the beneficial effect of REM sleep later in the night seems to be dependent on the uninterrupted completion of a short perod of REM sleep early in the night. If true, could this be subserved by slow processes involving protein synthesis, initiated early in the night and continued periodically in REM sleep periods throughout the night? Comparing the brain to an automatic washing machine might be an oversimplification as a general model, but it seems a useful metaphor to explain this sort of cyclical, programmed process.

Research originating in the study of visual processing has given further support to the REM-consolidation hypothesis. Karni and Sagi (1991) investigated the acquisition and retention of a basic visual discrimination skill, involving the recognition of very simple visual features in a large array. It was somewhat surprising that any learning at all should be evident in adult subjects on a pattern discrimination task. Furthermore, it was apparent that learning was not immediate, but was only evident after 10–24 hours, suggesting a period of consolidation. Experiments involving partial sleep deprivation revealed the following. First, performance improved after a normal night's sleep. Second, REM sleep deprivation removed any sign of improvement after sleep, whereas non-REM (stage 3 and 4) sleep deprivation resulted in significant improvement, comparable to that found after an undisturbed night. Finally, REM sleep deprivation had no detrimental effects on performance by subjects who had engaged in the learning task weeks before (Karni *et al.*, 1994). Taken together, these results give further support to the theory that learning is consolidated during REM sleep. Stickgold *et al.* (2000) have confirmed that learning in this sort of visual discrimination task improves with sleep, and that delayed sleep (after a night of sleep deprivation) comes too late to provide any benefit.

Smith (1995) has reviewed the work on memory and REM sleep conducted in the 1980s and early 1990s on both animals and humans, much of it in his own laboratory. He makes the distinction, in the human work, between cognitive procedural tasks, which are vulnerable to REM sleep loss, and declarative tasks, which are not. 'Procedural' tasks are represented by more complex learning, for instance, learning how to solve a problem, while 'declarative' memory tasks are represented by word-list learning. Plihal and Born (1999) have also found that early sleep, dominated by short-wave sleep facilitates declarative memory whereas late sleep, dominated by REM sleep, facilitates the consolidation of non-declarative memory.

Positron emission tomography (PET) studies of the brain during the various sleep states have also shown that during REM sleep the structures implicated in memory processing are indeed highly activated. It has been known for some time that the brain is generally more activated during REM sleep than during slow-wave sleep, and that its metabolic demand is as high as during wakefulness. Studies of sleeping humans, using PET scans, have shown that the areas of the brain that receive increased blood flow during REM sleep are in the hindbrain and midbrain (the pontine tegmentum, the left thalamus, both amygdaloid complexes, the anterior cingulate cortex and the right parietal operculum) while blood flow is reduced bilaterally in the prefrontal cortex and parietal cortex (Maquet *et al.*, 1996). Maquet *et al.* suggest that, 'given the role of the amygdaloid complexes in the acquisition of emotionally influenced memories, the pattern of activation in the amygdala and the cortical areas provides a biological basis for the processing of some types of memory during REM sleep'.

All in all, evidence that REM sleep plays an important role in the consolidation of complex, non-declarative memory is still mounting, 30 or so years after the first reports of the effects of REM sleep deprivation on learning and memory processes.

Is sleep a waste of time?

During the early 1970s the commonsensical theories of restorative sleep were being enshrined as scientific fact (long before they had been proven), but then a number of dissenting voices started to question their whole basis. The most fully developed proposal was presented by Meddis (1975, 1977), who argued that sleep is a period of enforced inactivity, reducing metabolic demands and keeping the organism out of trouble during periods of the day when other essential needs have been satisfied. According to this view, sleep mechanisms are instincts that have evolved in the same way as those controlling the court-ship and mating of birds and fish. Their sole function is to control behaviour. This provocative theory graphically illustrated the weakness of the evidence supporting the restorative theories, and hence a thorough reconsideration of all the assumptions underlying the thinking about sleep function was required to address its arguments. Even if this was all the theory would achieve, it would have done a great service.

Obviously, all animals' sleep mechanisms must have evolved, and any credible theory has to explain the variety of day-to-day patterns among modern species, including very large differences in total sleep time. If we were to take the 'waste of time' proposition seriously, it would be difficult to explain why this particular instinct has become universal, while other instincts are as diverse as the habitats of the creatures exhibiting them. In particular, it does not explain how this particular instinct remains a determinant of stereo-typed behaviour in mammals when the role of learning has become crucial to the expression of all other mammalian instincts. Nor does it explain why almost every known mammal shows the same pattern of sleep (although there is great variation in the total quantity taken). Despite enormous differences in living patterns, all mammals have to find time for a minimum amount of sleep. As discussed earlier, the porpoise has even evolved a system of sleeping where the two sides of the brain sleep alternately (Mukhametov and Polyakova, 1981). If there were no other evidence for the absolute necessity of sleep, this would be eloquent enough on its own. It clearly suggests that sleep has acquired an essential role in physiology, whatever the evolutionary pressures that led to its appearance in primeval reptiles.

A more critical test of the essential nature of sleep is to consider the effects of sleep deprivation. Preventing the expression of some instincts (such as by crowding chickens into small cages) does not result in death, but may produce faster growth and egg-laying. Interfering with sleep, however, is a much more serious matter. Writing over a hundred years ago, Marie de Manaceine (1897) reported that

> Direct experiment has shown that animals entirely deprived of food for twenty days, and which have then lost more than half their weight, may yet escape death if fed with precaution – that is to say, in small amounts often repeated. On the other hand, I found by experimenting on ten puppies that the complete deprivation of sleep for four or five days (96 to 120 hours) causes irreparable lesions in the organism, and in spite of every care the subjects of these experiments could not be saved. Complete

absence of sleep during this period is fatal to puppies in spite of the food taken during this time, and the younger the puppy the more quickly he succumbed.

With an experiment like this, it is crucially important to know how much physical ill-treatment the dogs were subjected to in order to ensure wakefulness, and Manaceine wrote little to reassure one in this respect. Early American work on rats (Patrick and Gilbert, 1896) involved keeping the animals awake by revolving their cage. All died from bites inflicted on each other, and of course little can be said about the role of sleep from results like that! The puppy experiment was repeated by Nathanial Kleitman (1927) using 12 animals deprived of sleep for two to seven days. Unlike Manaceine, Kleitman gave full details of the methods he used to enforce wakefulness, stressing the importance he attached to avoiding any physical damage being inflicted on his dogs. A slight pull on the chain and a short walk would result in wakefulness that persisted for some time. Control puppies (allowed *ad lib* sleep) were introduced to play with the experimental puppies, and this often banished somnolence entirely. Despite this relatively gentle regime, two of the puppies died, and like Manaceine's dogs, all showed a marked drop in red blood cells.

Allan Rechtschaffen and his colleagues conducted a comprehensive set of experiments on sleep deprivation in the rat (Bergmann *et al.*, 1989b). They used pairs of rats, housed in cages whose floors were composed of discs suspended above water, divided in two by a partition. With one rat on each side of the division, the partition was rotated whenever the experimental animal went to sleep, or entered one of the sleep stages specifically being denied it. Both rats were then impelled to walk in order to avoid falling in the water. While the control rats had the same physical treatment as the experimental ones, they were permitted to sleep whenever the other rat was naturally awake.

The effects of total sleep deprivation (TSD) and paradoxical sleep deprivation (PSD) were found to be essentially similar (Everson *et al.*, 1989a; Kushida *et al.*, 1989). Death was inevitable in the experimental animals, but the control animals suffered little if at all. The TSD rats survived for 11–32 days and the PSD rats for 16–54 days. As the animals became more and more sleep deprived their appearance changed, their fur becoming thin and dishevelled. They also typically developed sores on their tails in a regular pattern corresponding to the vertebral bones, as well as sores on their feet. In addition to eating more than usual (80–100 per cent above baseline in the last quarter of survival), they had a weight loss of about 20 per cent. This anomaly was not due to inefficient digestion (as judged from tests on faeces), and indirect calorimetry confirmed that the animals had increased their rate of energy expenditure in a way that could not be simply explained by their increased activity: to double baseline level by the final quarter of the survival period (Bergmann and Rechtschaffen, 1989). Eight animals that were deprived of sleep and developed all the symptoms of sleep loss described above, were allowed sleep *ad lib* before the final moribund stages. Three of them died within a few days, but the other five recovered completely, with energy expenditure returning to normal after 24 hours. They also showed massive rebounds of paradoxical sleep.

Rechtschaffen *et al.* (1989a) dismiss the notion that, in the rat at least, sleep is merely a behavioural adaptation – the catastrophic consequences of deprivation must imply an important function for sleep. The only function that the pattern of symptoms developed by their animals suggests is that of thermoregulation. Specifically, they suggest that loss of paradoxical sleep gives rise to excessive heat loss, and that loss of non-REM sleep results in an increase in the preferred 'setpoint' of body temperature, increasing the need for greater energy expenditure to maintain that temperature. While their hypotheses are commendably restricted to the facts observed in their studies, they leave much unexplained. In the first place, it seems implausible that such a complex system as sleep should have evolved simply to maintain a particular body temperature – something that could be dealt with by a much simpler mechanism, one would have thought.

Although most studies of sleep deprivation in humans have only involved one or two nights of deprivation, there are some in which sleep has been denied for as long as ten days – and without fatal consequences. Is the function of human sleep, therefore, different from the sleep of the rat? Rechtschaffen argues that the rate of development of sleep loss symptoms can be expected to be longer in human beings. Rats sleep 13.6 hours per day, humans 8.0 hours – thus symptom development should be 1.7 times slower in the human. It can be argued that other factors increase this differential. The small size of the rat gives it a much greater surface to mass ratio than the human, therefore it loses heat more quickly and is perhaps six times more vulnerable to disruptions in thermoregulation than humans. Relative survival times for starvation are 17 days for rats and 62 days for humans, suggesting that humans might survive sleep loss by a factor of 3.7 compared with rats, or 77 days of total sleep loss compared with the rat's 21 days.

These arguments are all well-supported, but in the end we have to admit that we do not know whether sleep deprivation on its own is lethal for humans, and we will probably never find out. The only indications come from the 'natural experiments', discussed in Chapter 7, with individuals suffering from 'fatal familial insomnia' (Manetto *et al.*, 1992). The indication from these cases is that the insomnia caused by damage to the thalamus may well have played a part in the death of the patients, but again it is difficult to attribute the precise cause of death when there was severe atrophy of brain structures as important as the ventral and mediodorsal thalamic nuclei. Systematic measures of energy expenditure and food intake were not recorded from the patients, but they did have symptoms that were consistent with an elevation in metabolic rate similar to that found in Allan Rechtschaffen's rats – pyrexia (high fever, or a resetting of the thermoregulatory thermostat upwards), tachycardia and hypertension.

Even if sleep deprivation does kill, this does not prove that sleep is restorative in function – it is vital to understand the mechanisms involved as well. The contention that sleep serves no function, has been useful in forcing a critical re-examination of our, sometimes unwarranted, preconceptions and assumptions about the role of sleep; but in the light of the evidence on the fatal effects of its deprivation and its ubiquity throughout the mammalian class, it seems safe to reject it. The Oswald theory has been particularly useful in respect of theories' role of tying facts into bundles – almost everything we know about sleep fits in with the theory. Continual confirmation of the theory through correlational evidence is no proof of its correctness, however, and only a complete understanding of the physiology of sleep will ultimately reveal what it is actually for. The impulse to ascribe a functional role to sleep will obviously not be satisfied until we have a clearer understanding of the inter-actions of the slow neurophysiological swings that punctuate our circadian cycle. The attribution of functions to a process is never easy, boiling down to a matter of understanding and judgement, and the scientific ground rules are rather obscure on this point!

A weaker version of the 'waste of time' theory has been suggested by Jim Horne (1988). In *Why We Sleep* he distinguishes core sleep, which is necessary, from optional sleep, which is not. Evidence from sleep deprivation experiments – both partial and total – has shown that accumulated sleep 'debts' are repaid to some extent on recovery nights, but never entirely. For example, the REM rebound after REM sleep deprivation accounts for approximately 50 per cent of the amount of REM sleep lost during a period of selective awakenings. Horne argues that evidence such as this indicates that only the first three hours of sleep during the night is truly necessary (core sleep) and that the remainder – optional sleep – has no physiological function, although in animals that sleep for longer than three hours it serves the function of reducing energy expenditure and keeping the animal immobile.

Horne rejects evidence that implicates sleep in bodily restorative processes, on the ground that most of the experiments showing increased protein synthesis and cell growth during sleep have been conducted on small rodents. These animals, he argues, are rarely active when awake, so the sleep period is the only time when these processes can occur. Larger mammals, including human beings, are inactive and resting for much of the time, so protein synthesis and cell division can take place during the day as well as the night. On the other hand, Horne suggests that the deep slow-wave sleep stages may have a role in the recovery of brain tissue in mammals, such as ourselves, with high degrees of encephalization.

Is this distinction between core and optional sleep useful in furthering our understanding of the functions of sleep? I would argue that it is not. Most of us eat more than we need to keep body and soul together, in both variety and quantity, but no biologist would consider it useful to say that because a proportion of feeding is optional, feeding is only partly functional. Rather, this reflects the operation of drive mechanisms serving ingestion. An understanding of the physiology of nutrition and its role in metabolism has given us a very good idea of the function of feeding, and in the same way we can hope one day to have a definitive account of the functions of sleep.

Evolution and sleep

The orthodox view of the origins of sleep is that slow-wave sleep developed first, and paradoxical sleep (as REM sleep is called in animals) then evolved in warm-blooded animals: 'it is at least clear that in the course of evolution slow wave sleep preceded paradoxical sleep. The latter seems to be a more recent acquisition' (Jouvet, 1967). Elisabeth Hennevin and Pierre Leconte (1971) similarly asserted that

> Paradoxical sleep does not exist in fishes, reptiles or amphibians ... It has been recorded in birds (the chicken, the pigeon), but its proportion is less than 0.3% of orthodox sleep ... except among predatory birds ... in fact paradoxical sleep does not appear with all its characteristics except in mammals. (My translation)

This is consistent with the idea that REM sleep is concerned with protein synthesis in the central nervous system (Oswald, 1969), or with memory processes or the elaboration of fixed, instinctive responses (Jouvet, 1978) in that mammals have much better-developed nervous systems than reptiles.

The nature of sleep in animals is obviously of some theoretical importance, and questions about the evolution of sleep and temperature-regulation mechanisms have become crucial in the debate about sleep function in man. There is evidence to suggest that the sleep of modern reptiles may be more similar to human REM sleep than to human short-wave sleep. This alternative analogy has the advantage of explaining both the anomaly of the appearance of REM sleep before short-wave sleep in the human foetus (when in embryology ontogeny normally follows phylogeny) and the loss of thermoregulation during paradoxical sleep in mammals (Heller and Glotzbach, 1977). (That is, during REM sleep we become reptilian-like in respect of not making any compensation, by shivering or sweating, for changes in body temperature.)

However, there are problems with this idea in that birds (which exhibit unequivocal slow-wave sleep) are conventionally viewed as having evolved, along with dinosaurs and pterosaurs, in parallel to the evolution of mammals from a common primeval reptile. Thus, as Meddis (1975) says, 'the stem reptiles ancestral to birds, mammals, turtles and crocodiles must have been pre-adapted to develop this kind of sleep pattern (SWS) under certain conditions (such as homeothermy)'. If we accept the persuasive evidence that dinosaurs were warm-blooded animals (Desmond, 1977), then perhaps this problem could be rationalized by hypothesizing a common warm-blooded ancestor to mammals, dinosaurs and birds that engaged in slow-wave sleep and diverged from the reptilian stem in prehistory (see Fig. 11.1). In the absence of any possibility of obtaining evidence about the sleep patterns of animals now extinct, one person's speculation is as good as another's!

The available evidence on the nature of modern reptilian sleep is by no means unambiguous. Most laboratory studies of the EEG of the reptile (discussed in Chapter 10) have found few signs of slow waves during periods of quiescence. This has been taken as evidence that REM sleep is 'reptilian' in origin, and that slow-wave sleep is an evolutionarily recent mammalian development. Evidence of EEG slow waves in eight-month-old crocodiles that were allowed to sunbathe, suggests that thermoregulatory behaviour (increasingly recognized as a major determinant of the temperature of cold-blooded animals) may be necessary for the production of slow-wave sleep, and that this may be common to all reptiles, including the ancestral stem reptiles from which

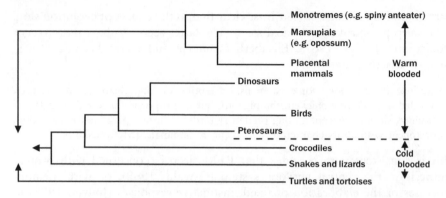

Figure 11.1   The evolutionary tree (from Meddis, 1983)

birds, mammals, dinosaurs and modern reptiles evolved. This is a more parsimonious explanation than the ones involving either multiple stem ancestors or preadaptations. That is, all vertebrates share the same sleep mechanisms. Some of the difficulties involved in assessing the natural sleep of wild animals were discussed in Chapter 10. It seems that we must wait for further evidence on reptilian sleep before reaching any firm conclusions about its nature.

What determines how mammals sleep? Systematic comparisons between mammalian species with respect to sleep and other stable characteristics, (size, metabolic rate, life span and so on) ought to give an answer to this question, and provide clues to the evolution and function of sleep. Zepelin and Rechtschaffen (1974) have examined the correlations between sleep length, metabolic rate, life span, brain weight and other relevant variables for 53 species and found a strong relationship between metabolic rate and total sleep taken. This can be interpreted in terms of sleep being merely a mechanism for reducing energy consumption, as it can be argued that animals with high metabolic rates save much-needed energy reserves during sleep (Walker and Berger, 1980). As Oswald (1980) points out, it is also consistent with the view that sleep is a period of active recuperation, with high levels of metabolic activity demanding longer periods of sleep. Oswald also argues that since, in humans, long sleepers have higher body temperatures than short sleepers, longer sleep may be associated with higher metabolic rates even within a species. In this context, the experiments by Horne and Reid (1985) (discussed in Chapter 9) showing that heating the body (by lying in a warm bath before bedtime) increases stage 4 sleep acquire a new significance, and provide support for Oswald's position.

As we saw in Chapter 10, there can be great discrepancies between different laboratories' findings on animals' sleep patterns, and calculations based on data from laboratory studies must be treated with caution. In addition, while correlations provide a description of the extent to which different measures (such as sleep length and metabolic rate) vary together, any inferences about whether one is caused by the other, or whether both are caused by a third factor, are inevitably speculative. Nevertheless, further analyses of this sort have been made, for example by Allison and Cicchetti (1976) and Meddis (1983).

In their analysis, Allison and Cichetti included ratings of the degree of danger typically experienced by 39 species, and correlated these ratings, together with a number of other variables, with the amounts of REM and non-REM sleep that these animals reportedly took in the laboratory. The amount of REM sleep taken correlated negatively with total danger (−0.69), as did non-REM sleep (−0.40), indicating the importance of life style and habitat in determining sleep patterns. Body size was negatively correlated with both non-REM sleep (−0.63) and REM sleep (−0.40). Thus, the body weight of an animal is the best predictor of how much non-REM sleep it takes, with larger animals sleeping less; and overall danger is the best predictor of the time spent in REM sleep every day, with animals with the most precarious lives sleeping least in this state.

A particular problem with this analysis is that Alison and Cichetti have included large grazing animals, which spend much of their time feeding, and also habitually doze rather than sleep. Should dozing be counted as sleep or wakefulness? In addition, as grazing animals' sleep is shorter and qualitatively differently from that of most other mammals, does it make sense to include them in a statistical procedure that assumes a certain homogeneity? Meddis (1983) argues that grazers ought not to have been included. When they are removed from the correlations, the relationship between sleep length and body size (and metabolic rate) dwindles disappointingly, while the amount of REM sleep in the adult seems to be predicted best by the maturity of the animal at birth (its precocity). Meddis's contention is somewhat controversial, and Zepelin (1983), strongly argues that it would be arbitrary indeed to remove the ungulates from the analysis while leaving other grazers such as gorillas, rabbits, beavers and guinea pigs.

It is perhaps overoptimistic to expect too much from correlations across species like this, as many of our estimates of sleep patterns are still somewhat unreliable. Precocity at birth, for instance, is commonly thought by biologists to be one way of resisting predation in animals that give birth in insecure habitats. Thus, cats are born blind and immature, while some of their potential prey, such as guinea pigs, are born ready to run about. Precocity at birth may thus predict timidity in the adult, not only because such animals are largely preyed upon, but also because they are typically vulnerable from an early age. An inability to sleep soundly in a laboratory environment would, therefore, be unsurprising. An artefact like this could well have inflated the negative correlation between precocity and REM sleep. Meddis (1983) is undoubtedly correct in being doubtful about correlations that are relatively small, even if statistically 'significant', but his re-analysis of the data without the ungulates (whatever the merits of the argument for doing so) does point up the difficulties inherent in this sort of exercise.

This chapter has set out to describe the sorts of theory that have been proposed, and to make some critical assessments of them. In an attempt to provide a balanced perspective of sleep functions, Shapiro (1982) comments:

Most systems of the body appear to be multi-functional, that is, having several 'operations' to perform and it seems reasonable to expect the same, a priori, of sleep.

It would seem quite possible that sleep is subserving several processes simultaneously and when one is studying a single facet, the changes in sleep patterns one observes may be being dampened by the other (unaffected) inputs that normally comprise the 'summated' pattern seen in sleep records.

The variety of alternative ideas (all plausible, and many compelling) advanced for the functions of sleep, illustrate the degree of our ignorance, despite the wealth of available data on sleep patterns and sleep mechanisms. To return to the basics, sleep appears to be ubiquitous and necessary, and is a complex function of the brain that involves far-reaching changes in bodily physiology as well as brain physiology. It is difficult to believe that it does not have an important function, and the restorative theories provide a coherent account of what this might be.

Readers will have to decide for themselves whether sleep is good for them, or is a waste of time, although it might be advisable to keep an open mind on the subject – it is just possible that one day soon a new insight into sleep function will be achieved that will make us wonder why it seemed such a mystery for so long. Until then, perhaps the safest thing would be to assume that it does do us some good, and to get as much sleep as we can. (Later they might bring out a pill to abolish sleep, turn all bedrooms into offices and workshops, and condemn us to working Victorian mill hours – so make the most of it while you can!)

Part IV
Sleep Disorders

12

Adult Sleep Disorders

The nature and scale of sleep disorders

The commonest types of sleep disturbance are caused by psychological problems, although there are some rarer syndromes that have medical causes, or seem to be innately determined. The use of EEG/EOG recordings has been crucial in increasing our understanding of these sleep disorders, and has contributed to the development of a precise system of classification of such disorders, based on psychophysiological as well as medical critera. In the US in particular, sleep disorder clinics have been set up that rely largely on EEG/EOG recordings, and their professional organization has used the results of this research to draw up an authoritative set of guidelines on the diagnosis of sleep disorders, some of which are extremely rare (Association of Sleep Disorders Centers, 1979).

How many people sleep badly? Two sources of information are the answers provided in surveys and the number of hypnotics (sleeping pills) prescribed by doctors, although, as we shall see, prescription rates are not as informative as they might seem. What is the matter with the sleep experienced by these people? Laboratory studies of people complaining of insomnia have the potential to identify types of sleep disorder, but, again as we shall see, they do not necessarily explain why particular individuals complain about their quality of sleep. The effects of the drugs taken to alleviate sleep problems are also highly relevant to the development of sleep disorders.

Insomnia and the sleeping pill habit

Sleep disturbance in adults is extremely common. In a survey of over 1000 households in Los Angeles in 1979, 38 per cent of the adult respondents complained of some sleep disorder (Bixler *et al.*, 1979). Dissatisfaction with sleep appeared to increase with age, especially among women. This confirmed the findings of a Scottish survey of a comparable size, conducted almost 20 years earlier (McGhie and Russell, 1962). The American survey also enquired into the general and mental health correlates of sleep disorder, and found that over 50 per cent of those who reported insomnia had other recurring health problems. They were also significantly more likely to complain of tension, loneliness, depression and the need for help with emotional problems, but were not more likely than others to have made use of mental health facilities.

The general picture is thus of sleep disturbance being related to poor physical health, unhappiness and anxiety. A history of sleep disorder does not make it more likely that an individual will have received treatment for psychiatric illness (although it is of course commonplace for people suffering from emotional disorders also to have problems with sleeping).

How many people regularly take a sedative before going to bed? Statistics on the number of prescriptions presented for various preparations can be obtained from pharmacists. Doctors, however, are not normally required to report what their patients complain of, or what they prescribe for them, and, of course, the profession jealously preserves its reputation for confidentiality. Consequently, our assessment must rely on a certain amount of guesswork about the purpose for which tablets have been prescribed, the proportion actually ingested, and by whom. At the time of a survey in Dundee and Glasgow (1961), the sedatives normally prescribed were barbiturates, and the respondents reported increasing dependence on them with age, especially in the case of women – over 25 per cent of women aged 45 and over were in the habit of taking a sedative, while only about 15 per cent of 45-year-old men did so (McGhie and Russell (1962). In a survey in France, of more than 1000 respondents (Quera-Salva et al., 1991), 10 per cent of the sample used hypnotics, 6 per cent on a heavy and frequent basis. Usage increased dramatically with age – between 45 and 54 for women and 65 and over for men.

Estimates of British consumption levels (Williams, 1983) show a very marked change in prescribing habits between 1960 and 1980 – of 14 million prescriptions for hypnotics in 1960, almost all were for barbiturates, while by 1973 the proportion of non-barbiturate hypnotics prescribed had increased to almost half the total, and by 1978 barbiturate prescriptions accounted for considerably less than half. A continuing survey of the prescribing habits of all 859 doctors who had entered general practice in the UK in the period 1969–70, clearly shows that by 1976 these doctors were prescribing barbiturates essentially only to patients who had become dependent on them, and practically all new prescriptions for hypnotics were of the non-barbiturate variety (Birmingham Research Unit, 1978).

Information on prescribing levels tells us when certain drugs cease to be prescribed (as with the barbiturates) but does not necessarily indicate which drugs have taken their place. This problem is particularly acute with the hypnotics, since so many preparations can be prescribed to patients who complain of sleeplessness. Rare evidence of the medical profession's response to patients presenting themselves with insomnia, is provided by a survey of five GPs at the Aldermoor Health Centre, attached to the Southampton University Medical School (Freeman, 1978). Of the 250 patients dealt with, only four were prescribed barbiturates, and the most popular drugs were nitrazepam (Mogadon), diazepam (Valium) and other benzodiazepines. Almost half the prescriptions for the under-14s were for antihistamines, and nearly a third of those for the over 65s were for chlormethiazole, a powerful barbiturate-like sedative. (It is known that some milder drugs, such as nitrazepam, can cause confusion in the elderly, so this rather potent sedative was probably the lesser of two evils for these patients.) Chloral derivatives and antidepressants were also prescribed quite often, the former mainly to the under-14s and the latter to patients in middle age or older.

No single group of these preparations can be classed as 'hypnotic', and the doctors were obviously attempting to match the prescriptions to their patients' specific needs, and so made use of a wide variety of drugs, some of which may have also been prescribed for other reasons. This flexibility of usage means that data for the number and types of prescription must be interpreted with some caution. Over the years, the benzodiazepines have become the most widely used psychotropic drugs, with the total number of prescriptions dispensed in the UK levelling off at about 30 million in the mid-1970s. About 13 million of these were drugs marketed as hypnotics; however, an unknown number of the remaining 17 million 'anxiolytics' will have been prescribed as hypnotics (in the Southampton study diazepam was freely prescribed as a hypnotic) and, of course, the use that the patients made of these drugs is not known.

Until 1982, the Department of Health carried out an annual survey of one in 200 prescriptions dispensed in England and Wales, and one in 100 in Scotland. Since 1982, there has been an actual record of the number of prescriptions dispensed in England. The data show a general increase in the dispensation of anxiolytic benzodiazepines (marketed as antianxiety drugs, normally intended to be taken during the day) from the 1960s, peaking in 1977. Over the following six years, their dispensation underwent a pronounced drop, while the number of prescriptions for hypnotics continued to rise. This may reflect an increasing tendency to prescribe specifically hypnotic benzodiazepine drugs for sleep problems, rather than diazepam (for example, Valium) or other anxiolytic benzodiazepines. An indication of the trend in England between 1980 and 1999, is provided in Figure 11.1 (also referred to in Chapter 9 on the effects of drugs). Prescriptions for hypnotics, largely benzodiazepines, increased until 1987, but declined somewhat thereafter. Prescriptions for anxiolytic benzodiazepines underwent a much more dramatic reduction.

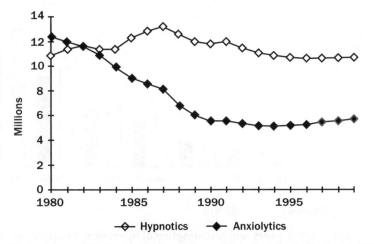

Figure 12.1   Prescribing rates for hypnotics and anxiolytics in England, 1980–99 (data supplied by Department of Health Statistical Office)

Official statistics on prescribing levels cannot provide more than a very rough idea of the number of people taking hypnotic drugs. Dividing the number of prescriptions by the number of adults in the population in England, and assuming about 30 tablets for each prescription, suggests that all adults take a sedative one night in ten. However, relatively few individuals on repeat prescriptions, in fact, account for a disproportionate number of total prescriptions, and most people do without hypnotics. In addition, even when prescribed and dispensed, the drugs may be left on the bathroom shelf, given to somebody else or thrown away, rather than being taken as instructed. The only reliable way of finding out how many people do take sleeping pills is to ask them systematically. A survey of psychotropic drug consumption in the general UK population in 1977 (Murray *et al.*, 1981) found that only 11 per cent of adults had taken sedatives in a two-week period, the same percentage as that reported eight years previously (see Dunnell and Cartwright, 1972) despite a large increase over the same period in the number of prescriptions. One explanation of this might be that the number of people with repeat prescriptions had increased. Another possibility (and there is some evidence for this) is that there was a decline in the proportion of patients taking the drugs prescribed to them, and the development of a degree of scepticism towards medical authority between 1969 and 1977, so that patients became more likely to take drugs when they felt the need for them, rather than as the doctor ordered.

Despite the lower than expected levels of consumption, this survey confirmed previous British and American evidence (Association of Sleep Disorders Centers, 1979; Bixler *et al.*, 1979) that women were much more likely than men to take hypnotics, and that this difference increased with age. Figure 12.2, which is based on a West German survey, illustrates both these trends very well. Paradoxically, this finding contradicts evidence on the quality of sleep

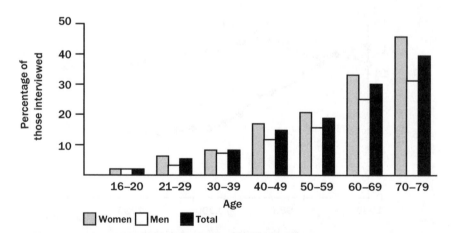

Figure 12.2   Age in years and consumption of hypnotics. A survey conducted in Germany asked respondents if they 'sometimes' took sleeping medication (from Spiegel and Azcona, 1985)

achieved, in general, by elderly men and women in the laboratory. There, men have almost twice as many awakenings and disturbances during the night as women, and it would, therefore, follow that a greater proportion of men would become sufficiently dissatisfied with their sleep to demand hypnotics.

Are women generally more neurotic than men as they get older, or is this specifically a sleep problem? The survey evidence shows that the proportion of women taking anxiolytic or antianxiety drugs (such as Librium or chlordiazepoxide) actually decreases with age. This demonstrates a lack of association between sleep disorder and general anxiety level, and contradicts the idea that the increase in sleep disorders with age amongst women is yet another symptom of a generally higher degree of neuroticism in women as they get older. No simple explanation can be offered for this sex difference.

The sleep of insomniacs

Psychophysiological studies of the sleep of insomniacs – that is, people who complain to doctors of sleeping badly – have consistently shown that self-reports of sleep quality are not reliable indicators of quantity or quality of sleep, as assessed in the laboratory. Most people overestimate the time it takes to get to sleep (Lewis, 1969). Insomniacs tend to have a longer latency to sleep onset, and do achieve less overall sleep than normal controls (Karacan *et al.*, 1971; Monroe, 1967). However, their complaints of lack of sleep, or of failure to get to sleep, are often contradicted by psychophysiological evidence, and some insomniacs even report wakefulness when roused from stage 4 sleep (Rechtschaffen and Monroe, 1969).

Ogilvie *et al.* (1989) suggest that sleep onset is not all-or-nothing, but that there is what they call a 'sleep onset period' – a gradual transition between wakefulness and sleep. Sleep laboratory studies by this group on both normals and insomniacs have shown that the best estimate of an insomniac's definition of sleep onset is the beginning of the first 15 minutes of uninterrupted stage 2 sleep, rather than stage 2 sleep onset *per se*, which they confirm as being the best estimate of subjective sleep onset in normals. Insomniacs, therefore, not only achieve less or worse sleep than normals, but their perception of it makes the problem worse. Some people who demand sedatives may not be deprived of sleep at all, merely the experience of unconsciousness. Many normals have less sleep than most self-declared insomniacs, without complaint. This four-fold typology is illustrated in Figure 12.3.

Types of sleep disorder

This section will generally follow the taxonomy of sleep disorders arrived at by the Association of Sleep Disorders Clinics, based on psychophysiological evidence as well as medical considerations. Of course, some sleep disorder syndromes are very common, while others are very rare, even if very interesting from a theoretical point of view. (Readers who have a personal interest in the matter should bear in mind that the most intractable sleep disorders tend to be extremely rare.)

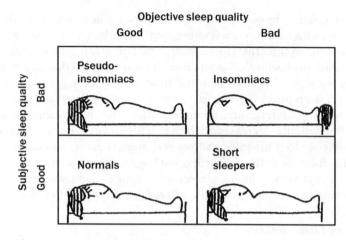

Figure 12.3 Types of sleeper. Satisfaction with sleep does not necessarily correlate well with objectively determined sleep quality

Disorders of initiating sleep

In the Los Angeles survey referred to earlier (Bixler *et al.*, 1979), almost half of those who reported insomnia had difficulty falling asleep. Worry and anxiety are commonly given as reasons for staying awake in bed. However, normal levels of anxiety and stress do not seem to have any simple effect on the time taken to fall asleep in the laboratory. In one study, insomniacs and good sleepers who were stressed by being required to do mental arithmetic problems after lights-out in the laboratory, took no longer than usual to get to sleep afterwards – the insomniacs taking slightly less time than before, and the non-insomniacs taking more (Haynes *et al.*, 1981). Another study compared the thoughts reported by non-insomniacs and insomniacs upon falling asleep (Freedman and Sattler, 1982). Many of the patients had complained of being unable to get to asleep because they could not turn off their minds. Reports of mental content during the period before sleep onset did not provide convincing evidence that worry or anxiety was causing the real delay in sleep onset shown by the insomniacs (44 minutes versus 13 minutes among the control group). The authors of this study conclude that 'excessive rumination may be an epiphenomenon of sleeplessness', rather than its cause.

According to Rosa *et al.* (1983), subjects declared to be highly anxious sleep slightly less, more lightly and have fewer awakenings than a control group, but generally have no problem getting to sleep. The relationship between anxiety and this sleep disorder is obviously not simple. Priest (1983) reports that in his clinical experience as a psychiatrist specializing in sleep problems, strong emotions of resentment or anger prevent sleep more commonly than does anxiety.

Very high levels of anxiety or worry must, however, be incompatible with sleep, and sleep always suffers during psychiatric crises, but the relationship between sleep and arousal is not simple, and can be paradoxical. For instance, Oswald (1959b) points out how bodily restraints and rhythmic stimulation can induce 'animal hypnosis' in a variety of species, and that this state of immobility is accompanied by EEG signs of sleep. His own experiments on human volunteers confirmed that sleep could be induced in conditions that could only otherwise be described as highly arousing. 'Nervous yawning' is a very commonplace observation. Quite inappropriately, we have an over-whelming desire to yawn when in some crisis, when in fact we have every reason to be extremely anxious. All this is consistent with the Pavlovian notion that impossible tasks or very disagreable conditions can result in 'inhibitory experimental neuroses' – including withdrawal and sleep. A similar explana-tion, applied to infantile sleep behaviour by the neo-Freudian psychiatrist Harry Stack Sullivan, is the 'dynamism of somnolent detachment', whereby the infant withdraws from anxiety-provoking situations (such as the absence of its mother) by falling asleep. Anxiety can thus actually cause sleep, although it also frequently prevents it (Sullivan, 1955).

One interpretation of the aetiology of sleep-onset insomnia is Elliot Weitzman's (1981) suggestion that it may be caused by a disturbance of biological rhythm. The syndrome of regularly not going to bed until the early hours of the morning, and then being unwilling to get up until lunchtime, is quite common among students. These individuals are clearly getting plenty of sleep, but at the wrong time of day. The draconian cure proposed for people with a chronic inability to fall asleep at a particular clock time ('chron-otherapy') is to reset their circadian rhythms with a progressive phase delay of bedtime by three hours each week until the desired bedtime is arrived at. It is unclear, however, how many patients have been sufficiently persistent (and have had a sufficiently flexible lifestyle) to complete the course of treatment. Simply buying a loud alarm clock and getting up an an appropriate time every morning might achieve the same end – one's biological rhythms would settle down in a few days, just as after a transatlantic flight.

A more serious circadian rhythm disorder is suffered by some totally blind people whose visual systems do not register light and dark in any way. (Interestingly, there may still be some effect from light even when light is not perceived at all.) As described in Chapter 9, the administration of melatonin may help reset the circadian cycle in these people, giving them better sleep at night and less need to nap.

To sum up, difficulty in getting to sleep that is not due to pain or discomort from physical illness can sometimes be attributed to excessive anxiety (in particular, apprehension about forthcoming and potentially stressful events) but is commonly caused either by feelings of resentment accompanied by rumination or by the lack of any pressure for sleep.

Disorders of maintaining sleep

Almost three quarters of the Los Angeles survey's insomniacs (Bixler *et al.*, 1979) reported difficulty staying asleep, and just under half reported early awakening. These two symptoms increase in frequency with age, especially the early awakenings. Arousals to light stage 1 sleep or wakefulness typically occur at the end of REM sleep periods in normals (Langford *et al.*, 1974) but are not usually remembered because they are brief. Awakenings have to be longer than two minutes or so to be clearly recalled the next day.

Lightened sleep and relatively early awakenings are normal features of old age, and do not normally result in daytime sleepiness. Persistent maintenance insomnia in middle age or earlier is commonly associated with affective illness (depression and mania), drug abuse, alcoholism and respiratory illnesses. Affective disorders are associated with shortened REM latency (the time between sleep onset and the first REM sleep period) and reduced stages 3 and 4. Monopolar depression (periodic depression with no manic episodes) is also associated with reduced sleep, repeated awakenings and early arousal (Gillin et al., 1979; Kupfer, 1976). Conventional wisdom in psychiatry has always attributed early awakenings to endogenous (severe, or psychotic) depression, and failure to get to sleep with exogenous (neurotic) depression. This 'classic' relationship has never been confirmed in the laboratory, despite the fact that these considerations have presumably been taken into account whenever these sorts of diagnosis have been made (Costello and Selby, 1965; Mendels and Hawkins, 1967).

Alpha–delta sleep

A minority of patients who complain of insomnia actually suffer from 'alpha–delta' sleep, in which the EEG patterns of wakefulness (the 10 Hz alpha rhythm) persist during slow-wave sleep, and the 12–15 Hz spindling of stage 2 is superimposed on the low-voltage, mixed-frequency EEG of REM sleep (Hauri and Hawkins, 1973). These patients report not having slept at all, and feel that they derive little benefit from sleep, although they regularly sleep uninterruptedly for six hours or more. This syndrome is characteristic of patients suffering from fibrositis, as described in Chapter 11.

Sleep apnoea syndrome

The routine use of a measure of respiration in the night-time assessment of the sleep of patients complaining of maintenence insomnia, led to the discovery that the cause of insomnia in some people is entirely respiratory (Guillemi-nault et al., 1973). This fact is usually unknown by sufferers and their doctors, and typically they have a lengthy history of taking a variety of hypnotics that only make their problems worse. These people suffer from sleep apnoea, in which respiration ceases during sleep until the build-up of carbon dioxide in the blood causes them to wake up gasping for air.

It was thought that the prevalence of sleep apnoea syndrome (SAS) in the UK was extremely low compared with the US, as judged by medical referrals (Guilleminault et al., 1973), but this has been challenged on the ground that the problem may have been systematically underdiagnosed (Apps et al., 1983), rather than that Americans are more likely to be obese (McNicholas et al., 1982). It is now accepted that sleep apnoea affects 1–2 per cent of adults in the UK, as much as in the US (Nasser and Rees, 1992).

There is no clear demarcation between SAS, snoring and normal sleep. Careful studies of blood oxygen saturation and of related hypopnoeas (reduction rather than complete cessation of airflow) and apnoeas during the night have shown that many normal subjects suffer from periodic but short-lived breathing difficulties, without any serious disruption of sleep (Bert *et al.*, 1970; Guilleminault and Dement, 1978). However, as these snorers get older, gain weight, take sedatives or drink, the symptoms may become more severe and ultimately result in significant blood oxygen desaturation, multiple awakenings, a significant reduction in REM sleep and the virtual elimination of deep slow-wave sleep stages 3 and 4. Men are eight times more likely to be affected than women until the menopause, when the incidence amongst women increases. In the long term, SAS is associated with intellectual and memory impairment and a higher incidence of cardiovascular disease.

Parkes (1985) distinguishes four categories of SAS:

- *Central apnoea*: respiratory movements are absent and there is no oronasal airflow;
- *Obstructive apnoea*: the diaphragm and chest wall move with changes in intrathoracic pressure but there is no airflow at the nose or mouth;
- *Mixed apnoea*: respiratory movements and airflow are absent early in the episode, followed by resumption of unsuccessful breathing. The opposite pattern does not occur;
- *Subobstructive apnoea*: reduced airflow with increased respiratory effort.

Parkes (ibid.) states that over 90 per cent of all cases of sleep apnoea are associated with airway obstruction, and that purely centrally mediated respiratory failure (with no mechanical obstruction to airflow) is relatively rare. Most of the cases of airway obstruction involve men over 40, many of them with a weight problem. More specifically, it seems that a thick short neck is highly associated with snoring and, more seriously, with apnoea during sleep (Katz *et al.*, 1990).

Drug withdrawal

Alcoholics drying out and suffering from delirium tremens have been found to have fitful sleep for six to eight days, with 50–100 per cent REM sleep accompanied by hallucinatory dreams (Allen *et al.*, 1971). Sleep disturbance continues for up to six months after the first 'good night's sleep', with delayed sleep onset and multiple awakenings through the night. Similar symptoms result from withdrawal from barbiturates (Oswald and Priest, 1965). It has been argued that tolerance to central nervous system depressants (such as alcohol, barbiturates and opiates) produces a syndrome of its own – drug dependency insomnia – and the beneficial sleep-inducing properties of, for instance, barbiturate hypnotics are lost after a few weeks of use (Kales *et al.*, 1969). It now seems that some benzodiazepines (minor tranquillizers) have a similarly disruptive effect on sleep upon withdrawal. Drugs taken initially to deal with transient sleep problems (such as sleep onset insomnia caused by some life crisis) can thus become the mainstay of a drug-dependent pattern of sleep – inducing a classic iatrogenic illness, whereby a course of medical treatment itself causes an illness.

Restless legs syndrome

Finally, maintenance insomnia can be caused by periodic jerking movements or 'restless legs syndrome'. These are persistent and exaggerated forms of the twitches (myoclonal jerks) that most people occasionally experience upon going to sleep, often associated with a sensation of falling. Myoclonal jerks are as mysteriously involuntary as hiccups are when we are awake, and little is known about the determinants of either. In this condition, they occur every 20–30 seconds during slow-wave sleep, disrupting sleep onset and causing disturbance throughout the night. There is no known cure for this condition, and as with sleep apnea, heavy sedation is not beneficial.

Disorders of arousal

Somnambulism, enuresis and night terrors

This group of disorders – somnambulism (sleepwalking), enuresis (bedwetting) and night terrors – have been classified together by Broughton (1968) as disorders associated with deep slow-wave sleep.

Sleepwalking has already been discussed in Chapter 8. It is fairly common: 15 per cent of all children have at least one episode, and up to 6 per cent suffer from frequent attacks (Anders and Weinstein, 1972). Typically the sleeper sits up in bed or gets up in stage 3 or 4 sleep, following some particularly large EEG slow waves. Episodes generally last less than 15 minutes, and after some apparently non-purposive, often repetitive activity sleepwalkers either go back to sleep – often in their own bed – or wake up. There is anecdotal evidence that this disorder runs in families, and there is evidence that enuresis, night terrors and somnambulism may all be genetically associated (Kales *et al.*, 1966).

Enuresis is of course invariable in babies. 'Primary' enuresis is defined as the persistence of bed-wetting into childhood and 'secondary' enuresis as its reappearance after a period of successful bladder continence. Broughton (1968) estimates that 10–15 per cent of 'nervous' children and 30 per cent of institutionalized children wet their beds. In addition, 1 per cent of US naval recruits are enuretic (despite screening for this, amongst other disorders), as are 24 per cent of naval recruits discharged on psychiatric grounds (ibid.). Studies of children have confirmed, as these figures suggest, that enuresis is associated with emotional stress, and often reappears as late as adolescence. Enuresis typically occurs after a period of deep slow-wave sleep. Recordings of bladder pressure have shown that bedwetting is preceded by an increasingly strong series of bladder contractions (which could also be stimulated by clicks, handclaps or other noises), quite unlike the patterns of bladder pressure recorded in normal controls. These excessive contractions do not always result in bedwetting, but have invariably preceded the episodes that have been recorded, which always occurred during slow-wave sleep arousals. This problem is almost certainly caused by overactivity in the autonomic nervous system, which controls all involuntary muscle activity (including the 'smooth muscle' of the guts and bladder, and the heart muscle) (Anders and Weinstein, 1972).

Nightmares should be distinguished from night terrors. The former consist of a frightening dream about some anxiety-laden subject, and normally occur during REM sleep. Waking up from an anxiety nightmare of this sort can be just as frightening as from a night terror, with the difference that reassurance is possible, as the fear is caused by the subject matter and plot of the dream. With night terrors it seems that the fear comes first, with no 'supporting' dream scenario. Typically, a child wakes its parents with an ear-splitting scream, and remains inconsolably terrified for 10 or 15 minutes before falling back into a deep sleep. The next morning, only the parents can remember the incident. Adults can also suffer from night terrors, although less commonly and less spectacularly.

Another disorder of arousal, unrelated to autonomic system activity, is sleep paralysis, in which the flaccid paralysis of REM sleep intrudes into wakefulness. Attacks last up to 10 minutes, and can occur at sleep onset or during the night's sleep at the end of an REM sleep period. Sleep paralysis can be very frightening, especially if accompanied by hallucinations or preceded by a nightmare. The idea of pressure on the chest or immobility, in the notions of 'incubus' and 'cauchmar', signifying being lain upon and pressing down upon, must surely refer to sleep paralysis rather than the other two varieties of nightmare. It is, of course, very common indeed in patients suffering from narcolepsy (being one of the four defining symptoms associated in this syndrome), but it is also relatively common in normal adolescence. In a sample of medical and nursing students, 5 per cent reported sleep paralysis as having occurred at least once in the past year (Goode, 1962). More recently, almost 30 per cent of 870 university students asked about hypnagogic and hallucinoid experiences reported at least one sleep paralysis incident (Cheyne *et al.*, 1999). Fear tends to be associated with the hallucinatory concomitants of sleep paralysis, rather than the experience of paralysis *per se*. It has also been reported that people who regularly suffer from attacks may gain some 'lucidity', so that they recognize what is happening to them and wait for the resumption of control over their bodies in relative tranquillity (Hishikawa, 1976).

REM sleep behaviour disorder (RBD)

Individuals with RBD make movements during REM sleep, sometimes violent but always vigorous, and have accompanying nightmarish dreams (Schenck *et al.*, 1986). This syndrome is associated with conditions where brain damage is implicated, such as dementia, Parkinson's disease, multiple sclerosis and multiple system failure (Ferini-Strambi and Zucconi, 2000). However, no single site of lesion has been identified as responsible for the disorder, and brain imaging and other neurological examinations have been less than helpful in revealing the underlying disorder (Olson *et al.*, 2000). Many of those who suffer from RBD have no specific brain damage. It has been found that clonazepam, a benzodiazepine, is an effective treatment in low doses.

The violent behaviour associated with RBD typically causes injuries to patients themselves, and has been blamed for injuries to others. Broughton *et al.* (1994) report a successful legal defence in a case where a young man committed murder during a sleepwalking episode. In another case, polysomnographic investigation of an alleged RBD sufferer who had killed a two-year-old girl, established that this was an unlikely explanation of the death, and 'sleepwalking' was withdrawn as a defence by the accused's lawyers (Kayumov *et al.*, 2001).

The hypersomnias

Excessive daytime sleepiness is commonly the result of a lack of adequate night-time sleep, caused, for example, by pain, jetlag or the effects of stimulant drugs at night. Sleep apnoea, although rare, is, of course, incompatible with normal sleep patterns, and most patients suffering from sleep apnoea also complain of sleepiness during the day (Guilleminault *et al.*, 1973).

Permanent daytime sleepiness may be a symptom of narcolepsy. This is a rare condition characterized by a tetrad of symptoms – sleep attacks and daytime somnolence, cataplexy, hypnagogic hallucinations and sleep paralysis. EEG/EOG studies of narcoleptic patients have been crucial in furthering our understanding of this disorder. The night-time sleep of sufferers is essentially normal, with the important difference that wakefulness is typically immediately followed by REM sleep, rather than a steady progression through the slow-wave sleep stages (Rechtschaffen *et al.*, 1963). The tendency to do this is more marked in patients who also complain of cataplexy, and is common in daytime sleep attacks and night-time sleep onset.

Cataplexy is an extreme form of the helplessness that can be experienced by anybody who is laughing hilariously or being 'tickled to death'. Any extreme of emotion causes narcoleptics to fall down, with flaccid paralysis of all muscles except the respiratory and oculomotor ones, just as in REM sleep. Hypnagogic hallucinations – the visual and auditory images that many people experience with the onset of sleep – are always reported by narcoleptics. Sleep paralysis, as noted above, is common in adolescence, but persists throughout life in patients suffering from narcolepsy, and is an awakening in which the flaccid paralysis of REM sleep is maintained.

Narcolepsy has long been assumed to be largely genetically determined but, because of its rarity, it has been difficult to quantify the genetic component of its aetiology. Kaprio *et al.* (1996) report a Finnish study of all twin pairs of the same gender born before 1958 and still alive in 1967: 3785 pairs of twins aged 33–60 responded to the Ullanlinna narcolepsy scale and two subscales of sleepiness and cataplexy-like symptoms. By including respondents who had no symptoms, and others who did not suffer from full narcolepsy but reported some of the symptoms, and essentially treating the condition as variable in severity, it was possible to perform regression (correlational) analyses as well as structural equation modelling. On the narcolepsy scale, the correlation between monozygotic (MZ) males was 0.36, and for dizygotic (DZ) males it was 0.07. For women the correlations were MZ, 0.38, and DZ, 0.16. Thus, identical (MZ) twins did not report identical symptoms, but they reported very much more similarly than non-identical (DZ) twins. It was calculated that genetic effects accounted for 35 per cent of the variance in the incidence of these symptoms in men, and 39 per cent in women.

It is unclear whether environmental factors may contribute to the development of this syndrome, which remains a life-long condition that cannot be cured but can be controlled with the help of stimulants during the day.

Cures and palliatives

Treatments for sleep apnoea syndrome (SAS)

Patients suffering from SAS should not be sedated at night, either by hypnotics, antihistamines or alcohol (Nasser and Rees, 1992). Peripheral airway obstruction is the primary cause in the vast majority of cases. Obesity, defined as a body weight 20 per cent greater than that dictated by height in actuarial tables, is present in 60–70 per cent of patients, and the worst symptoms of SAS are often completely eliminated by weight loss alone (Guilleminault et al., 1976).

Obstructive sleep apnoea can be treated surgically in an operation called uvulopalatopharyngoplasty, in which the back of the soft palate is removed, together with some other tissue in the throat. It is reported to produce good reductions in both sleep disturbance and daytime somnolence in about 60 per cent of patients. For a major operation such as this, with all the risks of any surgery with total anaesthetic, it is important to identify those patients who are most likely to benefit. It seems that the best results are obtained with those who do not have the worst symptoms at night (with apnoea/hypopnoea indices of under 30) and are not obese (Kryger et al., 1989).

A second, less drastic treatment is a mechanical aid called nasal continuous positive airway pressure (nCPAP), where at night the patient wears a mask attached to a source of positive air pressure (Sullivan et al., 1981). Both inhalation and exhalation occur at high pressure, so neither receives any assistance from a pump. Rather, the effect of the high pressure is to inflate the pharynx and maintain an airway. This treatment is highly effective and has become the medical profession's treatment of choice, although compliance may be a problem.

Hypnotic drugs

The dramatic change in prescribing habits in hypnotics in the late 1960s was not only a response to an epidemic of deaths through overdose and the availability of relatively non-toxic alternatives, but because of advances in understanding the effects of barbiturates on sleep, and of their addictiveness, gained through EEG/EOG studies.

In the mid-1960s Oswald and Priest (1965) had shown that barbiturates reduced the amount of REM sleep when first taken, like many other drugs.

As tolerance developed over a few days, the level of REM sleep returned to normal, but on withdrawal, the habitual user experienced vivid dreams and nightmares, with frequent night-time awakenings caused by a massive REM sleep rebound, with double the usual amount of REM sleep, lasting for five or six weeks. As discussed earlier, these symptoms often caused patients to return to their doctors for repeat prescriptions of the sedatives, ensuring drug dependency in otherwise healthy people. The change to prescribing minor tranquillizers or benzodiazepine-based hypnotics reduced the number of casualties from barbiturate overdose, and initially it was assumed that these alternative drugs were not habit-forming and induced a more 'natural' pattern of sleep.

Statistics on the number of prescriptions dispensed for hypnotic drugs do not support the view that the new drugs were any less habit-forming than the old ones: more or less the same number of prescriptions for hypnotics was dispensed in 1975 as in 1965 in the UK, and there was no great change in the number of hypnotic users over the age of 40 (who are more liable to suffer from sleep problems). If the new drugs were indeed less habit-forming, the number of prescriptions should have gone down as the benzodiazepine-based hypnotics were introduced.

The immediate effects on sleep of benzodiazepine-based hypnotics were discussed in Chapter 9. Their effects, especially in contrast with barbiturates, appear relatively harmless. However, there is evidence that commonly used hypnotics may cause hangovers the next day, to the extent of measurably impairing performance on simple psychological tasks (Johnson and Chernik, 1982). Their half-life in the blood (the time taken for peak concentrations to be reduced by half) can be as much as 100 hours for diazepam and 30 hours for nitrazepam. A nightly dose will not have dissipated by morning, and consistent use of these drugs results in the gradual build-up of the drug in the body, so that the regular user of sleeping pills is permanently drugged. There is also evidence that withdrawal from benzodiazepines causes anxiety and sleeplessness, and this is often more acute than the level of sleeplessness the drug was originally taken to remedy (Petersson and Lader, 1981).

Some hypnotics have a very short half-life, for example, triazolam. Are their effects any less severe? Morgan and Oswald (1982) assessed the effects of two such drugs, one with a half-life of 15 hours (loprazolam) and another with a half-life of only three hours (triazolam). Their subjects were middle-aged and elderly people who suffered from poor sleep. Triazolam made the subjects feel more and more anxious during the day over a three-week period, while loprazolam made them feel calmer. On withdrawal from triazolam, they felt less anxious, but on their first drug-free day they still felt significantly more anxious than they had before they started to take the drug. The longer-lasting effect of loprazolam resulted in increased anxiety on the third day after withdrawal. Low doses of these drugs did not impair performance on vigilance tasks during the day. However, Morgan et al.'s (1984) elderly subjects did report incidents of absent-mindedness during the day, resulting in four accidents, three of which were associated with taking triazolam.

In another study (Adam et al., 1984), elderly poor sleepers who took one of these two drugs over a similar period, experienced an immediate improvement

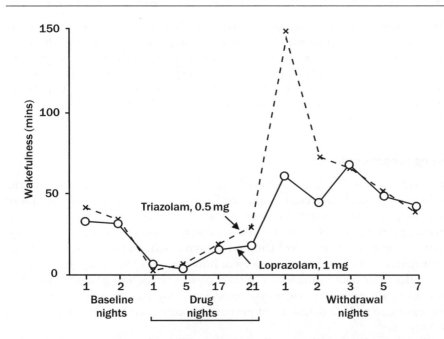

Figure 12.4   Minutes of wakefulness after first sleep onset before, during and after intake of loprazolam (1 mg) or triazolam (0.5 mg) by the same nine subjects. Note the immediate rebound after triazolam (from Adam *et al.*, 1984)

in sleep quality, although this was not maintained when the drug in question was triazolam – by the third week the subjects were sleeping almost as little as they had before they started. Upon withdrawal, sleep tended to be worse than before, especially when triazolam had been taken (Figure 12.4). The authors suspect that the adverse effects of such drugs, in respect of increased anxiety and sleeplessness after withdrawal, may be particularly great amongst elderly people.

Findings such as the ones described above caused many doctors to become increasingly sceptical about the benefits of benzodiazepine hypnotics, especially when taken for any length of time. The Committee on Safety of Medicines in the UK, which regularly publishes advice to doctors, reported in 1988 that dependence on benzodiazepines was becoming increasingly worrying. Withdrawal symptoms included anxiety, depression, tremor and even confusion and fits, as well as insomnia. These symptoms could even occur after short periods of treatment, and it was suggested that up to half the patients who had taken these drugs for any length of time, would develop withdrawal symptoms if they stopped. With regard to their use as hypnotics, the Committee recommended that benzodiazepines 'should be used to treat insomnia only when it is severe, disabling, or subjecting the individual to extreme distress'. In addition, treatment should be intermittent rather than continuous.

It is hard to believe that it is necessary to issue 15 million prescriptions to induce sleep every year, or that all the patients who are prescribed these drugs will be severely distressed or disabled if they do not take them. As many as 70 per cent of prescriptions for minor tranquillizers (including the most popular hypnotics) are repeat prescriptions. Consequently a large number of people in the UK have been taking benzodiazepines for months, if not years. Any attempt to reduce the usage of these drugs will have to allow patients to reduce their dosages gradually, in order to avoid the most unpleasant withdrawal symptoms.

Sleep disorder clinics

It is well known that laboratory subjects' recollections of awakenings in the night are extremely inaccurate, and similarly they are rather imprecise about how long it took to get to sleep, or even of whether they were asleep (according to EEG/EOG criteria) or awake at any moment. Those who consult their doctor about a sleep problem may be in no position to provide such basic information as to how long they sleep or how often they wake up. Patients can only offer their own impressions of their night's sleep, and describe how they feel. Even the most conscientious physician must rely on guesswork when attempting to make a diagnosis of primary insomnia on the basis of a patient's self-report.

In the US, a large number of sleep disorder clinics have been founded, offering routine night-time EEG/EOG assessment and giving objective information on the amount and quality of sleep achieved by any particular patient. There were only one or two of these in the UK at the time the first edition of this book was published (1989), but their number has grown since then. What benefits can they offer the patient?

A report from the US on the effects of referral to one such clinic provides some indication (Ancoli-Isreal et al., 1981). Almost a third of 170 consecutive patients were dealt with by interview and spend no nights in the clinic, but 117 of them were deemed to require polysomnographic assessment (including EEG/EOG recordings together with measures of respiration). Fifty-one of these were found to have sleep apnoea, which was obstructive in origin for 37 of them. The patients with apnoea were significantly older (average 52 years) than those without (average 42 years) and a good number of them were obese. Nine were treated surgically by tracheostomy, which was successful for eight of them. Eight patients were admitted and put on a strict slimming diet, and three of the four who did achieve normal weight had fewer apnoeic attacks. The seriousness of this condition is demonstrated by the fact that two of these patients died in their sleep, one of whom was aged 47 and had no other medically recognized disease. Twelve of the patients assessed in the clinic suffered from 'restless legs' syndrome.

In summing up the benefits of the clinic, Ancoli-Israel et al. (ibid.) stress the importance of discouraging unnecessary referrals, and of limiting EEG/EOG and respiratory recordings to those patients 'for whom a clinical indication is strong'. They ascribe to this selectivity their success in achieving specific diagnoses in 90 per cent of the cases recorded. Several of the patients suffering from sleep apnoea or narcolepsy were able to resume work, with treatment appropriate to their conditions. None of the patients who were given treament died during the course of the study, but five of the untreated patients did die.

It is clear that a few selected patients can benefit enormously from this sort of assessment, and after a lifetime of taking inappropriate, highly potent drugs can at last be given some real relief from their symptoms. However, since it is only for apnoea that EEG/EOG and respiratory evidence is crucial in making a diagnosis, and few sleep disorders are life-threatening, this could be taken as an argument for not pursuing this sort of assessment, which is both costly and laborious. Nonetheless, in view of the widespread suffering caused by sleep disorders in general, and the extensive use of hypnotics, it could be argued that some relatively inexpensive system of recording EEG, EOG, EMG and respiration at home would improve both the accuracy of diagnosis and the suitability of prescribing for patients who seem to be chronically in need of sedation.

Trends in the UK seem to indicate increasing awareness of the prevalence and importance of sleep apnoea. In 2000 Neil Douglas stated at the British Sleep Society's annual conference that the Edinburgh Sleep Service had experienced a huge increase in the number of referrals for respiratory problems over ten years (Douglas, 2000). Limiting themselves to accepting patients suffering from sleepiness during the day, the service was currently taking 30 referrals per week, and had about 2000 patients on CPAP (continuous positive airway pressure). The number of dedicated sleep assessment facilities in the UK is limited, and in many parts of the country hospitals' ear nose and throat departments conduct assessments for the prescription of CPAP.

Home recording devices exist that use reuseable magnetic tape to store the EEG/EOG and respiratory recordings. Since most of the cost of this sort of assessment arises from paying technicians to stay up all night in the sleep laboratory to monitor the equipment, and from the purchase of non-reuseable materials such as paper (a third of a mile of paper per night), a home-recording system would be relatively inexpensive. A sleep assessment service based on home recordings could be provided by psychologists attached to group practices or health services. The application of psychological techniques to the management of sleep disorders will be discussed in Chapter 13.

Enough is now known about the aetiology of sleep disorders to show that the palliatives offered in the past were ineffective, and in some cases positively harmful. While there have certainly been great pharmacological improvements, in that modern sedatives are rarely lethal in overdose, they are almost as habit-forming as the drugs they replaced, and their long-term effects (over periods of years) have not been fully assessed.

13

The Psychological Treatment
of Insomnia*

Insomnia is one of the most ubiquitous human experiences and, since time immemorial, humans have devised strategies to precipitate sleep in the face of insistent consciousness. Passed from one generation to the next, the old childhood panacea of 'counting sheep' is graven deep into the Western collective conscious and may represent one of the earliest attempts at ameliorating the problem of sleep-onset insomnia.

This chapter begins with a brief discussion of the nature and theories of insomnia, followed by an outline of what is entailed in its clinical assessment in the individual case. The range of psychological and behavioural interventions devised to address the problem is then reviewed.

A note on the nature of insomnia

As discussed in Chapter 12, there is no direct relation between objective characteristics of sleep and subjective reports of sleep quality and dissatisfaction (Espie, 1991; Lundh, 1998). It has been demonstrated that most insomnia sufferers overestimate the extent of their sleep disturbance: numerous studies show that people who complain of poor sleep overestimate sleep onset latency, where sleep onset has been determined objectively using polysomnography (Chambers and Keller, 1993).

In general, individuals who complain of insomnia experience fatigue or cognitive difficulties, such as concentration impairment, during the daytime, and it is such problems that lead them to seek treatment for sleep disturbance. These problems can also be a function of affective disturbance or frank clinical depression, which can also be the primary cause of the sleep disturbance itself. Daytime cognitive and affective problems can be a function of chronic difficulties such as chronic fatigue syndrome or dysthymia. It is clear that there are many individuals whose sleep is just as disrupted, but because they are untroubled by daytime difficulties they do not seek referral and view their awakenings as a minor inconvenience rather than as causing serious impairment of their quality of life. Note that a distinction should be made between

---

* By Michael Wang.

daytime concentration impairment, mood disturbance and cognitive fatigue, and the more obvious problem of daytime sleepiness. Surprisingly, the latter is a much less common complaint amongst those presenting with insomnia (Stepansky *et al.*, 1986).

In general, the central nervous system is extremely good at regulating the amount and quality of sleep required, and short of insistent and continuous external interference, in the long run, the vast majority of individuals will, because of the homeostatic nature of the neurophysiological systems which control sleep and sleep architecture, obtain the sleep that is needed to maintain daytime bodily and cognitive function. However, these general principles are overlaid on the human developmental canvas of a general decline in sleep quality with age; particularly in respect of the decline in slow wave sleep and the consequent decline in the perceived degree of restoration provided by sleep. Thus, Lichstein and Fischer (1985) have suggested that most insomniacs are individuals who overestimate their sleep requirement and consequently spend much of their time in bed feeling anxious and frustrated at their inability to fall asleep. A frequent context of complaints of insomnia is that of individuals entering old age and continuing to expect the eight hours of unbroken sleep they enjoyed in their early adult life. Older adults who complain of insomnia, commonly take little or no account of the number and duration of 'catnaps' they take during the day, and fail to include such sleep when considering total daily sleep duration; the homeostatic mechanisms referred to above make no such omission.

Aetiological theories

Despite doubts about the objective reality of complaints of sleep loss, a number of theories have been proposed to explain sleep disturbance. These generally focus on the notion of aberrant hyperarousal as the obstacle to sleep onset and maintenance. Two forms can be distinguished: cognitive arousal or hyperactivity (Borkovec, 1982), and physiological or autonomic arousal (Freedman, 1987; Monroe, 1967). In the case of cognitive hyperactivity, individuals may engage in problem solving, planning future activities, ruminating over the day's events or anticipating the following day. In the case of physiological arousal, the person may be cognitively fatigued but bodily activation such as high muscle tone, rapid heart rate and other signs of autonomic arousal prevent sleep onset.

Empirical support for these theories is equivocal. Insomniacs are not a homogeneous group and it is likely that there are a number of distinct subgroups. Hence, there may be those whose difficulties are largely a function of cognitive activation, others for whom excessive autonomic arousal is the problem, and conceivably a third group who are troubled by a combination of both. Studies that have attempted to prove or disprove the cognitive versus physiological arousal hypotheses, have not commonly taken this into account, and variations in the character of insomniac study samples may explain the divergent findings.

Within the cognitive activation hypothesis, some commentators further distinguish between cognitive and emotional arousal (Espie, 1991). For example, whilst some individuals find that as soon as they turn out the bedroom light involuntary problem-solving mentation begins, others are besieged by affect-laden thoughts and memories that are equally effective in preventing sleep onset. The latter group includes those who suffer frank affective disorders, such as clinical depression.

While the majority of insomniacs attribute their inability to fall asleep to troubling or activating thoughts (Lichstein and Rosenthal, 1980), the presence of such mental activity prior to sleep onset does not prove that it is the cause of insomnia: it is perfectly possible to view such cognition as an epiphenomenon of insomnia. In order to address this matter, some studies have deliberately induced cognitive arousal in normal sleepers and demonstrated resultant delayed sleep onset, in comparison with a control group (for example, Gross and Borkovec, 1982).

Assessment

Given the above considerations, detailed assessment of sleep disturbance and insomnia takes on a crucial and sometimes controversial importance. A comprehensive sleep assessment will include both subjective and objective measures of sleep duration, pattern and quality, as well as reports of daytime function (Espie, 1991; Van Brunt et al., 1996).

The starting point for the assessment of insomnia is the interview with the sufferer. It is important to note the specific nature of patients' discomfiture and their subjective impression of the nature of their difficulties. It is also important to consider their mental state and to reach preliminary conclusions on whether their sleep disturbance is primary, or secondary to an existing mood disorder. Some patients may have primary physical disorders that interfere with sleep as a secondary consequence. It is extremely useful to obtain a collateral account of a person's difficulties from, say, a spouse or partner, while bearing in mind that there is no such thing as an unbiased objective description of the problem. Despite the latter, it is helpful to have two independent perspectives on the phenomenology of the complaint.

It is advisable to obtain a detailed history of the patient's insomnia and general sleep pattern. It is important to enquire about any medical history because of the potential for medical complaints to precipitate and/or exacerbate sleep disturbance. Any history of psychological difficulties is also highly relevant. Furthermore, the therapist will need to discover what treatment (if any) has been obtained previously, and the effect of this.

As a matter of routine, the therapist should ask about the use of alcohol and other drugs, such as sedatives and illicit psychotropics. Most of these substances interfere with the normal rhythm and diurnal pattern of sleep. People often self-prescribe medication that is perceived as soporific; but in the long run, because of pharmacological tolerance and withdrawal effects, this may end up being a major cause of, rather than a cure for, sleep disturbance.

Although the effects of caffeine, as a stimulant of the central nervous system, are perhaps exaggerated, it is sensible to ask about the patient's consumption of coffee, tea, cola and other caffeine-containing drinks and foods. It is important to note that the results of empirical dose-response studies suggest that the early effects of caffeine are, paradoxically, sedative. Autonomic activation reaches a peak approximately three to six hours after the consumption of caffeine. Thus, individuals who consume a drink that is high in caffeine shortly before midnight may find themselves waking up at around 5–6 a.m. as a direct result of their bedtime drink.

A number of formal psychometric instruments designed to investigate the nature and severity of sleep disturbance are available, and it is often useful to employ one of these in order to obtain a reliable and valid quantitative representation of the problem (for a review of these, see Bootzin and Engle-Friedman, 1981; Evans 1977; Johns, 1975). Such an assessment will provide the basis for further discussion with the patient about the nature and type of the problem experienced, and will also provide baseline data with which to compare follow-up assessment data after intervention has taken place.

Invariably, self-monitoring is essential in the assessment of insomnia. The subject is asked to keep a sleep diary or log for the duration of the baseline assessment and subsequent intervention. Such a record will be partly tailored to the type of complaint in question; however, in general, it will include time of retirement to bed, time of sleep onset, number of awakenings and the approximate times of these and their duration, time of final awakening and rising, and some kind of rating of the degree of refreshment obtained. The therapist may also require information on activities and eating and drinking patterns from the early evening onwards. It may also be useful to ask for collateral monitoring of the same variables by the spouse or partner.

The patient may also be asked to keep a record of thoughts and the cognitive phenomena that occur during the sleep onset latency period, and to keep a notebook next to the bed to record any dreams or nightmares that interrupt sleep. All of these data should be brought to the treatment sessions and used to plan intervention and monitoring.

Lundh (1998) suggests focusing on three cognitive aspects during assessment: (1) degree of fear about insufficient sleep and its daytime consequences; (2) the beliefs implicated in these fears; and (3) the person's standard of performance in interpersonal and professional functioning (this is often unrealistically perfectionist in insomniacs).

Intervention

Almost all psychological insomnia treatments address the problem of initial insomnia (extended latency of sleep onset at the beginning of the intended sleep period), rather than that of maintenance insomnia or early morning waking. They can be broadly categorized according to aetiological emphasis: thus, progressive muscular relaxation training stems from an emphasis on aberrant somatic autonomic arousal as the primary impediment to sleep onset, whereas cognitive distraction techniques, such as image focusing, relate to an emphasis on worrying and rumination (cognitive activation) as the primary cause.

Sleep hygiene

Sleep hygiene includes simple guidance and advice on avoiding waking behaviours that are likely to interfere with subsequent sleep onset, and encouraging those which are likely to facilitate sleep onset. There is no common underlying theoretical rationale to these diverse recommendations, other than the need to avoid behaviours that increase autonomic activation and engage in those which reduce arousal. For example, there is dietary advice: the person is exhorted to avoid caffeine, particularly after 5 p.m., and is educated in the identification of caffeine-containing drinks and foods. Heavy meals are discouraged after 6 p.m., but a light snack accompanied by a milky drink shortly before retiring to bed is advocated. The person is advised to avoid strenuous or cognitively demanding activity after 8 p.m. and encouraged to engage in soporific activity such as light reading prior to bedtime; however, some outdoor physical activity earlier in the day is encouraged.

Progressive muscular relaxation (PMR)

The origins of PMR can be traced back to the American physician Jacobson (1929), who devised a complex and lengthy method of reducing resting muscle tone in all the major voluntary muscle groups of the body. He reasoned that since resting muscle tone is intimately related to autonomic activation, the reduction of muscle tone by external means ought to result in a comparable reduction in autonomic arousal. The innovation here was the paradoxical use of isometric muscle contraction as the prelude to muscle relaxation. Thus, Jacobson's method involved tensing and relaxing, in turn, 64 separate muscle groups. As many as 40 training sessions might be required. There were two effects that Jacobson sought to harness: first, the subject should learn to distinguish the proprioceptive sensations associated with the contrasting conditions of muscle contraction and muscle relaxation, leading to a heightened awareness of muscle state at any time; and second, the physiology of muscle fibre is such that strong isometric contraction followed by sudden release leads to a greater reduction in resting muscle tone than that arising from the release of muscle tension in the absence of a previous isometric contraction.

Later the South African psychiatrist Joseph Wolpe, in his influential book *Psychotherapy by Reciprocal Inhibition* (1958), introduced a much abbreviated version of PMR that could take as few as 10–15 training sessions of 30 minutes each with the therapist, using the same principles of tensing and relaxing muscle groups in a systematic, progressive manner. This modification constituted a much more practical and realistic improvement on Jacobson's original method whilst retaining its essential characteristics, and since its inception it has become widely used by clinical psychologists for anxiety management, and also by physiotherapists and midwives to prepare pregnant women for labour and childbirth.

The progressive muscular relaxation procedure

The following exercises are best practised either lying on the floor with a pillow under the head, or sitting in a comfortable armchair with a back that is high enough to support the head.

For each of the exercises, tightly contract the set of muscles in question for 10 seconds and then let go *suddenly and rapidly*. Spend the following 20 seconds concentrating on the sensations you experience from the part of the body concerned. Look out especially for feelings of warmth and tingling. Repeat this procedure another two times, and then go on to the next exercise. It should take at least 15 minutes to complete the whole set.

1. Clench the fists, with elbows resting on the chair arms or floor,
2. Press down the palms of the hands onto the chair arms or floor,
3. Press the heels of the feet backwards onto the floor,
4. Lift the feet off the floor, straighten the legs and point the toes,
5. Raise the eyebrows, looking 'surprised',
6. Screw up the eyes, lifting the corners of the mouth at the same time,
7. Press the back of the head against the back of the chair or the floor, raising the shoulders,
8. Press the chin into the chest,
9. Tense the muscles of the stomach/abdomen.

When PMR is applied to insomnia, the subject is first trained in the clinic and then asked to practise at home, perhaps three times a day. Subjects tend to improve their technique and to increase the potency and duration of the relaxation effect. They are then encouraged to engage in the PMR exercises either immediately before retiring to bed, or whilst lying in bed before expected sleep onset.

A large group of empirical studies have demonstrated the effectiveness of PMR as a treatment for insomnia. Borkovec (1982) has reviewed a number of studies and concludes that in the treatment of insomnia, despite its somatic focus, the most important effect of PMR is to induce a reduction in *cognitive* arousal. It is this cognitive effect that is primarily responsible for the induction of sleep.

Biofeedback

Biofeedback involves the provision of a physical indication (to which the subject attends) of the level of an autonomic parameter that is not normally available to conscious introspection. The subject then attempts, by means of cognitive effort, to alter the autonomic parameter in a particular direction (up or down) and the indicator provides knowledge of results. The most widely used parameter in connection with the treatment of insomnia is the electromyogram (EMG); that is, the provision of quantitative information on the level of electrical activity in a muscle, commonly the frontalis. Typically, electrodes are placed on the forehead, and the signal from the electrode leads is amplified in a box that includes a visual display, providing a quantitative indication of changes in the EMG signal on, for example, a dial or numerical light emitting diode. The visual display is placed in front of the subject, who is encouraged to concentrate on reducing the reading, which in turn should result in the progressive reduction of the EMG signal. Alternatively, auditory feedback may be provided in the form of continuous clicks that increase or decrease in frequency and pitch as a function of the physiological signal. Patients are often provided with a biofeedback machine to use at home. In the treatment of insomnia, the subject uses the machine immediately before retiring to bed at night to reduce autonomic arousal and thus increase the probability of sleep onset.

Biofeedback is essentially an operant conditioning intervention in which changes in the desired direction of the measured parameter are reinforced, initially by the therapist and subsequently by the subject him- or herself. Although biofeedback – as a general approach to the reduction of automatic arousal – was extremely fashionable in the early 1970s, it rapidly declined in popularity from the early 1980s, partly because it never lived up to its early promise in terms of potency of effect, and also because a number of studies published in the 1970s demonstrated that it was no better than relaxation training in terms of autonomic deactivation effects (Freedman and Papsdorf, 1976; Haynes *et al.*, 1977).

Hypnosis

Despite the literal meaning of the Greek root of the word, it is only in recent times that hypnosis has been used as a treatment for insomnia. Typically, the patient is hypnotized by the therapist in the clinic, and then in subsequent sessions is taught self-hypnosis. Generally, the patient is taken through a set sequence of images or scenes that deepen the hypnotic state and provide a cognitive focus. The procedure involves careful attention to self-induction and self-termination of the hypnotic state, along with education on the nature of the hypnosis and the ease of spontaneous emergence from it. Once the patient has practised self-induction and self-termination of hypnosis in the clinic with the therapist, he or she is encouraged to practise self-hypnosis at home (whilst lying in bed before sleep onset) as a means of reducing autonomic arousal, counteracting unhelpful cognitive activity and worry, and in effect, creating the cognitive and autonomic conditions that are most conducive for sleep.

Autogenic training

Autogenic training has been described as a hybrid of somatic relaxation and hypnosis. The patient practices self-statements that suggest that a particular limb is becoming increasingly heavy or warm whilst lying down or sitting in a comfortable armchair. The patient is encouraged to be vigilant of such sensations and to concentrate on these. A type of respiratory control is also taught. Effectively, the technique amounts to a form of self-hypnosis. When applied to insomnia, the autogenic training exercises are practised whilst in bed awaiting sleep onset. Nicassio and Bootzin (1974) compared autogenic training with progressive muscular relaxation training in a group of older adults with insomnia. Autogenic training was found to be as effective as relaxation.

There is much overlap between autogenic training and meditation, which has also proved to be effective in the treatment of insomnia (Woolfolk *et al.*, 1976).

Sleep restriction

The sleep restriction approach to insomnia begins with the recording of total subjective sleep duration for one week. These data are then used to plan a daily routine or schedule, which can result in a dramatic reduction in the time spent lying awake, since the time the patient spends in bed is restricted to the average duration of actual sleep time per night. In practice, time asleep increases progressively from the relatively short time-in-bed baseline. This approach is based on the assumption that those who complain of insomnia spend excessive amounts of time lying in bed. The aim of the intervention is to match more accurately the patient's bedtime routine with the actual sleep requirement.

Spielman *et al.* (1987) conducted a trial on sleep-restriction intervention using 35 participants. They found that although there was a worsening of total sleep time during the first two weeks of treatment, by the end of the treatment the average total sleep time had increased by 23 minutes, despite the fact that the participants were spending 86 minutes less in bed. However, there was a high drop-out rate in that 16 per cent of the original sample withdrew because of difficulty with complying with the rigorous schedule.

Paradoxical intention

Paradoxical intention was made popular by the American psychotherapist Viktor Frankl, but more latterly it has been adopted by behaviour therapists. The essence of the approach is that patients are instructed to reproduce cognitively the very problem they seek to eliminate. The rationale is that in most cases, anxiety and arousal are generated by deliberate attempts at amelioration; but if the individual concentrates on creating or worsening the problem, performance anxiety is avoided, leaving the naturally occurring response to emerge spontaneously. When applied to the problem of insomnia, patients are instructed to lie in bed with the light out but to keep their eyes open and direct all their cognitive effort towards staying awake as long as possible. This often results in a rapid reduction in sleep onset time. Initially the patients may be able to keep themselves awake for some hours, but by the second, third or fourth night they find it increasingly difficult to remain awake (Ascher and Turner, 1979). However, Espie and Lindsay (1985) found considerable variation in individual responses to paradoxical intention. In three of the six cases reported the patients achieved a rapid and robust improvement, but for the other three the insomnia worsened. Lundh (1998) points out that prior to intervention it is impossible to predict who will, and who will not, benefit from paradoxical intention, and on this basis does not recommend it as a treatment for persistent insomnia.

Stimulus control

The stimulus control approach to the management of insomnia, rests on the basic principle of associative conditioning (classical or Pavlovian conditioning). As in Pavlov's classic canine demonstration, an involuntary or autonomic response such as salivation can be prompted by a previously neutral stimulus such as a ringing bell, following a period of training in which the neutral stimulus is consistently presented immediately before the natural onset of the involuntary response (salivation). Bootzin (1972) first described the application of this principle to sleep and the problem of insomnia. Physical settings related to bedtime and the bedroom are seen as conditioned stimuli, associated on the one hand with sleep (in the case of the healthy somnolent) and on the other with worry and agitated wakefulness (in the case of the insomniac). Typically, the insomniac spends so much time lying awake in the bedroom, often in an agitated state, that the physical setting becomes associated with insomnia and worry rather than sleep. Thus, just lying down in bed automatically prompts sleep anxiety and inhibition.

One obvious example of this is the way in which the presence of a clock in the bedroom can exacerbate sleep anxiety and hence insomnia: insomniacs see the clock face and are immediately aware of how long they have been waiting to get off to sleep and how little time is left before they need to get up to start the new day. Thus, the clock face becomes associated with anxiety and inhibition of sleep onset.

In essence, the stimulus control approach involves the strict manipulation of associations between the physical setting of the bedroom and sleep onset. Insomniacs are advised not to use the bedroom for any activity other than sleep – thus eating, reading, watching television and so on are prohibited in the bedroom. All clocks are removed. Furthermore, a time limit of approximately 15 minutes (as estimated by the patients) is placed on each attempt to get off to sleep. When this period has elapsed and there is no sign of sleep, the patients are required to get out of bed, move to another room and engage in a potentially soporific activity, such as light reading or progressive muscular relaxation, until they begin to feel sleepy. They should then return to the bedroom and lie down in bed. If sleep onset again fails to occur within 15 minutes, the procedure is repeated.

For chronic insomniacs, the first week of this type of intervention is characterized by nights punctuated with repeated risings from and returns to bed, with little improvement (and sometimes a worsening) of the total time asleep. Generally, however, by the second week a substantial gain in sleep time and quality becomes evident.

Cognitive techniques

A number of classical cognitive therapy techniques have been recruited to treat insomnia. Here, the focus is on unhelpful worry- or problem-related thinking, which is thought to maintain insomnia. This includes thought-stopping, 'time out' from worry, rational appraisal or cognitive restructuring, image focusing and problem solving.

Thought stopping

The thought-stopping technique begins with asking the patient to articulate concisely the essence of her or his worry or preoccupation in one or two sentences, which she or he may be asked to write on a card. Next, the therapist reads out the written worry whilst the patient concentrates on recreating it in her or his mind. When the patient indicates that the worry is occurring with some intensity, the therapist suddenly bangs the table with the palm of the hand and simultaneously shouts 'stop!' This should have the effect of disrupting, in a rather dramatic way, the patient's thought progression or rumination. The procedure is repeated a number of times, and then the patient is encouraged to take over the therapist's role, initially by shouting out the word 'stop!' her- or himself, and eventually by internalizing this activity so that the thought sequence is disrupted and terminated without any sound being made. When applied to insomnia, the patient is asked to identify the most common and recurrent worries or ruminations that prevent sleep onset. Thought stopping is then practised in the clinic, based on these particular worries. Next, the patient is encouraged to use the thought-stopping technique at the first sign of such worries or ruminations occurring during the night.

Two studies have demonstrated the effectiveness of thought stopping in the treatment of insomnia, but only as one of a number of techniques in a combined package (Mitchell, 1979; Mitchell and White, 1977). The authors consider that thought stopping, along with the other cognitive control techniques, is more effective than PMR in the treatment package.

Thought substitution

An alternative approach aimed at curtailing thoughts that interfere with sleep onset is to substitute these with alternative thoughts that are more commensurate with sleep. The patient is asked to keep a record of all the thoughts that seem to be preventing sleep onset, perhaps writing them in a notebook placed at the bedside. The patient takes these records to the clinic and discusses them with the therapist. The patient and the therapist then 'brainstorm' a variety of alternative thoughts that are more conducive to sleep, and the patient is encouraged to switch rapidly from the sleep-interfering thoughts to the substitutes. The patient may be asked to practise this substitution both in the clinic and also at home.

Worry control

Espie and Lindsay (1987) describe a technique called 'worry control'. Patients are asked to reflect on their day and to write down all possible worries that might arise and interfere with their sleep onset at night. They are expected to think through each problem and write down any action they might take to help resolve the problem. Espie and Lindsay recommend that this phase of problem noting and resolution should take place in the early evening, immediately after the evening meal. No more than 30 minutes each evening should be spent on the task, which should not take place in the bedroom.

The authors describe a case in which this procedure was used. There was an average improvement of 38 minutes to sleep onset (from 52 minutes to 14 minutes) and this was reported as being maintained at the three- and 12-month follow-up sessions.

Articulatory suppression

This technique is described by Levey *et al.* (1991). The patient is required to repeat out loud a relatively meaningless word such as 'the', rather like a Buddhist mantra, varying the rhythm so that it is irregular, with inconsistent intervals from one vocalization to the next. Levey *et al.* describe a case study in which they combined sleep hygiene, stimulus control, progressive muscular relaxation training, worry control and articulatory suppression in separate phases, thus allowing a degree of partition of the effect of each component. They tentatively conclude that the articulatory suppression phase gave rise to the greatest gain in sleep onset latency.

Problem solving

The basic pattern of problem solving is described by d'Zurilla and Goldfried (1971). It is a generic approach that is applicable to a large range of clinical and non-clinical situations. In the first phase, the problem is identified and expressed in concrete, specific and operational terms. The second phase involves 'brainstorming' a number of alternative solutions to the problem. Classical brainstorming involves the generation of numerous alternatives without criticism, examination or analysis of how realistic and practical such generated alternatives are. Evaluation of each potential solution takes place in the third stage, when the patient and therapist collaboratively choose the most practical and effective of the alternatives. In the fourth phase, the chosen solution is broken down into detailed steps; in other words, a task analysis is conducted. The task analysis translates a general solution into a detailed series of actions that are specific, concrete and have a high probability of being implemented by the patient. The fifth stage includes a careful examination, with the patient, of where implementation might break down or encounter significant obstacles. Further discussion and planning then takes place to pre-empt such problems. Finally, the patient is encouraged to implement the chosen solution, and the success and difficulties encountered are evaluated in subsequent sessions.

When applied to insomnia, the patient is asked to keep a record of the worries and problems that prevent sleep onset. These are discussed at the therapy session and the classical problem-solving approach is applied to each in turn. The aim is to pre-empt cognitive worry by engaging in a programme of active problem solving that removes the affective intensity of such thoughts.

Image focusing

As mentioned earlier, one of the oldest techniques for engendering sleep is 'counting sheep', where the would-be sleeper imagines a field of sheep and either counts the number present or counts them in turn as they jump over a fence, keeping a tally of the total. The essential characteristics of this are the cognitive focus the image provides, distracting the person from sleep-inhibiting thoughts, and the repetitive and somewhat monotonous nature of the image, which induces hypnosis. This general approach is known as 'image focusing' and there are a number of variations of the theme. For example, Coates and Thoresen (1979) describe a case in which the patient was instructed to focus on a single pleasant image – it was suggested to the patient that she could consider her problems during the following day. The package of treatment also included progressive relaxation training, although this was used mainly in the early phase of the treatment, prior to the image focusing. Coates and Thoresen report a reduction of sleep onset latency from 33 minutes to just two minutes, and there was also some improvement in sleep efficiency. They followed up this patient over a four-year period, during which time the improvement was maintained.

Rational appraisal or cognitive restructuring

Traditional cognitive therapy approaches, in which the underlying beliefs and assumptions from which spring worries and rumination are identified and challenged systematically, have been applied to cognition that inhibits sleep onset. These techniques are forms of rational appraisal or combative restructuring and may include the correcting of unrealistic sleep expectations, revising false beliefs about the causes of insomnia, and reappraising perceptions of consequences on daytime functioning.

Ideographic analysis of thought content

Much of the above points to the importance of detailed, intensive, individualized analysis of thought content during periods of wakefulness. There are large individual differences in the types and nature of the worry and rumination that preoccupy individuals whilst awaiting sleep onset. Although sometimes overlooked, a fundamental characteristic of cognitive behavioural intervention in whatever setting is the individualized approach. Each client and each problem is considered unique. Competent cognitive behavioural intervention begins with a detailed analysis, using numerous sources of information, including self-monitoring, and individualized treatment is a direct function of such analysis. In the case of insomnia where recurrent thoughts prevent sleep onset, detailed assessment of these is required, along with consideration of the patient's underlying concerns, automatic thoughts and silent assumptions. Such areas need to be considered in great detail during sessions with the therapist and a detailed programme of intervention that addresses these cognitive phenomena should be developed and implemented.

Meta-analyses of outcome studies

Two major analytic studies of the effectiveness of psychological treatments for insomnia have been published. Morin's (1993) analysis suggests that sleep restriction brings about the greatest improvement, although the number of sleep restriction studies included in the analysis was small in comparison with those for relaxation and stimulus control. On the other hand, Murtagh and Greenwood (1995) conclude that combination treatment that includes relaxation and cognitive components produces the best improvements in total sleep time. In terms of individual components, stimulus control was found to have the most beneficial effect on ratings of sleep quality, and paradoxical intention had the largest effect on total sleep time.

Conclusion

This chapter has reviewed the diverse psychological and behavioural techniques that have been devised or borrowed to treat insomnia. In practice, it is unusual for such treatments to be used in isolation – rather they are usually part of a multiple component package. There is considerable empirical evidence of the effectiveness of these treatments, in combination or alone, mainly in comparative or placebo-controlled trials. Nevertheless, such research, whilst helpful in the general evaluation of treatment, is somewhat misleading in that it implies homogeneity among the individuals who complain of insomnia, and in the nature of their problems. Whilst a treatment may result in the improvement of objective indices of sleep, such as sleep onset latency and total sleep time, the individual may remain dissatisfied because of his or her continuing subjective perception of poor sleep quality or, more pertinently, the absence of improvement in daytime functioning. All this points to the importance of a careful and detailed ideographic assessment and analysis of each individual's problems, focusing on night-time thoughts, concerns and underlying beliefs and taking account of daytime functioning and other factors (in addition to sleep disturbance) that may be contributing to daytime problems.

It is common for those complaining of insomnia to have erroneous beliefs about the nature of sleep and the effects of sleep deprivation: they may overestimate how much sleep they actually require; they may erroneously attribute aspects of daytime functioning and mental state to disturbed sleep; and they may have unrealistically high expectations of daytime performance. These factors require careful and skilled examination and assessment – drawing on multiple sources of information – before decisions are made about intervention, which should follow directly from the conclusions drawn from the ideographic analysis.

14

Children's Sleep Problems

Assessment of the nature of sleep problems in children poses different problems from those faced when assessing adult sleep disorders. As we saw in Chapter 12, it is not always easy to judge what is wrong with adults' sleep merely by listening to their own impressions of how they spend their nights. Many adults who sleep little or badly do not complain, while others whose sleep appears normal in the laboratory do complain of poor sleep. As far as children are concerned, their opinions may not even be sought on whether they are sleeping well or badly – it is the parents who generally decide whether a sleep problem exists, rather than the child. Parents' expectations of how much children ought to sleep, and when, will obviously determine whether they see their child as having a sleep problem. Furthermore, this is often treated within the family as a matter of managing the child, or of discipline, rather than something to be treated by the family doctor.

Essentially, therefore, a child's sleep problem is a parental problem. In the very young it may even be one that the child is unaware of. On the other hand, children aged four to 12 or so may be well aware that that they are causing difficulties, but 'their' sleep problem is only felt acutely by their parents. While the rarer syndromes of sleep disorder suffered by adults, such as sleep apnoea, may also affect small children, instances of this are mercifully rare. Breathing difficulties are commoner amongst premature babies or those with a very low birth weight, and these individuals are usually identified early in life by medical professionals. For very young babies, breathing difficulties are potentially life-threatening and ought to be treated in hospital. This chapter will not consider the rarer, more serious sleep disorders associated with medical conditions, but will confine itself to the far more common problems of sleep that confront many parents.

Infancy

During the first few weeks of life babies sleep as much during the day as during the night, waking up every three or four hours around the clock. From the age of six weeks some infants settle down at night and do not make any demands on their parents until morning, while others continue to wake up and cry at night for three months or longer. Laboratory evidence (discussed in Chapter 2) has shown that infants do not necessarily sleep through the night after they

209

have stopped demanding attention during the night. Rather they periodically wake up, but remain quiet. Babies vary in temperament, some being content to lie awake in relative silence in a darkened room even if moderately wet and slightly hungry, while others invariably summon their mothers at the tops of their voices.

Colic

Where a baby screams for no apparent reason, it is all too easy to imagine that something is seriously amiss. The colicky baby is inconsolably irritable for at least three hours a day. Weissbluth (1987) reports that colic is very common indeed, although the severity of the attacks and their length vary considerably. Typically, the attacks begin after the second week of life; 50 per cent of infants will have settled down by their second month, and only 10 per cent will still be showing the symptoms after four months of age. Interestingly, premature babies do not show signs of colic until they reach the age they would have been if the pregnancy had been full term, rather than their age since birth, giving support to the view that these periodic paroxysms of screaming are an inevitable consequence of the development of the nervous system in some babies. There is no evidence that colic is associated with any particular of child-rearing practices, and it is certainly not a consequence of neglect.

Little can be done to prevent or cure colic, and it is important to remain calm and patient, even when the baby screams and screams. Merely holding and cuddling the baby often has little effect. One tactic is to put a nappy on your shoulder, hold the baby so that it faces over your shoulder, and then walk up and down, singing softly. Eventually the crying will cease. Of the three that I have been involved in bringing up, only one (fortunately) suffered from colic, and at her worst she could only be quietened by a ride in her carrycot in the car. (On one occasion this ride had to continue for 30 miles, although more commonly a trip around the block was enough.)

Most importantly, one must recognize when the child is beginning to leave this difficult stage. At that point it is vital to establish a regular routine at bed-time in order to facilitate the transition to normal, trouble-free nights. It has been suggested that it is the most solicitous mothers who do the most to prevent the development of normal sleep patterns – that is, the mother maintains the infant's disrupted sleep pattern by continuing to pick it up at the slightest sound even after it has recovered from its colicky phase, eventually making the child dependent on the mother's constant physical presence (Ogden, 1985).

Toddlers

Origins of common sleep disorders in toddlers

Between the age of three months and three years there is a great reduction in the total amount of sleep taken by the child. Most of this reduction is during the day, with naps becoming shorter and fewer. Spock (1979) observed that towards the end of the first year most babies are down to two naps a day, and by the time they are 18 months old they will have dropped one of these. Sleep during the night becomes uninterrupted. At this stage, many children wake up rather earlier in the mornings than their parents would like them to – for instance, between 5 am and 6 am. As with awakenings during the night, there is no reason why a toddler should not be able to amuse itself in its cot until its parents feel it is a reasonable time to get up, and if the parents are not too quick to run to the toddler at the first sound, it often transpires that it is perfectly happy to remain on its own, murmuring and muttering to itself.

Parental tolerance of night wakenings in one-year-old toddlers varies considerably. Messer and Richards (1993) report the findings of a postal survey that asked mothers how frequently their babies awoke, and whether they thought there was a night-waking problem. Of those mothers whose babies woke five times a week or more at night, 10 per cent regarded this as normal. Of those whose babies woke less frequently than this, 37 per cent felt that night waking was a real problem. According to Messer and Richards, between a third and a fifth of infants continue to wake at night during their preschool years.

The definition of 'sleep problem' in this age group is thus most unclear – some parents see multiple awakenings during the night as perfectly normal, while others do not. It is possible, however, to try to determine the incidence of disturbed sleep during infancy, and to correlate this with any psychosocial factors that may be relevant. Zuckerman et al. (1987) conducted a longitudinal study based on interviews with over 300 mothers in London. Ten per cent of mothers reported three or more wakenings per night when their babies were eight months old, and 22 per cent reported one awakening per night. The interviews were repeated when the children were three years old, when the mothers were asked about other behavioural problems, as well as sleep problems. Twenty-nine per cent of three-year-olds were reported to have sleep problems, with 18 per cent having difficulty getting to bed or to sleep, and 22 per cent waking up at night. One third of the children who had been reported as having a sleep problem at eight months still had a sleep problem at the age of three –many more than would be expected by chance, and demonstrating good evidence of consistency in sleeping badly at both ages.

It was also found that the three-year-olds who slept badly were more likely to have other behavioural problems – having tantrums or being more difficult to manage in general. A range of demographic and psychosocial measures failed to show that the circumstances of the poor sleepers were worse than those who slept well, although the mothers of poor sleepers tended to be more depressed. Naturally one might ask whether they were depressed because they were being kept awake every night by their infant. That is, given an association between depression in the mother and a sleep disorder in the child, was the depression the cause or the consequence of the sleep problem? The authors investigated this by comparing the rate at which depression had developed amongst mothers who had not been depressed at the eight-month interview. With regard to the likelihood of becoming depressed, there was no difference between those whose children had sleep problems at that age and those whose children had not, indicating that it was perhaps depression in the mother that had somehow caused at least a proportion of the children to develop sleep problems – a conclusion supported by the findings of two other studies (Lozoff *et al.*, 1985; Richman, 1981). It would be surprising indeed if only one factor (such as maternal depression) is responsible for all sleep problems in infancy and childhood, and it is highly likely that temperamental differences account for a large number of overactive, difficult and wakeful individuals.

Children may refuse to go to bed, or persistently wake up and summon their parents at night for no apparent or good reason. Ferber (1987) estimates that 15–35 per cent of young children behave like this. Ferber suggests that anxiety and oversolicitousness on the part of parents dealing with a colicky baby may result in a toddler continuing to demand attention during the night, long after there is any real need for it. While a small baby may need to be rocked to sleep, a two-year-old generally should not. It is more usual for a young child to have achieved enough independence to go to sleep and stay asleep all night without further attention.

Some objective evidence in support of this interpretation comes from a study that compared the night-time waking rates of children whose parents were routinely with them when they fell asleep (33 per cent of the sample of 122) with those whose parents were not (Adair *et al.*, 1991). The nine-month-old infants who always had one parent with them when they fell asleep were twice as likely to wake during the night as those whose parents left them to fall asleep on their own (6.2 versus 3.1 awakenings a week). While suggestive, this finding cannot be regarded as conclusive, as of course it may be that the more difficult children (those who were more likely to wake up later in the night) were more likely to elicit more attention from their parents, including sitting with them while they went to sleep.

Theoretical and clinical background to treatments

A fundamental concept in the management of sleep problems in babies and young children is that of behavioural extinction. The assumption is that parental attention following natural awakenings by the child reinforces both the intensity of the child's crying (to draw attention to the fact that it is awake) and the frequency of such awakenings. The pragmatic solution to this state of affairs is to deny the child such parental attention, and a number of sound empirical studies bear testimony to the effectiveness of this approach. However, many parents find this too harsh, and leaving the baby to cry for long periods of time – particularly during the first few nights of this treatment, when there is often a paradoxical worsening of the problem (known as the 'post-extinction response burst') – is more than they can bear. There is concern about the ethics of such treatment and some parents worry that there may be harmful long-term consequences (despite there being no evidence whatsoever that this is the case). These considerations have led to modifications of the basic extinction approach, in which intervention is made more gentle whilst preserving the underlying extinction principle.

For example, a graded approach may be adopted, in which parents gradually reduce the immediacy and duration of their response to the child's crying. They may systematically increase the time between crying onset and attending to the child, or they may gradually reduce the time spent with the child after an awakening. Alternatively, parents may be advised to check their child briefly and at regular intervals during the period of crying, but without making physical contact or communicating with the child. A parent may be asked to remain in the same room as the child, sleeping in a separate bed, but again witholding physical contact and communication with the child during the early phase of the treatment. This has the effect of reassuring the parent that no harm is coming to the child, but at the same time the parent is not responding to the child's attempts to gain attention and physical interaction.

Scheduled awakening

Scheduled awakening first involves making a baseline recording of the infant's pattern of sleep disturbance. The child is then deliberately woken at scheduled points during the night, timed to occur prior to each expected awakening. Over the subsequent weeks the time between these scheduled awakenings is gradually increased, until a lengthy period of sustained sleep is achieved.

Stimulus control

Stimulus control principles, as described in Chapter 13 in respect of psychological treatments for adult sleep disorders, have also been used in the treatment of children's sleep problems. This includes careful and consistent management of activities prior to bedtime, setting fixed bedtime and rising patterns, and maintaining an exclusive sleep environment.

Practical treatments of common sleep disorders in toddlers

Bidder *et al.* (1986) assessed the usefulness of one child sleep disorder clinic and examined the nature of the sleep problems experienced by the children referred to it. The 44 clients referred to the clinic ranged from seven months to four years of age, although most were younger than two. In general, they either suffered from frequent awakenings during the night, or a combination of freqent awakenings and difficulty in settling. Difficulty in settling on its own was not common. The treatment consisted of advice being given by child development advisers to the parents, and continuous monitoring of the child's progress by means of sleep diaries kept by the parents.

A typical eight-month-old with settling and frequent waking problems was put on a regime of quiet play before bed, a last bottle in bed, and soothing and relaxing techniques to help it settle. The relaxation techniques were repeated when the child woke in the night, but with minimal stimulation; for example, quiet music could be played but there should be no light, change, drinks or talking. The child could only be picked up and soothed very quietly. By the end of three weeks there had been a great improvement, and there was only one difficult night in the fourth week. Before treatment began the child had typically taken an hour and a half to get to sleep, and had woken at least three times every night for about half an hour.

In this case the treatment was entirely successful. The techniques used were similar to those which many parents adopt spontaneously as a matter of 'common sense'. There may be other ways of dealing with small children that are equally effective in reassuring them and promoting uninterrupted sleep. For instance, therapists at another sleep disorder clinic (Richmann *et al.*, 1985) advised parents to discuss the problem with their two-year-olds and to set agreed targets (such as sleeping in their own bed, and going to bed at an agreed time). They rewarded the children with surprises under the pillow if they went to bed at the right time, stories for settling quickly, and promises of surprise activities in the morning after an uninterrupted night.

The advantage of following treatment programmes such as these is that they establish a consistency of approach from night to night. When parents say, 'We've tried everything!', they probably mean it only too literally and have changed their approach from night to night. While treatment programmes differ in some of their approaches, it is agreed that it is essential to calm toddlers down before expecting them to go to sleep, and to avoid turning a minor disagreement about bedtime into a battle. Calm firmness and consistency are essential. In addition, as Bidder *et al.* (1986) point out, it is important not to allow these sleep problems to continue after the age of two: the older their clients with sleep problems, the longer it took to establish normal sleep patterns.

A different approach to sleep problems in infants is to provide *all* parents with guidance on the management of their infants' sleep, not just those with problems. In one intervention study (Adair *et al.*, 1992) the parents of 164 four-month-old infants were visited, handed an information leaflet and given verbal instructions to put their babies to bed when they were awake and not stay with them until they went to sleep. The parents were asked to complete a daily sleep chart during the fifth month, and they had another consultation with the pediatrician at the sixth month. The outcome of all this at nine months was that the infants had only 2.5 awakenings per week compared with 3.9 in the control group (with no instructions). In addition, frequent night waking was twice as common in the control group as in the intervention group (27 per cent versus 14 per cent). These findings provide further support for the notion that many sleep problems in infants are attributable to parental over-anxiety or oversolicitousness.

Disorders of arousal

Disturbances of deep slow-wave sleep that result in bed-wetting, night terrors or sleepwalking are very much more prevalent amongst children than adults.

A longitudinal (follow-up) study of 212 normal, randomly selected children over a 10-year period found that sleepwalking was a very common occasional occurrence, reported by 75 of the children in the sample (Klackenberg, 1987). Thirty-five of these children were persistent sleepwalkers who continued to walk in their sleep throughout the period of the study, although only four or five of them walked in their sleep more than once a month. The seven children in the sample who reported night terrors all did so before the age of seven – interestingly, all of them later became sleepwalkers.

Regular bed-wetting (several times a week either regularly or periodically during the year) was more common in boys than girls between the ages of four and 16, although after the age of nine there were no girls who wet their beds and only two or three boys.

Suggestions for treatment

Persistent sleepwalking can be dangerous – for instance, children may roam outside the house or out of windows onto dangerous ledges. One solution is to tie the child to the bed by a piece of string attached to an ankle, so that it cannot get far without waking up. Episodes of sleepwalking tend to be associated with periods of worry or stress, in both adults and children. If there is an obvious source of worry, such as parental strife, then some reassurance may help relieve the child's mind.

While bed-wetting can be the result of a disorder of arousal associated with deep slow-wave sleep in the way described by Broughton (1968), it is now clear from studies at the Stanford Sleep Disorders Clinic (Nino-Murcia and Keenan, 1987) that many children wet their beds in other sleep stages, or even when awake, and this less specific pattern may in fact be more common than the one specifically associated with stage 4 sleep. The Stanford therapists initially train their young clients to control their bladders when awake. After drinking quantities of fluid, they have to withhold micturition for as long as possible. They also have to practise stopping in mid-stream, and starting again at will. After a few days of practise at controlling their bladders in this way most children stop wetting their beds. Those who do not may be provided with devices that detect wetness in the bed, setting off an alarm during the night. Finally, some children are prescribed imipramine, an antidepressant drug, one of whose side effects is to improve bladder control. Its mode of action is still uncertain, but it can be very useful in proving to the worried child that dry nights are indeed possible, and a short course of treatment may solve the problem.

Night terrors are not uncommon, but rarely persistent. They may not bother the child as much as its parents, as children frequently forget the whole episode if they are promptly reassured and settled back to sleep. Like sleepwalking, night terrors tend to occur during periods of worry, and daytime reassurance about family problems may be enough to stop these terrifying screaming episodes in the first half of the night. As a last resort a family practioner may prescribe a benzodiazepine antianxiety drug for a short period, which may not only relieve any anxiety the child may be experiencing, but also lighten slow-wave sleep.

Adolescence

Some teenage children rarely get up before noon at weekends, and frequently appear chronically sleepy. The obvious explanation is that for some reason connected with adolescence these young people need more sleep than they did when they were 11 or 12, when they got up earlier than their parents. Research from the Stanford Sleep Research Centre confirms that there are indeed changes in patterns of sleep during adolescence (Carskadon and Dement, 1987). Over a period of seven years young people were invited to attend a summer camp, where observations were made of their sleep habits and some of them were required to have their sleep monitored using EEG/EOG polygraphy. In total, 196 seven- to nine-year-olds, 121 10- to 11-year-olds, 124 12- to 13-year-olds and 168 18- to 22-year-olds took part.

The subjects were examined to determine their maturational stage, using a standardized classification system based on breast development and pubic hair growth in girls and genital development and pubic hair growth in boys. These examinations allowed the children to be classified into one of five categories ('Tanner stages'). Those at Tanner stage 1 (prepubertal) were on average 10.5 years old, and those at Tanner stage 5 (fully developed) were 16.9 years old. They were given the opportunity to sleep for 10 hours every night for three nights.

Measures of sleep patterns showed that the total amount of sleep taken remained constant across the five groups, but that the amount of deep slow-wave sleep (stages 3 and 4) declined by 40 per cent between Tanner stages 1 and 5. Daytime alertness, assessed by the multiple sleep latency test, showed a decline in alertness between the prepubertal and mid-adolescent stages, which remained low in late adolescence. (This test is based on the time taken to get to sleep during the day, given the opportunity.) This increase in daytime sleepiness (despite no reduction in the total amount of sleep taken) suggests that adolescence may indeed be associated with an increased need for sleep.

In a comparison of early adolescents who slept as much as they liked and young college students who slept for seven to nine hours (their preferred and habitual amounts of sleep) it was found that the college students were chronically sleepy during the day, some of them as sleepy as patients suffering from sleep disorders, while the early adolescents were wide awake and alert. As parents exert less control over adolescents' bedtimes there is a tendency for bedtime to become later and later. In a survey of adolescents' preferences, nearly two thirds of the sample endorsed the statement 'I enjoy staying up late' (Price *et al.*, 1978). The Stanford researchers speculate that many of the problems of adolescence, including communication problems with parents and the misuse of drugs, may have their origins in the normal adolescent's chronic sleepiness. They suggest that life for both parents and teenagers would greatly improve if only adolescents would sleep one hour longer every night.

Postscript and Further Reading

This book has provided some insight into the 'how' of sleep and dreaming. The psychophysiological methods of establishing a taxonomy of sleep stages, with their associated mental states, were established over thirty years ago, but they have proved remarkably reliable and have stood the test of time. We also know a great deal about the physiology of sleep, and the ways in which different brain structures interact during it, as well as their neurochemistry. An understanding of the architecture of sleep states has informed our understanding of a number of illnesses, and the use of psychophysiological methods has proved invaluable for the assessment of new drugs.

The 'why' of sleep still eludes us, however. Perhaps, like happiness, it should not be consciously sought, but will come to us if we live our lives fruitfully and continue to struggle towards an even better understanding of the 'how' – but perhaps not. In the final words of his book *Sleep*, Allan Hobson remarks: 'variations in sleep and its underlying brain mechanisms within and across species suggest a twofold purpose: to conserve energy and to organize information. Learning exactly how these functions are served is now the major agenda of sleep science.' This is a sentiment with which most sleep researchers would agree, although they might differ about the strength of the scientific evidence supporting it. When expressed so simply, it seems even more appropriate that psychology should be able to provide some answers to these major questions, as well as neurophysiology and other brain sciences. After all, what should psychologists be able to comment on except the organization of information? Similarly, ethological science should be central in explaining behavioural strategies, including sleep, to conserve energy. Only time will tell if our understanding of these major questions will be expanded, but it seems implausible that psychological explanation will not have an important part to play.

Printed below is a list of further reading for those who would like to take the subject further.

Sleep research

Rechtschaffen, A. and Kales, A. (eds) *A Manual of Standardized Terminology, Techniques and Scoring System for Sleep Stages of Human Adults*. Washington, DC, Public Information Service, US Government Printing Office, 1968.

Williams, R. L., Karacan, I. and Hursch, C. J. *Electroencephalography (EEG) of Human Sleep: Clinical Applications*. New York, Wiley, 1974.

The experience of sleep

Arkin, A. M., Antrobus, J. S. and Ellman, S. J. (eds) *The Mind in Sleep*, 2nd edn., Hillsdale, NJ, Lawrence Erlbaum Associates, 1990.

Behavioral and Brain Sciences, **23**, (no. 6, special issue on sleep and dreaming, December, 2000).

Freud, S., *The Interpretation of Dreams. Standard edition of the complete psychological works of Sigmund Freud*, vol. 4, ed. and trans. J. Strachey. London, Hogarth Press, 1960.

Hobson, J. A. *The Dreaming Brain*. New York, Basic Books, 1988.

Rycroft, C., *The Innocence of Dreams*. Oxford, Oxford University Press, 1979.

www.asdreams.org: this website has abstracts from the journal *Dreaming*, and provides the opportunity to discuss dream issues.

The physiology and natural history of sleep

Carlson, N. R. *Physiology of Behavior*. Boston, MASS, Allyn and Bacon, 1991, ch. 9.

Colquhoun, W. P. and Rutenfranz, J. (eds) *Studies in Shiftwork*. London, Taylor and Francis, 1980.

Hobson, J. A. *Sleep*. New York, Scientific American Library, 1989.

Horne, J., *Why We Sleep*. Oxford, Oxford University Press, 1988.

Monk, T. H. (ed.) *Sleep, Sleepiness and Performance*. London, Wiley, 1991.

Siegel, J. M. (1990) 'Mechanisms of sleep control'. *Journal of Clinical Neurophysiology*, **7**, 49–65.

Sleep disorders

Guilleminault, C. (ed.) *Sleep and its Disorders in Children*. New York, Raven Press, 1987.

Espie, C., *The Psychological Treatment of Insomnia*. Chichester, Wiley, 1991.

Kryger, M. H., Roth, T. and Dement, W. C. (eds) *Principles and Practice of Sleep Medicine*. Philadelphia, Saunders, 1989.

Morgan, K., *Sleep and Ageing*. London, Croom Helm, 1987.

Parkes, J. D., *Sleep and its Disorders*. London, Saunders, 1985.

Appendix: The Hull Sleep and Dreaming Questionnaire

The Hull questionnaire was completed by 149 respondents, including 28 university applicants, 19 students of nursing, 85 psychology students and 17 academic members of the university staff. This sample was in no way representative of the country as a whole, but the respondents' answers do provide some indication of what relatively well informed lay people think about sleep and dreaming.

The questions are reproduced below, together with the number of respondents who agreed with the alternative answers. (In the version given to the respondents these alternatives alternated in order, so that 'True', or 'Always', sometimes appeared on the left, sometimes on the right. Here, for ease of comprehension, affirmative answers are all given on the right.)

Responses to questionnaire on beliefs about sleep

	Never	Rarely Untrue	Perhaps Sometimes	Often True	Always
Sleep quality:					
1. Lack of sleep gives you rings under the eyes		20	49	80	
2. Children need sleep to help them grow		22	34	93	
3. A strong alcoholic drink at bedtime improves sleep		51	44	54	
4. Adults need some sleep to stay healthy		4	12	133	
5. The prolonged use of sleeping pills is bad for you		3	18	128	
6. One hour's sleep before midnight is worth two afterwards		78	53	17	
7. A good night's sleep improves one's appearance		9	52	88	
8. Exercise improves the quality of sleep		4	49	96	
9. A warm nourishing drink at bedtime helps you to sleep		25	66	58	
10. A warm nourishing drink at bedtime reduces awakenings during the night		61	79	9	
11. There are some people who need no sleep at all		108	14	27	

Continued

	Never	Rarely untrue	Perhaps sometimes	Often true	Always
Dreaming:					
12. Dreams occur only in the few moments before you wake up		108	22	18	
13. Dreams are caused by spirits visiting the body during sleep	128	12	4	0	0
14. Dreaming is accompanied by flaccid (relaxed) paralysis		48	47	54	
15. Preventing people from dreaming will drive them mad		57	59	32	
16. Dreams can foretell the future	48	45	52	4	0
17. Most dreams are trivial and haphazard		45	58	46	
18. Cheese can cause nightmares		78	56	14	
19. Nightmares are caused by evil spirits visiting the body during sleep	138	8	2	1	0
20. Dreams are messages from the unconscious mind		6	72	71	
21. Interpreting dreams can throw light on mental processes		8	80	61	
22. Dreaming recurs three or four times every night		13	46	90	
23. The soul leaves the body and wanders during sleep	124	11	12	1	0

	No	Possibly	Certainly
24. In the holy scriptures of many religions there are accounts of messages from deities being received during dreams, and of dreams foretelling the future (e.g. Pharoah's dream in the Old Testament, Mary's dream in the New Testament). Do you believe any of these accounts to be literally true?	53	76	19

Correlational analysis

Cluster analysis of correlation coefficients between responses to the questions suggests that the answers fell into two principle groups or types. (That is, if a subject answered one question in a particular way it tended to predict how she or he would respond to the other questions in its group, but not how she or he might answer the questions in the other group.) These two clusters included 17 of the 23 questions.

Cluster analysis types

- *Type 1*: questions 16, 23, 24, 14, 19, 20(-), 9(-).
- *Type 2*: questions 15, 18, 21, 11, 17(-), 2(-), 12, 3(-), 10, 7.

The first group (Type 1) included questions about the ability of dreams to foretell the future, whether dreams are caused by spirits and so on, as well as (surprisingly) the proposition that dreaming is commonly accompanied by flaccid (relaxed) paralysis. That is, people who agreed with this statement tended to agree that dreams could be supernatural. Their belief in this proposition was therefore hardly likely to be based on the scientific evidence for it, which happens to be strong!

The second group (Type 2) of questions included those dealing with sleep being good for you, or necessary. People who subscribed to this view also endorsed the view that deprivation of dreaming sleep can drive you mad, and that cheese causes nightmares. Again, while some of their beliefs may have scientific support, others do not, and one cannot say that either of these clusters, or factors, represents a dimension of well-informed opinion.

References

Achermann, P. and Borbely, A. A. (1990) 'Simulation of human sleep: ultradian dynamics of electroencephalographic slow-wave activity'. *Journal of Biological Rhythms*, 5, 141–57.

Adair, R., Bauchner, H., Philipp, B., Levenson, S. and Zuckerman, B. (1991) 'Night waking during infancy: role of parental presence at bedtime'. *Pediatrics*, 87, 500–4.

Adair, R., Zuckerman, B., Bauchner, H., Philipp, B. and Levenson, S. (1992) 'Reducing night waking in infancy: a primary care intervention'. *Pediatrics*, 89, 585–8.

Adam, K. (1980) 'Sleep as a restorative process and theory to explain why'. *Progress in Brain Research*, 53, 289–305.

Adam, K. and Oswald, I. (1983) 'Protein synthesis, bodily renewal and the sleep–wake cycle'. *Clinical Science*, 65, 561–7.

Adam, K., Oswald, I. and Shapiro, C. (1984) 'Effects of loprazolam and of triazolam on sleep and overnight urinary cortisol'. *Psychopharmacology*, 82, 389–94.

Agnew, H. W., Webb, W. B. and Williams, R. L. (1964) 'The effects of stage four sleep deprivation'. *Electroencephalography and Clinical Neurophysiology*, 7, 68–71.

Agnew, H. W., Webb, W. B. and Williams, R. L. (1966) 'The first night effect: an EEG study of sleep'. *Psychophysiology*, 2, 263–6.

Ajilore, O., Stickgold, S., Rittenhouse, C. D. and Hobson, J. A. (1995) 'Night: laboratory and home-based evaluation of a portable sleep monitor'. *Psychophysiology*, 32, 92–8.

Akerstedt T. (1984) 'Hormones and sleep' in Borbely, A. A. and Valatz, J.-L. (eds). *Sleep Mechanisms*. Berlin, Springer-Verlag, 193–203.

Akerstedt, T., Czeisler, C. A., Dinges, D. and Horne, J. A. (1994) 'Accidents and sleepiness: a consensus statement'. *Journal of Sleep Research*, 3, 195,

Akerstedt, T. and Folkard, S. (1996) 'Predicting sleep latency from the three-process model of alertness regulation'. *Psychophysiology*, 33, 385–9.

Akerstedt, T., Palblad, J., De La Torre, B. and Marana, R. (1980) 'Adrenocortical and gonadal steroids during sleep deprivation'. *Sleep*, 3, 23–30.

Allen, R. P., Wagman, A., Faillace, L. A. and MacIntosh, M. (1971) 'EEG sleep recovery following prolonged alcohol intoxication in alcoholics'. *Journal of Nervous and Mental Disease*, 152, 424–33.

Allison, T. and Cicchetti, D. V. (1976) 'Sleep in mammals: ecological and constitutional correlates'. *Science*, 194, 732–34.

Allison, T. and Goff, W. R. (1968) 'Sleep in a primitive mammal, the spiny anteater'. *Psychophysiology*, 5, 200.

Ancoli-Isreal, S., Kripke, D. F., Menn, S. J. and Messin, S. (1981) 'Benefits of a sleep disorders clinic in a veterans administration medical center'. *The Western Journal of Medicine*, 135, 14–18.

Anders, T. F. , Emde, R. and Parmelee, A. (eds) (1971) *A Manual of Standardized Terminology, Techniques and Criteria for Scoring of States of Sleep and Wakefulness in*

Newborn Infants. Los Angeles, CA, UCLA Brain Information Service, NINDS Neurological Information Network.

Anders, T. F. and Weinstein, P. (1972) 'Sleep and disorders in infants and children – a review'. *Pediatrics*, 50, 312–24.

Angus, R. R., Heslegrave, R. J. and Myles, W. S. (1985) 'Effects of prolonged sleep deprivation, with and without chronic physical exercise, on mood and performance'. *Psychophysiology*, 22, 276–82.

Antrobus, J. S. (1986) 'Dreaming: cortical activation and perceptual thresholds'. *Journal of Mind and Behavior*, 7, 193–212.

Antrobus, J. S. (1990) 'The neurocognition of sleep mentation: rapid eye movements, visual imagery, and dreaming' in Bootzin, R., Kihlstrom, J. and Schacter, D. (eds) *Sleep and Cognition.* Washington, DC, American Psychological Association, 904–6.

Antrobus, J. S. (1991) 'Dreaming: cognitive processes during cortical activation and high afferent thresholds'. *Psychological Review*, 98, 96–121.

Antrobus, J. S. (2000) 'How does the dreaming brain explain the dreaming mind?' *Behavioral and Brain Sciences*, 23, (6)

Antrobus, J. S., Dement, W. and Fisher, C. (1964) 'Patterns of dreaming and dream recall: an EEG study'. *Journal of Abnormal and Social Psychology*, 69, 341–4.

Apps, M. C. P., Moore Gillon, J. C. and Stradling, J. R. (1983) 'Underdiagnosis of obstructive sleep apnoea in Britain'. *The Lancet*, 1, 1054.

Arendt, J., Middleton, B., Stone, B. and Skene, D. (1999) 'Complex effects of melatonin: evidence for photoperiodic responses in humans'. *Sleep*, 22, 625–35.

Arkin, A. M. (1966) 'Sleep-talking: a review'. *Journal of Nervous and Mental Disease*, 143, 101–22.

Arkin, A. M. (1978) 'Sleeptalking' in Arkin, A. M., Antrobus, J. S. and Ellman, S. J. (eds) *The Mind in Sleep: Psychology and Psychophysiology.* Hillsdale, New Jersey, Lawrence Erlbaum.

Arkin, A. M., Toth, M. G., Baker, J. and Hastey, J. M. (1970) 'The degree of concordance between the content of sleep talking and mentation recalled in wakefulness'. *Journal of Nervous and Mental Disease*, 151, 375–93.

Arnold, G. W. (1985) 'Rest and Sleep' in Fraser, A. F. (ed.) *Ethology of Farm Animals.* Amsterdam, Elsevier.

Ascher, L. M. and Turner, R. M. (1979) 'Paradoxical intention and insomnia: an experimental investigation'. *Behavior Research and Therapy*, 17, 408–11.

Aschoff, J. (1965) 'Circadian rhythms in man'. *Science*, 148, 1427–32.

Aschoff, J. (1979) 'Circadian rhythms: general features and endocrinological aspects' in Krieger, D. T. (ed.) *Endocrine Rhythms.* Raven Press, New York.

Aschoff, J. (1980) 'Circadian rhythms: inference with and dependence on work–rest schedules' in Johnson, L. C., Tepas, D. I., Colquhon, W. P. and Collingham, M. J. (eds) *The 24 Hour Workday. A Symposium on Variations in Work–Sleep Schedules.* Washington, DC, National Institute for Occupational Safety and Health.

Aserinsky, E. and Kleitman, N. (1953) 'Regularly occuring periods of eye motility, and concomitant phenomena, during sleep'. *Science*, 118, 273–4.

Aserinsky, E. and Kleitman, N. (1955) 'A motility cycle in sleeping infants as manifested by ocular and gross bodily motility'. *Journal of Applied Physiology*, 8, 11–18.

Aserinsky, E., Lynch, J. A., Mack, M. E., Tzankoff, S. P. and Hurn, E. (1985) 'Comparison of eye motion in wakefulness and REM sleep'. *Psychophysiology*, 22, 1–10.

Association of Sleep Disorders Centers (1979) 'Diagnostic classification of sleep and arousal disorders'. *Sleep*, 2, 1–137.

Aston-Jones, G. (1985) 'Behavioural functions of locus coeruleus derived from cellular attributes'. *Physiological Psychology*, 13, 118–26.

Aston-Jones, G. and Bloom, F. E. (1981) 'Norepinephrine-containing locus coeruleus neurons in behaving rats exhibit pronounced responses to non-noxious environmental stimuli'. *Journal of Neuroscience*, **1**, 887–900.

Aston-Jones, G., Ennis, M., Pieribone, V. A., Nickell, W. T. and Shipley, M. T. (1986) 'The brain nucleus locus coeruleus: restricted afferent control of a broad efferent network'. *Science*, **234**, 734–7.

Baekeland, F. and Laski, R. (1966) 'Exercise and sleep patterns in college athletes'. *Perceptual and Motor Skills*, **23**, 1203–7.

Bakin, H. (1970) 'Sleep walking in twins'. *The Lancet*, **2**, 446–7.

Barber, B. (1966) 'Factors underlying individual differences in dream reporting'. *Psychophysiology*, **6**, 247–8.

Becker, R. de (1968) *Dreams, or the Machinations of the Night*, trans. Michael Heron. Allen & Unwin, London.

Belvedere, E. and Foulkes, D. (1971) 'Telepathy and dreams: a failure to replicate'. *Perceptual and Motor Skills*, **33**, 783–9

Belyavin, A. and Nicholson, A. N. (1987) 'Rapid eye movement sleep in man: modulation by benzodiazepines'. *Neuropharmacology*, **26**, 485–91.

Benca, R. M., Kushida, C. A., Everson, C. A., Kalski, R., Bergmann, B. M. and Rechtschaffen, A. (1989) 'Sleep deprivation in the rat: VII. Immune function'. *Sleep*, **12**, 47–52.

Berger, R. J. (1961) 'Tonus of extrinsic laryngeal muscles during sleep and dreaming'. *Science*, **134**, 840.

Berger, R. J. (1963) 'Modification of dream content by meaningful verbal stimuli'. *British Journal of Psychiatry*, **109**, 710–40.

Berger, R. J. (1984) 'Slow wave sleep, shallow torpor and hibernation: homologous states of diminished metabolism and body temperature'. *Biological Psychology*, **19**, 305–26

Berger, R. J., Olley, P. and Oswald, I. (1962) 'The EEG, eye movements and dreams of the blind'. *Quarterly Journal of Experimental Psychology*, **14**, 183–6.

Berger, R. J. and Oswald, I. (1962a) 'Effects of sleep deprivation on behaviour, subsequent sleep, and dreaming'. *Journal of Mental Science*, **108**, 457–63.

Berger, R. J and Oswald, I. (1962b) 'Eye movements during active and passive dreams'. *Science*, **137**, 601–3.

Berger, R. J. and Walker, J. M. (1972) 'Sleep in the burrowing owl (Speotyto cunicularia hypugaea)'. *Behavioural Biology*, **7**, 183–94.

Bergmann, B. M., Everson, C. A., Kushida, C. A., Fang, V. S., Leitch, C. A., Schoeller, D. A., Refetoff, S. and Rechtschaffen, A. (1989a) 'Sleep deprivation in the rat: V. Energy use and medication'. *Sleep*, **12**, 31–41.

Bergmann, B. M., Everson, C. A., Kushida, C. A., Gilliland, M. A., Obermeyer, W. and Rechtschaffen, A. (1989b) 'Sleep deprivation in the rat: II. Methodology'. *Sleep*, **12**, 5–12.

Bergmann, B. M. and Rechtschaffen, A. (1989) 'Sleep deprivation in the rat: III. Total sleep deprivation'. *Sleep*, **12**, 13–21.

Berry, D. T. R., Webb, W. B. and Block, A. J. (1984) 'Sleep apnea syndrome: a critical review of the apnea index as a diagnostic criterion'. *Chest*, **84**, 529–41.

Bert, J., Kripke, D. F. and Rhodes, J. M. (1970) 'Electroencephalogram of the mature chimpanzee: 24 hour recordings'. *Electroencephalography and Clinical Neurophysiology*, **28**, 368–73.

Besterman, T. (1933) 'Report of an inquiry into pre-cognitive dreams'. *Proceedings of the Society for Psychical Research*, **41**, 186–204.

Betts, T. A. and Alford, C. (1985) 'Beta-blockers and sleep: a controlled trial'. *European Journal of Clinical Pharmacology*, **28**, 65–8.

Bidder, R. T., Gray, O. P., Howells, P. M. and Eaton, M. P. (1986) 'Sleep problems in pre-school children: community clinics'. *Child: Care, health and development*, **12**, 325–37.

Birmingham Research Unit of the Royal College of General Practitioners (1978) 'Practice activity analysis, 4. Psychotropic drugs'. *Journal of the Royal College of General Practitioners*, **28**, 122–4.

Bixler, E. O., Kales, A., Soldatos, C. R., Kales, J. D. and Healey, S. (1979) 'Prevalence of sleep disorders in the Los Angeles metropolitan area'. *American Journal of Psychiatry*, **136**, 1257–62.

Bjerner, B. (1949) 'Alpha depression and lowered pulse rate during delayed actions in a serial reaction test: a study in sleep deprivation'. *Acta Physiologica Scandinavica*, **19**, Supplement 65, 1–93.

Blake, H. and Gerard, R. W. (1937) 'Brain potentials during sleep'. *American Journal of Physiology*, **119**, 692–703.

Bleuler, E. (1930) *Textbook of Psychiatry*, trans. A. A. Brill. New York, Macmillan.

Bokert, E. (1968) 'The effects of thirst and related auditory stimulation on dream reports'. *Dissertation Abstracts*, **28**, 122–31.

Bonnet, M. (1982) 'Performance during Sleep' in Webb, W. B. (ed.) *Biological Rhythms, Sleep and Performance*. Chichester, Wiley, ch. 8.

Bootzin, R. R. (1972) 'Stimulus control treatment for insomnia'. *Proceedings of the American Psychological Association*, **7**, 395–6.

Bootzin, R. R. and Engle-Friedman, M. (1981) 'The assessment of insomnia'. *Behavioral Assessment*, **3**, 107–26.

Borbely, A. (1986) *Secrets of Sleep*, trans. Deborah Schneider. London, Longman.

Borbely, A. A. and Neuhaus, H. U. (1979) 'Sleep-deprivation: effects on sleep and the EEG in the rat'. *Journal of Comparative Physiology*, **133**, 71–87.

Borbely, A. A. and Tobler, I. (1989) 'Endogenous sleep-promoting substances and sleep regulation'. *Physiological Reviews*, **69**, 605–70.

Borkovec, T. D. (1982) 'Insomnia'. *Journal of Consulting and Clinical Psychology*, **50**, 880–95.

Bosinelli, M., Cicogna, P. and Molinari, S. (1974) 'The tonic-phasic model and the testing of self-participation in different stages of sleep'. *Italian Journal of Psychology*, **1**, 35–65.

Boyar, R. M. (1978) 'Sleep-related endocrine rhythms' in Reichlin, S., Baldessarine, R. J. and Martin, J. B. (eds) *The Hypothalamus*. New York, Raven Press, 373–86.

Bradley, C. and Meddis, R. (1974) 'Arousal threshold in dreaming sleep'. *Physiological Psychology*, **2**, 109–14

Brazier, M. A. B. (1961) *A History of the Electrical Activity of the Brain*. New York, Macmillan.

Breger, L. (1967) 'Function of dreams'. *Journal of Abnormal Psychology*, **72**, 1–28.

Breger, L., Hunter, I. and Lane, R. W. (1971) *The Effect of Stress on Dreams*. New York, International Universities Press.

Brezinova, V. and Oswald, I. (1972) 'Sleep after a bedtime beverage'. *British Medical Journal*, **2**, 431–3.

Broughton, R. J. (1968) 'Sleep disorders: disorders of arousal?' *Science*, **159**, 1070–8.

Broughton, R. J., Bullings, R., Cartwright, R. and Doucette, D. *et al.* (1994) 'Homicidal somnambulism: a case report'. *Sleep*, **17**, 253–64.

Browman, C. P., Gordon, G. C., Tepas, D. I. and Walsh, J. K. (1977) 'Reported sleep and drug use of workers: a preliminary report'. *Sleep Research*, **6**, 111.

Bunnell, D. E., Bevier, W. and Horvath, S. M. (1983) 'Effects of exhaustive exercise on the sleep of men and women'. *Psychophysiology*, **20**, 50–8.

Buysse, D. J. (1991) 'Drugs affecting sleep, sleepiness and performance' in Monk, T. H. (ed.) *Sleep, Sleepiness and Performance*. London, Wiley.

Caekebeke, J. F. V., Van Dijk, J. G. and Van Sweden, B. (1990) 'Habituation to K-complexes or event-related potentials during sleep'. *Electroencephalography and Clinical Neurophysiology*, Supplement 41, 168–72.

Callaway, C. W., Lydic, R., Baghdoyan, H. A. and Hobson, J. A. (1987) 'Pontogeniculocipital waves: spontaneous visual system activity during rapid eye movement sleep'. *Cellular and Molecular Neurobiology*, 2, 105–49.

Campbell, S. (1977) 'Double blind psychometric studies on the effects of natural oestrogens on postmenopausal women' in Campbell, S. (ed.) *Management of the Menopause and the Postmenopausal Years*. Lancaster, MTP Press, 149–58.

Carey, W. B. (1974) 'Night-waking and temperament in infancy'. *Journal of Pediatrics*, 84, 756–8.

Carlson, N. R. (1991) *Physiology of Behavior*, 4th edn. Boston, Allyn & Bacon.

Carskadon, M. A. and Dement, W. C. (1975) 'Sleep studies on a 90-minute day'. *Electroencephalography and Clinical Neurophysiology*, 39, 145–55.

Carskadon, M. A. and Dement, W. C. (1981) 'Cumulative effects of sleep restriction on daytime sleepiness'. *Psychophysiology*, 18, 107–13.

Carskadon, M. A. and Dement, W. C. (1987) 'Sleepiness in the normal adolescent' in Guilleminault, C. (ed.) *Sleep and its Disorders in Children*. New York, Raven Press.

Cartwright, R. (1977) *Night Life*. Englewood Cliffs, NJ, Prentice-Hall.

Casper, R. F. and Yen, S. S. C. (1981) 'Menopausal flushes: effect of pituitary gonadotropin desensitization by a potent luteinizing hormone-releasing factor agonist'. *Journal of Clinical Endocrinology and Metabolism*, 53, 1056–8.

Casper, R. F., Yen, S. S. C. and Wilkes, M. M. (1979) 'Menopausal flushes: a neuroendocrine link between pulsatile luteinizing hormone secretion'. *Science* 205, 823–5.

Caton, R. (1875) 'The electric currents of the brain'. *British Medical Journal*, 2, 278–82.

Chambers, M. J. and Keller, B. (1993). 'Alert insomniacs: are they really sleep deprived?' *Clinical Psychology Review*, 13, 649–66.

Chenen, A. M. L., van Hulzen, Z. J. M. and van Luijtelaar, E. L. J. M. (1983) 'Paradoxical sleep in the dark period of the rat: a dissociation between electrophysiological and behavioural characteristics'. *Behavioural and Neural Biology*, 37, 350–6.

Cheyne, J. A., Newby-Clark, I. R. and Rueffer, S. D. (1999) 'Relations among hypnagogic and hypnopompic experiences associated with sleep paralysis'. *Journal of Sleep Research*, 8, 313–17.

Cistulli, P. A., Grunstein, R. R. and Sullivan, C. E. (1994) 'Effect of testosterone administration on upper airway collapsibility during sleep'. *American Journal of Respiratory and Critical Care Medicine*, 149, 530–2.

Coates, T. J. and Thoresen, C. E. (1979) 'Treating arousals during sleep using behavioural self-management'. *Journal of Consulting and Clinical Psychology*, 47, 603–5.

Cohen, D. B. and Wolfe, G. (1973) 'Dream recall and repression: evidence for an alternative hypothesis'. *Journal of Consulting and Clinical Psychology*, 41, 349–55.

Committee on Safety of Medicines (1988) 'Benzodiazepines, dependence and withdrawal symptoms'. *Current Problems*, 21, January.

Corcoran, D. W. J. (1962) 'Noise and loss of sleep'. *Quarterly Journal of Experimental Psychology*, 14, 178–82.

Costello, C. G. and Selby, M. M. (1965) 'The relationship between sleep patterns and reactive and endogenous depression'. *British Journal of Psychiatry*, 111, 497–501.

Crick, F. and Mitchison, G. (1983) 'The function of REM sleep'. *Nature*, **304**, 111–14.

Crick, F. and Mitchison, G. (1986) 'REM sleep and neural nets'. *Journal of Mind and Behavior*, 7, 229–49.

Crisp, A. H. and Stonehill, E. (1977) *Sleep, Nutrition and Mood*. London, Wiley.

Crown, S., Crisp, A. H. (1979) *Manual of the Crown–Crisp Experiential Index*. London, Hodder & Stoughton.

Czeisler, C. A., Allan, J. S., Strogatz, S. H., Ronda, J. M., Sanchez, R., Rios, C. D., Freitag, W. O., Richardson, G. S. and Kronauer, R. E. (1986) 'Bright light resets the human circadian pacemaker independent of the timing of the sleep–wake cycle'. *Science*, **233**, 667–71.

Czeisler, C. A., Johnson, M. P., Duffy, J. F., Brown, E. N., Ronda J. M., and Kronauer, R. E. (1990) 'Exposure to bright light and darkness to treat physiologic maladaptation to night work'. *The New England Journal of Medicine*, **322**, 1253–9.

Czeisler, C. A., Kronauer, R. E., Allan, J. S., Duffy, J. F., Jewett, M. E., Brown, E. N. and Ronda, J. M. (1989) 'Bright light induction of strong (type O) resetting of the human circadian pacemaker'. *Science*, **244**, 1328–33.

Daan, S., Beersma, D. G. M. and Brobely, A. A. (1984) 'The timing of human sleep: recovery process gated by a circadian pacemaker'. *American Journal of Physiology*, **246**, R161–78.

Darwin, E. (1796) *Zoonomia, or, The Laws of Organic Life*, 2nd, corrected edn. London, J. Johnson.

Daurat, A., Benoit, O. and Buguet, A. (2000) 'Effects of zopiclone on the rest/activity rhythm after a westward flight across five time zones'. *Psychopharmacologia*, **149**, 241–5.

Davis, H., Davis, P. A., Loomis, A. L., Harvey, E. N. and Hobart, G. (1937) 'Human brain potentials during the onset of sleep'. *Journal of Neurophysiology*, **1**, 24–37.

De Andres, I., Gutierrez-Rivas, E., Nava, E. and Reinoso-Suarez, F. (1976) 'Independence of sleep–wakefulness cycle in an implanted head "encephale isole"', *Neuroscience Letters*, **2**, 13–18.

Deary, I. J. and Tait, R. (1987) 'Effects of sleep disruption on cognitive performance and mood in medical house officers'. *British Medical Journal*, **295**, 1513–16.

DeFazio, J., Meldrum, D. R., Laufer, L., Vale, W., Rivier, J., Lu, J. K. H. and Judd, H. L. (1983) 'Induction of hot flashes in premenopausal women treated with a long-acting GnRH agonist'. *Journal of Clinical Endocrinology and Metabolism*, **56**, 445–8.

Delorme, F., Vimont, P. and Jouvet, D. (1964) 'Etude statistique du cycle veille-sommeils chez le chat'. *Comptes rendus société biologique* (Paris), **58**, 2128–30.

Dement, W. C. (1960) 'The effect of dream deprivation'. *Science*, **131**, 1705–7.

Dement, W. C. (1965) 'Studies on the function of rapid eye movement (paradoxical) sleep in human subjects' in Jouvet, M. (ed.) *Aspects anatomo-functionnels de la physiologie du sommeil*. Paris, Editions du Centre National de la Recherche Scientifique, 571–608.

Dement, W. C. (1972a) *Some Must Watch While Some Must Sleep*. Stanford, CA, Stanford University Press. Reprinted, San Francisco, Freeman, 1974.

Dement, W. C. (1972b) 'Sleep deprivation and the organization of the behavioral states' in Clemente, C. D., Purpura, D. P. and Mayer, F. E. (eds) *Sleep and the Maturing Nervous System*. New York, Academic Press, 319–55.

Dement, W. and Kleitman, N. (1957) 'The relation of eye movements during sleep to dream activity: an objective method for the study of dreaming'. *Journal of Experimental Psychology*, **53**, 339–46.

Dement, W. and Wolpert, E. A. (1958) 'The relation of eye movements, body motility, and external stimuli to dream content'. *Journal of Experimental Psychology*, **55**, 543–53.

Desmond, A. J. (1977) *The Hot-Blooded Dinosaurs*. London, Futura.

Dexter, D. D. and Dovre, E. J. (1998) 'Obstructive sleep apnea due to endogenous testosterone production in a woman'. *Mayo Clinic Proceedings*, **73**, 246–8.

Dickson, P. R. (1984) 'Effect of a fleecy woolen underlay on sleep'. *Medical Journal of Australia*, **140**, 87–9.

Doering, C. H., Kraemer, H. C., Brodie, K. H. and Hamburg. D. A. (1975) 'A cycle of plasma testosterone in the human male'. *Journal of Clinical Endocrinology Metabolism*, **40**, 492.

Douglas, N. (2000) 'Future of sleep medicine in the U.K.' Paper presented at the 12th Annual Scientific Meeting of the British Sleep Society, University of Surrey, 13–14 July 2000.

Driver, H. S., Dijk, D. J., Werth, E., Biedermann, K. and Borbely, A. A. (1996) 'Sleep and the sleep electroencephalogram across the menstrual cycle in young healthy women'. *Journal of Clinical Endocrinology and Metabolism*, **81**, 728–35.

Dunleavy, D. L. F. and Oswald, I. (1973) 'Phenelzine, mood response and sleep'. *Archives of General Psychiatry*, **28**, 353–6.

Dunleavy, D. L. F., Oswald, I., Brown, P. and Strong, J. A. (1974) 'Hyperthyroidism, sleep and growth hormone'. *Electroencephalography and Clinical Neurophysiology*, **36**, 259–63.

Dunne, J. W. (1927) *An Experiment with Time*. New York, Macmillan.

Dunnell, K. and Cartwright, A. (1972) *Medicine Takers, Prescribers, and Hoarders*. London, Routledge & Kegan Paul.

D'Zurilla, T. J. and Goldfried, M. R. (1971). Problem-solving and behavior modification'. *Journal of Abnormal Psychology*, **78**, 107–26.

Easton, P. A., West, P., Meatherall, R. C., Brewster, J. F., Lertzman, M. and Kryger, M. H. (1987) 'The effect of excessive ethanol ingestion on sleep in severe chronic obstructive pulmonary disease'. *Sleep*, **10**, 224–33.

Eguchi, K. and Sato, T. (1980a) 'Characterization of the neurons in the region of solitary tract nucleus during sleep'. *Physiology and Behavior*, **23**, 99–102.

Eguchi, K. and Sato, T. (1980b) 'Convergence of sleep–wakefulness subsystems onto single neurons in the region of cats' solitary tract nucleus'. *Archives Italiennes de Biologie*, **118**, 331–45.

Ellingson, R. J. (1964) 'Studies of the electrical activity of the developing human brain'. *Progress in Brain Research*, **9**, 26–53.

Ellis, H. D. and Young, A. W. (1990) 'Accounting for delusional misidentifications'. *British Journal of Psychiatry*, **157**, 239–48.

Emerson, R. W. (1884) *Lectures and Biographical Sketches*, Boston, MASS, Houghton Mifflin.

Emmons, W. H. and Simon, C. W. (1956) 'The non-recall of material presented during sleep'. *American Journal of Psychology*, **69**, 76–81.

Empson, J. A. C. (1977) 'Periodicity in body temperature in man'. *Experientia*, **33**, 342–3.

Empson, J. A. C. and Clarke, P. R. F. (1970) 'Rapid eye movements and remembering'. *Nature*, **227**, 287–8.

Empson, J. A. C., Hearne, K. M. T. and Tilley, A. J. (1981) 'REM sleep and reminiscence' in Koella, W. P. (ed.) *Sleep 1980: Circadian Rhythms, Dreams, Noise and Sleep*. Basel, S. Karger.

Empson, W. (1964) 'The Ancient Mariner'. *Critical Quarterly*, 6, 4. Republished in Empson, W. (1987) *Argufying: Essays on Literature and Culture*. Edited with an introduction by Haffenden, J. Iowa City, University of Iowa Press.

Ephron, H. S. and Carrington, P. (1966) 'Rapid eye movement sleep and cortical homeostasis'. *Psychological Review*, 73, 500–26.

Erlik, Y., Tataryn, I. V., Medrum, D. R., Lomax, P., Bajorek, J. G. and Judd, H. L. (1981) 'Association of waking episodes with menopausal hot flushes'. *Journal of the American Medical Association*, 245, 1741–4.

Espie, C. (1991) *The Psychological Treatment of Insomnia*. Chichester, Wiley.

Espie, C. and Lindsay, W. R. (1985). 'Paradoxical intention in the treatment of chronic insomnia: six case studies illustrating variability in therapeutic response'. *Behaviour Research and Therapy*, 23, 703–9.

Espie, C. and Lindsay, W. R. (1987) 'Cognitive strategies for the management of severe sleep-maintenance insomnia: a preliminary investigation'. *Behavioural Psychotherapy*, 15, 388–95.

Evans, F. J. (1977) 'Subjective characteristics of sleep efficiency'. *Journal of Abnormal Psychology*, 86, 561–4.

Evans, F. J., Gustafson, L. A., O'Connell, D. N., Orne, P. T. and Shor, R. E. (1970) 'Verbally induced behavioral responses during sleep'. *Journal of Nervous and Mental Diseases*, 150, 171–87.

Everson, C. A., Bergmann, B. M. and Rechtschaffen, A. (1989a) 'Sleep deprivation in the rat: III. Total sleep deprivation'. *Sleep*, 12, 13–21.

Everson, C. A., Gilliland, M. A., Kushida, C. E., Pilcher, J. J., Fang, V. S., Refetoff, S., Bergmann, B. M. and Rechtschaffen, A. (1989b) 'Sleep deprivation in the rat: IX. Recovery'. *Sleep*, 12, 60–7.

Fagen, J. W. and Rovee-Collier, C. (1983) 'Memory retrieval: a time-locked process in infants'. *Science*, 222, 1349–51.

Falkenstein, M., Hohnsbein, J., Hoormann, J. and Blanke, L. (1991) 'Effects of cross-modal divided attention on late ERP components: II error processing in choice reaction tasks'. *Electroencephalography and Clinical Neurophysiology*, 78, 447–55.

Faraday, A. (1972) *Dream Power*. London, Hodder & Stoughton.

Faraday, A. (1975) *The Dream Game*. London, Maurice Temple Smith.

Feinberg, I., Fein, G. and Walker, J. M. (1979) 'Flurazepam effects on sleep EEG'. *Archives of General Psychiatry*, 36, 95–102.

Feinberg, I., Koresko, R. L. and Heller, N. (1967) 'EEG sleep patterns as a function of normal and pathological aging in man'. *Journal of Psychiatric Research*, 5, 107.

Feldman, J. M., Postlethwaite, R. W. and Glenn, J. F. (1976) 'Hot flashes and sweats in men with testicular insufficiency'. *Archives of Internal Medicine*, 136, 606–8.

Ferber, R. (1987) 'The sleepless child' in Guilleminault, C. (ed.) *Sleep and Its Disorders in Children*. New York, Raven Press.

Ferini-Strambi, L. and Zucconi, M. (2000) 'REM sleep behavior disorder'. *Clinical Neurophysiology*, 111, S136–40.

Firth, H. (1973) 'Habituation during sleep'. *Psychophysiology*, 10, 43–51.

Flanigan, W. F. Jr (1973) 'Sleep and wakefulness in chelonian reptiles: 1. The red-footed tortoise'. *Sleep Research*, 2, 82.

Flanigan, W. F. Jr, Wilcox, R. H. and Rechtschaffen, A. (1973) 'The EEG and behavioral continuum of the crocodilian, *Caiman sclerops*'. *Electroencephalography and Clinical Neurophysiology*, 34, 521–38.

Folkard, S. and Monk, T. H. (1981) 'Individual differences in the circadian response to a weekly rotating shift system' in Reinberg, A., Vieux, N. and Andlauer, P. (eds) *Night and Shift Work: Biological and social aspects*. Oxford, Pergamon Press, 365–74.

Foulkes, D. (1982) 'A cognitive–psychological model of REM dream production'. *Sleep*, 5, 169–87.

Foulkes, D. (1985) *Dreaming: a cognitive–psychological analysis*. Hillsdale, NJ, Lawrence Erlbaum.

Foulkes, D., Pivik, T., Steadman, H. S., Spear, P. S. and Symonds, J. D. (1967) 'Dreams of the male child: An EEG study'. *Journal of the American Psychoanalytical Association*, 18, 747–82.

Foulkes, D. and Pope, R. (1973) 'Primary visual experience and secondary cognitive elaboration in state REM: a modest confirmation and extension'. *Perceptual and Motor Skills*, 37, 107–18.

Foulkes, D. and Rechtschaffen, A. (1964) 'Presleep determinants of dream content: Effects of two films'. *Perceptual and Motor Skills*, 19, 983–1005.

Foulkes, D. and Vogel, G. (1966) 'Mental activity at sleep onset'. *Journal of Abnormal Psychology*, 70, 231–43.

Fowler, M. J., Sullivan, M. J. and Ekstrand, B. R. (1973) 'Sleep and memory'. *Science*, 179, 302–4.

Frankfurt, M., Gould, E., Wooley, C. S. and McEwen, B. S. (1973) 'Gonadal steroids modify dendritic spine density in ventromedial hypothalamic neurons: a Golgi study in the adult rat'. *Neuroendocrinology*, 51, 530–5.

Frazer, J. G. (1918) *Folk-lore in the Old Testament*, vol. 2. London, Macmillan.

Frazier, K. (ed.) (1986) *Science Confronts the Paranormal*. New York, Prometheus.

Freedman, R. (1987) 'Chronic insomniacs: replication of Monroe's findings'. *Psychophysiology*, 24, 721–2.

Freedman, R. and Papsdorf, J. (1976) 'Biofeedback and progressive relaxation treatment of sleep-onset insomnia: a controlled all-night investigation'. *Biofeedback and Self regulation*, 1, 253–71.

Freedman, R. R. and Sattler, H. L. (1982) 'Physiological and psychological factors in sleep-onset insomnia'. *Journal of Abnormal Psychology*, 91, 380–9.

Freeman, G .K. (1978) 'Analysis of primary care prescribing – a "constructive" coding system for drugs'. *Journal of the Royal College of General Practitioners*, 28, 547–51.

Freemon, F. R., McNew, J. J. and Ross Adey, W. (1971) 'Chimpanzee sleep stages'. *Electroencephalography and Clinical Neurophysiology*, 31, 485–9.

Freud, S. (1922) *Introductory Lectures on Psycho-Analysis*, translated by Joan Rivière. London, Allen & Unwin.

Freud, S. (1932) *The Interpretation of Dreams*, translated by A. A. Brill. London, George Allen & Unwin.

Freud, S. (1966) *Project for a Scientific Psychology* (first published in 1895), in *Complete Psychological Works, Standard Edition*, vol. 1, translated and edited by J. Strachey. London, Hogarth Press, 294–397.

Friedman, L., Benson, K., Noda, A. and Zarcone, V. (2000) 'An actigraphic comparison of sleep restriction and sleep hygiene treatments for insomnia in older adults'. *Journal of Geriatric Psychiatry and Neurology*, 13, 17–27.

Friedman, R. C., Bigger, J. T. and Kornfeld, D. S. (1971) 'The intern and sleep loss'. *New England Journal of Medicine*, 285, 201–3.

Friedman, S. and Fisher, C. (1967) 'On the presence of a rhythmic, diurnal, oral instinctual drive cycle in man: a preliminary report'. *Journal of the American Psychoanalytic Association*, 15, 317–43.

Friedmann, J., Globus, G., Huntley, A., Mullaney, D., Naitdi, P. and Johnson, L. (1977) 'Performance and mood during and after gradual sleep reduction'. *Psychopsysiology*, 14, 245–50.

Fuller, C. A., Lydic, R., Sulzman, F. M., Albers, H. E., Pepper, B. and Moore-Ede, M. C. (1981) 'Circadian rhythm of body temperature persists after suprachiasmatic lesions in the squirrel monkey'. *American Journal of Physiology*, 241, R385–91.

Gahagan, L. (1936) 'Sex differences in recall of stereotyped dreams, sleep-talking and sleep-walking'. *Journal of Genetic Psychology*, 48, 227–36.

Gaillard, J.-M. and Blois, R. (1989) 'Differential effects of flunitrazepam on human sleep in combination with flumazenil'. *Sleep*, 12, 120–32.

Gaillard, J.-M., Nicholson, A. N. and Pascoe, P. A. (1989) 'Neuro-transmitter systems' in Kryger, M. H., Roth, T. and Dement, W. C. (eds) *Principles and Practice of Sleep Medicine*. Philadelphia, W. B. Saunders, ch. 19.

Galton, F. (1883) *Inquiries into the Human Faculty and its Development*. London, Macmillan.

Gambetti, P. and Lugaresi, E. (1998) 'Conclusions of the symposium'. *Brain Pathology*, 8, 571–5.

Gander, P. H., Kronauer, R. E. and Graeber, R.C. (1985) 'Phase shifting two coupled circadian pacemakers: implications for jet lag'. *American Journal of Physiology*, 249, R704–19.

Garber, M. B. (1974) *Dream in Shakespeare*. New York, Yale University Press.

Garfield, P. L. (1974) *Creative Dreaming*. New York, Simon & Schuster.

Gauthier, P. and Gottesmann, C. (1983) 'Influence of total sleep deprivation on event-related potentials in man'. *Psychophysiology*, 20, 351–5.

Giannocorou, M. (1984) 'Sleep loss and the CNV'. MSc dissertation, University of Hull.

Gillberg, M., Anderzen, I., Akerstedt, T. and Sigurdson, K. (1986) 'Urinary catechol-amine responses to basic types of physical activity'. *European Journal of Applied Physiology*, 55, 575–8.

Gilliland, M. A., Bergmann, B. M. and Rechtschaffen, A. (1989) 'Sleep deprivation in the rat: VIII. High EEG amplitude sleep deprivation'. *Sleep*, 12, 53–9.

Gillin, J. C., Duncan, W., Pettigrew, K. D., Frankel, B. L. and Snyder, F. (1979) 'Successful separation of depressed, normal and insomniac subjects by EEG sleep data'. *Archives of General Psychiatry*, 36, 85–90.

Globus, G. G., Gardner, R. and Williams, T. A. (1969) 'Relation of sleep onset to rapid eye movement sleep'. *Archives of General Psychiatry*, 21, 151–4

Glover, T. R. (1909) *The Conflict of Religions and the Early Roman Empire*. London, Methuen.

Goldsmith, O. (1811) *A History of the Earth and Animated Nature*, vol. 1. Liverpool, Nuttal & Dixon.

Goode, G. B. (1962) 'Sleep paralysis'. *A.M.A. Archives of Neurology*, 6, 228–34.

Goodenough, D. R. (1978) 'Dream recall: history and current status' in Arkin, A. M., Antrobus, J. S. and Ellman, S. J. (eds) *The Mind in Sleep*. New Jersey, Lawrence Erlbaum Associates.

Goodenough, D. R., Shapiro, A., Holden, M. and Steinschriber, L. (1959) ' "Dreamers" and "non-dreamers" '. *Journal of Abnormal and Social Psychology*, 59, 295–302.

Goodenough, D. R. , Witkin, H. A., Koulack, D. and Cohen, H. (1975) 'The effects of stress films on dream affect and on respiration and eye-movement activity during REM sleep'. *Psychophysiology*, 12, 313–20.

Gorer, G. (1966) 'Psychoanalysis in the world', in Rycroft, C. (ed.) *Psychoanalysis Observed*. London, Constable.

Gresham, S. C., Webb, W. B. and Williams, R. L. (1963) 'Alcohol and caffeine: effect on inferred visual dreaming'. *Science*, 134, 1226–7.

Griffin, M. L. and Foulkes, D. (1977) 'Deliberate pre-sleep control of dream content: an experimental study'. *Perceptual and Motor Skills*, 45, 660–2.

Griffin, S. J. and Trinder, J. (1978) 'Physical fitness, exercise and human sleep'. *Psychophysiology*, 15, 447–50.

Griffith, R. M., Miyagi, O. and Tago, A. (1958) 'The universality of typical dreams: Japanese vs. Americans'. *American Anthropologist*, 60, 1173–9.

Gross, R. T. and Borkovec, T. D. (1982) 'The effects of a cognitive intrusion manipulation on the sleep onset latency of good sleepers'. *Behavior Therapy*, 13, 112–16.

Gross, J., Byrne, J. and Fisher, C. (1965) 'Eye movements during emergent stage 1 EEG in subjects with lifelong blindness'. *Journal of Nervous and Mental Disease*, 141, 365–70.

Guilleminault, C. and Dement, W. C. (1978) 'Sleep apnea syndrome and related sleep disorders' in Williams, R. L. and Kornean, I. (eds) *Sleep Disorders: Diagnosis and Treatment*. New York, Wiley, 9–28.

Guilleminault, C., Eldridge, F. L. and Dement, W. C. (1973) 'Insomnia with sleep apnea: a new syndrome'. *Science*, 181, 856–8.

Guilleminault, C., Tilkian, A. and Dement, W. C. (1976) 'The sleep apnea syndromes'. *Annual Review of Medicine*, 27, 465–84.

Haider, I., and Oswald, I. (1971) 'Effects of amylobarbitone and nitrazepam on the electrodermogram and other features of sleep'. *British Journal of Psychiatry*, 118, 519–22.

Hakkanen, H. and Summala, H. (2000) 'Sleepiness at work among commercial truck drivers'. *Sleep*, 23, 49–57.

Halberg, F. (1969) 'Chronobiology'. *Annual Review of Physiology*, 31, 675–725.

Halberg. F., Halberg, E., Barnum, C. P. and Bittner, J. J. (1959) in Withrow, R. B. (ed.) *Photoperiodism and Related Phenomena in Plants and Animals*. Washington, DC, AAAS.

Hall, C. S. (1951) 'What people dream about'. *Scientific American*, 184, 60–3.

Hamilton, P., Wilkinson, R. T. and Edwards, R. S. (1972) 'A study of four days partial sleep deprivation' in Colquhoun, W. P. (ed.) *Aspects of Human Efficiency: Diurnal rhythm and loss of sleep*. London, English Universities Press.

Hansel, C. E. M. (1980) *ESP and Parapsychology: a Re-evaluation*. New York, Prometheus.

Harrison, Y. and Horne, J. A. (1996) 'Long-term extension to sleep – are we really chronically sleep deprived?' *Psychophysiology*, 33, 22–30.

Hartmann, E. (1968) 'The effect of four drugs on sleep in man'. *Psychopharmacologia*, 12, 346–53.

Hartmann, E. (1973) *The Functions of Sleep*. New Haven, CT, Yale University Press.

Hartmann, E. (1976) 'Long-term administration of psychotropic drugs: effects on human sleep' in Williams, R. L. and Karacan, I. (eds) *Pharmacology of Human Sleep*. New York, Wiley, 211–23.

Hartmann, E. (1978) *The Sleeping Pill*. New Haven, CT, Yale University Press.

Haslam, D. R. (1981) 'The military performance of soldiers in continuous operations: exercises "early call" I and II' in Johnson, L.C., Tepas, D. I., Colquhoun, W. P. and Colligan, M. J. (eds) *Biological Rhythms, Sleep and Shift Work*. New York, Spectrum, 435–58.

Haslam, D. R. (1982) 'Sleep loss, recovery sleep, and military performance'. *Ergonomics*, 25, 163–78.

Hauri, P. (1966) 'Effects of evening activity on early night sleep'. *Psychophysiology*, 4, 267–77.

Hauri, P. and Hawkins, D. R. (1973) 'Alpha-delta sleep'. *Electroencephalography and Clinical Neurophysiology*, **34**, 233–7.

Hauri, P. and Olmstead, E. (1983) 'What is the moment of sleep onset for insomniacs?' *Sleep*, **6**, 10–15.

Hayes, F. J. and Crowley, W. F. (1998) 'Gonadotropin pulsations across development'. *Hormone Research*, **49**, 163–8.

Haynes, S. N., Adams, A. and Franzen, M. (1981) 'The effects of presleep stress on sleep-onset insomnia'. *Journal of Abnormal Psychology*, **90**, 601–6.

Haynes, S. N., Sides, H. and Lockwood, G. (1977) 'Relaxation instructions and frontalis electromyographic feedback intervention with sleep-onset insomnia'. *Behavior Therapy*, **8**, 644–52.

Hebb, D. O. (1968) 'Concerning imagery'. *Psychological Review*, **75**, 466–74.

Heller, H. C. and Glotzbach, S. F. (1977) 'Thermoregulation during sleep and hibernation: environmental physiology II'. *International Review of Physiology*, **15**, 147–88.

Hennevin, E. and Leconte, P. (1971) 'La fonction du sommeil paradoxal'. *Annee Psychologique*, **72**, 489–505.

Herman, J. H., Ellman, S. J. and Roffwarg, H. P. (1978) 'The problem of NREM dream recall re-examined' in Arkin, A. M., Antrobus, J. S. and Ellman, S. J. (eds) *The Mind in Sleep*. New York, Wiley.

Hishikawa, Y. (1976) 'Sleep paralysis' in Guilleminault, C., Dement, W. C. and Passuant, P. (eds) *Narcolepsy*. New York, Spectrum.

Hobson, J. A. (1989) *Sleep*. New York, Scientific American Library.

Hobson, J. A. (1990) 'Activation, input source, and modulation: a neurocognitive model of the state of the brain-mind' in Bootzin, R. R., Kihlstrom, J. F. and Schacter, D. L. (eds) *Sleep and Cognition*. Washington, DC, American Psychological Association, 25–42.

Hobson, J. A. (1992) 'A new model of brain-mind state: Activation level, input source and mode of processing' in Antrobus, J. and Bertini, M. (eds) *The Neuropsychology of Sleep and Dreaming*. Hillsdale, Erlbaum, 227–45.

Hobson, J. A., Pace-Schott, E. F. and Stickgold, R. (2000) 'Dreaming and the brain: toward a cognitive neuroscience of conscious states'. *Behavioral and Brain Sciences*, **23**, 6, 793–842.

Hobson, J. A. and McCarley, R. W. (1977) 'The brain as a dream state generator: an activation-synthesis hypothesis of the dream process'. *American Journal of Psychiatry*, **134**, 1335–48.

Hockey, G. R. J. (1970a) 'Effect of loud noise on attentional selectivity'. *Quarterly Journal of Experimental Psychology*, **22**, 28–36.

Hockey, G. R. J. (1970b) 'Changes in attention allocation in a multi-component task under loss of sleep'. *British Journal of Psychology*, **61**, 473–80.

Holt, R. R. (1972) 'On the nature and generality of mental imagery' in Sheehan, P. (ed.) *The Function and Nature of Imagery*. New York, Academic Press.

Hong, C. C.-H., Gillin, J. C., Dow, B. M., Wu, J. and Buchsbaum, M. S. (1995) 'Localized and lateralized cerebral glucose metabolism associated with eye movements during REM sleep and wakefulness: a positron emission tomography (PRT) study'. *Sleep*, **18**, 570–80.

Hong, C. C.-H., Potkin, S. G., Antrobus, J. S., Dow, B. M., Callaghan, G. M. and Gillin, J. C. (1997) 'REM sleep eye movement counts correlate with visual imagery in dreaming: a pilot study'. *Psychophysiology*, **34**, 377–81.

Hopfield, J. J., Feinstein, D. I. and Palmer, R. G. (1983) ' "Unlearning" has a stabilizing effect in collective memories'. *Nature*, **304**, 158–9.

Horne, J. A. (1981) 'The effects of exercise upon sleep: a critical review'. *Biological Psychology*, **12**, 241–90.

Horne, J. (1988) *Why We Sleep: The Functions of Sleep in Humans and Other Mammals*. Oxford, Oxford University Press.

Horne, J. A. and Moore, V. J. (1985) 'Sleep EEG effects of exercise with and without additional body cooling'. *Electroencephalography and Clinical Neurophysiology*, **60**, 33–8.

Horne, J. A. and Pettit, A. N. (1985) 'High incentive effects on vigilance performance during 72 hours of total sleep deprivation'. *Acta Psychologica*, **58**, 123–39.

Horne, J. A. and Porter, J. M. (1976) 'Time of day effects with standardized exercise upon subsequent sleep'. *Electroencephalography and Clinical Neurophysiology*, **40**, 178–84.

Horne, J. A. and Reid, A. J. (1985) 'Night-time sleep EEG changes following body heating in a warm bath'. *Electroencephalography and Clinical Neurophysiology*, **60**, 154–7.

Horne, J. A. and Reyner, L. A. (1996) 'Counteracting driver sleepiness: effects of napping, caffeine and placebo'. *Psychophysiology*, **33**, 306–9.

Horne, J. A. and Wilkinson, R. T. (1985) 'Chronic sleep reduction: daytime vigilance performance and EEG measures of sleepiness, with particular reference to "practice" effects'. *Psychophysiology*, **22**, 69–77.

Horton, R. H. (1963) *Stories of the Early Church*, vols 1–4. London, Edward Arnold.

Hull, C. L. (1962) 'Psychology of the scientist: IV. Passages from the "idea books" of Clark L. Hull'. *Perceptual and Motor Skills*, **15**, 807–22.

Humble, R. (1975) *Marco Polo*. London, Weidenfeld & Nicolson.

Hume, K. I. (1986) paper presented at the December 1986 meeting of the Psychophysiology Society (UK), Charing Cross Hospital.

Hume, K. I. and Mills, J. N. (1977) 'Rhythms of REM and slow-wave sleep in subjects living on abnormal time schedules'. *Waking and Sleeping*, **1**, 291–6.

Huntley, A. C. and Cohen, H. B. (1980) 'Further comments on "sleep" in the desert iguana, *Dipsosaurus dorsalis*'. *Sleep Research*, **9**, 111.

Immelman, V. K. and Gebbing, H. (1962) 'Schlaf bei Giraffen'. *Zeitscrift Tierpsychologisch*, **19**, 84–92.

Inouye, S.-I. T. and Kawamura, H. (1979) 'Persistence of circadian rhythmicity in a mammalian hypothalamic "island" containing the suprachiasmatic nucleus'. *Proceedings of the National Academy of Sciences (USA)*, **76**, 5962–6.

Ishizuka, Y., Pollak, C. P., Shirakawa, S., Kakuma, T., Azum, K. and Usui, A. (1994) 'Sleep spindle frequency changes during the menstrual cycle'. *Journal of Sleep Research*, **3**, 26–9.

Jackson, J. H. (1874) 'On hallucinations'. *Medical Times London*, **1**, 123. Reprinted in Taylor J., Holmes, G. and Walshe, F. M. R. (eds) *Selected Writings of Hughlings Jackson*, vol. 2. New York, Basic Books.

Jacobs, L., Feldman, M. and Bender, M. B. (1972) 'Are the eye movements of dreaming sleep related to the visual images of the dreams?' *Psychophysiology*, **9**, 393–401.

Jacobson, E. (1929) *Progressive Relaxation*. Chicago, University of Chicago Press.

James, W. (1896) *The Will to Believe, and Other Essays*. London, Longmans.

Jewett, M. E., Dijk, D.-J., Kronauer, R. E. and Dinges, D. F. (1999) 'Dose-response relationship between sleep duration and human psychomotor vigilance and subjective alertness'. *Sleep*, **22**, 171–9.

Johns, M. W. (1975). 'Factor analysis of subjectively reported sleep habits and the nature of insomnia'. *Psychological Medicine*, **5**, 83–8.

Johns, M. W. and Masterton, J. P. (1974) 'Effects of flurazepam on sleep in the laboratory'. *Pharmacology*, **11**, 358–64.

Johnson, L. C. and Chernik, D. A. (1982) 'Sedative-hypnotics and human performance'. *Psychopharmacology*, **76**, 101–13.

Johnson, L. C. and Lubin, A. (1967) 'The orienting reflex during waking and sleeping'. *Electroencephalography and Clinical Neurophysiology*, **22**, 11–21.

Johnson, L. C., Naitoh, P., Moses, J. M. and Lubin, A. (1974) 'Interaction of REM deprivation and stage 4 deprivation with total sleep loss: experiment 2'. *Psychophysiology*, **11**, 147–59.

Jones, H. S. and Oswald, I. (1968) 'Two cases of health innsomnia'. *Electroencephalography and Clinical Neurophysiology*, **24**, 378–80.

Jouvet, M. (1967) 'Neurophysiology of the states of sleep'. *Physiological Review*, **47**, 117–34.

Jouvet, M. (1972) 'The role of monoamines and acetylcholine containing neurons in the regulation of the sleep-waking cycle'. *Revue Physiologique*, **64**, 166–307.

Jouvet, M. (1978) 'Does a genetic programming of the brain occur during paradoxical sleep?' in Buser, P. and Buser-Rogeul, A. (eds) *Cerebral Correlates of Conscious Behaviour*. Amsterdam, Elsevier/North Holland.

Jouvet, M., Denoyer, M., Hitahama, K. and Sallanon, M. (1989) 'Slow wave sleep and indolamines: a hypothalamic target' in Wauquier, A. (ed.) *Slow Wave Sleep: Physiological, Pathophysiological and Functional Aspects*. New York, Raven Press, 91–108.

Jouvet, M. and Renault, J. (1966) 'Insomnie persistante après lesions des noyaux du raphe chez le chat'. *Comptes Rendus de la Société Biologie* (Paris), **160**, 1461–5.

Kahn, E., Dement, W. C., Fisher, C. and Barmcak, J. E. (1962) 'Incidence of colour in immediately recalled dreams'. *Science*, **137**, 1055–6.

Kahn, E. and Fisher, C. (1969) 'The sleep characteristics of the normal aged male'. *Journal of Nervous and Mental Disorders*, **148**, 477–82.

Kales, A. (1969) 'Psychophysiological and biochemical changes following use and withdrawal of hypnotics' in Kales, A. (ed.) *Sleep Physiology and Pathology*. Philadelphia, Lippincott.

Kales, A., Hewser, G., Jacobson, A., Kales, J. D., Hanley, J., Zweizig, J. R. and Paulson, M. J. (1967) 'All night sleep studies in hypothyroid patients before and after treatment'. *Psychosomatics*, **14**, 33–7.

Kales, A., Jacobson, A., Paulson, M. J., Kales, J. and Walter, R. D. (1966) 'Somnambulism: psychophysiological correlates'. *Archives of General Psychiatry*, **14**, 586–94.

Kales, A., Malmstrom, E. J., Scharf, M. B. and Rudin, R. T. (1969) 'Psychophysiological and biochemical changes following use and withdrawal of hypnotics' in Kales, A. (ed.) *Sleep Physiology and Pathology*. Philadelphia, Lippincott.

Kales, A., Tan, T. L., Kollar, E. J., Naitoh, P., Preston, T. A. and Malmstrom, E. J. (1970) 'Sleep patterns following 205 hours of sleep deprivation'. *Psychosomatic Medicine*, **32**, 189–200.

Kaprio, J., Hublin, J., Partinen, M., Heikkila, K. and Koskenvuo, M. (1996) 'Narcolepsy-like symptoms among adult twins'. *Journal of Sleep Research*, **5**, 55–60.

Karacan, I., Salis, P. J. and Hursch, C. J. (1971) 'New approaches to the evaluation and treatment of insomnia'. *Psychosomatics*, **12**, 81–8.

Karni, A. and Sagi, D. (1991) 'Where practice makes perfect in texture discrimination: evidence for primary visual cortex plasticity'. *Proceedings of the National Academy of Sciences (U.S.A.)*, **88**, 4966.

Karni, A., Tanne, D., Rubenstein, B. S., Askenasi, J. J. M. and Sagi, D. (1994) 'Dependence on REM sleep of overnight improvement of a perceptual skill'. *Science*, 265, 679–82.

Katayama, Y., DeWitt, D. S., Becker, D. P., and Hayes, R. L. (1986) 'Behavioral evidence for cholinoceptive pontine inhibitory area: Descending control of spinal motor output and sensory input'. *Brain Research*, 296, 241–62.

Katz, I., Stradling, J., Slutsky, A. S., Zamel, N. and Hoffstein, V. (1990) 'Do patients with obstructive sleep apnea have thick necks?' *American Review of Respiratory Disease*, 141, 1228–31.

Katznelson, L., Riskind, P. N., Saxee, V. C. and Klibanski, A. (1998) 'Prolactin pulsatile characteristics in postmenopausal women'. *Journal of Clinical Endocrinology and Metabolism*, 83, 761–4.

Kayumov, L., Pandi, P. S. R., Fedoroff, P. and Shapiro, S. M. (2001) 'Diagnostic values of polysomnography in forensic medicine'. *Journal Forensic Science*, 45, 191–4.

Key, B. J. and Marley, E. (1962) 'The effect of the sympathomimetic amines behaviour and electrocortical activity of the chicken'. *Electroencephalography and Clinical Neurophysiology*, 14, 90–105.

Keys, A. (1986) *The Biology of Human Starvation*. Minneapolis, University of Minnesota Press.

King-Hele, D. (1986) *Erasmus Darwin and the Romantic Poets*. London, Macmillan.

Kjellberg, A. (1977) 'Sleep deprivation and some aspects of performance: I. Problems of arousal changes. II. Lapses and other attentional effects. III. Motivation, comment and conclusions'. *Waking and Sleeping*, 1, 139–43; 145–8; 149–53.

Klackenberg, G. (1987) 'Incidence of parasomnias in children in a general population' in Guilleminault, C. (ed.) *Sleep and Its Disorders in Children*. New York, Raven Press.

Klein, R. and Armitage, R. (1979) 'Rhythms in human performance: 1.5 hour oscillations in cognitive style'. *Science*, 204, 1326–7.

Kleitman, N. (1927) 'Studies on the physiology of sleep: V. Some experiments on puppies'. *American Journal of Physiology*, 84, 386–95.

Kleitman, N. (1969) 'The basic rest-activity cycle in relation to sleep and wakefulness' in Kales, A. (ed.) *Sleep: Physiology and Pathology*. Philadelphia, Lippincott.

Kluvitse, C. D. (1984) 'The effects of sleep loss on ERPs'. MSc dissertation, University of Hull.

Knauth, P., Landau, K., Droge, C., Schwitteck, M., Widynski, M. and Rutenfranz, J. (1980) 'Duration of sleep depending on the type of shiftwork'. *International Archives of Occupational and Environmental Health*, 46, 167–77.

Koestler, A. (1966) *The Act of Creation*. London, Pan, 213–14.

Kohlschutter, E. (1862) 'Messungen der Festigheit des Schlafes'. *Zeitschrift fur Rechtscmedizin*, 17, 209–53.

Kohsaka, M., Fukuda, N., Honma, K., Honma, S. and Morita, N. (1992) 'Seasonality in human sleep'. *Experientia*, 48, 231–3.

Koukkou, M. and Lehmann, D. (1968) 'EEG and memory storage in sleep experiments with humans'. *Electroencephalography and Clinical Neurophysiology*, 25, 455–62.

Krahn, L. E., Lin, S. C., Wisbey, J. and Rummans, T. A. (1997) 'Assessing sleep in psychiatric inpatients: nurse and patient reports versus wrist actigraphy'. *Annals of Clinical Psychiatry*, 9, 203–10.

Kristal, M. B. and Noonan, M. (1979) 'Note on sleep in captive giraffes (*Giraffa camelopardalis reticulata*)'. *South African Journal of Zoology*, 14, 108.

Kronauer, R. E., Czeisler, C. A., Pilato, S. F., Moore-Ede, M. C. and Weitzman, E. D. (1982) 'Mathematical model of the human circadian system with two interacting oscillators'. *American Journal of Physiology*, 242, R3–17.

Kryger, M. H., Roth, T. and Dement, W. C. (eds) (1989) *Principles and Practice of Sleep Medicine*. Philadelphia, Saunders.

Kupfer, D. J. (1976) 'REM latency: a psychobiologic marker for primary depressive disease'. *Biological Psychiatry*, 11, 159–74.

Kushida, C. A., Bergmann, B. M. and Rechtschaffgen, A. (1989) 'Sleep deprivation in the rat: IV. Paradoxical sleep deprivation'. *Sleep*, 12, 22–30.

Kushida, C. A., Everson, C. A., Suthipintharm, P., Sloan, J., Soltani, K., Bartnicke, B., Bergmann, B. M. and Rechtschaffen, A. (1989) 'Sleep deprivation in the rat: VI. Skin changes'. *Sleep*, 12, 42–6.

Lamond, N. and Dawson, D. (1999) 'Quantifying the performance impairment associated with fatigue'. *Journal of Sleep Research*, 8, 255–62.

Langford, G. W., Meddis, R. and Pearson, A. J. D. (1972) 'Spontaneous arousals from sleep in human subjects'. *Psychonomic Science*, 28, 228–30.

Langford, G. W., Meddis, R. and Pearson, A. J. D. (1974) 'Awakening latency from sleep for meaningful and non-meaningful stimuli'. *Psychophysiology*, 11, 1–5.

Lefebure, Molly (1974) *Samuel Taylor Coleridge: A Bondage of Opium*. London, Gollanz.

Lehman, M. N., Silver, R., Gladstone, W. R., Kahn, R. M., Gibson, M. and Bittman, E. L. (1987) 'Circadian rhythmicity restored by neural transplant: immunocytochemical characterization with the host brain'. *Journal of Neuroscience*, 7, 1626–38.

Lehmann, D, and Koukkou, M. (1974) 'Computer analysis of EEG wakefulness–sleep patterns during learning of novel and familiar sentences'. *Electroencephalography and Clinical Neurophysiology*, 37, 73–84.

Levey, A. B., Aldaz, J. A., Watts, F. N. and Coyle, K. (1991). 'Articulatory suppression and the treatment of insomnia'. *Behaviour Research and Therapy*, 29, 85–9.

Levi, P. (1960) *If This is a Man*, translated by Stuart Woolf. London, Orion Press.

Levi, P. (1965) *The Truce*, translated by Stuart Woolf. London, Bodley Head,.

Levine, B. Roehrs, T., Zorick, F. and Roth, T. (1988) 'Daytime sleepiness in young adults'. *Sleep*, 11, 39–46.

Lewis, B. (1980) *The Assassins: A Radical Sect in Islam*. New York, Octagon Books.

Lewis, H. B., Goodenough, D. R., Shapiro, A. and Sleser, I. (1966) 'Individual differences in dream recall'. *Journal of Abnormal Psychology*, 71, 52–9.

Lewis, S. A. (1969) 'Subjective estimates of sleep: an EEG evaluation'. *British Journal of Psychology*, 60, 203–8.

Lichstein, K. L. and Fisher, S. M. (1985) 'Insomnia' in Hersen, M. and Bellak, A. S. (eds) *Handbook of Clinical Behavior Therapy with Adults*. New York, Plenum, 319–52.

Lichstein, K. L. and Rosenthal, T. L. (1980) 'Insomniacs' perceptions of cognitive versus somatic determinance of sleep disturbance'. *Journal of Abnormal Psychology*, 89, 105–7.

Lindsley, D. B., Schreiner, L. H., Knowles, W. B. and Magoun, H. W. (1950) 'Behavioral and EEG changes following chronic brain stem lesions in the cat'. *Electroencephalography and Clinical Neurophysiology*, 2, 483–98.

Lisper, H.-O. and Kjellberg, A. (1972) 'Effects of 24 hours sleep deprivation on rate of decrement in a 10 minute auditory reaction time task'. *Journal of Experimental Psychology*, 96, 287–90.

Lister, S. J. (1981) 'A theoretical formulation of the effects of sleep loss', PhD thesis, University of Hull.

Lockley, S. W., Skene, D. J., James, K., Thapan, K., Wright, J. and Arendt, J. (2000) 'Melatonin administration can entrain the free-running circadian system of blind subjects'. *Journal of Endocrinology*, 164, no. 1.

Loomis, A. L., Harvey, E. N. and Hobart, G. A. (1937) 'Cerebral states during sleep as studied by human brain potentials'. *Journal of Experimental Psychology*, 21, 127–44.

Lozoff, B., Wolf, A. W. and Davis, N. S. (1985) 'Sleep problems seen in pediatric practice'. *Pediatrics*, 75, 477–83.

Lubin, A., Moses, J. M., Johnson, L. C. and Naitoh, P. (1974) 'The recuperative of REM sleep and stage 4 sleep on human performance after complete sleep loss: experiment 1'. *Psychophysiology*, 11, 133–46.

Lugaresi, E., and Gambetti, P. (1992) 'Fatal familial insomnia: clinical and pathologic study of five new cases'. *Neurology*, 42, 312–19.

Lugaresi, E., Medori, R., Montagna, P., Baruzzi, A., Cortelli, P., Lugaresi, A., Tinuper, P., Zucconi, M. and Gambetti, P. (1986) 'Fatal familial insomnia and dysautonomia with selective degeneration of thalamic nuclei'. *New England Journal of Medicine*, 315, 997–1003.

Lukas, J. S. and Kryter, K. D. (1970) 'Awakening effects of simulated sonic booms and subsonic aircraft noise' in Welch, B. L. and Welch, A. S. (eds) *Psychological Effects of Noise*. New York, Plenum Press.

Lundh, L.-G. (1998) 'Cognitive-behavioural analysis and treatment of insomnia'. *Scandinavian Journal of Behaviour Therapy*, 27, 10–29.

Lydic, R., Scroene, W. C., Czeisler, C. A., and Moore-Ede, M. C. (1980) 'Suprachiasmatic region of the human hypothalamus: homolog to the primate circadian pacemaker?' *Sleep*, 2, 355–61.

Lyman, C. P. (1982) 'Why bother to hibernate?' in Lyman, C. P., Willis, J. S., Malan, A. and Wang, L. C. H. (eds) *Hibernation and Torpor in Mammals and Birds*. New York, Academic Press.

Macdonald, D. G., Schicht, W. W. and Frazier, R. E. (1975) 'Studies of information processing in sleep'. *Psychophysiology*, 12, 624–9.

MacNeice, L. (1982) *The Strings are False*. London, Faber, 198.

Magnes, J., Moruzzi, G. and Pompeiano, O. (1961) 'Synchronization of the EEG produced by low-frequency electrical stimulation of the region of the solitary tract'. *Archives Italiennes de Biologie*, 99, 33–67.

Mahowald, M. W. and Schenck, C. H. (1989) 'REM sleep behavior disorder' in Kruger, M. H., Roth, T. and Dement, W. C. (eds) *Principles and Practice of Sleep Medicine*. Philadelphia, Saunders, 389–401.

Manaceine, M. de (1897) *Sleep: Its Physiology, Pathology, Hygiene and Psychology*. London, Walter Scott.

Manber, R. and Bootzin, R. R. (1997) 'Sleep and the menstrual cycle'. *Health Psychology*, 16, 209–14.

Manetto, V., Medori, R., Cortelli, P., Montagna, P., Tinuper, P., Baruzzi, A., Rancurel, G., Hauw, J.-J., Vanderhaeghen, J.-J., Mailleux, P., Bugiani, O., Tagliavini, F., Bouras, C., Rizzuto, J., Lugaresi, E. and Gambetti, P. (1992) 'Fatal familial insomnia: clinical and pathologic study of five new cases'. *Neurology*, 42, 312–19.

Manseau, C. and Broughton, R. J. (1984) 'Bilaterally synchronous ultradian EEG rhythms in awake adult humans'. *Psychophysiology*, 21, 265–73.

Maquet, P., Peters, J. M., Aerts, J., Delfiore, G., Degueldre, C., Luxen, A. and Franck, G. (1996) 'Functional neuroanatomy of human rapid-eye-movement sleep and dreaming'. *Nature*, 383, 163–6.

Maury, A. (1861) *Le Sommeil et les Rêves*, Paris.

Mavromatis, A. (1987) *Hypnagogia: the Unique State of Consciousness Between Wakefulness and Sleep*. London, Routledge.

McCarley, R. W. and Hobson, J. A. (1977) 'The neurobiological origins of psychoanalytic dream theory'. *American Journal of Psychiatry*, 134, 1211–21.

McCarley, R. W. and Massaquoi, S. (1986) 'A limit cycle mathematical model of the REM sleep oscillator system'. *American Journal of Physiology*, **251**, R1011–29.

McGhie, A. and Russell, S. M. (1962) 'The subjective assessment of normal sleep patterns'. *Journal of Mental Science*, **8**, 642–54.

McGinty, D. J. and Harper, R. M. (1976) 'Dorsal raphe neurons: depression of firing during sleep in cats'. *Brain Research*, **101**, 569–74.

McGregor, D. (1964) *The Dream World of Dion McGregor*. New York, Geis.

McKellar, P. (1957) *Imagination and Thinking*. London, Cohen & West.

McKellar, P. (1972) 'Imagery from the standpoint of introspection' in Sheehan, P. (ed.) *The Function and Nature of Imagery*. New York, Academic Press.

McNicholas, W. T., Tarlo, S. M. and Phillipson, E. A. (1982) 'Is sleep apnoea more common in North America?' *The Lancet*, **1**, 458.

Meddis, R. (1975) 'On the function of sleep'. *Animal Behaviour*, **23**, 676–91.

Meddis, R. (1977) *The Sleep Instinct*. London, Routledge & Kegan Paul.

Meddis, R. (1983) 'The evolution of sleep' in Mayes, A. (ed.) *Sleep Mechanisms and Functions*. Wokingham, Van Nostrand.

Meddis, R., Pearson, A. J. D., and Langford, G. (1973) 'An extreme case of healthy insomnia'. *Electroencephalography and Clinical Neurophysiology*, **35**, 391–4.

Meglasson, M. D. and Huggins, S. E. (1979) 'Sleep in a crocodilian, *Caiman sclerops*'. *Comparative Biochemistry and Physiology*, **63**, 561–90.

Meier-Ewart, K., Matsubayashi, K. and Benter, L. (1985) 'Propranolol: longterm treatment in narcolepsy-cataplexi'. *Sleep*, **8**, 95–104.

Meldrun, D. R., Erlin, Y., Lu, J. K. H. and Judd, H. L. (1981) 'Objectively recorded hot flushes in patients with pituitary insufficiency'. *Journal of Clinical Endocrinology and Metabolism*, **52**, 684–7.

Meldrun, D. R., Tataryn, I. V., Frumar, A. M., Erlik, Y., Lu, K.H. and Judd, H. L. (1980) 'Gonadotropins, estrogens, and adrenal steroids during the menopausal hot flash'. *Journal of Clinical Endocrinology and Metabolism*, **50**, 685–9.

Mendels, J. and Hawkins, D. R. (1967) 'Sleep and depression'. *Archives of General Psychiatry*, **16**, 344–54.

Mendelson, W. B., Jacobs, L. S. and Gillin, J. C. (1983) 'Negative feedback suppression of sleep-related growth hormone secretion'. *Journal of Clinical Endocrinology and Metabolism*, **56**, 486–8.

Merrick, A. W. and Sharp, D. W. (1971) 'Electroenchephalography of resting behavior in cattle, with observations on the question of sleep'. *American Journal of Veterinary Research*, **32**, 1893–7.

Messer, D. and Richards, M. (1993) 'The development of sleeping difficulties' in St James-Roberts, I., Harris, G. and Messer, D. *Infant Crying, Feeding and Sleeping*. Hemel Hempstead, Harvester Wheatsheaf.

Michelson, E. (1897) 'Intersuchungen uber die Tiefe des Schlafes'. *Psychologic Arbeiten*, **2**, 84–117.

Middleton, W. C. (1942) 'The frequency with which a group of unselected college students experience colour dreaming and colour hearing'. *Journal of General Psychology*, **27**, 221–9.

Mitchell, K. R. (1979) 'Behavioral treatment of pre-sleep tension and intrusive cognitions in patients with severe pre-dormital insomnia'. *Journal of Behavioral Medicine*, **2**, 57–69.

Mitchell, K. R. and White, R. G., (1977) 'Self-management of severe pre-dormital insomnia'. *Journal of Behavior Therapy and Experimental Psychiatry*, **8**, 57–63.

Moldofsky, H., Scarisbrick, P., England, R. and Smythe, H. (1975) 'Musculoskeletal symptoms and non-REM sleep disturbance in patients with "fibrositis syndrome" and healthy subjects'. *Psychosomatic Medicine*, 37, 341–53.

Molinari, S. and Foulkes, D. (1969) 'Tonic and phasic events during sleep: psychological correlates and implications'. *Perceptual and Motor Skills*, 29, 343–68.

Molnar, G. W. (1975) 'Body temperatures during menopausal hot flushes'. *Journal of Applied Physiology*, 38, 499–503.

Monk, T. H., Buysse, D. J. and Rose, L. R. (1999) 'Wrist actigraphic measures of sleep in space'. *Sleep*, 22, 948–54.

Monod, J. and Guidasci, S. (1976) 'Sleep and brain malformation in the neonatal period'. *Neuropaediatrie*, 7, 229–49.

Monroe, L. J. (1967) 'Psychological and physiological differences between good and bad sleepers'. *Journal of Abnormal Psychology*, 72, 255–64.

Moore, R. Y. and Eichler, V. B. (1972) 'Loss of a circadian adrenal corticosterone rhythm following suprachiasmatic lesions in the rat'. *Brain Research*, 42, 201–6.

Morgan, K., Adam, K. and Oswald, I. (1984) 'Effects of loprazolam and of triazolam on psychological function'. *Psychopharmacology*, 82, 386–8

Morgan, K. and Oswald, I. (1982) 'Anxiety caused by a short-life hypnotic'. *British Medical Journal*, 284, 942.

Morin, C. M. (1993) *Insomnia: Psychological Assessment and Management*. New York, Guilford.

Moruzzi, G. and Magoun, H. W. (1949) 'Brain stem reticular formation and activation in the EEG'. *Electroencephalography and Clinical Neurophysiology*, 1, 455–73.

Moscovitz, E. and Berger, R. J. (1969) 'Rapid eye movements and dream imagery: are they related?' *Nature*, 224, 613–14.

Mukhametov, L. M. and Polyakova, I. G. (1981) 'EEG investigation of the sleep in porpoises (*Phocoena phocoena*)'. *Zhurnal Visshei Nerundi Deyatelnosti Pavlova*, 31, 333–9.

Mukhametov, L. M., Supin, A. Y. and Polyakove, I. G. (1977) 'Interhemispheric asymmetry of the electroencephalographic sleep patterns in dolphins'. *Brain Research*, 134, 581–4.

Mullaney, D. J., Johnson, L. C., Naitoh, P., Friedmann, J. K, and Globus, G. G. (1977) 'Sleep during and after gradual sleep reduction'. *Psychophysiology*, 14, 237–44.

Mullaney, D. J., Kripke, D. F., Fleck, P. A. and Johnson, L. C. (1983) 'Sleep loss and nap effects on sustained continuous performance'. *Psychophysiology*, 20, 643–51.

Murray, J., Dunn, G., Williams, P. and Tarnopol, A. (1981) 'Factors affecting the consumption of psychotropic drugs'. *Psychological Medicine*, 11, 551–60.

Murtagh, D. R. R. and Greenwood, K. M. (1995) 'Identifying effective psychological treatments for insomnia: a meta-analysis'. *Journal of Consulting and Clinical Psychology*, 63, 79–89.

Naitoh, P. (1992) 'Minimal sleep to maintain performance: the search for the sleep quantum in sustained operations' in Stampi, C. (ed.) *Why We Nap*. Boston, Birkhauser, 198–219.

Naitoh, P., Johnson, L. C. and Lubin, A. (1971) 'Modification of surface negative slow potential (CNV) in the human brain after total sleep loss'. *Electroencephalography and Clinical Neurophysiology*, 30, 17–22.

Nasser, S. and Rees, P. J. (1992) 'Sleep apnoea: causes, consequences and treatment'. *British Journal of Clinical Practice*, 46, 39–43.

Nathan, P. W. (1969) *The Nervous System*. Harmondsworth, Penguin.

Needham, J. (1956) *Science and Civilisation in China*, vol. 2. Cambridge, Cambridge University Press.

Nelson, R. A., Wahner, H. W., Jones, J. D., Ellefson, R. D. and Zollman, P. E. (1973) 'Metabolism of bears before, during and after winter sleep'. *American Journal of Physiology*, **224**, 491–6.

Ngubane, H. (1976) *Body and Mind in Zulu Medicine*. London, Academic Press.

Nicassio, P. M. and Bootzin, R. R. (1974) 'A comparison of progressive relaxation and autogenic training as treatments for insomnia'. *Journal of Abnormal Psychology*, **83**, 253–60.

Nielsen, T. A. (2000) 'A review of mentation in REM and NREM sleep: "covert" REM sleep as a possible reconciliation of two opposing models'. *Behavioural Brain Science*, **23**, 815–66.

Nino-Murcia, G. and Keenan, S. (1987) 'Enuresis and sleep' in Guilleminault, C. (ed.) *Sleep and Its Disorders in Children*. New York, Raven Press.

Norton, R. (1970) 'The effects of acute sleep deprivation on selective attention'. *British Journal of Psychology*, **61**, 157–61.

Ogden, T. H. (1985) 'The mother, the infant and the matrix: interpretations of aspects of the work of Donald Winnicott'. *Contemporary Psychoanalysis*, **21**, 346–71.

Ogilivie, R. D., Wilkinson, R. T. and Allison, S. (1989) 'The detection of sleep onset: behavioural, physiological, and subjective convergence'. *Sleep*, **12**, 458–74.

Olson, E. J., Boeve, B. F. and Silber, M. H. (2000) 'Rapid eye movement sleep behaviour disorder: demographic, clinical and laboratory findings in 93 cases'. *Brain*, **123**, 331–9.

Omwake, K. and Loranz, M. (1933) 'Study of ability to wake at a specified time'. *Journal of Applied Psychology*, **17**, 468–74.

Oswald, I. (1959a) 'Sudden bodily jerks on falling asleep'. *Brain*, **82**, 92–103.

Oswald, I. (1959b) 'Experimental studies of rhythm, anxiety and cerebral vigilance'. *Journal of Mental Science*, **105**, 269–94.

Oswald, I. (1969) 'Human brain protein, drugs and dreams'. *Nature*, **223**, 893–7.

Oswald, I. (1980) 'Sleep as a restorative process: human clues'. *Progress in Brain Research*, **53**, 279–88.

Oswald, I. and Adam, K. (1980) 'The man who had not slept for 10 years'. *British Medical Journal*, **281**, 1684–5.

Oswald, I., Merrington, J. and Lewis, S. (1970) 'Cyclical "on demand" oral intake by adults'. *Nature*, **225**, 959–60.

Oswald, I. and Priest, R. G. (1965) 'Five weeks to escape the sleeping pill habit'. *British Medical Journal*, **2**, 1093–5.

Oswald, I., Taylor, A. M. and Treisman, M. (1960) 'Discriminative responses to stimulation during human sleep'. *Brain*, **83**, 440–53.

Padgam, C. A. (1975) 'Colours experienced in dreams'. *British Journal of Psychology*, **66**, 25–8.

Papakostopoulos, D. and Fenelon, B. (1975) 'Spatial distribution of the Contingent Negative Variation (CNV) and the relationship between the CNV and reaction time'. *Psychophysiology*, **12**, 74–8.

Parker, A. (1980) *States of Mind: ESP and Altered States of Consciousness*. New York, Taplinger.

Parker, D. C., Rossman, L. G., Kripke, D. F., Hershman, J. M., Gibson, W. and Davis, C. (1980) 'Endocrine rhythms across sleep-wake cycles in normal young men under basal state conditions' in Orem, J. and Barnes, C. D. (eds) *Physiology in Sleep*. New York, Academic Press.

Parker, D. C., Rossman, L. G. and Vanderlaan, E. F. (1974) 'Relation of sleep-entrained human prolactin to REM-nonREM cycles'. *Journal of Clinical Endocrinology and Metabolism*, **38**, 646–51.

Parkes, J. D. (1985) *Sleep and its Disorders*. London, Saunders.

Parkes, J. D. and Lock, C. B. (1989) 'Genetic factors in sleep disorders'. *Journal of Neurology, Neurosurgery and Psychiatry*, special supplement, 101–8.

Parmelee, A., Wenner, W. H., Akiyama, Y., Stern, E. and Flescher, J. (1967) 'Electroencephalography and brain maturation' in Minkowski, A. (ed.) *Symposium on Regional Development of the Brain in Early Life*. Philadelphia, Davis.

Parry, B. L., Mendelson, W. B., Duncan, W. C., Sack, D. A., Wehr, T. A. (1989) 'Longitudinal sleep EEG, temperature, and activity measurements across the menstrual cycle in patients with premenstrual depression and age matched controls'. *Psychiatry Research*, 30, 285–303.

Pasnau, R. O., Naitoh, R., Stier, S. and Killar, E. J. (1968) 'The psychological effects of 205 hours of sleep deprivation'. *Archives of General Psychiatry*, 18, 496–505.

Patrick, J. and Gilbert, J. A. (1896) 'On the effects of loss of sleep'. *Psychological Review*, 3, 469–98.

Petersson, H. and Lader, M. H . (1981) 'Withdrawal from long-term benzodiazepine treatment'. *British Medical Journal*, 283, 643–5.

Pfaff, D. W. and McEwen, B. (1983) 'Actions of oestrogens and progestones on nerve cells'. *Science*, 219, 808–14.

Pieron, H. (1913) *Le Problème Physiologique du Sommeil*. Paris, Masson.

Pivik, R. T., Bylsma, F. W. and Cooper, P. (1986) 'Sleep–wakefulness rhythms in the rabbit'. *Behavioural and Neural Biology*, 45, 275–86.

Plihal, W. and Born, J. (1999) 'Effects of early and late nocturnal sleep on priming and spatial memory'. *Psychophysiology*, 36, 571–82.

Polo-Kantona, P., Erkkola, R., Helenius, H., Irjala, K. and Polo, O. (1998) 'When does estrogen replacement therapy improve sleep quality?' *American Journal of Obstetrics and Gynecology*, 178, 1002–9.

Portnoff, G., Baekeland, F., Goodenough, G. R., Karacan, I. and Shapiro, A. (1968) 'Retention of verbal materials perceived immediately prior to onset of NREM sleep'. *Perceptual and Motor Skills*, 22, 751–8.

Prechtl, H. F. R. (1974) 'The behavioural states of the newborn infant (a review)'. *Brain Research*, 76, 185–212.

Price, V. A., Coates, T. J., Thoresen, C. E. and Grinstead, O. A. (1978) 'Prevalence and correlates of poor sleep among adolescents'. *American Journal of Disorders of Childhood*, 143, 583–6.

Priest, R. G. (1983) 'Sleep and its disorders' in Gaine, R. N. and Hudson, B. L. (eds) *Current Themes in Psychiatry*. London, Macmillan.

Priest, R. G., Terzano, M. G., Parrino, L. and Boyer, P. (1997) 'Efficacy of zolpidem in insomnia'. *European Psychiatry*, 12, Supplement 1.

Purdie, D. W., Empson, J. A. C., Crichton, C. and MacDonald, L. (1995) 'Hormone replacement therapy, sleep quality and psychological wellbeing'. *British Journal of Obstetrics and Gynaecology*, 102, 735–9.

Quera-Salva, M. A., Orluc, A., Goldenberg, F. and Guilleminault, C. (1991) 'Insomnia and use of hypnotics: study of a French population'. *Sleep*, 14, 386–91.

Ralph, M. R., Foster, R. G., Davis, F. C. and Menaker, M. (1990) 'Transplanted suprachiasmatic nucleus determines circadian period'. *Science*, 247, 975–8.

Ravnikar, V. A., Schiff, I. and Regestein, Q. R. (1983) 'Menopause and sleep' in Buchsbaum, H. J. (ed.) *The Menopause*. New York, Springer-Verlag.

Rebar, W. and Spitzer, I. B. (1987) 'The physiology and measurement of hot flushes'. *American Journal of Obstetrics and Gynecology*, 156, 1284–8.

Rechtschaffen, A. (1978) 'The singlemindedness and isolation of dreams'. *Sleep*, 1, 97–109.

Rechtschaffen, A., Bergmann, B. M., Everson, C. A. and Gilliland, M. A. (1989a) 'Sleep deprivation in the rat: X. Integration and discussion of the findings'. *Sleep*, 12, 68–87.

Rechtschaffen, A., Bergmann, B. M., Everson, C. A., Kushida, C. A. and Gilliland, M. A. (1989b) 'Sleep deprivation in the rat: I. Conceptual issues'. *Sleep*, 12, 1–4.

Rechtschaffen, A. and Kales, A. (eds) (1968) *A Manual of Standardized Terminology, Techniques and Scoring System for Sleep Stages of Human Adults*. Washington, DC, Public Information Service, US Government Printing Office.

Rechtschaffen, A. and Monroe, L. (1969) 'Laboratory studies of insomnia' in Kales, A. (ed.) *Sleep: Physiology and Pathology*. Philadelphia, Lippincott.

Rechtschaffen, A., Wolpert, E. A., Dement, W. C., Mitchell, S. A. and Fisher, C. (1963) 'Nocturnal sleep of narcoleptics'. *Electroencephalography and Clinical Neurophysiology*, 15, 599–609.

Reinberg, A., Andlauer, P., DePrins, J., Malberg, W., Vieux, N. and Baurdeleau, P. (1984) 'Desynchronization of the oral-temperature circadian-rhythm and intolerance to shift work'. *Nature*, 308, 272–4.

Reyner, L. A. and Horne, J. A. (1997) 'Suppression of sleepiness in drivers: combination of caffeine with a short nap'. *Psychophysiology*, 34, 721–5.

Richmann, N. (1981) 'A community survey of characteristics of 1 to 2-year-olds with sleep disruptions'. *Journal of the American Academy of Child Psychiatry*, 20, 281–91.

Richmann, N., Douglas, J., Hunt, H., Lansdown, R. and Levere, R. (1985) 'Behavioural methods in the treatment of sleep disorders – a pilot study'. *Journal of Child Psychology and Psychiatry*, 26, 581–91.

Robertson, J. (1981) *The Ladybird New Testament*. London, Ladybird Books.

Roehrs, T., Timms, V., Zwyghuizen-Doorenbos, A. and Roth, T. (1989) 'Sleep extension in sleepy and alert normals'. *Sleep*, 12, 449–57.

Roffwarg, H. P., Dement, W. C., Muzio, J. N. and Fisher, C. (1962) 'Dream imagery: relationship to rapid eye movements of sleep'. *Archives of General Psychiatry*, 7, 235–58.

Roger, H. (1932) *Les Troubles du Sommeil – Hypersomnies, Insomnies, Parasomnies*. Paris, Masson.

Rosa, R. R. Bonnet, M. H. and Kramer, M. (1983) 'The relationship of sleep and anxiety in anxious subjects'. *Biological Psychology*, 16, 119–26.

Rubin, R. T., Gouin, P. R., Lubin, A. and Poland, R. E. (1975) 'Nocturnal increase of plasma testosterone in men: relation to gonadotropins and prolactin'. *Journal of Clinical Endocrinology and Metabolism*, 40, 1027–33.

Ruckebusch, Y. (1972a) 'The relevance of drowsiness in the circadian cycle of farm animals'. *Animal Behaviour*, 20, 637–43.

Ruckebusch, Y. (1972b) 'Development of sleep and wakefulnes in the foetal lamb'. *Electroencephalography and Clinical Neurophysiology*, 32, 119–28.

Ruckebusch, Y., Barbey, P. and Guillemot, P. (1970) 'Les états de sommeil chez le cheval (*Equus caballus*)'. *Comptes Rendus Seances Société Biologique*, 164, 658–64.

Rundell, O. H., Lester, B. K., Griffiths, W. J. and Williams, H. L. (1972) 'Alcohol and sleep in young adults'. *Psychopharmacologia*, 26, 201–18.

Rycroft, C. (1979) *The Innocence of Dreams*. Oxford, Oxford University Press.

Sanders, N. K. (1960) *The Epic of Gilgamesh*. Harmondsworth, Penguin.

Sassin, J. F., Franz, A. G., Weitzman, E. D. and Kapen, S. (1972) 'Human prolactin: 24-hour pattern with increased release during sleep'. *Science*, 177, 1205–7.

Sassin, J. F., Parker, D. C., Johnson, L. C., Rossman, L. G., Mace, J. W. and Gotlin, R. W. (1969) 'Effects of slow wave sleep deprivation on human growth hormone release in sleep: preliminary study'. *Life Science*, 8, 1299–1307.

Saul, L. J. and Curtis, G. C. (1967) 'Dream form and strength of impulse in dreams of falling and other dreams of descent'. *International Journal of Psychoanalysis*, **48**, 281–7.

Schacter, D. L. (1976) 'The hypnagogic state: a critical review of the literature'. *Psychological Bulletin*, **83**, 452–81.

Scharf, M. B., McDannold, M. D., Stover, R., Zretsky, N. and Berkowitz, D. V. (1997) 'Effects of estrogen replacement therapy on rates of cyclic alternating patterns and hot-flush events during sleep in postmenopausal women: a pilot study'. *Clinical Therapeutics*, **19**, 304–11.

Scheffers, M. K., Humphrey, D. G., Stanny, R. R., Kramer, A. F. and Coles, M. G. H. (1999) 'Error-related processing during a period of extended wakefulness'. *Psychophysiology*, **36**, 149–157.

Schenck, C. H., Bundlie, S. R., Ettinger, M. G., and Mahawald, M. W. (1986) 'Chronic behavioral disorders of human REM sleep: a new category of parasomnia'. *Sleep*, **9**, 293–308.

Schiff, I., Regestein, Q., Tulchinsky, D. and Ryan, K. J. (1979) 'Effects of oestrogens on sleep and psychological state of hypogonadal women'. *Journal of the American Medical Association*, **242**, 2405–7.

Schlehuber, C. J., Flaming, D. G., Lange, G. D. and Spooner, C. E. (1974) 'Paradoxical sleep in the chick (*Gallus domesticus*)'. *Behavioral Biology*, **11**, 537–46.

Schneerson, J. M. (1999) *Handbook of Sleep Medicine*. Oxford, Blackwell.

Schneider, E. (1975) *Coleridge, Opium and Kubla Khan*. New York, Octagon Press.

Seligman, M. E. P. and Yellen, A. (1987) 'What is a dream?' *Behavioural Research and Therapy*, **25**, 1–24.

Shanon, B. (1979) 'Semantic processing during sleep'. *Bulletin of the Psychonomic Society*, **14**, 382–4.

Shapiro, C. M. (1982) 'Energy expenditure and restorative sleep'. *Biological Psychology*, **15**, 229–39.

Shapiro, C. M., Catteral, J. R., Oswald, I. and Flenley, D. C. (1981) 'Where are the British sleep apnea patients?' *Lancet*, **2** (8245), 534–5.

Shapiro, C. M., Catteral, J., Warren, P., Oswald, I., Trinder, J., Paxton, S. and East, B. W. (1986) 'Lean body mass and non-rapid eye movement sleep'. *British Medical Bulletin*, **294** (22), 537–46.

Shulman, S. (1979) *Nightmare*. London, David & Charles.

Siegel, J. M. (1985) 'A behavioral approach to the analysis of reticular formation unit activity' in Robinson, T. E. (ed.) *Behavioral Approaches to Brain Research*. New York, Oxford University Press.

Siegel, J. M. (1990) 'Mechanisms of sleep control'. *Journal of Clinical Neurophysiology*, **7**, 49–65.

Siegel, J. M. and McGinty, D. J. (1977) 'Pontine reticular formation neurons: relationship of discharge to motor activity'. *Science*, **196**, 678–80.

Smith, C. (1995) 'Sleep states and memory processes'. *Behavioural Brain Research*, **69**, 137–45.

Snyder, F. (1970) 'The phenomenology of dreaming' in Madow, J. and Snow, L. H. (eds) *The Psychodynamic Implications of the Physiological Studies on Dreams*. Springfield, ILL., Charles C. Thomas.

Sokolov, E. N. (1963) *Perception and the Conditioned Reflex*. New York, Pergamon Press.

Sokolov, E. N. and Paramonova, N. P. (1961) 'Progressive changes in the orienting reflex in man during the development of sleep inhibition'. *Pavlov Journal of Higher Nervous Activity*, **11**, 217–26.

Soldatos, C. R., Kales, J. D., Scharf, M. B., Bixler, E. O. and Kales, A. (1980) 'Cigarette smoking associated with sleep difficulty'. *Science*, 207, 551–3.

Solms, M. (1997) *The Neuropsychology of Dreams*. New Jersey, Lawrence Erlbaum.

Solms, M. (2000) 'Dreaming and REM sleep are controlled by different brain mechanisms'. *Behavioral and Brain Sciences*, 23, 823–850.

Sontag, S. (1969) *Trip to Hanoi*. London, Panther.

Spiegel, R. and Azcona, A. (1985) 'Sleep and its disorders' in Pathy, M. S. J. (ed.) *Principles and Practice of Geriatric Medicine*. London, Wiley.

Spielman, A. J., Saskin, P. and Thorpy, M. J. (1987) 'Treatment of chronic insomnia by restriction of time in bed'. *Sleep*, 10, 45–56.

Spock, B. (1979) *Baby and Child Care*. London, W. H. Allen.

Steiger, A., Holsboer, F. and Benkert, O. (1987) 'Effects of brofaremine (CGP 11 305A), a short-acting reversible, and selective inhibitor of MAO-A on sleep, nocturnal penile tumescence and nocturnal hormonal secretion in three healthy volunteers. *Psychopharmacology*, 92, 110–14.

Stepansky, E. J., Zorick, F., Sicklesteel, J., Young, D. and Roth, T. (1986) 'Day time alertness-sleepiness in patients with chronic insomnia'. *Sleep Research*, 15, 174.

Stephan, F. K. and Zucker, I. (1972) 'Circadian rhythms in drinking behavior and locomotor activity of rats are eliminated by hypothalamic lesion'. *Proceedings of the National Academy of Sciences, U.S.A.*, 69, 1583–6.

Steriade, M., Pare, D., Bouhassira, D., Deschenes, M. and Oakson, G. (1989) 'Phasic activation of lateral geniculate and perigeniculate thalamic neurons during sleep with ponto-geniculo-occipital waves'. *Journal of Neuroscience*, 9, 2215–29.

Stickgold, R., James, L. T. and Hobson, J. A. (2000) 'Visual discrimination learning requires sleep after training'. *Nature Neuroscience*, 3, 1237–8.

Stone, B. M. (1980) 'Sleep and low doses of alcohol'. *Electroencephalography and Clinical Neurophysiology*, 48, 706–9.

Strohl, K. P., Hensley, M. J., Saunders, N. A. and Scharf, S. M. (1981) 'Progesterone administration and progressive sleep apneas'. *Journal of the American Medical Association*, 245, 1230–2.

Strunz, F. (1993) 'Preconscious mental activity and scientific problem-solving: a critique of the Kekulé dream controversy'. *Dreaming*, 3, 281–94.

Sturdee, D. W., Wilson, K. A., Pilili, E. and Crocker, A. D. (1978) 'Physiological aspects of menopausal hot flush'. *British Medical Journal*, 2, 79–80.

Sullivan, C. E., Issa, F. G., Berthon-Jones, M. and Eves, L. (1981) 'Reversal of obstructive sleep apnoea by continuous positive airway pressure applied through the nares'. *The Lancet*, 1, 862–5.

Sullivan, H. S. (1955) *The Interpersonal Theory of Psychiatry*. London, Tavistock.

Sutton, F. D., Zwillich, C. W. and Creagh, C. E. (1975) 'Progesterone for outpatient treatment of Pickwickian syndrome'. *Annals of Internal Medicine*, 83, 476–9.

Szymusiak, R. and McGinty, D. (1986) 'Sleep-related neuronal discharge in the basal forebrain of cats'. *Brain Research*, 370, 82–92.

Szymusiak, R. and McGinty, D. (1989) 'Sleep-waking discharge of basal forebrain projection neurons in cats'. *Brain Research Bulletin*, 22, 423–30.

Takahashi, Y., Kipnis, D. M. and Daughaday, W. H. (1968) 'Growth hormone secretion during sleep'. *Journal of Clinical Investigation*, 47, 2079–90.

Tataryn, I. V., Meldrun, D. R., Lu, K. H., Frumar, A. M. and Judd, H. L. (1979) 'FSH and skin temperature during the menopausal hot flash'. *Journal of Clinical Endocrinology and Metabolism*, 49, 152–4.

Taub, J. M. and Berger, R. (1969) 'Extended sleep and performance: the Rip Van Winkle effect'. *Psychonomic Science*, 16, 204–5.

Taub, J. M. and Berger, R. (1973) 'Performance and mood following variations in the length and timing of sleep'. *Psychophysiology*, **10**, 559–70.

Taub, J. M. and Berger, R. (1976) 'Effects of acute sleep pattern alteration depend on sleep duration'. *Physiological Psychology*, **4**, 412–20.

Taub, J. M., Globus, G. G., Phoebus, E. and Drury, R. (1971) 'Extended sleep and performance'. *Nature*, **233**, 142–3.

Tauber, E. S., Rofas-Ramire, J. and Hernandez-Peon, R. (1968) 'Electrophysiological and behavioural correlates of wakefulness and sleep in the lizard *Ctenosaura Pectinata*'. *Electroencephalography and Clinical Neurophysiology*, **24**, 424–33.

Thomson, J. and Oswald, I. (1977) 'Effect of oestrogen on the sleep, mood and anxiety of menopausal women'. *British Medical Journal*, **2**, 1317–19.

Tilley, A. J. and Empson, J. A. C. (1978) 'REM sleep and memory consolidation'. *Biological Psychology*, **6**, 293–300.

Tilley, A. J. and Wilkinson, R. T. (1982) 'Sleep and performance of shiftworkers'. *Human Factors*, **24**, 629–41.

Tinbergen, N. (1951) *The Study of Instinct*. London, Oxford University Press.

Tobler, I. and Schwierin, B. (1996) 'Behavioural sleep in the giraffe (*Giraffa camelopardalis*) in a zoological garden'. *Journal of Sleep Research*, **5**, 21–32.

Toutain, P.-L. and Ruckebusch, Y. (1972) 'Secretions nasolabiales au cours du sommeil paradoxal chez les bovins'. *Comptes Rendus de l'Académie Sciences* (Paris), **274**, 2519–22

Trulson, M. E. and Jacobs, B. L. (1979) 'Raphe unit activity in freely moving cats: correlation with level of behavioral arousal'. *Brain Research*, **163**, 135–50.

Turnbull, R. (1961) *The Forest People*. London, Jonathan Cape.

Twain, M. (1943) *The Adventures of Tom Sawyer* (originally published in 1876). London, Dent, 64–5.

Ullman, M., Krippner, S. and Vaughan, A. (1973) *Dream Telepathy*. New York, Macmillan.

Ursin, R. (1968) 'Sleep stages in the cat'. *Brain Research*, **11**, 347–56.

Van Brunt, D. L., Reidel, B. W. and Lichstein, K. L. (1996) 'Insomnia' in Van Hasselt, V. B. and Hersen, M. (eds.) *Sourcebook of Psychological Treatment Manuals for Adult Disorders*. New York, Plenum, 539–66.

Van Twyver, H. (1973) 'Polygraphic studies of the American alligator'. *Sleep Research*, **2**, 87.

Vogel, G. W., Thurmond, A., Gibbons, P., Sloan, K., Boyd, M. and Walker, M. (1975) 'REM sleep reduction effects on depression syndromes'. *Archives of General Psychiatry*, **32**, 765–80.

Waldstreicher, J., Duffy, J. F., Brown, E. N., Rogacz, S., Allan, J. S. and Czeisler, C. A. (1996) 'Gender differences in the temporal organization of prolactin (PRL) secretion: Evidence for a sleep-independent circadian rhythm of circulating PRL levels – a clinical research center study'. *Journal of Clinical Endocrinology and Metabolism*, **81**, 1483–7.

Walker, J. M. and Berger, R. J. (1980) 'Sleep as an adaption for energy conservation functionally related to hibernation and shallow torpor'. *Progress in Brain Research*, **53**, 255–78.

Walker, J. M., Floyd, T. C. and Fein, G. (1978) 'Effects of exercise on sleep'. *Journal of Applied Physiology*, **44**, 945–51.

Walker, J. M., Glotzbach, S. F., Berger, R. J. and Heller, H. C. (1977) 'Sleep and hibernation in ground squirrels (*Citellus spp*): electrophysiological observations'. *American Journal of Physiology*, **233**, R213–21.

Walter, W. G. (1953) *The Living Brain*. London, Duckworth.

Walters, W. J. and Lader, M. H. (1970) 'Hangover effects of hypnotics in man'. *Nature*, 229, 637–8.

Ward, D. (ed. and trans.) (1981) *The German Legends of the Brothers Grimm.* Philadelphia, ISHI; London, Millington Books.

Warner, B. F. and Huggins, S. E. (1978) 'An electroencephalographic study of sleep in young caimans in a colony'. *Comparative Biochemistry and Physiology*, 59A, 139–44.

Webb, W. B. (1969) 'Partial and differential sleep deprivation' in Kales, A. (ed.) *Sleep: Physiology and Pathology.* Philadelphia, Lippincott.

Webb, W. B. and Agnew, H. W. (1964) 'Sleep cycling within twenty-four hour periods'. *Journal of Experimental Psychology*, 74, 158–64.

Webb, W. B. and Agnew, H. W. (1975a) 'The effects on subsequent sleep of an acute restriction of sleep length'. *Psychophysiology*, 12, 367–70.

Webb, W. B. and Agnew, H. W. (1975b) 'Are we chronically sleep deprived?' *Bulletin of the Psychonomic Society*, 6, 47–8.

Wehr, T. A., Moul, D. E., Barbato, G., Giesen, H. A., Seidel, J. A., Barker, C. and Bender, C. (1993) 'Conservation of photoperiod-responsive mechanisms in humans'. *American Journal of Physiology*, 265, R846–57.

Weissbluth, M. (1982) 'Sleep duration and infant temperament'. *Journal of Pediatrics*, 99, 817–19.

Weissbluth, M. (1987) 'Sleep and the colicky infant' in Guilleminault, C. (ed.) *Sleep and its Disorders in Children.* New York, Raven Press.

Weitzman, E. D. (1981) 'Sleep and its disorders'. *Annual Review of Neuroscience*, 4, 381–417.

Weitzman, E. D., and Pollak, C. P. (1982) 'Effects of flurazepam on sleep and growth hormone release during sleep in healthy subjects'. *Sleep*, 5, 343–9.

West, J. L. (1962) 'A General Theory of Hallucinations and Dreams' in West, J. L. (ed.) *Hallucinations.* New York, Grune & Stratton.

Wilkinson, R. T. (1959) 'Rest pauses in a task affected by lack of sleep'. *Ergonomics*, 2, 373–80.

Wilkinson, R. T. (1961) 'Interaction of lack of sleep with knowledge of results, repeated testing and individual differences'. *Journal of Experimental Psychology*, 62, 263–71.

Wilkinson, R. T. (1962) 'Muscle tension during mental work under sleep deprivation'. *Journal of Experimental Psychology*, 64, 565–71.

Wilkinson, R. T. (1970) 'Methods for research on sleep deprivation and sleep function'. *International Psychiatry Clinics*, 7, 369–81.

Wilkinson, R. T., Tyler, P. D. and Varey, C. A. (1975) 'Duty hours of young hospital doctors: effects on the quality of work'. *Journal of Occupational Psychology*, 48, 219–29.

Williams, H. L. (1972) 'Alcohol and sleep in young adults'. *Psychopharmacologia*, 26, 201–18.

Williams, H. L., Lubin, A. and Goodnow, J. J. (1959) 'Impaired performance with acute sleep loss'. *Psychological Monographs*, 73 (14, whole no. 484).

Williams, P. (1983) 'Psychotropic drug prescribing'. *The Practitioner*, 227, 77–81.

Williams, R. L., Agnew, H. W. and Webb, W. B. (1964) 'Sleep patterns in young adults: an EEG study'. *Electroencephalography and Clinical Neurophysiology*, 17, 376–81.

Williams, R. L., Karacan, I. and Hursch, C. J. (1974) *Electroencephalography (EEG) of Human Sleep: Clinical Applications.* New York, Wiley.

Wilson, S. J., Bell, C., Coupland, N. J. and Nutt, D. J. (1995) 'Sleep in depressed outpatients during treatment with fluvoxamine – a home-based study'. *European Neuropsychopharmacology*, 5, 303–7.

Wolff, P. H. (1959) 'Observations on newborn infants'. *Psychosomatic Medicine*, **21**, 110–18.

Wolpe, J. (1958) *Psychotherapy by Reciprocal Inhibition*. Stanford, CA, Stanford University Press.

Wood, A. J. J. (1984) 'Pharmacologic differences between beta blockers'. *American Heart Journal*, **108**, 1070–7.

Woodward, S., Freedman, R. R. (1994) 'The thermoregulatory effects of menopausal hot flashes on sleep'. *Sleep*, **17**, 497–501.

Woolfolk, R. L., Carr-Kaffashan, L., McNulty, T. F. and Lehrer, P. M. (1976) 'Meditation training as a treatment for insomnia'. *Behavior Therapy*, **7**, 359–65.

Wynn, V. T. (1972) 'Measurements of small variations in absolute pitch'. *Journal of Physiology* (London), **220**, 627.

Yules, R. B., Freedman, D. K. and Chandler, K. A. (1966) 'The effect of ethyl alcohol on man's electroencephalographic sleep cycle'. *Electroencephalography and Clinical Neurophysiology*, **20**, 109–11.

Zepelin, H. (1983) 'Note by Harold Zepelin' in Mayes, A. (ed.) *Sleep Mechanisms and Functions*. London, Van Nostrand, 93.

Zepelin, H. and Rechtschaffen, A. (1974) 'Mammalian sleep, longevity, and energy metabolism'. *Brain, Behaviour and Evolution*, **10**, 425–70.

Zir, L. M., Smith, R. A. and Parker, D. C. (1971) 'Human growth hormone release in sleep: effect of daytime exercise on subsequent sleep'. *Journal of Clinical Endocrinology*, **32**, 662–5.

Zuckerman, B., Stevenson, J. and Bailey, V. (1987) 'Sleep problems in early childhood; continuities, predictive factors, and behavioural correlates'. *Pediatrics*, **80**, 664–71.

Zung, W. W. K. and Wilson, W. P. (1971) 'Time estimation during sleep'. *Biological Psychiatry*, **3**, 159–64.

Index

activation-synthesis model of dreaming, 69, 75, 78, 109
active sleep (neonatal), 3–36
Adam, K., 33, 166, 184, 192–3
Adler, A., 19
adolescence, 36, 188, 190, 215–16
after-images, 52, 53, 74
alertness, *see* cortical arousal
alligator, 160–1
alpha rhythm of the EEG
  defined, 22
  development of, 35
  dreaming, 79
  predicting recall, 134
  sign of drowsiness, 116
alpha-delta sleep, 165, 186
amitryptyline, 149
amphetamine, 144
amphibians, 173
Ampiaraus of Oropus, 8
anabolic processes, 142, 164–5
animal hypnosis, 160, 185
animal sleep patterns, 152–9
  birds 159
  insecurity, 174
  mammals, 153–9
  reptiles, 160
  rituals, 152
  see also hibernation
anorexia nervosa, 142, 165
anthropology, 16
anti-anxiety drugs, *see* drugs, benzodiazepines
anxiety and sleep quality, 184, 192
anxiolytics, *see* drugs, benzodiazepines
apnoea, 186, 191, 195
appetitive behaviour, 152–3
apprehension and sleep disturbance, 185
APRE (Army Personnel Research Establishment), 125
archetypal dreams, 64
arousal, *see* autonomic arousal, cortical arousal, sleep disorders (disorders of arousal)

arousal, neural control of, 81, 106–7
arousal thresholds, 138
  in reptiles, 160
Artemidorus, 10–11, 17–8, 64
ascending reticular activating system (ARAS), 82, 107
Aschoff, J., 85–8, 99
Aserinsky, B., 25, 47
assassins' dreams of paradise, 8–9, 12
astrology, 16
attention
  control of, 72
  during sleep, 128, 134
  lapses of after sleep loss, 135, 189
A-type thinking, *see* primary process thinking
autonomic arousal, 129, 134, 197, 199–202
autonomous problem-solving, 68
awakening thresholds, *see* arousal thresholds

babies, *see* neonatal sleep, sleep disorders (children)
basic rest activity cycle (BRAC), *see* biological rhythms
bedwetting, *see* enuresis
beliefs about dreaming
  in antiquity, 5–13
  modern, 13–19
benzodiazepines, *see* drugs and sleep
biblical dreams, 15
biological rhythms
  basic rest activity cycle 94, 96, 104
  circadian, 85–93
  infradian, 97–8
  ultradian, 93–7
blind
  dreams of, 47
  circadian rhythms disorder, 99, 149, 185
brainstem, 75, 77, 80, 108–9
bruxism, 137